GW00683923

God Needs Salvation

A New Vision of God for the
Twenty-First Century

The idea of God has been an evolving human construct since the dawn of history. Sometimes forces conspire to freeze that evolutionary process in a moment of history but the process cannot be stopped. Hugh Rock seeks to move that process along past the theisms of yesterday as he seeks to find a God that can live in the 21st century. It is a noble task. One hopes it will be successful.
John Shelby Spong, author of The Fourth Gospel: Tales of a Jewish Mystic

Hugh Rock brings great breadth of reading in arguing his case for a 'Community God'. He works in the tradition of Martin Buber's 'I and Thou' and John MacMurray's Gifford Lectures 'Persons in Relation'.
Brian Mountford, Vicar of the University Church Oxford, Fellow of St Hilda's College, author of Christian Atheist: Belonging without Believing

God Needs Salvation

Salvation

A New Vision of God for the
Twenty-First Century

Hugh Rock

CHRISTIAN
ALTERNATIVE

Winchester, UK
Washington, USA

First published by Christian Alternative Books, 2014
Christian Alternative Books is an imprint of John Hunt Publishing Ltd.,
Laurel House, Station Approach,
Alresford, Hants, SO24 9JH, UK
office1@jhpbooks.net
www.johnhuntpublishing.com
www.christian-alternative.com

For distributor details and how to order please visit the 'Ordering' section on our website.

Text copyright: Hugh Rock 2013

ISBN: 978 1 78279 399 1

A CIP catalogue record for this book is available from the British Library.

Design: Stuart Davies

Printed and bound by CPI Group (UK) Ltd, Croydon, CR0 4YY

We operate a distinctive and ethical publishing philosophy in all areas of our business, from our global network of authors to production and worldwide distribution.

Contents

To Marie and Gordon with grateful thanks for a
happy Catholic childhood.

Preface

Before setting out on a journey it is useful to know the direction in which one is headed. To save the reader the trouble of working out the bearings as we go along here at the start are the principles that guide this book.

The mission is to rescue our idea of what religion is from its present abuse and to salvage the character of God from the wreckage.

It is nonsense to say that life today is no longer religious and has become secular. Such talk tells only the fact that our idea of what religion is has been broken in pieces. Today's culture is an inarticulately religious protest against religion. How could it be otherwise when so much that is repugnant is shouted in the name of religion? And so much that is good quietly done by the 'I am not religious'? To put the pieces back together I find religion in what is done, not what is believed. Some readers will decide that this is a book about God written by an atheist. But I repudiate the whole divisive scenario of 'unbelief.'

We need to diagnose our religious past if we are to attain the catharsis from which we can move forward with confidence. To bury the whole lot might appear to be a solution but the powers involved are too strong. The repression would remain a liability to psychosis. This journey is a liberal critique of liberal ideas which have done a lot of burying. Nothing short of frank discussion will establish a firm foundation for the future. God must stand up on its own and cannot be shored up by privilege of reserved matters.

There is nothing to fear from such honest appraisal. Our idea of God will emerge refreshed from any interrogation because it represents something real in human life. We just need to work out what that real thing is. That is the direction in which this book is headed.

Acknowledgments

I want to thank Christopher Rowland who kindly acted as a much needed conversation partner with regard to the history of Christianity. Thomas Noble generously read a draft as a test case for a lay reader and made useful suggestions. No thinker can form their ideas in isolation from the tradition and for this grounding I thank the staff of the Department of Politics at Birkbeck College and the Department of Theology and Religious Studies at King's College London. All have been unfailingly stimulating to the student. I would like to thank Joan Taylor in particular for encouragement. It was her module on the Last Things which prompted my revolt against the current valuation of the Apocalypse. A big thank you to the staff of Henley Library for the great service in obtaining books. My wife Felicity has been ever supportive and forborne more than I will ever know.

A note on the notes
The majority of the notes give reference sources only. In the instances where further material is included the superscript numeral has been marked with an asterisk *.

Introduction and Preview

1.1. Two Gods and Hopefully One More
1.2. Three Giant Figures in Twentieth-Century Theology. And a Fourth
1.3. Fifty Years of Revisioning Christianity
1.4. The Layout of the Book
1.5. Three Foundational Standpoints

1.1. Two Gods and Hopefully One More

My mission in this book is to put forward a new vision of God that will serve the twenty-first century. This will be a century in which the problems for the established religions that emerged in the twentieth century are going to be exacerbated. New qualities are needed for a God that would serve the twenty-first century. Four qualities at least are paramount.

God must not give rise to the accusations of exclusivity and cultural restriction which were the subject of agonized debate within Christianity for most of the twentieth century. God must be acceptable to and welcoming of people from any religion without the least claim to be the sole possession of one particular group.

God must be acceptable to the new generation of people with no religion. That is to say that this God must be able to close the artificial conceptual divide between people who are religious and people who are not religious, between people who believe in God and people who do not believe in God. That means a God to serve the twenty-first century must be *a concept believable by atheists.* This might seem a crazy demand on a new vision of God but I am convinced that the difficulty is only an apparent difficulty, a genuinely artificial difficulty. My conviction is that Christianity has produced a conceptual blockage as to what God is supposed to be. To put it bluntly our conceptual framework of God is as wrecked as the site of a plane crash. It will take the whole of this book to explain that, so much refabrication is there to be done to piece a framework back together.

The third quality required is that this new God must be recognizably a close relative of the old God. That is to say that the new God should not really be new but must embody something essential that was in the old. It is imperative to retain sympathetic connection with the God of previous generations. Without that connection we are placed in the position of counting our ancestors as dupes and elevating ourselves to a smug superiority. Would that really be a true relation to generations of sincere people whose lives were motivated by those visions?

This book is an attempt to elicit that new God with this quality of continuity by finding something powerfully good in the old God that is the same as some powerfully good force running in society today, a power that is the same as the old God but not recognized as such.

By the standard of traditional respect it is impertinent to set a specification for God. It is impertinent to shop around for the best product match as though these were choices on a supermarket shelf. Isn't it God who tells us the spec? Isn't there only one God? Free discussion is however the fourth quality that the new God must accommodate. Any God who relies on privilege and cannot be openly appraised is no God for the twenty-first century.

If it is impertinent to set a new specification then my mission is not alone but stands in good company. The liberal intellectual vanguard that has been engaged in revisioning Christianity has for long been writing the new specification. It dislikes the specification of the old God and it has already chosen the new God for the twenty-first century. The votes have been cast, the polling booths are closed and the election is over. The God of the Bible, the God of Everyman in the Pew, has been rejected in favor of the Greek Philosophical God of the Intellectuals in the Academy.

This sets a problem for my mission to propose a new God that is neither of these two because it seems too late. I want to contest the result of this election because we have only been offered two candidates chosen by an elite caucus. It has been like a communist election where the result is a foregone conclusion. There are at present two parties which field all candidates for the place of Biblical God and Philosophical God. They are the parties of revealed theology and natural theology. Revealed theology comprises God revealed to humans through the medium of other humans and then incorporated into texts. It could be described as the word of mouth party. Natural theology comprises God revealed to humans through the governing laws and the creative processes of the universe. It is the deductive party. The revealed party may be understood by analogy as the Tory party in theology. With its element of possession of special knowledge it is naturally suited to ecclesiastical hierarchy. The natural party is the Whig opposition. With its philosophical bent it is apt to view revelation as hearsay. It prefers to offer knowledge of God which each of us may obtain directly.

I want to break open this cosy cartel by founding a new party that comprises God revealed to us, in each of us, directly through the dynamic of the person. I could have used the phrase 'human relationships' there but that is too vague. By dynamic of the person I mean especially that the person itself, from the moment of birth, *is a relationship*. We are constituted by the creative enterprise of other people. It is in the ideal possibilities of this creative adventure of life, this unique character of human existence where we each create the lives of each other that I see God revealed to us as a direct experience. This fact of life so naturally accommodated that, like the seventy thousand miles per hour velocity of the earth, we are barely conscious of it, must necessarily surface like the four seasons, as a fundamental aspect of human existence. It is this fact, whether we name it God or not, whether we express it in a humanist or supernatural frame that gives rise to our concept and experience of God. The old voted out God, poor thing in the face of constant cultural abuse, was trying to represent something of this to us. I name this new party 'Social Theology'. Its character will become apparent through the discussion of the person in chapter eight, in its platform set out in chapters six and seven, and in its contrast with the character of the other two parties set out in chapters one and two.

So, if the God vacancy genuinely is to be thrown open let's have some more candidates. The current victor for revisioning is unacceptable by the standard of our third named quality of continuity. If the Greek Philosophical God succeeds by means of a platform to suppress the God of the Bible, if it simply ditches one tradition in favor of another, then it does not fulfill the necessary qualification. In response to this accusation of abandoning the tradition of the old God the electors of the establishment would object that I am mistaken because the two Gods are really one. The Greek Philosophical God is, according to this objection, a complementary understanding of the God of the Bible. At this point unfortunately we enter the murkiest waters. The mix up began the day that Paul was laughed at in Athens and vowed to show the Greeks that their unknown God was one with Yahweh.[1*] But it was a vain boast and a typical instance of Paul's browbeating argumentative style. It set off the assault of one culture upon another that would be looked askance were it begun today.

The academy ignores the contrasted characters of the two Gods with which it has to deal. But unless we are able to know properly the characters of the two Gods currently on offer there can be no hope of properly assessing the value of any proposed new candidate. I wish that it were possible to plunge straightaway into setting out the new vision of God that begins in the second part of this book but the present morass of polemic, embarrassment and wishful hopes makes a profoundly unsatisfactory situation from which to move forward. The joke about the Irishman asked to give directions to Tipperary holds a truth pertinent to the current departure point of liberal Christianity. The respondent replied, 'if I were going to Tipperary I wouldn't start from here.' It is a precondition of any potential advance in thought that it should depart from a position of clarity on what has gone before. There is then a prior task of elucidation that has to be undertaken in the first part of this book. Though I would like immediately to address the vision to the new generation of 'non-religious' people for whom the word God is an annoyance it is an inescapable requirement for the mission first to engage with twentieth-century argument over that nuisance word.

A brief note on vocabulary is necessary before going any further. In theological language the understanding of God represented by the Greek philosophical God is known as panentheism; pan-en-theism, that is, God everywhere-in-the-world. This is contrasted with the God of the Bible, known as theism or, often encountered now, as classical theism;[2] this is understood to be a God who directs-from-outside-the-world. The difference between the two types is thus reduced in its bare essentials to a God who is separate from the world or a God who is integrally part of the world. The long debated standoff between theism and panentheism has been framed largely on the basis of this distinction.[3] This dichotomy loads the electoral dice from the outset. Who would not prefer a God who is in relationship with us to a God who barks commands?

I won't be using either of these names, except where it is necessary to do so in quoting other writers. The distinction 'in' or 'separate', 'intimate' or 'remote figure' is itself questionable but the primary reason for refusal is that the distinction trivializes the real difference between these interpretations. It suggests this might be the same God operated in different modes, of which we must choose the correct mode. This is how the academy likes to present the matter. The distinction between the two is much more deeply rooted. There are here two different Gods. I will be referring to the God of the Bible as the God of Mother Community, Community God for short. The God of Greek philosophy is referred to as the God of Mother Nature, Nature God for short.

The full explanation of these characterizations will not become apparent till some way through chapter two but as an indication in anticipation the Biblical Community God evolved from Yahweh, the war God of the Old Testament, who smote Pharaoh to liberate the captive Israelites and won the battle against the Philistines by causing havoc at Mishmash. This is a God of the fortunes of the tribe. The Greek Nature God evolved from the harvest festivals of ancient Greece that were philoso-phized by Plato. This is the God of the cosmos, the earth God. Reference to the Nature God in this book includes as synonymous both panentheism and Platonism. It also includes the existentialist readings of God as 'being itself' that were fashionable approximately from the 1940s to the seventies. It includes the companion to 'being itself' the stock phrase 'Ultimate Reality.' The choice of these two names, Community and Nature, is intended to highlight the separate origins of the two Gods of Christianity and to begin to explain that nothing but violence has been done to our understanding by rolling these two personalities into one. The distinction between the two will situate home base for our new departure point.

The distinction Nature and Community does not however sound the depths of the difference between these two Gods. The two Gods have divergent temperaments and originate exclusive types of religion. The philosophized Nature God allies naturally with Buddhism and is allergic to the apocalyptic character of the Community God arising from Judaism. Far from being one person in two disguises these two could not even share the same house together. No proper understanding of the contemporary debate or the choices available today can be achieved without a review of these two religions that were brought together in Christianity and have ever since been involved in a tussle for supremacy. That review is the task of the first part of the book and the basis for the title, A Tale of Two Religions. The history takes us back two thousand seven hundred years to the Bacchanalian rites of ancient Greece and to the origin of apocalyptic in the murderous suppression of Jewish identity by Antiochus Epiphanes (c175-164 BCE).

Any proposal for a new God must start with a clear perspective on what proposals have gone before. My perspective is that the liberal vote to run for the future with the Nature God and to ditch the Community God is unfortunate on a number of counts. The motive is wrong. It is driven by a sense of embarrassment about the Community God and all his preposterous doings. The insight is wrong. It proposes that the Community God is really a version of the Nature God. This means that the excellent characteristics of the Community God are dismissed as a source of potential for the future. The result is wrong. There is in the liberal position at present a tragic sense of homelessness. Liberals have been dispossessed of the wonderful home that the Community God gave to generations of believers. They now find themselves uncertain where to go. Nor will any new home ever be satisfactory so long as it provides shelter at the cost of denying the original home. We must own our heritage if we are ever to feel properly grounded. My mission then is to rescue something of the rejected Community God. Hence the title of the book: God Needs Salvation.

To fill out that perspective on the past it is necessary to come up to date on twentieth-century liberal theology. The key to the nature of that project and the key figures that frame it are presented briefly in the next two sections.

1.2 Three Giant Figures in Twentieth-Century Theology. And a Fourth.

There is a cast of three giant forces acting out twentieth century liberal theology. Their influence is pervasive and still flowing strongly today. These three are the signposts to the way through that century and it is useful to have a firm grasp of their directions before embarking on the survey that is to be presented. They are encountered at every turn but often disguised in someone else's thought. Whole swathes of theology are derivative from them. Where one of them appears on stage the other two are always in the wings. They work as a team but their association often escapes notice because of three factors. They inhabit different eras. Their characters are divergent. Their writings are strongly colored in contrasting shades. These differences disguise the fundamental thought that unites them. They are mystics. They found their sense of God on direct intuition of another plane of existence, a fifth dimension, which we may sense but can never describe. They can perhaps be best understood as a combination of Wordsworth and Plato. They combine Wordsworth's sensual nature rapture with Plato's philosophical nature rapture. They have the same sense of Plato's ideal real world of which this material world is but an imperfect and transient copy. They hum the theme tune of Platonism the distinction between the finite and the infinite. These three giant influences are one and the same mystical thought presented in different clothing.

That mystical thought has profound consequences. It refuses all rational structures of religion. That means that it dispenses with Christian doctrinal apparatus, but not quite. It views the incarnation, resurrection, atonement, second coming, judgment, heaven and hell as poor attempts to give reality to the mystical feeling that cannot be described. That mystical feeling is ambiguous in its effect on doctrine. On one hand it is proposed to validate it by association with a higher principle. On the other hand the direct line to God places all doctrine and the authority of the bible in suspension. It is not possible to serve two masters. Mysticism ultimately discounts ecclesiasticism. Although all three attempt to tie doctrine in with the mystical feeling it produces a condescending understanding of Christianity. That mystical thought also makes the character of God ambiguous. Depending on which way one wants to look at it God might be an impersonal potentiality present in the universe or God might be an intelligent agent. These twin features of discount of doctrine and the sophistication of an *It* God are the attraction which the Nature God holds for liberal theology and the means to berate the Community God.

The cast list of giants is Friedrich Schleiermacher (1768-1824), Rudolph Otto (1869-1937), and Paul Tillich (1886-1965). Tillich is the ostensible main influence on the latter half of the twentieth century. This is because his existentialist version of the mystical feeling caught the fashionable philosophy of the time and associated theology with the fashion.

For many people Tillich well merits the accolade 'the incomprehensible Tillich;'[4] there are good reasons for this. Tillich inhabits two eras, ancient and modern. In reading him it is never certain which era he is in and he was not certain himself. The first era is the nineteenth century before the First World War. It is the idyllic childhood in the ancient village of Starzeddel where his father was pastor and God held the world safely in the palm of his hand. The second era is a shattered world, a shattered confidence in God and a personality shaken after serving as pastor in the trenches. It is the world of a socialist intellectual escaped to exile from the Nazis. It is the post World War Two era of nuclear anxiety in America. Tillich's existentialism is an attempt to reclothe with the security of the original world.

Tillich's work is apt to confuse because it is written in a dual language of the traditional mixed up with existentialism. The key to Tillich is that his stock phrases 'ultimate concern' and 'God is being-itself, not *a* being,'[5*] refer to the mystical feeling. Neither of these two concepts is arrived at by abstruse philosophical reasoning although it is easy to form the impression that that is what Tillich is doing. Tillich was explicit that he was inspired by Schleiermacher and Otto.[6*] He was an exponent of perfectly indescribable mystical feeling that is freely available to anyone regardless of intellectual ability. The mystical feeling founds the parallel language that Tillich speaks. In one voice he wishes to leave undisturbed the traditional believers. In the other voice he speaks to the audience of his personal mission, 'those in a situation of doubt,'[7*] by means of a code running through the traditional doctrines that correlates them to a higher understanding through the mystery.

If Tillich is a repeat of Schleiermacher how did he become famous as an original? Tillich is the theologian of anxiety.[8*] The quest to salve his own anxious personality coincided with the American national anxiety of the cold war years. Tillich's huge intellectual stature brought a soothing note to the anxiety and he was adopted as religious godfather to the American nation. Tillich's influence reverberates through the theological radicals at the end of the twentieth century although for the lay person feminist concerns quickly displaced his existentialism as the cultural focus.

Schleiermacher is the great junction through which the confluence of Platonic and medieval mystical influences come together and flow out again into the modern era. Schleiermacher has immense stature. He is variously described as 'an intellectual giant,'[9] 'the founder of modern Protestant thought,'[10] 'pioneer of modern theology,'[11] 'epoch-making thinker.'[12] From the point of view of the presentation in this book it is curious that such an ancient idea should be fêted as an advance. Schleiermacher, however, like Tillich, caught the spirit of his times. His was the era of romanticism. He addressed the cultured doubts about the doctrines of Christianity and with overwhelming eloquence presented his mystical solution of a direct intuition of God.

There is a peculiarity in Schleiermacher's reputation on two counts. He presented the idea of a mystical feeling as his own and did not root it in Plato or in the suppressed mystical tradition that it represents. His particular content of the mystical experience, a 'feeling of absolute dependence' gave his thought the appearance of something new. On the second count although his world of a mystery that can be sensed but not described is pure mysticism he does not find a place in the compilations of the Christian mystical tradition.[13] This is because he is a traitor to the mystical spirit. Instead of using the mystery to put doctrines into suspense Schleiermacher contrives to found a vast doctrinal scheme upon it. He is revered as a pillar of the church establishment which he supported from his chair in theology at the new university of Berlin. To read Schleiermacher is to enter a den of theological opium dreams. He is a weaver of spells so subtly persuasive that one gradually loses all sense of one's own volition. It is best not to go near him unless, like Ulysses with the Sirens, one has taken the necessary precautions.

Otto was a biblical scholar with special interest in comparative religion. His short book *Das Heilige* was translated into English with disregard for its intention as *The Idea of the Holy*.[14] It should be *The Feeling of the Holy* because it is about mystical sense experience. Otto admired Schleiermacher's attempt to overcome rationalism by founding religion in feeling[15] but starts out from disagreement as to the procedure and content. According to Otto Schleiermacher should not have read his feeling as a feeling of absolute dependence. This is secondary. It should have been a primary feeling of worthless self-abasement from which the sense of dependence would follow.[16] Otto thus injects into Schleiermacher's method a particular brand of abject Puritanism. He creates an exaggerated distance between the sacred and the profane using his vocabulary of the *mysterium tremendum et fascinans*. In this way he updates the romanticism of

Schleiermacher's era with the profane guilt of the times. Otto's book, published in 1917, became a bestseller in post World War One Germany. It appealed to a longing for return to the sacred. Otto is not well known to the general Christian public but he has immense influence in the twentieth century liberal academy.

A feature of this trio of theologies is that the same thought appears in different costume. By this means it succeeds in appeal to the spirit of its time. It is a cultural chameleon. The thought seems to be endlessly adaptable and ramifies in all directions. John Robinson transformed Tillich's existentialist anxiety into love.[17] Don Cupitt hybridizes Schleiermacher with Eastern mysticism to produce a Buddhist style cosmic consciousness.[18] In comparison to the usefully adaptable blankness of Tillich's philosophical ultimate concern, Otto's strong puritan characterization is less adaptable. However, Otto is the route through which the thought enters today's sociology of religion. While the Puritan abasement is too specific for sociology the sacred profane distinction is wonderfully universalizable. It backs up and becomes a cipher for Plato's mystical dualism which Otto admired.[19] Mircea Eliade (1907-1986) picked up on Otto's sacred and profane[20] and from his seat at Chicago influenced a whole generation of sociologists. It is through Eliade that stems the syndrome in the sociology of religion today of 'theology speaking sociology' which comes up for discussion in chapter six. Nor is the chameleon thought restricted to religious metaphysics. The atheist Julian Huxley admired Otto's basis for religion and used it to found his humanist religion on a perfectly rational mystical feeling of the sanctity of human existence.[21] To say that the thought ramifies is an understatement, it is pervasive.

This cast list of Schleiermacher, Otto and Tillich is encountered extensively in the following pages. There is occasion to use a shorthand reference to it as 'The Triumvirate.'

Who is the fourth giant influence? It is Plato. Plato is ancestor to the Triumvirate but although he is two thousand five hundred years old there is nothing ancient about Plato. He has found the secret of eternal youth. Plato possesses the gene for perpetual metamorphosis. Where Schleiermacher, Otto and Tillich reproduce Plato, each in their culturally transient way, Plato retains the universal gene that continues to reproduce in any culture. It is through this power that Plato still busies about directing the proceedings in today's theology with the hormones of an adolescent.

The problem with Plato's influence today is that most insidious of all problems. It is a determining influence which is not recognized as such. His metaphysical viewpoint is so much considered to be the actual fact of what religion is and what God must be that it is never examined as an assumption. That assumption is that religion is defined by the leaven of metaphysics. It is the assumption that ethical relations without metaphysics added to them cannot constitute religion. Plato's metaphysic of the Forms, the distinction between the permanent ideal real world and the transient material corrupted world; between the sacred and the profane; between the spiritual and the material; between mind and matter; between the religious and the secular, has a stranglehold on both theology and sociology as to what qualifies as religion. Plato is the director general who decides what is allowed to be religion today. Present day liberal theology and the sociology of religion are his puppets. Apart from the handful of relegated thinkers that I seek to retrieve in chapter eight I have not been able to discover any liberal ideas of God that are not directed by him.

This unexamined metaphysical assumption about what qualifies as religion sets a problem for understanding religion in the twenty-first century where ancient metaphysics has evaporated. It is on account of the conceptual blockage produced by this metaphysical definition that religion can seem in theory to have disappeared. The understanding that I will be proposing, that religion arises directly out of the dynamics of the human person in relation *is not permitted to be a religious understanding.* Yet it is in those dynamics that I see religion in society today bubbling away inarticulate to itself and unrecognized by theology.

The problem is more definitive than stated so far. The modern understanding is that the universe is indifferent to human existence. Humans, therefore, generate their own moral structure in the face of that indifference. In this understanding there is only one reality. There are not two worlds. Ethical principles guiding human relationships are not beamed to us like a radio signal out of another dimension of the universe. This modern understanding, however, is just as much a metaphysic as Plato's metaphysic. It is just a different understanding of the fundamental nature of existence. The sum total of Plato's influence is then not just that religion must be defined by metaphysics; it is that *only one variety of metaphysic is permitted to be religious.* Plato *forbids* that the natural world of human relationships can be the source of religion. It is his acolytes today who scorn any such idea as shallow secularism.

Both liberal theology and the sociology of religion have been up against this conceptual impasse for about the past hundred years. In order to break the hold of Plato's philosophical artifice a complete conceptual switch is necessary. That switch can be said to be a precondition of a place for the God proposed in this book. Nothing is going to move forward in our understanding of religion until this tyranny has been overthrown. It is a tyranny that I name the 'metaphysical remnant.' This hangover from the past determines the belief that our society is now secular and is no longer a religious society.

It necessarily becomes a critical part of my mission to assist Plato to a suitable place of rest. Old age, decline and death are a feature of biological existence necessary to give way to renewal. The same is true of ideas. While Plato remains in charge of theology there can be no houseroom for a new God for the twenty-first century. Although this book is not about Plato it is obliged to cross him. The skirmish with him runs as a counter-point theme throughout. Chapter two identifies the metamor-phosing gene in Plato. Chapters three and four show in more detail the extensive saturation of Plato into the liberal strands of Christianity. Chapter five examines the result. Chapters six and seven propose the liberation of theology and sociology from the dictatorship of the sacred and the profane. Chapters eight through to twelve present an alternative.

1.3. Fifty Years of Revisioning Christianity

In order to show my proposal in proper relief it is necessary to set it against the context of what has gone before. A brief account of the liberal efforts of the last fifty years will help bring out the situation as it stands today.

A concerted movement has been underway since just after the First World War to remodel God in a way that will effect the revisioning of Christianity that is needed to take the religion forward. This came to a head fifty years ago with the radical 'Death of God' movement which burst into the theological world in the mid 1960s and whose fiftieth anniversary is upon us. Thomas Altizer and William Hamilton's *The Death of God*, [22*] published in 1965, gathered together previously published articles and gave a focal point to currents which had not up till then been brought together as a movement. That year also saw the death of Paul Tillich to whom the book was dedicated and who has since been confirmed as the undisputed figurehead of the movement. Tillich's influence continues undiminished through a recently departed generation on to the current gener-ation of revisioners. In 1966 the infamous title Death of God made the front page of *Time* Magazine, the weekly barometer of topical intellectual themes in America, and in this manner a conversation within the theological academy achieved, as it occasionally does, a measure of public notice.

The distinctive peculiarity of the movement was that the title 'Death of God' was misleading. It was not about the death of God. It was about the death of *a* God. The God of the Bible was to be killed off in favor of the Greek Philosophical God. This strident element ran out of impetus during the eighties but its stance has been carried on with no less momentum in the great contemporary turn of the academy toward the mystical tradition of Christianity. This contemporary turn is couched in terms of remodelling God instead of death of God. On all counts however and from all liberal points of view the God of the philosophers has triumphed and the God of the Bible is despised and rejected.

In the intervening fifty years the theme Nature God trumps Community God has been continuously reiterated. It was the basis of Bishop John Robinson's *Honest to God*. It was the basis of Don Cupitt's 1980s' landmark *Taking Leave of God*.[23*] The title took popular hold as a catchphrase that summed up all that seemed objectionable in the theology. Lloyd Geering's *Christianity without God* [24] refreshed the momentum at the turn of the century.

The death of God throughout this period was consistently not the death of God but the exchange of one God for another. The confused self-perception of this movement is illustrated in the frequent reference to Dietrich Bonhoeffer's enigmatic 'religionless Christianity.'[25] This was for Bonhoeffer a tentative hypothesis in his endeavor to work out where religion had transcribed itself and what religion could be in a world 'come of age.' But his hypothesis tended to be taken as a fact. Altizer's opening question, 'is it possible to conceive of a form of Christianity coming to expression without a belief in God'[26] was deceptive. It was not a religionless proposition at all. 'Death of God' was a good marketing title but poor explanation. The intention was to replace the God of the Day of Judgment with the mystical philosophical God; Nature God trumped Community God; the anthropomorphic, irascible, sacrifice demanding, arbitrarily interfering God was to be replaced by the 'indestructible relevance'[27] of the God of Ultimate Reality; Yahweh was replaced by Tillich's 'Ground of Being.' In Robinson's rephrasing of Tillich the God 'up there and out there' is replaced by God 'in the depths.'[28]

These few works are only a sample of a broad movement united in the thread of a common purpose to trump the Community God with the Nature God. Many works every bit as radical escaped the label because they did this under cover of less provocative titles. Karen Armstrong's *The Case for God* is a representative of this genre.[29*] It could as well be titled *The Case against God*. Here the repudiation is disguised because the philosophical God is presented as the real essence of the Community God who is treated as a mistake of naive understanding.

A separate scientific tributary to the Nature God runs through the twentieth century in the form of the influential process theology. Scientists consider that they have a special contribution to make to the Nature God alongside philosophers. This is to be expected. The Greek word *Physis* unites the senses nature and physics the knowledge of which was itself the original philosophy. Pythagoras, for instance, is inseparably a philosopher, scientist and religious leader. Alfred North Whitehead, Bertrand Russell's partner in their work *Principia Mathematica*, set up as mathematician turned theosopher [30*] and gave new scientific input to Nature God religion in the 1930s. His process theology updated Pythagoras' harmony of the spheres and Newton's mechanical universe with Einstein's theory of relativity.[31*] The relativity of Einstein's theory has been a boon to feminist and ecological revisionings that posit relation, mutuality and reciprocity in place of the command of the Community God.[32*]

Each repetition of the 'radical' story has provoked a riposte from the guardians of the establishment. Robinson was counted an atheist by Alasdair MacIntyre.[33] Cupitt's leave taking was

countered by Keith Ward's *Holding Fast to God*.[34] Anthony
Freeman's *God in Us* [35] earned the riposte of Richard Harries' *The
Real God*.[36] These defensive works had difficulty in spotting the
real target. In retrospect there never was any such thing as
radical theology: Death of God represented the attempt to swap
the two thousand five hundred year old tradition from Mount
Sinai for the two thousand five hundred year old tradition from
Mount Olympus. It is surprising that this endeavor, which re-
enacts for today a history of eighteen hundred years of tension
within Christianity, should, by the self-estimation of the radicals,
be presented as new. It is surprising also that, with Platonism so
well-placed in the echelons of the establishment, the religion
should be reacted to by that establishment as radical or objectionable. The antipathies, in so far as they were promoted by the
assumption of novelty, were artificial and stem in large part from
the failure of the radicals to reach a mature perspective on the
nature of their endeavor.

The whole scenario represents an unfortunate lack of
theological and historical overview of the fact that Christianity,
since the days of Clement and Origen in third-century
Alexandria, has been a composition of two different religions.
Perhaps this is due to the way the same ancient Platonism can
deceive by disguising itself each time as new in the costume of
Christianity then existentialism, postmodernism or science?
Perhaps it is due to the way one generation forgets the
movements of the previous? Who took, for instance, the
Cambridge Platonists of the seventeenth century as an observation point for seventies radicalism? Who understands Don
Cupitt's Nature God driven Christian Buddhism and joyously
expressive Solar Ethics as a postmodern remix of Alan Watts'
beat generation rejection of guilt ridden religion? Perhaps we
simply have not yet achieved clarity on the distinct characters of
the Nature God and the Community God due to their
embroilment in polemical tensions? The first two chapters of this

book are a necessary exercise to bring out the bare historical groundings of this missing overview as an aid to analysis in what follows.

If radical theology was discussed as radical in its context from the sixties through to the eighties that context and discussion now has a dated air so much has its candidate Nature God become the new orthodoxy of today's vanguard with its great revival of interest in the mystics. Gone is the situation in 1984 when Alan Stephenson, writing the history of the Liberal Anglican Church, could speak of 'the Modernists pushed out of the scene by the new radicals.'[37] In retrospect, Stephenson recorded the last stand of early liberalism to protest the incoming tide of the Nature God. It is a phrase of Sarah Coakley, Professor of Divinity at Cambridge that can be taken to sum up the Nature God mysticism of the scene today. It is, 'the profound Dionysian influence on contemporary theological developments.'[38]

1.4. The Layout of the Book

To continue the theme that any new proposal must start out from a perspective on the current situation, the other aspect of this grounding is to consider whether the Nature God vote can achieve the result expected of it. That is the subject of chapter five. My doubt about the Nature God vote for revisioning the future is that it defeats its own object. It is an attempt to address the modern personality that cannot believe the old myths of human existence as the center of cosmic purpose. This personality accepts that human existence is an accident in a random part of the universe. It accepts that evil is a fact, not a theological issue to be resolved by religious theory. The Nature God vote aspires to revision religion in such a way that it may renew its appeal to an audience of those disenchanted within Christianity and to those comprising a fresh audience drawn from outside. It hopes also to be comprehensive of all religions and end what is considered now, in the environment of pluralism, to be the stigma of exclusivity. The revisioning offered, however, is not really the address to this era that it purports to be. It is the instalment of an ancient brand of specifically western philosophy which contains its own quota of mantras and mysteries.

Ancient provenance is not of itself a disqualification for the relevance of a philosophy to address the twenty-first century. But the question needs to be asked whether the religion of Orpheus, mystically mathematicized by Pythagoras, philosophized by Plato, tidied up by Plotinus, allegorized into Christianity by Clement and descended to the present through Dionysius/ Tillich,[39*] really is the revitalizing tonic that it is made out to be.

The situation in which the Nature God campaign finds itself with regard to critical appraisal is the somewhat luxurious situation of judge in its own cause. It enjoys the luxury of the party in opposition which is privileged to claim that all bad things are the product of the incumbents and that under its own rule all will be different. The divine status of Jesus, for instance, has been suggested to carry the blame for the persecution of the Jews, Imperialist exploitation of Third World peoples and denial of the saving effectiveness of other religions.[40] For good measure the Community God's grant, in Genesis, of human dominion over nature, is responsible for ecological disaster.[41] All would by implication have been different under the hypothetical gover-nance of the Nature God.

The Nature God campaign turns a withering intellectual power on the dissection of the Community God and its doctrines but the same percipience is not exercised with regard to itself. Any critique must, therefore, come from other quarters which have so far proved inadequate to the task. That appraisal from the quarter of the Community God is long running but is restricted to repulsion of the three horrors, enthusiasm,[42*] pantheism and panentheism. The defensive nature of the argument, which parades the obvious fears of ecclesiastical authority, disqualifies it as anything worthy of the name critique. Nor does the sociology of religion provide any proper appraisal. It is the Community God and institutional religion which, because they constitute the immediately apparent data, bear the brunt of attention from sociology just as much as they do from the Nature God. Sociology is so much disinclined to do theology that it does not register the current division within Christianity.

Yet if the Nature God is to fulfill hopes of revisioning and to be more than a private conversation between theologians or confined to a liberalism within Christianity doomed, as the sociologist Steve Bruce sees it, to a membership parasitic on discontented orthodoxy,[43] then what is needed and to be welcomed is an appraisal by the hypothetical consumer in the culture and century which it aspires to address.

Chapter five is an attempt to outline this missing appraisal by taking up a number of critical perspectives. It should be made clear, to prevent potential misunderstanding, that this is not a book 'against the Nature God.' I wish to leave the followers to the unquestioned enjoyment of their beautiful religion. What is put into question is the claims made for the Nature God to universalize a religion with renewed relevance to the twenty-first century. This occasions the speaking of a number of harsh truths which otherwise might have been left unspoken.

There is a view that it is intellectually and spiritually fruitless to attempt to separate Platonic and Christian influences in the wish to adjudicate orthodoxy and that it is time to move on from Adolf Harnack's (1851-1930) antipathetic separation of the Christian kernel from the Greek husk.[44] The premise adopted in the argument of this book is that there is intellectual mileage to be gained from an approach which has no concern with orthodoxy. The benefit of this premise derives from analyzing the two religions on the basis of two out of three of the fundamental religious types for the resolution of evil: the apocalyptic, the cyclical and the permanently dualist irresolution. It is then possible to examine more clearly the tensions and fractures, still unfinished business today, which result from the association of incompatibles. The hoped for payoff is a better perspective for present day choice and for Christianity's understanding of itself. This two religions approach is the new ground to be established as my starting point. It provides a useful diagnostic tool. It was, for instance, cultural pressures which in the twentieth century handed the advantage to the promotion of the Platonic in suppression of apocalyptic. The profound mystical/Dionysian influence on contemporary theological developments is not an independent event but a responsive apologetic strategy toward today's cultural environment.

To pick out just two of these critical perspectives as a preliminary indication, the philosophy introduces a disadvantage not contained in the religion discarded. Mystical and ecstatic experience which is the ultimate validation of this religion is agreed to be a rare occurrence. It is not given to all and is available, if at all, after a course of ascetic practices of purification, illumination and union.[45] It is, therefore, permanently exclusive by temperament and tends also to be exclusive by class and education. This esoteric elitism confines it to minority status which cannot serve as the basis of a new church open and appealing to all people. The measure of its success will only be the measure of deepening class division among Christians. It cannot fulfill the non-exclusiveness quality number one for a God to serve the twenty-first century.

As to ecumenism this philosophy's hopeful accommodation of pluralism is based on the conceit that it is a higher synthesis of all religions.[46*] This constitutes in reality an equality of disrespect for all religious traditions, a disrespect that begins at home with the disparagement of its host. It is impossible that a higher philosophical understanding of the plain truths of Christianity, however much it is hoped to claim this as an ally and philosophical sustainer,[47] should not be supercilious to those truths.

What is more, the universalizing claims reproduce, albeit unwittingly and with good intentions, a version of the same Christian imperialism that is objected to in the Community God. The new God proposed in the second part of this book is content to allow that there are different religions and different Gods. It accepts the conclusion of comparative religion that no principle synthetic of all religions can be discovered. The desire to synthesize all religions is viewed as a misguided ambition for the religious impetus of the twenty-first century. We will gain a better basis for unity by acknowledging the irreconcilable nature of our different cultural heritages.

These defects in the Nature God claims, together with various others, are brought out in chapter five which concludes with a summary of my challenge to the claim of this campaign to address the twenty-first century: it attempts to replace the myths of the Community God with its own myths. It strains at the gnat of the Community God but swallows the camel of grandiose claims for a particular western philosophical nature mysticism. On the basis of these questionable claims it asks that the old God of the Bible should be put away. God Needs Salvation: God needs to be saved from disposal by the Platonists.

In order to arrive at a position to assess the options for the future it is necessary to examine the different liberal branches of Christianity as they stand today. To present that assessment needs some preliminary groundwork. If radical is an epithet that serves more to confound than to enlighten our understanding of the last fifty years of conversation how should we understand the relations between the various currents of thought that constitute Christianity today? A classificatory scheme of four types is proposed: Christians, Platonists, Christian Mystics, and Jesusologists. This review of the present scene is the task of the first four chapters. The intention is to show that once the various currents flowing today are analyzed it is not possible to describe one of them as radical in relation to the others. There are only the two main streams. These are the two longstanding different religions of the Christian and the Platonist, with which the Christian Mystics and Jesusologists coalesce in various alliances. Before embarking on this classification, however, the thorny question of defining what is Christian presents itself. A base camp of orthodoxy is an absolute precondition to any triangulation on the relationship to other currents. Such a base camp is obligatory in order to reference how a new God might fulfill the requisite third named quality of being both the same and different. Without such a reference point the task of saying anything useful is made hopeless and no part of the thesis to be presented could get underway. This definition is undertaken in the first chapter.

This first step of definition may seem doomed when so many authorities will not admit any such possibility. Ernst Troeltsch (1865-1923), the great friend of Max Weber, refused any fixed essence. From his towering historian's perspective he saw Christianity as a shifting series of chronological developments.[48] Maurice Wiles (1923-2005), Regius Professor of Divinity at Oxford, similarly saw the history of doctrine as one of continuous change in response to cultural requirements.[49] Adolf Harnack considered the essence of Christianity to be eternal life too sublime to pin down to any dogma.[50] Some, like Karen King, count any definition as exclusive and relish sheer pluralism as a resource.[51] For John Hick (1922-2012) the search for essence is not an appropriate approach to Christian identity.[52] Hick considered that Christianity is an enormously complex phenomenon and that to pick out any one strand as authentic would be to hold up only a locally dominant point of view.[53] Keith Ward considers that it is important not to insist on one true inalienable core of faith: the term Christianity can only be used to signify some sort of continuity with historic origins.[54]

I am not so doubtful that a keystone in the architectural structure of Christianity cannot or ought not to be identified.

There must be some principle that coordinates any social body. This is proposed not out of pedantic insistence that doctrine is irrevocable or that we should not develop our materials in whatever way may give them renewed vitality for faith today. Indeed it is just that which I aim to do in the second part of this book. What is insisted on is that if we are to reinterpret these materials we should first know what it is that is to be reinterpreted and not simply trample the materials in a polemical stampede.

In face of the postmodern fashion that everything in religion is plastic, determined only by cultural forces and therefore freely remoulded into new work,[55*] I want to demonstrate the fixed structural elements in different religions. Different originating materials and different starting premises generate particular structures of thought. These structures remain inherent for all time unless the premises themselves are removed. In the event of removal the character of 'reinterpretation' defeats itself because it becomes no longer a modification of the structural features but the exchange of one edifice for another. All too much of the recent history of revisioning tinkers with doctrines as though they can be tackled independently of their structural relations. The switch from the Community God to the Nature God, without acknowledging the fact, swaps round the basic premises and so cannot count as the reinterpretation that it purports to be. Three different religions are portrayed in this book. These are the two founding religions of Christianity together with my modern interpretation of the foundational Community God religion. Although these three are convergent in respect of their result for the ethics of human relations they arrive at this result from distinct premises which determine their separate characters.

The polemical motive in the attempt to fudge definition should not pass without notice. Wiles and Hick both state their refusal as a prelude to introducing their own definitions: they wish to make the concept of divine incarnation give way to a fully human Jesus as the basis of Christian inspiration. Ward makes his statement in the context of introducing some elements of Hinduism as part of his desire for 'unrestricted development.' Don Cupitt's claim that 'a smallish group of creative individuals made it all up'[56] is a prelude to his creation of a Christian Buddhist theory of religion.[57] When Karen Armstrong informs us that the Supreme Being is 'an idea that was quite alien to the religious sensibility of antiquity' and that there is 'no clear, consistent image of God in Genesis,'[58] this is a prelude to her wish to trade in the personal God the Father for the impersonal God Ultimate Reality.

The refusal of definition serves admirably as a prelude to install Platonist ideas of God but the field of struggle between emotionally interested parties is not the field that serves the interest of theological analysis. If the battle for the intellectual high ground of Christianity currently underway is to be understood then it is necessary first to understand the fundamental ideas that give rise to the conflict. Good detective work requires the collection and examination of clues, not their cavalier disposal.

An example of this disposal of clues and the obliteration of analysis by wishful intentions is provided by William Inge, Dean of St Paul's in the 1920s, who long preceded the current generation of revisioners as the champion of Platonism's claim to be the 'true heir to the original Gospel.'[59] In discussing the philosophy of Plotinus, the key personality in the migration of Platonism into Christianity, he noted, 'the doctrine of the evolution of Souls, and their re-incarnations, does not agree well with the belief in rewards and punishments in a super-terrestrial world. But attempts to combine incompatible theories are characteristic of all eschatology.'[60]

What Inge glosses over here is two different theological schemes, the apocalyptic which proposes a once and final collective resolution of the problem of evil and the religion of

Orpheus which proposes a continuous individualist process of cyclical resolution. One scheme holds to the once and for all incarnation, identity and resurrection of souls, the other has permanent souls traveling through many identities in spiritual ascension toward perfection. One believes that the quantity of evil in the world can be reduced or increased by human action, the other believes in a fixed quantity of evil inherent in matter.

Inge disregards the fact that the question of evil, its propitiation, expiation, or resolution is the main business of religion and that the different objectives and methods adopted found different types of religion. Inge has happened upon two different schemes of resolution which produce two mutually exclusive types of religion. The Day of Judgment cannot be mixed with Orphism any more than oil can be mixed with water. The airy dismissal of incompatibility by Inge works to the detriment of his understanding. He is convinced of the natural sympathy of Platonist ideas with the Christian but it is with some puzzlement that he has to recognize the weighty history of revolt against them.[61]

Mention of the Day of Judgment is a reminder of the apocalyptic basis of Christianity, the end toward which the religion is directed. This is the keystone in the architectural structure of Christianity. To ascertain the character of Christianity as my defining reference point I return to the Apostles' Creed as a test of faith as did David Strauss (1808-1874) in *The Old Faith and the New* when, nearly one and a half centuries ago, he asked of his times 'are we still Christians.'[62] In the Apostles' Creed the affirmation 'he will come again to judge both the living and the dead' is apocalyptic. Judgment, the future rectification of the moral deficit of human existence, is the prime identifier of apocalyptic in general. The second coming identifies the specifically Christian variant. Such is the nominalism with which the creed is treated today that perhaps only lip service may now be paid to that belief but I take it as the test of what Christianity at least has been for most of its time, or is nominally supposed to be, and so take up apocalyptic as the essential character of what is Christian. The explanation of this is the objective of chapter one.

The validation of apocalyptic encounters a massive task of retrieval because of its rejection by the concerted effort of a hundred years of embarrassed twentieth-century theology responding to its cultural circumstances. It needs to be explained why apocalyptic continues, denied and unrecognized, to be the theological hard core of the Christians. I risk appearing to invest the millennialist sects with guardianship of 'True Christianity' but nothing could be further from my intention. It needs to be explained why the strict millennialist sects are an aberration from the psychology of the distinctively Christian progression of apocalyptic, which on account of the inauguration in Christ, exchanges imminence for its close relation certainty. It needs to be explained why that certainty is no less apocalyptic than imminence and why Christianity has not been de-eschatologized, as is commonly supposed, but remains wholly within an apocalyptic framework, one which is albeit so relaxed that it is not recognized as such. It needs also to be explained why it is permitted to wear the badge of an apocalyptic Christian with pride. The timeless theological message has to be disengaged from its fearsome literary expression in the Revelation of John. *The apocalypse is not the end of the world.* Apocalyptic does not necessarily entail the destruction of earth in a hail of fire; the cataclysm is not the direct focus of apocalyptic; apocalyptic is energizing not apathetic; universal salvation for all can be articulated within apocalyptic just as well as eternal damnation for some.

There is a mountain of false preconceptions to be cleared away. The task ought to have been unnecessary and is all something of a detour but it is made necessary by the disservice of scholarship. Under the influence of Platonist forces scholarship has removed this backbone from Christianity, an excision of character necessary to facilitate the implant of its own structures. Chapter one, therefore, is obliged to cover some theory and some history. The theological necessity of apocalyptic is stated together with a brief outline of the history of twentieth-century rejection. The apocalyptic basis of Christianity, once established, is the key triangulation point of orientation toward the other categories.

1.5. Three Foundational Standpoints

The book is intended to be constructive. The job of critical analysis, though vital for a clear starting point, is only preliminary to the proposal of a new vision of God. A number of foundational standpoints are in play.

Firstly this book is a protest against the trivial definition of religion maintained in contemporary sociology. The discipline has regressed to its infancy pre Durkheim. Prior to Durkheim the principal viewpoint was that religion represented unscientific, irrational beliefs and so would inevitably be superseded. Durkheim's reflexive understanding sited religion as the product of a social reality which it sought to express. This was the first genuinely sociological definition of religion. Durkheim opposed it to all varieties of psychological and primitive theories of religion. In this Durkheim produced a new potential for analysis to focus primarily on human relationships as the source of religion. The great advance of the reflexive principle is that it founds religion as a permanent feature of human life independent of the forms by which it is articulated. The social reality, if it can be identified, must prove no less religious for being articulated in its originating form. For this reason I take Durkheim to be a profound validator of religion and not the skeptic that theology takes him for.

The sociology of religion has abandoned this conclusion from Durkheim with the result that its trivial definition of religion yields only a trivial conclusion. Religion is defined as 'belief in supernatural beings.'[63] Declining belief in supernatural beings therefore means decline in religion.

My complaint can be illustrated by an analogy. Over the past thirty years handwritten ledgers for business accounts have been superseded by software programs such as Quickbooks and Sage. No one would conclude from the decline of book ledgers that accountancy has disappeared. Yet such a ridiculous line of reasoning about religion is adopted by sociology. By analogy to the sociological line of argument accountancy would be defined as 'hand-writing numbers in ledgers.' Handwriting in ledgers has declined, therefore, accountancy has declined. The reason that we know such a conclusion about accountancy cannot be valid is that hand ledgers and software programs are known to be different operating programs to effect the same purpose. Accountancy is a permanent requirement of business regardless of the operating programs used to effect it. There could be no business without accountancy. Religion similarly effects a permanent purpose in human relationships. Accordingly I make a distinction in religion between purpose and operating program. Religion is what is done. Religion is not the operating programs that implement the doing. In this new scheme institutionalized beliefs are defined as the operating programs that put into effect the religious purpose. What that purpose consists of is the subject of chapter six, further expanded in the chapters which follow.

A number of useful discussions are opened up by this analytic distinction between purpose and operating program. It is apparent that the 'ideal potential of human relationships', which I use to define the purpose of religion, is a permanent feature of human existence. It is a social feature and it is a visionary feature that will occur to every generation. This means that I do not share the ecclesiastical fears that the adoption of a basis for God arising wholly within the parameters of human relationships results in a shallow secularism or 'empty radical humanism.'[64] Nor do I share the prediction of sociology that such a natural basis would end talk of God and dissolve theology as a subject.[65] If the social referent of God can be identified then there is no reason for it to be any less religious when carried in a new operating program than when it is carried in one of the traditional programs.

There is no reason that the independent territory of God and of religion should not be identified and take its place alongside sociology. I mean specifically alongside and not subsumed within sociology because I consider religion occupies a permanently independent domain. The automatic assumption under the current conceptual regime is that once the domain of 'the sacred' is disconnected from metaphysics then religion reverts to a sociological subject. As I contest this it is incumbent on this work to demonstrate the matter differently. This can only be done by providing a replacement conceptual framework. Building up that framework occupies chapters six through to twelve.

This proposal of the permanently independent domain of religion cannot be properly illustrated without defining the counterpart of what that domain stands independent of. The conventional distinction is between the religious and the secular. The secular merges into and might be named the political but the distinction between the religious and the political domains, though much considered, has never been exactly specified and remains in a state of fluidity. The proposal that Christianity is definitively not a political ideology is half recognized but obscured by the general perception that it is 'about everything.' It is obscured by the claim of pope to appoint emperor and for the archbishop to anoint the Queen. The proposal has been particularly confounded in recent history by the urge of twentieth-century Christianity, upstaged by the prophet Marx, to claim political credentials.

I propose that the real division in human actions is not between the religious and the secular but between the religious and the political. A clear criterion that distinguishes the two forms of action is necessary. To do this I make use of one of the many definitions of political that is available, but one which is much more extensive than what is commonly understood to constitute politics and political. To produce this clear distinction a clue is taken up from the notorious problem of the timing of the arrival of the Kingdom of God. The Kingdom of God as it is presented in the New Testament is simultaneously here present amongst us but also still to be anticipated. This perplexing feature has generated a mass of inconclusive discussion in biblical scholarship. I refer to it as the 'semi-final puzzle.' What does it mean in social terms that great responsibility to implement this Kingdom is given to all, but an element is reserved to the action of God? This two component constitution of the Kingdom is taken to found the distinction between the political and religious domains. This piece of bible study concludes the book in chapter twelve.

For a large proportion of people today all religious operating programs appear to have been abandoned, not just Quickbooks and Sage but the ledger and abacus for good measure. Yet with the religious purpose posited as permanent there must in fact be a program operating it that we have not so far been able to spot. The prime task of theology today is to elicit what the new program is. Working with the twin principles that God is reflexive of a social reality and that the social purpose of religion is unchangeable, the detective mission is to identify God and religion in contemporary secular culture. The assumption guiding this mission is that God and the new religion in secular culture will turn out to be *fundamentally the same thing.*

The plan of campaign for this mission is to marry up and cross fertilize various clues. As a first clue a small group of largely overlooked theologians is considered. These discover God directly in the dynamic of the human person. They are decidedly not followers of Plato. This group might be described as sociological theologians in contrast to mystical theologians. I take them as exemplary of the new 'Social Theology' proposed in chapter seven. This group, which provides vital insight of God as a presence between persons, is taken up in chapter eight. The second clue comes from a minority of sociologists who have sought to discover religion migrated and hidden in the forms of present day culture. These attempts are reviewed and expanded in chapter nine. Guiding this plan of campaign the assumption of sociology that God has evaporated, because the supernatural program has fallen into disuse, is rejected as shamefully unsociological: God Needs Salvation. God needs to be rescued from trivialization by sociology.

To summarize this first foundational standpoint, concerted use is made of Durkheim's reflexive validation of religion. Several new propositions are developed from Durkheim which have consequences for a reorientation of fundamental ideas about the origin of religion. These consequences are presented in chapter six; The Sociology of Religion is the Puppet of Plato, and in chapter seven, By What Authority? Is this the End of Theology?

The second foundational standpoint is that, in seeking to discover the new operating program for God, there is an unworked mine of clues to be had from the old Community God. This book is fundamentally an attempt to retrieve the valuable directions to human relationships that are embodied in the old theism. This is not to preclude that the Nature God may not yield the same value. It is only that my temperament inclines to the Community God and sees readily transferable connections available from the supernatural format of expression. Besides which, it is necessary in any case to work from the Community God in order to preserve a relationship to our religious heritage. This heritage is abandoned by the revisioning advocacy of the Nature God vote which displays a wish to jump ship rather than steer that ship into the new waters of the twenty-first century. I hope, although this may prove naïve, that a new natural God may live alongside and in solidarity with the old supernatural God.

There is surely something vital that distinguishes Christianity and that has acted as such a powerfully inspiring force in the lives of countless millions of people across two thousand years? Surely those believers were not merely pawns of a cultural captivity which we can now discount as a fraud? Surely Christianity was not passed down only by rote of inheritance but contained a vivifying quality that was renewed afresh in each person who received its memes? To claim that it is merely plastic; that it never had any firm character; that it was all a bad dream; that all along it really represented something else; that with no roots in the conditions of human existence it was all something we just made up in the continuous process of making things up; that it is in liberal fashion 'the religion above all others with which one can do what one wants',[66] is a useless hypothesis. Theological science must assume something solid behind such a staggeringly powerful inheritance. It must assume something solid if we are to identify connections between what we can have now and what we had in the past.

For a third clue that offers potential to cross fertilize clues one and two, chapter ten turns to the unusual but beautiful and fertile practice of those Christians who believe in the demandingly reciprocal religion of the Authority of No Authority. That defines the religion of the Society of Friends or Quakers in colloquial usage. The small membership of this Society bears no relation to the universal esteem with which its religious practice is held and it is in the Friends that the modulating point between the religious and a 'secular' God is discovered. It is a special feature of the Friends that they combine the most vividly religious understanding of God with the most vividly secular understanding. With their refusal to define religion by its operating programs they are exemplars of my definition of religion as what is done, not what is believed.

The brilliant clue for our purposes is provided by the founder George Fox. The highly distinctive social peculiarities of his faith give direct access to the character of the 'inward light.' The refusal of hat honor, the adoption of plain dress and the principle of absolute non retaliation, which drove the culturally accommo- dated Christians of England to an apoplexy of cruel abuse, is a flat contradiction of the hierarchical conventions of society. The egalitarian principles of Fox demonstrate that the inward light is no vague and incommunicable mystical experience but a magnif- icent social vision of the equal value of all persons: the theological and the sociological visions cross each other's bound- aries and become identical.

In the vocabulary of social theory the religion of the Authority of No Authority is known as Anarchism. This is a clue to the cross referencing of the religious practice with the political practice that I name in chapter eleven as the Religious Vision of Political Anarchism. Political Anarchism is decisively atheist so the proposal that it could be associated with religion might seem to some readers a startling claim. All the authorities on Anarchism are, however, unanimous that it is more like a religious than a political creed. Anarchism is uncompromisingly utopian. The disqualification of Anarchism as a principle of political organi- zation is confirmed by political theory. All government is based on power but Anarchism denies the legitimacy of any power of one individual over another. Anarchism was finally defeated as a political force by the Spanish Civil War but it is precisely the practical impossibility of it ever succeeding as a political force that qualifies it as a religious force.

Anarchism admits as the legitimate basis for society only the spontaneous cooperation of individuals. In this utopian relation of the individual to the state, it cross links to Christianity and reproduces Luther's Anarchist freedom of the Christian. 'A Christian is a perfectly free lord of all, subject to none. A Christian is a perfectly dutiful servant of all, subject to all.'[67] For

Luther the restraint of law is superfluous to the perfect Christian and the sword of secular authority is but an interim provision made necessary by the weakness of human nature and present failure to live up to that ideal. For the Anarchists government is similarly superfluous. The law itself is a perversion of natural human relationships. The essential cross-fertilizing principle between Anarchism and Christianity is that both envisage the ideal fulfillment of human potential in *a society that does not need any laws*. Political Anarchism is every bit as much an exercise of faith as Christianity.

Such is the prevalent image of Anarchism, encountered today in its demented form of provocative destruction, that the task of retrieving and validating its religious basis is as daunting as that of reclaiming apocalyptic. That retrieval is the task of chapter eleven. Suffice it to say for the interim that the portrait of 'The Anarchists' has suffered, like the caricature of 'The Jews' in Matthew's gospel, to be drawn by the victorious rivals. 'Supernatural nonsense... Herculean pillars of absurdity' and 'opportunist scum' was bruiser Lenin's harangue before he proceeded to liquidate in jail the remaining visionaries of a devolved society that had once been the rival model to state socialism.[68]

As part of the task of reclaiming Anarchism, Alexander Berkman's *ABC of Anarchism* is examined.[69] Berkman wished to dispel the slanders perpetrated on Anarchism. He provided a description of the Anarchist Kingdom that could as well be titled *ABC of the Kingdom of God* such is its incorporation of every feature that might be expected to be found in that Kingdom. The mild and charming Russian Prince Peter Kropotkin, with his faith in the biological examples of mutual aid as the model of human society and his mission as a scientist to improve the agriculture of subsistence farmers on the Steppes, provides the example of an Anarchist saint.

It is to the principle of the authority of no authority that I look for the secular synergy with the ideals of human conduct commanded by and contained in the Community God. This synergy is more readily observed in Islam with its strict One God than it is in Christianity with its incipiently hierarchical Trinity. As Said Qutb insisted the very declaration of Muslim faith is a declaration of Anarchism. 'No deity except God, "La ilaha illa Allah" means 'no sovereignty except God's... no authority of one man over another... all are equal under the banner of God.'[70] It is a pity that Qutb's was a restricted Anarchism exclusive to the male and internal to the Muslim Brotherhood. The true spirit of Anarchism refuses to be vandalized in such manner. Mohamed Taha, martyred for his efforts, expounded the principle in a form more worthy as a statement of the great One God egalitarian vision of Islam.[71] For Taha the flourishing of the individual is the purpose of society. The current regulatory conditions of Islam are a temporary measure instituted by the Prophet in consideration of the weak nature of humanity and the first stage of Mu'minin (believers). The blessed Qur'an still awaits the realization of its ideal and the redundancy of all rules, in a nation of true Muslimin (submitters in intelligent surrender to God). In Christianity the no authority principle is expressed in attractively universal terms by the direct relation of every soul to God, its maker, for whom each one, utterly without qualification, is of supreme and equal importance.

The third foundational standpoint already skirted in the foregoing but which needs to made explicit, is a belief that the idea that we live in a secular society that has dispensed with religion is a chimera. Our society is religious to the core. The fact that we cannot identify in what way that is so is what I mean by the conceptual blockage. The long running secularization thesis that has covered sociology with embarrassment is a misconceived conceptual artefact. If the religious basis of society cannot be identified then this is not confirmation that the society is not religious but confirmation that there is a conceptual blockage as to what constitutes religion. To investigate this new religion hidden in the culture the work of a small band of sociologists is taken up, including the pioneering work of Don Cupitt's religion of everyday life.[72] This minority voice declines mainstream sociology's retarded definition of religion as 'belief in supernatural beings' and searches for the metamorphosis of religion within popular culture.

This inspiration is taken up in combination with Durkheim's concept of mechanical solidarity as the basis of social cohesion. A 'Super Ethic' is identified at work among today's young people. This Super Ethic is an inarticulately religious protest against religion. It cuts across all cultural, gender and class boundaries. There is in this an intuitive sense that such boundaries create artificial divisions between people and that direct action must be taken to counter this. This Super Ethic is respect for the autonomous self-determination of every individual with the co-operation of all others. The Super Ethic completes a four part cross referencing of an essentially religious idea in today's culture, in political theory, embodied in the Community God and expressed in religious practice. Each one is an expression of the religion of the Authority of No Authority. They are all in essence Anarchist.

So finally, to indicate the direction of the conclusion from these discussions which, in the nature of the vast re-orientation of our conceptual apparatus that is attempted, are necessarily rather wide-ranging, my proposal is a newly named natural God elicited from the supernatural God. This is not the anthropomorphic person of the Community God, nor the impersonal, cosmic 'Ultimate Reality' of the Nature God, but a vision directly rooted in the ideal potential of human relations. This is characterized by the ideal of self-determination, the ideal of auto-nomy, the authority of no authority, the authority of an-archy. It is the demandingly reciprocal God in each one of us who is also the ideal potential of every one of us. It is a perennial God not an eternal God. It is a fragile God which must be renewed in every person in every generation. It is the God of no superiority of one person over another. It is the God of no power. It is the newly elicited and newly named, but not at all new, God of the Religion of the Authority of No Authority.

It is in this God that I see a religious continuation of the identical command to human relations that the Community God tried to represent to us. It is in this that I see preserved the links to a religious heritage that ought to be cherished and in which Christianity might take pride in the realization of a successor. It is in this source that I identify, in the secular domain independent of Christianity, an already working but culturally unvoiced new religion, whose articulation is strangulated by the convention of what religion is supposed to be. This emerging religion is already based in cross-cultural appeal and has a prospect of attracting not only the disenchanted from the established world religions but newcomers to religion as well and will do so not by obliterating the individuality of those religions in a purported higher synthesis but by mutual respect of each religion for other religions.

Part One: A Tale of Two Religions

1

The House of the Christians

1.1. Introduction: The Apocalypse is not the End of the World
1.2. The Theological Imperative of the Apocalypse
1.3. The Architecture of the Apocalypse: The Ethic and its Articulation
1.4. The Reflexive Dynamic of the Apocalypse: The Energization of the Present
1.5. The Apocalyptic Resistance of the Twentieth Century
1.6. Conclusion: The Christians

1 1. Introduction: The Apocalypse is not the End of the World

> Then I looked and there was a white cloud, and seated on the cloud was one like the Son of Man, with a golden crown on his head, and a sharp sickle in his hand! Another angel came out of the temple, calling with a loud voice to the one who sat on the cloud, 'Use your sickle and reap, for the hour to reap has come, because the harvest of the earth is fully ripe.' So the one who sat on the cloud swung his sickle over the earth, and the earth was reaped.
>
> Then another angel came out of the temple in heaven, and he too had a sharp sickle.
>
> Then another angel came out from the altar, the angel who has authority over fire, and he called out with a loud voice to him who had the sharp sickle 'Use your sharp sickle and

gather the clusters of the vine of the earth, for its grapes are ripe.'

So the angel swung his sickle over the earth and gathered the vintage of the earth, and he threw it into the great wine press of the wrath of God. And the wine press was trodden outside the city, and the blood flowed from the wine press, as high as a horse's bridle, for a distance of about two hundred miles.

(The Revelation of Saint John the Divine, Chapter 14 verses 14 to 20)

The person who wrote The Revelation of Saint John, which has been preserved for us as the last book in the New Testament, was a dramatic genius with an over-fertile imagination. He recycled a lot of imagery from the Old Testament and much else besides, to produce a work so mesmerizing, evocative and enigmatic that its images of the Four Horsemen of Death, the Whore of Babylon, and the earth consumed in a hail of fire are still potent two thousand years later. In the days before television or cinema he produced what would be the equivalent of a blockbuster widescreen experience with three-dimensional sensurround. Saint John had the master touch of all good screenplay which draws the viewer into a fictional story as if it were for real. If he had lived to collect the film royalties he would find them still pouring in.

The imagery is so vivid that it has blinded biblical scholarship to the difference between the essential theological message which it conveys and the circumstantial means used to articulate that message: both have been taken to be one and the same. Biblical scholarship in most circumstances has become a discipline of fearsome dissection that is not afraid to question every last piece of detail presented in the bible however much that may unsettle the credibility of the Gospel and render unlearned believers distraught with doubt. However, in the case of the Apocalypse, in place of interpretation, Biblical scholarship has exercised the dullest literalism that takes the whole at face value. That face value of murderous and gloating revenge is repugnant today so the inevitable result is rejection of apocalyptic. The face value promotes a lather of apology at what seems a hideous specter associated with Christianity. Apocalyptic has thus become a subject of distaste that cannot be interpreted into modern theology. The history of twentieth-century theology is the history of rejection of the apocalyptic basis of Christianity either explicitly or implicitly. It is a history of what I name 'Apocalyptic Resistance Theology:' 'The Resistance' for short.

The strained interpretation of the New Testament produced by this rejection is a disgrace to the intelligence of scholarship, a disservice to our understanding of Christianity and a disservice to the community of believers. Apocalyptic is the essential, theologically imperative, basis of Christianity. Christianity was born from apocalyptic and remains today integrally apocalyptic. It needs to be explained that apocalyptic is not the sole preserve of a minority of fanatical millennialists. That it is not the peculiarity of a primitive thought world that we have superseded. That its badge is worn by all Christians displayed in the very name of the religion. It needs to be explained why the end of the world and eternal hellfire for the condemned are not necessary characteristics of apocalyptic and that thinkers today are at work, without being conscious that this is what they are doing, articulating new apocalypses suited to the sentiments of the twenty-first century.

It is a tall order to contradict the impetus of one hundred years of theological denial and the one hundred or so main works of embarrassment that comprise that history. Numerical weight of opinion is, however, no surety for the value of an opinion. The triumph of feminism in the twentieth century is the case in point. How many would have accepted, in the days when women students were permitted to sit in on lectures but barred from taking the examinations for professional qualification, that male students today would sit in class with starry eyed admiration for the intellectual prowess of their female professors? It is then with no sense of trepidation but only a sense of the magnitude of the task, that I am prepared to stand up as the one person ready to accept the apocalyptic basis of Christianity.

The thesis in this book, which is not centrally about apocalyptic but makes it a central point of reference, could ideally have done with founding upon the convenient reference of an account of the meaning of apocalyptic. This would ideally be accompanied by a historical and cultural account of the Apocalyptic Resistance. No such work exists so this extended first chapter will have to serve as a microcosm in its place. This is needed to establish the home triangulation point for the survey of the two different understandings of God on offer today. The value of apocalyptic and the unwarranted basis of its rejection needs to be illustrated from scratch. Without this vantage point the thesis cannot proceed. I have to ask the reader's patience for so much groundwork that needs to be undertaken before it is possible to reach the starting point.

These first four chapters together constitute the groundwork for reaching that starting point and it is worth previewing the argument just in case the reader should at any stage feel lost in the journey. The aim is to illustrate the two different Gods that historically came together to form Christianity. Although four main schools of Christianity can be identified in the contemporary spectrum the appearance of variety is deceptive. The three categories Platonists, Christian Mystics and Jesusologists are united against the apocalyptic Community God by their sympathetic allegiance to the philosophical Nature God. Four schools are based on only two understandings of God. From this vantage point, reached by the end of chapter four, it is possible to ask the two questions with which the rest of the book is concerned.

Looking backward which of these Gods has the best potential to bring Christianity into an understanding of itself and into a relationship of respect for its ancestral inheritance. Looking forward, which of these two has the better potential for a contributory relationship to the new religion of today, mistakenly known as secular society? Part one of the book tunnels through the inner sanctuary of recent discourse to establish the context of a new vision of God. The constructive aspect of that new vision gets under way in part two where there is freedom to range more widely and to be found, I' hope, a refreshing change of subject matter.

1.2. The Theological Imperative of the Apocalypse

Robert Henry Charles (1855-1931), Professor of Biblical Greek at Trinity College Dublin was one of the great pioneers in the rediscovery and translation of the lost apocalyptic literature around the turn of the century. This rediscovery provided the material which enabled Johannes Weiss (1863-1914)[1] and Albert Schweitzer (1878-1965)[2] to make their revolutionary proposal that Jesus' proclamation of the Kingdom of God was an apocalyptic proclamation. Charles' edition of the peripheral literature of the Old Testament remains today a standard reference work for students.[3] Charles had a distinctive grasp of the theological basis of apocalyptic. His analysis is retrieved and built upon here in the belief that it is a powerful perspective to focus a disparate literature. It enables us to understand not just the apocalyptic elements in the New Testament but the nature of the New Testament as a whole and the dynamic appeal of Christianity.

Charles' analysis seems to have been stillborn to the purposes of exegesis since the framework was established in his Jowett Lectures of 1898, *Eschatology: Hebrew, Jewish and Christian* [4] and presented in condensed form in *Religious Development Between the Old and the New Testaments* in 1914.[5] No statement of it can be found, for instance, in the Society of Biblical Literature's definitional project [6] nor in Christopher Rowland's *The Open Heaven*[7] which stands as a major recent interpretation of apocalyptic. A brief restatement of Charles is, therefore, in order.

Charles takes an evolutionary view of religious development; revelation is progressive.[8] There is a move to a 'loftier conception of God'[9] and a 'higher theology.'[10] The progression is from monolatry to monotheism, from the era of one God nationalism to one God universalism. It is unfortunate that this is framed in a Victorian Christian chauvinist perspective of a move from the 'heathenism of primitive Israel'[11] to a transfiguration complete in Christianity[12] but it has to be allowed that this was the permissible language of the time and does not affect the value of the result to be taken up. For Charles, progression is evidenced in an advance from prophecy to apocalyptic that is composed of three main elements. Firstly prophecy is concerned with the destiny of the nation but the apocalypticist advances to the doctrine of a blessed future life as 'a fundamental postulate of his belief in God.'[13] Secondly the doctrine of a new heaven and a new earth is an apocalyptic spiritualization and individualization of the corporate and materialist hopes of prophecy.[14] Thirdly prophecy takes up history in a limited fashion but 'the scope of apocalyptic is incommensurably greater.'[15] It seeks to penetrate the spiritual purposes and forces of events, to sketch 'in outline the history of the word and of mankind, the origin of evil, its course and inevitable overthrow, the ultimate triumph of righteousness and the final consummation of all things. It was thus, in short a Semitic philosophy of religion.'[16]

This brief exposition elicits the essential theme of apocalyptic. The 'inevitable overthrow of evil and the final consummation of all things' is, as I put it in short, the eventual revelation of God's justice. Charles adds to this prophetic build up a second component of propulsion toward apocalyptic by theological development. 'Apocalyptic... was the first to grasp the great idea that all history, alike human, cosmological, and spiritual is a unity – a unity following naturally as a corollary of the unity of God preached by the prophets. Such problems arose inevitably in Israel owing to Israel's belief in monotheism and the righteousness of God.'[17] To crystallize Charles' analysis, apocalyptic, the overall view of history, the eventual revelation of God's justice, *is a logical necessity of monotheism.* As Charles summed up,

> When once the great doctrine of monotheism emerged in Israel, all other beliefs, whether relating to the present life or the after-world, were destined to be brought into unison with it... By the rise of monotheism the relations of theology and eschatology were essentially transformed; for when Yahweh was once conceived as the Creator God of all the earth, the entire existence of men here and hereafter, came logically under His jurisdiction.[18]

A note on vocabulary is needed at this point. Charles uses the accepted theological description monotheism for this one universal God. The description does not however capture the two key preconditions of apocalyptic which is not singleness but omnipotence combined with perfect goodness. The Nature God, 'The One' of Platonic thought, which comes up for consideration in the next chapter, is just as much a monotheism as the Community God. This One however is more tolerant of evil because it is not omnipotent on account of being an abstract potency instead of an intelligence. It is also not necessarily perfectly good because its association with nature enables it to tolerate a measure of evil within itself. Monotheism is therefore too loose a description to discriminate an apocalyptic God from an un-apocalyptic God. I will not be using the term and prefer instead 'one God omnipotence' which will be used where monotheism would usually be considered appropriate.

Charles' understanding is backed up by that other great student of Judaism, Max Weber, who arrived at the same point of view by remarking a similar pressure of evolution toward omnipotence. Weber formulates the background to the problem of God's justice stated in the Book of Job:

> The legitimation of every distinctively ethical prophecy has always required the notion of a god characterized by attributes that set him sublimely above the world, and has normally been based on the rationalization of the god idea along such lines... but the more the development tends toward the conception of a transcendental unitary god who is universal, the more there arises the problem of how the extraordinary power of such a god may be reconciled with the imperfection of the world that he created and rules over... A recent questionnaire submitted to thousands of German workers disclosed the fact that their rejection of the god idea was motivated not by scientific arguments, but by their difficulty in reconciling the idea of providence with the injustice and imperfection of the social order.[19]

Weber names this problem of the not-apparent existence of God's justice as the problem of theodicy and proceeds to analyze the theoretical and historical solutions to the problem that an all-powerful God sets up, of which the Book of Job is a key expression:

> As people continued to reflect about the insoluble problem of the imperfections of the world in the light of God's omnipotence, one result was inevitable: the conception of an unimaginably great ethical chasm between the transcendental god and the human being... and this conception inevitably led to the ultimate theoretical conclusion, apparently assumed in the Book of Job, that the omnipotent creator god must be envisaged as beyond all the ethical claims of his creatures, his counsels impervious to human comprehension.[20]

Weber is right about this conclusion of disjunction to be found in Job. Job receives from God the rebuff of a non-answer which bypasses his pleas. Job retires from the conversation in resigned defeat. The implication of this is apocalyptic. God's plans for the resolution of evil are not vouchsafed to us and it is difficult, nigh impossible, to work out what the resolution might be. The only certainty is faith that the resolution of evil must and will eventually be revealed.

Weber's comparative perspective is useful in placing apocalyptic as one of three possible solutions to the problem of God's justice. These solutions found three different types of religion. The particular solution of apocalyptic is to propose an eventual just equalization. This is achieved by concrete retribution of justices and injustices on the basis of trial of the dead, 'generally conceived in the eschatological process as a universal day of judgment.'[21] For Weber the Indian doctrine of *karma* is the most complete and radical formal solution to the problem of God's justice. 'The world is viewed as a completely connected and self-contained cosmos of ethical retribution. Guilt and merit in this world are unfailingly compensated by fate in the successive lives of the soul.'[22] The third solution to the problem goes back to Charles' precursors of one God omnipotence. Under forms of dualism such as Zoroastrianism, Manichaeism or in the poly framework of one God for each tribe, the power of God is compromised by the autonomous power of rivals. In this circumstance the ethical discrepancy can be attributed to the fluctuating fortunes of this struggle beyond the realm of the human. In the dualist scheme evil is understood to be permanently irresolvable and subject to the ebb and flow of the tides of good and evil.

These are great and foundational schemes. Each one of them founds a type of religion with its own worldview, its own psychological dynamic for the adherents and its own distinctive practices. Apocalyptic characterizes Islam and Christianity. Judaism should be included although direct focus on the eventual revelation of God's justice has been suppressed in the religion since the catastrophe of the destruction of Jerusalem. The cyclical resolution of *karma* with its transmigration of souls and cycles of escape by spiritual ascension characterizes Buddhism in the Eastern tradition and the religion of Orpheus in the West.

To grade the psychological character of these three solutions to the problem of evil using a medical analogy, karma is stable, dualism is chronic, and one God omnipotence is acute. Several writers have confirmed the acute nature of the problem in one God omnipotence noting the liability of apocalyptic literature to break out in time of severe community stress.[23] D.S. Russell categorizes the literature as 'tracts for the times.' They are documents of crisis and anxiety such as the Book of Daniel which was a response to the suppression of Jewish culture by Antiochus.[24] The Revelation of Saint John has been interpreted as a response to a period of Roman repression of a Christian community under the emperor Diocletian.

To summarize, apocalyptic is a theologically driven imperative. The coherent feature of apocalyptic is not to be found exclusively in a literary genre, it is identified in the theological theme. The definition of apocalyptic adopted here, founded as a logical necessity of one God omnipotence is: *the eventual revelation of God's justice.*

Although this usage may not be prevalent in discussions of apocalyptic and has not been made much use of it cannot be claimed as new. It is found to pervade the work of many biblical scholars. Charles Moule (1908-2005), Lady Margaret Professor of Divinity at Oxford, stated it in the same terms as the above definition. 'Apocalypse... is a way of conveying pictorially and in symbol the conviction of the ultimate victory of God.'[25] The same definition was adopted by the Pannenberg Group.[26] In a previous generation Ethelbert Stauffer (1902-1979), Professor of New Testament Studies at Bonn, grasped theology as the coherent basis of apocalyptic[27] and used this to define New Testament theology. George Caird (1917-1984), Dean Ireland Professor at Oxford, in summarizing the theology of the Book of Revelation, elicited the principle of the apocalypse. Although the word is alien to his terminology[28] and the matter is not encapsulated in a single phrase, the defining principles are all present. 'The dominant symbols... introduce us to the central problem of all theology: how can God, in a sinful world, do equal justice to his sovereignty and his mercy?'[29] Caird noted that John speaks of Christ 'But the more important fact is that he is saying something about God.'[30] John reminds his readers 'that the events they must live through are part of an all-embracing purpose... because the future has been decreed in the predestining purpose of God.'[31]

Charles' analysis of apocalyptic as theologically driven is confirmed in Christopher Rowland's *The Open Heaven*. Rowland is not directly concerned to elicit this and adopts revelation as the coordinating feature which defines the customary body of apocalyptic literature, 'a Jewish literary genre of a fairly fixed type' with 'an underlying religious conviction, the direct revelation of the divine mysteries.'[32]

Nevertheless, when the content of those mysteries is examined it becomes clear that apocalyptic is in fact defined by the eventual revelation of God's justice. This jumps out repeatedly from Rowland's several summaries which paraphrase the apocalypse:

'Most of the material contained within the apocalypses can be understood as the direct consequence of the attempts... to understand God and his purpose for the world and man's place in it.'[33] 'The distinguishing features of the view of history in apocalyptic is the belief that the whole course of history is under God's control and conforms to the plan laid down by God before the foundation of the world.'[34] 'Jewish apocalyptic was concerned with the fate of mankind in the future, and particularly the destiny of the people of God.'[35]

'Eschatology [in 4 Ezra and Syriac Baruch] functions as a kind of final justification of God in the face of insoluble problems presented by existence.'[36] 'The revelation of the whole of history to the seer [in 2 Kings 18.9-12] in these "predictions" seems to have a theological point. The readers of the apocalypses are permitted to see that the experiences of the present must be related to the totality of human history, whose course is entirely directed by God.'[37] 'To know that the unsatisfactory situation which faces man in the present is a transitory phenomenon is one way of reaffirming the viability of religious belief.'[38]

To draw out the principle that unites these several statements, although apocalyptic is characterized as the revelation of divine mysteries in the plural, thus allowing potentially for several possible mysteries, there really is only one mystery, one secret, one piece of knowledge that commands interest: it is the eventual revelation of God's justice.

It is awkward to continue to discuss the subject by means of an adjective which by customary usage associates it with a literary style as in 'apocalyptic literature.' A noun would be preferable and because of its close association with apocalyptic 'the Apocalypse' is adopted here as the noun of shorthand reference for 'the eventual revelation of God's justice.' The adjective 'apocalyptic' is retained in use generally to refer to the subject matter that has historically been the object of rejection but also applied to the new usage proposed. The fact that catastrophe, commonly taken as the meaning of the Apocalypse, is neither a necessary nor an exclusive means to articulate this conviction, but is a means to articulate transition, is brought out later. I have to ask the reader to accommodate this different usage. This means to break, or set aside for the time being, the fascination that this unfortunate dominant popular image has gained. *The Apocalypse is not the end of the world.* That catastrophe of 'the end' is subordinated to 'the eventual revelation of God's justice' as a circumstantial articulation; it is an articulation historically and imaginatively circumscribed but not theologically fixed nor necessary. It is only one of many potential articulations whose possibilities are in principle open ended. The Book of Revelation has exercised too dominant an influence. It is one person's attempt to envisage the transition. It has no more authority than the imagination of one great dramatist.

While setting out definitions, it is understood here that the relations of prophecy, eschatology and apocalyptic, on which scholarship has expended much energy, are not mutually exclusive. The Apocalypse is necessarily eschatological, but eschatology and prophecy may at their option be apocalyptic. That is to say that the Apocalypse is a species within the genus eschatology. This follows Charles except for loosening his restrictive definition of prophecy as superseded by apocalyptic.[39] Caird holds to the broadest definition of eschatology 'the study of, or the corpus of beliefs held about the destiny of man and the world,' and admires the clarity of the OED definition 'the department of theological science concerned with the four last things, death, judgment, heaven and hell.'[40] Unfortunately the clarity is illusory. In practice, the anxious problem of evil raised by one God omnipotence fixes interest so much on the Apocalypse that, although possible in principle, it is difficult to find eschatology that is not directed to it. Indeed the inclusion of judgment in the OED definition of eschatology inescapably characterizes it as apocalyptic.

The Resistance dislike of apocalyptic has taken advantage of the overlapping and permeable boundaries in these categories and in approaching any writing on the subject it is necessary to bear this influence in mind. An extreme example is Walter Kümmel's Promise and Fulfilment. [41] In this work the polarizing equation is made: eschatological = all good, sober and true prognostications of the future, apocalyptic = all bad, fanciful and false prognostication. So we find that drama is bad apocalyptic, but hurrying urgently with news is eschatological.[42] Imminent expectation is apocalyptic but future expectation is eschatological.[43] Revelation is bad apocalyptic, message is good prophetic.[44] Specific dates and premonitory signs are apocalyptic, general expectation is eschatological.[45] Speculative and fanciful ideas about the future are apocalyptic. Predictions of sensible and definite future events are eschatological.[46] Revealing secrets of the Kingdom is apocalyptic but open pronouncement of its consummation is eschatological.[47] By this play between eschatology and apocalyptic the message of Jesus is figured by Kümmel as eschatological. By this means Jesus is protected from what Kümmel sees as the tar of apocalyptic. I will not be using the word eschatological, except where it is referred to by other writers, in the belief that it is superfluous and a source of obfuscation.

1.2. The Architecture of the Apocalypse: The Ethic and its Articulation

Returning to consideration of Charles and Weber I would like to build more of a conceptual frame for The Apocalypse and bring out in particular how it is a live and relevant issue, albeit not necessarily recognized for what it is, for Christian theologians today.

A feature emerging from Charles and Weber is that a certain amount of *structural articulatory apparatus* has to be built up to give effect to the implementation of God's justice. If the ethical deficit is delayed for remedy till after death then the structural feature of an afterlife becomes imperative. If there is to be ethical discrimination the event of an assize must be incorporated as a preliminary to this afterlife. If this assize is to be comprehensively fair it must be retrospective of all the dead since the beginning of creation. This in turn requires some scheme of an interim holding place for the dead, a temporary heaven or limbo.

It becomes necessary to retrieve the dead at the appropriate moment, hence the day of resurrection of the dead. It is the development and alignment of this necessary apparatus in accord with the gravitational pull of one God omnipotence that frames Charles' *Critical History of the Doctrine of a Future Life* (subtitle of his *Eschatology*, 1898).The evolution of Sheol illustrates this. Where Sheol was originally conceived as a place comprehensive of all the dead without moral selection there is no means for readjustment of rewards in the afterlife. God does not possess the power of adjustment in these circumstances. The power of God is doubly compromised under monolatry through lack of exclusive jurisdiction of Sheol. Other Gods may be consigning the dead of their own nations to its confines.

The principle that compels development of the apparatus of implementation is that the Apocalypse is an ethical goal. An ethic has no reality unless it is accompanied by the moral rules that would give effect to its implementation. Every ethic has two parts: the ethic and its articulation. The ethic states the goal that is to be achieved. The articulation frames the means to its realization. The questions of How? When? and For Whom? are implicit in the Apocalypse and demand answers. The human imagination is naturally curious for details of the practical means of implementation of this important event. From this curiosity is generated the apparatus of articulation; portents, introductory tribulations, the gathering in of the Gentiles, catastrophe, the messiah, the millennium, the resurrection of the dead, the day of judgment, the afterlife, the elect and any other ingredient that logic or unsatisfied curiosity might require.

A number of points need to be made about this ethic and its articulation. Firstly, although the ethic is fixed by the theological imperative its articulation, as imagined by its many hopeful interpreters, is immensely varied because it is impossible to imagine. That indeed is the nature of the problem. Paul's attempt to answer the question, 'How are the dead raised?'[48] and his

exasperated floundering in the process, is a charming example.
No one has privileged information in the matter. The articulation
is open to anybody's guess. We are incapable of an answer yet
there must be one, hence the bewildering variety of apocalyptic
material that has been inherited and the incompatibility of the
different schemes proposed. Paul alone grapples with three.[49]

Confronted with this variety the impression of irreducibly
eclectic and discrepant material is natural. As J. H. Leckie
presented the matter in his 1917 lecture to the United Free
Church College in Glasgow,

> The chief difficulty which besets this branch of study is *the
> immense variety and confusion of its forms*... We may reasonably
> doubt whether it will ever be possible to bring order out of all
> this perplexity, or to reduce to system the amazing variety of
> the eschatological forms.[50]

Or as Inge put the matter with more pith, 'All religious eschatology is a mass of contradictions.'[51]

Secondly, this articulatory material is *speculative*. Speculation,
not revelation, is its true provenance. The device of revelation is
only the means to dress speculation in authority. The speculation
is cast in the form of revelation from God directly communicated
to senior figures, in the guise of secrets and esoteric knowledge.
This is the clothing with which speculation is dressed in
authority and given the dramatic interest that has preserved it.
But revelation has no necessary connection to the Apocalypse.
The combination of speculative fertility with open ended
potential is the reason that the listing approach to the definition
of apocalyptic literature, though much attempted, has not proved
satisfactory.[52] As John Collins points out, the attempt to classify a
body of apocalyptic literature is an anachronistic project applied
to works which were not so identified at the time.[53]

The theological test is much safer ground for identification.

This eliminates some works in which apocalyptic is synonymous only with revelatory dreams but includes other works not usually identified. For instance Enoch's delightful tour of the machinery of heaven, as it were backstage at the theater, is excluded by the theological test. The New Testament, however, is included. The good news of the New Testament is that in Christ God has acted to initiate the eventual revelation of his justice. The New Testament as a whole is an Apocalypse despite the fact that it does not bear the name.

Thirdly the permanent theological imperative indicates that the Apocalypse cannot piecemeal be added to or subtracted from Christianity. It is an inherent feature of the religion. When Robert Funk (1926-2005), founder of the Jesus Seminar, set an agenda to 'exorcise the apocalyptic elements from Christianity'[54] this was not just a culturally embarrassed attempt to cauterize a blemish on the body of Christianity, it was a theological murder. Ernst Käsemann (1906-1998), Professor of New Testament at Tubingen, made a famous statement that set theology and apocalyptic apart, 'Apocalyptic was the mother of all Christian theology – since we cannot really class the preaching of Jesus as theology.'[55] But there is no such divide. The Apocalypse is theological and Jesus, in his apocalyptic proclamation, is doing theology.

The problem of the resolution of evil is no less an issue for today's thinkers. We should not be lulled into thinking that apocalyptic is the preserve of a pre-scientific worldview and ancient minds. The problem of the resolution of evil is still vital today and in this the permanent value of Weber and Charles' analyses is confirmed. As John Hick wrote, 'The enigma of evil presents so massive and direct a threat to our faith that we are bound to seek within the resources of Christian thought for a way, if not of resolving it, at least rendering it bearable by the Christian conscience.'[56] Today's theologians continue to theorize and construct apocalypses, although with the deficit in the current conceptual framework these are not recognized as such.

A number of examples may be cited. Vernon White reiterates the theological necessity of the Apocalypse in his book *Life Beyond Death*:

> The theological mind and imagination will be driven inevitably to afterlife. We are bound to conclude that for divine justice, creativity, and love to have full meaning, the world's evils 'must' be redeemed beyond what we see. Otherwise it would not be perfect justice and love. I repeat, the force of this 'must' is neither purely logical nor psychological: but it is fully theological.[57]

Jürgen Moltmann both confirms the theological imperative of the Apocalypse and speculates some new articulation:

> Think of the countless numbers of the raped and murdered and killed... where will their own lives be completed, and how? Can they somewhere be healed, complemented, lived to the full after they have died? The idea that for these people their death is 'the finish' would plunge the whole world into absurdity; for if their life has no meaning, has ours?... So I would like to think that eternal life gives the broken and the impaired and those whose lives have been destroyed space and time and strength to live the life which they were intended for, and for the sake of which they were born... I think this... for the sake of the justice which I believe is God's concern and his first option.[58] The 'Last Judgment'... is the most wonderful thing that can be proclaimed to men and women. It is a source of endlessly consoling joy to know, not just that the murderers will finally fail to triumph over their victims, but that they cannot in eternity even remain the murderers of their victims.[59]

Moltmann articulates the Apocalypse just as much as does The

Revelation of John. The cultural language of his articulation reflects the sentiments of the twentieth century in place of the resources of the Old Testament. On the same lines Tom Wright has contributed to the literature a full scale Apocalypse that goes by the title *Surprised by Hope*.[60] He reiterates the theological necessity. 'God is utterly committed to set the world right in the end. This doctrine, like that of the resurrection itself, is held firmly in place by the belief in God as creator on the one side and the belief in his goodness on the other.'[61] The book is framed by the concern to articulate what is meant by the ultimate future hope of the Christian gospel. Wright is confident to entertain much more detail than Paul but he nevertheless admits the speculative nature of the enterprise and the limitations to our knowledge occasioned by looking into the 'darkest theological mysteries.'[62] It is not possible, for instance, to ascertain whether our resurrected bodies will be reconstituted with or without their original defects.[63] Though it can be surmised that the Christian departed are in a state 'of restful happiness.' [64] It can be calculated that the earth will not be overcrowded when the dead are raised as half of all people who have populated the earth are alive today and huge tracts of land still remain unpopulated.[65]

For John Hick the Apocalypse is the essence of the gospel 'good news for all' and it is his complaint against humanist or non-theist theologians that their Christianity is elitist in its lack of provision for the Apocalypse:

If life terminates definitively at bodily death, then the universe is good only for a small minority of men and women. It does *not* sustain a religious message that is good news for all... the restrictions and pressures and often pathetic brevity of life, have prevented the great majority of human beings from making more than a small beginning towards the fulfilment of which the religions speak. If that potential is to be realised – and that it is to be realised is the meaning for human life of the ultimate goodness of the universe – then reality must be structured accordingly... even if the human situation should presently change markedly for the better... it would still be true that thousands have already lived and died, their highest potentialities unfulfilled – and, if the non-realists are right, permanently and irrevocably unfulfilled. This would negate any notion of the ultimate goodness of the universe.[66]

It is inconceivable that this comprehensive rectification of the backlog of the moral deficit of human existence could take place via a re-run on this planet or in these biological bodies as presently constituted, so these contemporary apocalypses confirm the continued requirement of articulatory apparatus such as a miraculous new earth, changed conditions of our biological bodies, or a new heaven together with a transition point, 'catastrophe' or 'end', that would inaugurate the necessary changed conditions. This condition is still accompanied by the assize necessary to adjudicate which persons are deemed to have been fulfilled in life and those who have not. The parameters of the articulatory problems set by the ethic remain the same today as they did in the apocalyptic literature of two thousand years ago.

Fourthly, no particular item of articulatory material has a fixed necessity for the implementation of the Apocalypse. The articulations are plastic. They are subject to cultural reformulation using the imaginative power, by tradition, of the seer or the visionary and today by anyone who cares to consider the matter. Judgment, for example, is the articulation most disliked by twentieth-century sentiment. For Robert Funk it is a 'crass, pathetic form... unworthy of the Galilean.'[67] Cecil Cadoux (1883-1947), Professor of Church History at Mansfield College, noted that the modern Christian conscience has given up eternal punishment in favor of universal salvation.[68] Moltmann, who shares this sentiment, articulates, as above, this universal salvation. Wright, a more stern traditionalist, is reluctant to abandon altogether some form of punishment and prefers to articulate the compromise of annihilationism whereby evil people, through their self-selected loss of qualification as human, do not pass on to immortal life.[69]

The literature inherits different cultural and literary streams of articulation and many influences on apocalyptic have been proposed; Persian,[70] Iranian,[71] Hellenistic,[72] a development of prophecy,[73] Jewish wisdom literature,[74] Pharisaism,[75] old Canaanite mythic lore,[76] and roundly dismissing all these, 'a stubbornly Jewish and Christian development.'[77] It is an interesting topic to trace the connections of imagery, which with the instinct of literary economy for a good story, is never discarded but taken up for recycling. But in terms of the thesis presented here there is no special result obtainable from tracing origins. The ethic itself is assumed potentially to arise spontaneously from the conditions of one God omnipotence.

To conclude the subject of the ethic and its articulation, the failure to separate the necessary theological ethic from the circumstantial articulation is the root cause of rejection of apocalyptic in the twentieth century and continuing today. The old articulations are simply embarrassing. They are now considered incompatible with modern feelings. The ethic is not recognized as the generating principle, the newly generated articulations are not recognized as apocalyptic and so the whole is thrown out with the unfortunate consequence that the possibilities for forging the connections between ancient worldviews and our own are denied.

The treatment of circumstantial articulations as a falsely definitive test of apocalyptic has been one of many standard gambits used to eliminate apocalyptic from Jesus. For example, in *Jesus and the Word* Rudolf Bultmann (1884-1976), Professor of New Testament at Marburg, noted the relative shortage of apoca-

lyptic details in Jesus' proclamation of the Kingdom of God.[78]
This enabled Bultmann to declare the message of Jesus unapocalyptic and to separate him from his Jewish background
preparatory to proposing his existentialist interpretation of the
Word. Günter Bornkamm (1905-1990), Professor of New
Testament at Heidelberg, similarly made use of the reticence on
detail to mark 'deep and fundamental' contrast between Jesus
and Jewish apocalypticism.[79] But the dearth of speculative details
is no test that the proclamation of the Kingdom of God is disqualified as an Apocalypse.

1.4. The Reflexive Dynamic of the Apocalypse: The Energization of the Present

The belief that the Apocalypse is synonymous with abdication of
action for a better world was a prevalent motivation for the
twentieth-century Resistance. For Paul Hanson apathy is the very
definition of apocalyptic. 'Prophetic eschatology is transformed
into apocalyptic at the point where the task of translating the
cosmic vision into the categories of mundane reality is
abdicated.'[80] In this Hanson echoes a general sense that it is
prophecy which offers the tradition of social critique considered
lacking in apocalyptic. Stephen Patterson, who pleads 'the end of
the apocalypse' claims 'the radically world-negating theology of
apocalyptic.'

The apocalyptic paradigm can also have its own debilitating
and self-serving tendencies. The repeated assertion that God's
decisive activity in the world belongs to the future and that until
God decides to act we must be content to live in an imperfect
world can lead to complacency about the problems we face as a
culture. In the face of such temporal theological dualism, in
which the present is given over to an imperfect humanity while
the future is placed in God's exclusive hands, one can only
conclude that any human attempt at reform is ultimately futile.
Moreover, it is unnecessary, for the security of God's intervention

in the future means that ultimately humanity will not have to deal with its current problems anyway. The idea of a father God who arrives just in time to save his unruly children from their own inevitable foolishness is an unhealthy starting point.[81] The same sentiment is felt by Marcus Borg. He takes it is a primary assumption that eschatology equals apathy. Borg considers that the association of Jesus with apocalyptic has, therefore, obscured the socialist critique of society that was made by Jesus and which Borg wants to bring to the fore.[82] St Paul can be enlisted to this view, recommending the suspension of normal commitments under expectation of the imminent end.[83]

This equation with apathy has spelt trouble for apocalyptic in the face of Christianity's urge to reclaim social relevance after the shock of being upstaged by Marx, the reigning prophet of the twentieth century. Stephen Liberty at the start of the century, when the attraction of communism and its prospects was more vital than it is now, entered a passionate plea, against the 'eschatological attack of the moment' and the 'pathetic helplessness on the part of the Christian Church.' Liberty called for a political Jesus 'to vindicate afresh the right of the Christian Church to hold up the example of its Master in dealing with the policies and social conditions of contemporary life.'[84] Liberty's anxiety can stand as figurehead for a worry driving through the whole of the twentieth-century theology's approach to apocalyptic. The question of whether Marxism has stolen the clothes from a Christianity that owns the original Marxism is one likely to occur to socialist Christians. It was brought to the fore by Karl Kautsky (1854-1938), Marxist theoretician and friend of Marx and Engels. Kautsky appropriated Jesus as the original Marxist in his 1908 work *Foundations of Christianity*.[85] The Christian Marxist philosopher Ernst Bloch (1885-1977) similarly framed early Christianity as the original communism and proved himself the inspiration of seventies liberation theology.[86]

The presumed tension between the vital aspirations of

socialism and the apathy of apocalyptic came to the longed for and ingenious resolution in Moltmann's *Theology of Hope*[87] in which he appropriated apocalyptic to socialism. Pirouetting on the parallelism of the word hope Moltmann turned the hope of God's action in the Apocalypse[88] into humanist hope for the sufficiency of human achievement. By this means Moltmann metamorphosed the apocalyptic Kingdom of God into the Socialist Kingdom. The Socialist Kingdom became a diverse spectrum exhibited in liberation theology and the humanist Jesus of the Westar Institute. Other writers with the same conviction that apocalyptic equates to political apathy prefer to avoid what might seem the sleight of hand in Moltmann's appropriation and take the more common line of simple rejection. Leon Morris, for instance, is unequivocal in his rejection of the apathetic apocalypse. 'The apocalypticists are content to abandon the present… and the historical process.'[89] They write off the world and have no 'workable political solutions' to contribute.[90] Christianity is really about the cross and so 'apocalyptic fails us at the heart of the faith… At base Christianity is the gospel, and "gospel" is not an apocalyptic term.'[91]

There is something almost wilfully contrary in exegesis that entails apocalyptic with apathy in the face of the obvious fact that John the Baptist, Jesus and Paul were characters hyper motivated by their mission, sufficiently, all three of them, to forfeit their lives for their beliefs. The source of this motivating energy is not hidden but lies on the face of the internal dynamic of the Apocalypse. The use to which we employ our creative talents in the present determines our situation and prospects on the critical Day of Judgment: *the dynamic of the Apocalypse is reflexive*. The more imminent the prospect of the Apocalypse the more vitalizing is the need for good actions. The need for genuine action and not lip service is the message of John the Baptist:

John said to the crowds that came out to be baptized by him,

'You brood of vipers! Who warned you to flee from the wrath to come? Bear fruits worthy of repentance. Do not begin to say to yourselves, "We have Abraham as our ancestor"...' And the crowds asked him, 'What then should we do?' In reply he said to them, 'Whoever has two coats must share with anyone who has none; and whoever has food should do likewise.'[92]

A place in the glorious future has to be earned. It is not something to be granted automatically. The opening line from John Donne's divine poem XIII captures this reflexive energization of the Apocalypse. 'What if this present were the world's last night?' Although the Apocalypse appears to focus our attention on future events the actual focus is now. This is because the last things are not in fact the last. The time of tribulation, the coming of the Lord, the judgment and the separation of the wicked from the elect are preliminaries to a new era linked by a continuous consciousness that threads through from the now into the hereafter. The dynamic connections of the Apocalypse link what happens to us in the future to our behavior in the present. Intensifying this it radicalizes and makes urgent that connection in three ways. It makes the connection important because on it depends a future of bliss or torment. It makes the connection vital because it is individualist: it proposes our sole personal responsibility for the outcome. It makes the connection urgent by its element of Russian roulette. We are given a number of chances to repent and take charge of this responsibility but we do not know when the hour is and by surprise our last chance will come upon us. The Apocalypse is urgently concerned with the present. Although we seem to be scanning the heavens for these signs as though through a telescope, the optical focus is reversed; it is the heavens that are focused on us as a subject scrutinized under a microscope.

The Apocalypse acts to energize the present. The primary

reflexive function of judgment is to found a close-knit community. It gives to the community a spirit of identity and purpose even in situations of distress where hopes and meaning seem to be contradicted. Philip Davies captures this effect. 'By means of the authority of ancient figures bearing divine revelations they consoled their flock with the assurance that God was in control of both history and nature; that evil had a rational explanation and an imminent end.'[93] From this spirit of community and trust in God stems the individual sense of identity, purpose and support.

The entailment of apathy is a psychologically and sociologically inept reading. There is no more potent force that has in fact served for two thousand years to inspire and direct the energies of Christians. The active nature of the religion with its belief that evil can and will be conquered is one of its centrally attractive qualities. It is a question to be addressed to any replacement liberal theology how its dynamic can match the energizing quality of the Apocalypse? It is doubtful that any theological principle of equivalent power could be produced.

It is difficult to locate a clue as to how, in the face of this obvious energizing quality, such a contrary interpretation of the Apocalypse has taken hold of exegesis. It may be to do with the loss of belief in the afterlife. Perhaps Leckie pinpointed the heart of the matter:

> The man who undertakes the discussion of any subject must be granted certain postulates... so it is quite a modest thing for me to begin the present study with the assumption that we are agreed on two matters of opinion. The first of these is that human personality survives death.[94]

Without a genuine belief in 'the life of the world to come' the crucial linkage between the present and future which generates the reflexive dynamic power is short circuited. The Apocalypse collapses into a lifeless thing: as much use as a bouncy castle with the fan blown.

1.5. The Apocalyptic Resistance of the Twentieth Century

The 'New Theology', as it was known at the turn of the nineteenth century, arose through the interpretations of Johannes Weiss and Albert Schweitzer. These read the newly discovered apocalyptic material into Jesus' proclamation of the Kingdom of God. This New Theology was accompanied by inauspicious portents from its birth. It was disliked by both parents who, although insisting on its legitimacy, disowned it as a proposition for their times. They were at heart attached to the un-apocalyptic liberal theology of the day. Neither Weiss nor Schweitzer were analysts of the Apocalypse and saw it as part of an ancient thought world. They did not pick up the theological basis and understood the end of the world with a literalism that inevitably made it difficult to appropriate. This assumption made Jesus seem alien. It posited an embarrassing disjunction between what were taken to be 'primitive Christians' and the presumed more sophisticated Christians of their day.

This pattern of acknowledging apocalyptic but having nothing constructive to say about it is still apparent a century later in one of the few scholars who has insisted on interpreting Jesus as a prophet of the Apocalypse. Dale Allison's recognition of the fact is still made 'reluctantly but without equivocation.'[95]

Schweitzer had humanist leanings and looked forward to the 'ruins of the supersensuous other-worldly system of thought' being swept away to make space for a new spiritual real world.[96] Weiss preferred the liberal position of his father-in-law Albrecht Ritschl that he had so effectively undermined. The translators of his book *Die Predigt* point out that 'He was ready to allow a radical hiatus to exist between Jesus's teachings and those of subsequent Christians. Indeed he could see no alternative to that position.'[97] For Weiss the liberal spiritualized Kingdom as a development of Christianity was inevitable and preferable. His protest against that liberal theology was directed to its origin not its substance. Weiss insisted that we should admit that we made it up ourselves and should not pretend that it comes from Jesus. The reception in the English speaking world fared no better. William Sanday (1843-1920), Dean Ireland Professor of Scriptural Exegesis at Queen's College Oxford, first introduced the New Theology in 1907. He simultaneously set out his reservations. Sanday explained his personal attachment to 'mediating theology', that is, ethics as an alternative focus to apocalyptic.[98] In this Sanday agreed with his friend and correspondent, Ernst Von Dobschütz (1870-1934), Professor at the University of Halle. Dobschütz gave voice to the charged atmosphere of emotional anxiety which drove the Apocalyptic Resistance through the twentieth century. Here is the salvo with which Dobschütz, addressing the 1909 summer school of theology at Oxford, greeted the 'favourite subject of the present moment.'[99]

If eschatology is the key to all gospel questions then it becomes the problem of problems how Christianity could go on without eschatology through so many centuries. If there was nothing in Jesus but eschatology, then he was a misguided enthusiast, and it would be almost impossible to explain how the name of an eccentric became the symbol for millions and millions of Christians who took from Him not only some vain hopes of the future, but a joyful experience of real salvation and an unexampled amount of moral energy.[100]

This heartfelt expression of concern that Jesus might be judged mistaken in predicting the imminent arrival of a kingdom that did not materialize can stand as example for dozens of similar expressions of anxiety that are encountered in New Testament commentary throughout the twentieth century; 'deluded visionary';[101] 'futile nonsense;'[102] 'dark cloudland of impressive but vague and barbarous ideas;'[103] 'Great source of weakness in our presentation of Christianity;'[104] 'deluded fanatic... a synthetic modern scholarly construction that we need to abandon;'[105] 'cul-de-sac... abandon either the Christian faith or the hypothesis;'[106] 'alien in a bizarre world of fanatic zeal and fantastic expectations;'[107] 'That bizarre idea, which has been touted around New Testament scholarship all this century should now be given a pauper's funeral.'[108] One hundred years after Dobschütz scholars are no better reconciled to 'The Mistake' and no more subtle in its solution than rejection of apocalyptic. The rescue plan of the Resistance is that Jesus himself must be preserved from apocalyptic however much the gospels may be saturated with it.

This problem of the Mistake taken as an apparent challenge to the credibility of Jesus runs concurrently through the twentieth century with Apathy as a challenge to his relevance. These twin forces combine to form what could be named 'apocalyptic allergy syndrome' which drives the Apocalyptic Resistance. But there is a force simultaneously opposing this urge to rejection. It is the need to accept the apocalyptic discovery which has been found difficult to challenge head on. The evidence is too strong. Rowland confirms that 'apocalyptic... and eschatological beliefs had a significant, perhaps central, role to play in early Christian belief.'[109] Thus Wright, a challenger of the Mistake, is prompted to say that 'Schweitzer was 100 percent right to say that Jesus must be understood in terms of Jewish apocalyptic.'[110]

The result of this intolerable tension of opposing forces is a variety of schizophrenia: rejection becomes acceptance. Dobschütz is an example of rejection masquerading as acceptance and his procedure is an example of the major Resistance gambit employed during the century. It can be summed up as 'apocalyptic is essential, but not important' or in the words of Morris, 'there is much more to Christianity than apocalyptic.'[111] This gambit founds the 'mediating theology' of Sanday and

Dobschütz. Apocalyptic is relegated in favor of ethics. Dobschütz can serve as an illustration of this anti-apocalyptic maneuver still current today in the elevation to pride of place of the Old Testament wisdom literature.

Dobschütz introduces his work as a response to the interest in the engaging debate of the time; he is concerned to accept the apocalyptic discovery. He recognizes a genuine stock of apocalyptic sayings in Jesus and rejects the method of circumventing their face value by spiritualizing interpretations. He intends to demonstrate the *real* significance of eschatology.[112] This sounds like a positive assessment, but the reader is in no position to know at this stage that this is going to turn out to be no significance whatsoever. His method is to follow the 'exaggerated consistency in a sounder way.'[113] The coat of arms of 'pure apocalyptic' is first diluted by quartering with 'non-eschatological moral material' and 'transmuted eschatology', that is, realized eschatology before Charles Dodd (1884-1964), Professor of Divinity at Oxford, coined the term. The significance is already reduced to one third. Each of these elements is now to be given its appropriate value and weight.[114] The non-eschatological material is promoted to the first rank because of its permanent value.[115] Eschatology is thus further diminished by relegation. It is now found that eschatology is a cultural husk which Jesus used because it was the common currency of expression.[116] Jesus used it for its motivational effect, not its content.[117] Jesus transformed the miraculous scheme into inward moral meaning.[118] Eschatology is thus further quartered by intellectual supercession. It is now down to perhaps one-sixteenth of its original importance and still the relegation continues. The transmuted eschatology of the Johannine Gospel 'best expresses Jesus' proper view.'[119] Much of what is found in the gospel is the common stock of Jewish ideas, not correctly traceable to Jesus.[120] It was a misunderstanding and 'declension' in primitive Christianity to exaggerate the eschatological.[121] Matthew, abetted by Mark and

Luke is the prime culprit in introducing this material.[122] 'However strong Jesus' belief in eschatology might have been it was only of secondary importance for His religious life, and for his teaching.'[123] The antipathy of Dobschütz which was initially veiled now begins to display itself. Scholars following the trend have divested themselves of modern ideas to assert a 'one-sided archaism'[124] and have got used to 'strange eschatological ideas.'[125] Apocalyptic, reduced from its original pride of place to a tiny quartering in the bottom corner of the shield is now to be ousted altogether as superfluous: 'The form of his expectation was unimportant even to himself.'[126]

The result of these maneuvers by Dobshütz is doublespeak. Jesus is made into an apocalyptic prophet who has no interest in the Apocalypse. Jesus expressed himself in eschatological terms but it was wrong for the early church to bring in eschatology. At the same time the early church was not eschatological. 'In the kernel of early Christian religious feeling, we shall find there is nothing eschatological about it.'[127] Eschatology is at once accepted in principle and rejected in fact. This is the schizophrenia of Apocalyptic Resistance Theology.

The overall result with Dobschütz is the assertion of immovable nineteenth-century orthodoxy. The Kingdom of God is restated in a repetition of words almost identical to Harnack, 'God dwelling inwardly in the hearts of the believers.'[128] The Kingdom of God has ceased to be the objective event brought in by God, which was the whole claim of the apocalyptic discovery. In this way the New Theology which reputedly unsettled forever the liberal theology of the nineteenth century did not at all unsettle that liberal theology. Having ring-fenced apocalyptic to its satisfaction, liberal nineteenth-century orthodoxy sailed unperturbed into the twentieth century. The Liberal Kingdom metamorphosed into the Socialist Kingdom, bypassed apocalyptic altogether and brings us to the present date.

It is notable that this early history prefigures most of the rejection gambits made use of throughout the century. These are: Jewish apocalyptic expression as a cultural husk within which Jesus has superior understanding;[129] a Jesus dissociated from his Jewish background, from his mentor John the Baptist and from his church;[130] the 'not only but also' separation of eschatology from ethics; the priority of a non-eschatological Q gospel;[131] the apocalyptic introductions of Matthew;[132] Mark [133] and Luke; Jerusalem as the local focus and saving vindication of Jesus' predictions;[134] the priority of the present over the future kingdom.[135] The repertoire springs up ready made in response to Schweitzer, because it has been in rehearsal in response to the earlier Weiss.[136*] The only scenario missing is the claim that we invented apocalyptic.

This early settlement of the repertoire gives an air of repetition to the rest of the century. The Resistance arguments of the Westar institute, for instance, are not new methods. They derive their apparent newness from the discoveries of new gospel material. These discoveries are adopted as the new canon but the principle is the same as the prioritization of Q.

In addition to the syndrome of the Mistake and Apathy what underlies Dobschütz in particular, and the Resistance in general, is the inability to see apocalyptic as ethical. There is a wish to source and prioritize ethical material from elsewhere. Charles countered this fallacy from its outset. The Apocalypse is the comprehensive ethical attempt:

> Prophecy has always been recognized as the greatest ethical force in the ancient world.
>
> Such also was apocalyptic in its time, yet an attempt has recently been made by advanced liberals to differentiate prophecy and apocalyptic on the ground that apocalyptic and ethics are distinct, that ethics are the kernel and apocalyptic the husk, which Christianity shed when it ceased to need it. But apocalyptic was essentially ethical... an ethics based on

the essential righteousness of God.[137]

The above completes the exposition of my understanding of the Apocalypse and the outline of the mistaken motives and means of its rejection. To bring up to the present the picture of the situation opened by Sanday and Dobschütz a tour of some of the later historical landmarks of Apocalyptic Resistance is needed.

Ernst Käsemann's already encountered statement 'Apocalyptic was the mother of all Christian theology' was made in the context of his rebellion against his teacher Bultmann's existentialist basis for theology. In calling time on existentialism Käsemann might seem to presage a turn to advocacy for apocalyptic but his insistence on the parentage was accompanied by his unease that this was so. Käsemann adopted some of the standard rejection gambits. Jesus himself was not very apocalyptic. The apocalyptic element was a development introduced by Paul and by the church after Easter.[138] Klaus Koch's *Rediscovery of Apocalyptic*,[139] is a staple text for students and considered a landmark of seventies revival of interest.[140] James Barr pointed out, however, that the English translation of the German title gives the wrong sense of the book's intention. *Ratlos* in the original would be better rendered as *'Not a Clue what to do with'* Apocalyptic. Such was the scene that Koch surveyed. His rallying call that apocalyptic might hold the clue which, 'in the face of the desperate situation of systematic theology and philosophy, provides aspects under which theology will again be convincingly possible in the future'[141] fell on deaf ears. Koch expressed only doubts that any integration would be made in the face of insurmountable theological embarrassment and singled out the 'complete lack of enthusiasm' of American theologians.[142]

That peculiarity of the Americans occasions an observation of the hidden cultural determinants on theology. If, as has been noted, apocalyptic comes to the fore in repressed communities under stress then it must be admitted to recede to insignificance in the nation which has achieved above all others in the history of the world the highest standard of living together with pride in the model of its political organization. More than one American theologian has equated American Democracy with the closest it is possible to get to the Kingdom of God on earth.[143*] It is fitting that the epicenter of recent Apocalyptic Resistance is situated in California. With not only the Americans in mind it can be said that the most interesting thing that twentieth-century theology says about apocalyptic is what it says about itself.

Exegesis today inherits Wright's theologically suspect masterpiece of hybrid acceptance/rejection. What could be named as the 'local' apocalyptic articulation of the destruction of Jerusalem is substituted in order to vindicate Jesus and acknowledge the inescapable apocalyptic element. With the same stroke apocalyptic is put in the past tense as a completed event and religion today is made safe from the culturally embarrassing universal apocalypse.[144]

This one hundred-year history of Apocalyptic Resistance Theology throws light on the latest focus of interest in the academy: Dionysius and the mystical tradition. These do not ostensibly have anything to do with the Resistance but that is because the situation has moved on. Both conservative interpretations of Christianity, as per Wright and radical interpretation as per the Nature God of Death of a God theology are united in agreement that Christianity will not be allowed to have been apocalyptic in the past and shall not be apocalyptic in the future. The ground has been so thoroughly prepared by the past one hundred years and the eradication of apocalyptic so universally agreed that this has become the premise on which today's theology is done. The fundamental attraction of Dionysius and the Nature God of the mystics is that they bear no trace of apocalyptic. The present fashion represents the triumph of the Resistance. It continues on a new plane where apocalyptic has so far been obliterated that it is no longer necessary even to mention it.

1.6. Conclusion: The Christians

Referring back to the question of a definition of Christianity that was raised in the introduction it remains to close this chapter with an explanation of why I consider that the Apocalypse is not only the central but the unique, and uniquely valuable, character of the religion. I hope to explain how Christianity effected a progression of the Apocalypse, how this produced an especially attractive psychology and why the Christian Apocalypse took the world by storm. It is necessary to bring out the special character of the Christian Apocalypse, in contrast to other types of Apocalypse. This special character is what I call the Relaxed Apocalypse. Its distinctive psychology can best be brought out by arguing against a prevalent view that apocalyptic was the preserve only of 'primitive Christians' and that today Christianity has been de-eschatologized.

The perception that eschatology was central to 'Primitive Christian Belief' but that there was later a dissolution of the eschatological framework which became the form that we inherit today is presented by Rowland in his textbook *Christian Origins* and is considered to hold immeasurable influence.[145]

Rowland adopted the thesis of Martin Werner (1887-1964), Lecturer in New Testament at Bern. The question of de-eschatologization is best approached by a consideration of Werner's argument. Werner takes to extreme degree the twin influences of the Hellenization thesis championed by Harnack at the end of the nineteenth century and of the delay that the second coming of Christ is purported to have had on early expectations. Werner's particular endeavor is to marry the two and explain Hellenization not *'from without'* but from 'the elucidation of the *inner causes.'*[146] This he does by harnessing the delay as the internal driving force of Hellenization. This compound he then applies with comprehensive singularity to the 'inevitable' de-eschatologizing of primitive Christianity.[147] Werner does not define eschatology so this has to be deduced from its application.

For Werner it is imminence that distinguishes the eschatological from what has been de-eschatologized. For Werner 'imminence of the end' or imminence of the second coming is the essential qualifying feature of what is eschatological. Relating this to basic definitions it is clear that imminence will not be adequate to the decisive performance Werner expects of it. Imminence is not an essential feature of Caird's 'corpus of beliefs held about the destiny of man and of the world.' Although the question of When? is inherent to the Apocalypse, imminence is only one possible articulation of the timing. On this basis imminence is not going to prove a useful tool to distinguish between eschatological and de-eschatologized concepts. Certainly the transition from imminence to deferral cannot bear the weight of the wholesale dissolution and abandonment of the eschatological doctrines of primitive Christianity; the collapse of the eschatological significance of the death and resurrection of Jesus;[148] to render 'hopelessly problematical' Jesus' conquest of the demonic powers;[149] and have a 'disintegrating effect' on the concept of the Messiah. [150] What Werner proves, if anything, is not that eschatology vanished but that the tense imminence with which it was originally vested became relaxed.

Werner's thesis is another example of apologetics defining eschatology. For Werner de-eschatologizing is not just what did happen it is something that rightly should happen. According to him the job of Protestantism today is to overturn the 'false-compromise forms' and 'mis-development of de-eschatologizing' undertaken by the Catholic Church.[151] This false compromise evolved Catholic mystery religion which is Werner's target.[152] Protestantism must replace this with a true de-eschatologizing understanding of 'the special revelation of God concerning the principle of human existence'[153] and to show the world 'what ultimately is the nature of Christian faith.'[154] 'The content of the apocalyptic-eschatological ideas of Primitive Christianity, in their original concrete form, are no more, as such, to be reckoned as

Christian truth.'[155] The apocalyptic aspect of Jesus was only the peculiar contemporary mode of expression which cannot be followed today and Protestantism has to abandon the dogma of the eschatological Christ.[156]

The de-eschatologizing apologetic of Werner is blind to the creative advancement of the articulation of the Apocalypse that Christianity effected and which remains its uniquely powerful basis of attraction. Rowland is close to the right track. He notes that the apocalyptic framework contains within itself the resource to cope with the delay.[157] As an example he notes Paul's relaxed attitude, enjoying the assurance of Christ enthroned in heaven. But what is not connected up is that this resource within the Apocalypse is a creative intensification not a departure. It is not a 'radical rethinking away from eschatology.'[158] On the contrary, the singular development in the Christian Apocalypse, and it is the feature displayed by Paul, is that *imminence* is transferred into its close relation *certainty of inauguration*. The second coming presupposes and takes its significance from the inauguration of the eventual revelation of God's justice. This inauguration has already been demonstrated with unshakeable certainty in the resurrection of Christ. Incarnation, atonement, the resurrection and the figure of Christ are all articulations of the Apocalypse. God has acted. The stage curtain on the final moral validation of life in this world has begun to draw aside. Full disclosure in due course is guaranteed. It is this certainty of inauguration that is the distinguishing and energizing feature of the Christian Apocalypse. Were the second coming to be discounted from these other four articulations it would have only a limited effect on the overall apocalyptic significance of Christ. Compared to this certainty of inauguration the second coming is an administrative formality. It remains only a supposedly logical deduction and it is a misreading of the psychology, that its delay was critical.

There may have been at an early stage in Christianity an

adjustment to a lower degree of imminence but to read into this inevitable pressure of de-eschatologization is the opposite of the advancement of eschatology that Christianity forged. Jewish apocalyptic was articulated by the expectation of the Messiah, historical events of catastrophe and Jesus' proclamation of the Kingdom of God. Christian apocalyptic forged the new articulations of the pre-existence of Christ, the logos entering the world, the incarnation, the resurrection, and the image of Jesus sitting at the right hand of God. There is a simple bi-polar transition in the articulation of the Apocalypse, between Jesus and the death of Jesus that founds Christianity. Jesus declared the good news of the *imminent* arrival of the Kingdom of God. At the death of Jesus, Christians declared the good news of the *certainty* that God has acted in Jesus himself as a step in the progress of his Apocalypse. The 'good news', as Hick insisted, is the good news that the eventual revelation of God's justice is now under way: The New Testament is an Apocalypse. Wright sums this up neatly, although as an anti-apocalyptic advocate the confirmation is inadvertent. 'Take away the resurrection and you lose the entire New Testament.'[159] For Wright, bodily resurrection is the point at which the doctrine of creation and the doctrine of God's justice meet.[160] That is to say that resurrection is significant because it is a progression of the revelation of God's justice. The transition from imminence to certainty is a feature inherent in the very conception of Christianity and not a later development. Although the burning coals of certainty may have been accompanied for a while by the embers of imminence the eventual extinction of these embers did not leave the Christian Apocalypse short of warmth or energy from the second of the two parents.

Although the proposal that the New Testament is an Apocalypse may seem surprising in comparison to what is generally understood to be apocalyptic literature it cannot be considered new. The description only gives a new name to the concept that has been readily identified in scholarship on the theology of the New Testament. The concept appears veiled in a variety of alternative words and phrases such as universal history, salvation history, predestination or determinism. Stauffer's apocalyptic basis for the New Testament has already been quoted. A couple of further illustrations will serve here. Oscar Cullmann (1902-1999), Professor of New Testament at Basel, adopted the expression *Heilsgeschichte*. He used this to coordinate 'the innermost nature of all New Testament Christology,'[161] and 'the decisive revelation of God's redemptive will.'[162] This is pure Apocalypse. Kümmel, in setting the problem of discovering unity in the very different voices of Jesus, Paul and the Gospel of John, found that unity in 'the divine conde-scension.'[163] This elliptic expression is, it can be discerned from Kümmel's exposition, none other than God's act of revealing his justice. Moule sees the Gospel as 'the first extant specimen of a new genre... it has no real parallels before it.'[164] There is an element of truth in this, but the newness derives not from the genre but its particular content and circumstances. The Jewish Apocalypses were 'good news' but in a subdued consolatory manner aching with hurt. In the agonizing and irresolvable context of the political situation of Israel they could be none other. But released from the drag of national circumstance, universalized and individualized, the Christian Apocalypse became unequivocally exuberant good news. There was every reason for it to take the world by storm.

The staggering power that the New Testament Apocalypse unleashed is a result of the brilliant advancement of the problem of the resolution of evil that it effects and the attractive psychology generated by the new articulation. Under the shelter of the incarnation and resurrection of Christ, Christians live *inside* the Apocalypse. They are no longer supplicants and bystanders in hopeful anticipation but enjoy the exciting and motivating assurance that they are participants. Their actions are supplementary contributions to the overall framework of God's plan. With the humanization of God in Christ, Christians are brought into intimate connection with the Apocalypse in the double facet of a role model and an intercessor. Freed from the corporate nature of the Jewish Apocalypse the Christian Apocalypse becomes wholly individualist. The corporate Jewish Apocalypse operates to restrain the personal power of the individual because one person's commitment can always be compromised by the action of others. For Christians the brakes are off. The responsibility is unmitigated individualism with the striking free empowerment and energization that this entails.

It was stated in the introduction that it would be explained how the strict millennialist sects are an aberration from the Christian Apocalypse. The explanation is that the installment of Christ and the imminent return of Christ, although they may be treated as one, are really two separate articulations of the Apocalypse. Inherent in the installment of Christ is the overwhelmingly convincing reassurance of God's action which founds the Relaxed Apocalypse characterized in the paragraph above. This is already realized from the earliest stage in Paul's blissful conception of being 'in Christ' and it represents the mainstream. In comparison the return of Christ does not offer any increment to this reassurance and it is effectively relegated. The strict millennialist sects, however, fixate on the return and so do not participate in the relaxed mainstream.

To sum up the classification of the Christians undertaken in this chapter I take the Apocalypse as the integral, joyous, energizing and uniquely characterizing keystone in the architecture of Christian theology. It might seem appropriate in order to facilitate distinctions of other types to name orthodoxy specifically as 'apocalyptic Christianity' but this would be tautological. God's action in the incarnation, the resurrection and installment of Christ 'seated at the right hand of God' places Christ as the central inauguration of the Apocalypse. The simple name 'Christian' is inextricably inclusive of the apocalyptic nature of the religion.

Can a modern understanding of God appropriate this Apocalypse? In strict terms it cannot. The Apocalypse is a product of artefactual theology (discussed in chapter seven). It is a secondary construction built on the premise of one God omnipotence. Once God is no longer personified as an intelligent and magically powerful agent the structure of a comprehensive and retrospective rectification of the moral deficit of human existence vaporizes. Referring back to the three solutions to the resolution of evil that found three different types of religion the removal of the conception of God as an omnipotent intelligent agent categorically removes the apocalyptic basis of the religion. A liberal revisioning of Christianity has to recognize the limitations of what can be revisioned. For itself this great aeon of the Apocalypse is over. A modern theology has to recognize that it is founded on a fourth solution to the problem of evil. This solution is that there will be no cosmic resolution of evil. Evil is a fact not a theological puzzle. What resolution there can be is partial not comprehensive. God is not going to make everything all right. We have to make it all right for each other. It is necessary to recognize that this forms a basis for religion that is fundamentally different from the Christian. Liberal theology is not a plain updating or reinterpretation. It is qualitatively different. We ought to be honest about this as a starting point.

Does this difficulty of appropriation mean that the value of apocalyptic is lost? Some small consolations are available. An understanding of this character of the religion provides the means to own our Christian heritage. That heritage is a reminder of the uniquely powerful ability of religion to frame people's worldview and direct their creative energies. An understanding of the beauty of the Apocalypse is a reminder of the sense of loss that any new liberal concept of God must bear. Although any new concept may equally frame a religious worldview it is doubtful whether it may do so with the same inspiration. The past fifty years of revisioning has disowned this heritage without understanding its value. That is what I mean by burying the past referred to in the preface.

All is by no means lost however. The Community God contains valuable resources independent of the artefactual constructions. It falls to the task of the second half of this book to take up the inspiration that can be retrieved from the House of the Christians. This turns out to be not a remainder but a determinative connection between the past and the future.

2

The House of the Platonists

2.1. Introduction: The Encounter of Two Incompatible Religions

With regard to the project to revision God that has gripped the intellectual vanguard for the past fifty years, it is not generally appreciated that the method of trumping the Community God with the Nature God is not new. It is a symptom of the long-standing clash between two incompatible religions that were brought into confluence eighteen hundred years ago to form Christianity. In this clash the Community God was made use of to trump the Nature God, but in a manner that turned out to be a pyrrhic victory.

When the raw wind of the Christians blew out from rural Galilee it encountered in cosmopolitan Alexandria the urbane breezes of the Greek philosophical/mystical thought of Plato and of Plotinus, his interpreter and key figure in the incorporation of

Platonism into Christianity. The new educated clientele in Alexandria were attracted to the moral conviction and buoyant psychology of the Christians, and, it must be said the wonderfully romantic story of God's Son saving the world. This contrasts with a certain dryness about the appeal of the philosophical God. This clientele needed a perspective on the new religion sympathetic to their Greek intellectual background. The Greek philosophy of the religion of Christianity that was forged from Platonism, by Clement of Alexandria, the first 'systematic theologian of the East,'[1] has since then been joined to the Christian religion in an embrace of mutual repulsion like the North and South poles of a magnet.

This incompatibility derives from a fundamental difference which Charles Bigg (1840-1908), Regius Professor of Ecclesiastical History at Oxford, pinpointed in his work *The Origins of Christianity*... 'Clement... set entirely on one side the Father of the New Testament and launched upon the Church the Neoplatonic doctrine of the Absolute god.'[2] This move set off the permanent tensions between the Community God and the Nature God that, as only the most recent of periodic outbursts, erupted in the Death of a God theology of the 1960s.

An additional note on vocabulary is appropriate here. The term panentheism which describes the Neoplatonic doctrine and which has been subsumed, for the purposes of this book, in the name Nature God, was coined relatively recently in 1832. It only came into more general use after the turn of the nineteenth century.[3] Writers before that date, and indeed many after, do not label themselves panentheists as such. But just as it is not necessary, as in the case of Wordsworth's nature rapture, to speak the language of Greek Philosophy to express Platonist ideas, so the name panentheist is not necessary to the expression of its fundamental idea. The exact characterization of that idea is reserved until it has been illuminated in the history to follow but as a temporary indication the name Nature God is to some extent self-explanatory, as previewed in the introduction. What needs to be added here are further terms to be subsumed in the name Nature God. These are Neoplatonism and mysticism (subject with this last, to the considerations of the next chapter). The name Nature God is also inclusive of the God of the Philosophers in general because the philosophical God has an irrepressible tendency to turn out to be Platonist.[4*] These six names, Platonism, Neoplatonism, panentheism, mysticism, the God of Greek Philosophy and the God of Philosophy in general are taken together as species within a particular class. They have different aspects, which will not concern us, united in the fundamental idea which does.

A qualification needs to be added to the name Nature God. This should strictly speaking be the Philosophized Nature God. But that is too much of a mouthful in a text that makes frequent reference. P/Nature God is shorter but seems ugly so I leave it to the understanding of the reader that reference to the Nature God here refers always to the Philosophized Nature God.

The distinction is important because there is also inspiration today from a revival of the primordial un-philosophized Nature God. This is the Pagan Goddess Mother Earth to which Starhawk, (Miriam Simos), gives voice for the New Age and Wicca spiritual movements.[5] Rosemary Reuther also revives this God for ecofeminism which draws inspiration from a revisit to Gaia the Greek Earth Goddess.[6] This Goddess can be distinguished by the name Native Nature God. This, probably the world over, preceded the Philosophized Nature God. Starhawk amply portrays the non-philosophical sensual nature of the Native Nature God. 'The Goddess tradition opened up new possibilities. Now my body, in all its femaleness, its breasts, its vulva, womb and menstrual flow, was sacred. The wild power of nature, the intense pleasure of sexual intimacy, took centre stage as paths to the sacred instead of being denied.'[7] 'One of the core principles of the thealogy presented here is that the earth is sacred.'[8] 'Erotic energy inherently generates and celebrates diversity. And Goddess religion, at its heart, is precisely about the erotic dance of life playing through all religion and culture.'[9]

To return to Bigg's view of Clement, what is the difference between the Father of the New Testament and the Neoplatonic doctrine of the Absolute God? Since the two are supposedly brought into synthesis in Christianity and thereby identical but in Bigg's opinion a displacement of one in favor of the other, the reasons that the two are not only different but originate two different religions that are irrevocably incompatible needs to be ascertained. Those reasons are found in the religious origins of Platonism.

Platonism is a non-apocalyptic religion. It is not and cannot be apocalyptic. The Apocalypse so much does not figure in Platonism that, were it not for the fact that we want to compare it to the Christians, the assertion, 'Platonism is a non-apocalyptic religion', would be as odd as the assertion that coffee is not tea. The non-apocalyptic conditions of Platonism are transparent in the *Timaeus* which serves in the religion as the scriptural canon of creation. *Timaeus* serves Platonism in the same role that Genesis serves the Christians.

The scheme of creation in the *Timaeus*, however, is different from that in Genesis. It is polytheistic. Responsibility is dissipated into a committee of Gods. There is no single omnipotent God responsible for the creation so the acute problem of the resolution of evil that arises for the Christians does not arise in Platonism. The Demiurge is the creator God who first orders the cosmos from the original chaos but he does not do the whole job himself. In this scheme each heavenly body becomes itself a God animated by soul. In turn other shadowy Gods create humans. The whole of this creation then becomes a God in its own right. It is a scheme of Gods within Gods within Gods composing another God. The *Timaeus* concludes as follows:

We can now claim that our account of the universe is complete. For our world has now received its full complement of living creatures, mortal and immortal; it is a visible living creature, it contains all creatures that are visible and is itself an image of the intelligible, and it has thus become a visible god, supreme in greatness and excellence, beauty and perfection, a single uniquely created heaven.[10]

That is to say that nature, or what might variously be described as the solar system, the cosmos or the universe, is itself a God. Unlike the creator in Genesis whose thunderous dissatisfaction hangs around and smashes the whole thing up on one occasion, the platonic Demiurge, after a job well done, disappears off stage never to be seen again. He leaves the Universe/God/Organism as the focus of attention.

Platonism does not discount the existence of evil and has its own scheme of resolution of evil. This is effected by the transmigration of souls and escape from the cycle of life, the wheel of birth and death, through spiritual ascension to a higher plane of existence. The soul which animates a body may pass to this existence here and now without need to wait for 'The End'. There is no end point or goal to the totality of Platonic creation and there can be no Day of Judgment. The resolution of evil in Platonism is through a spiral of ascent or descent, endlessly cyclical, not driving to a specific end. For example, the first incarnation of humanity was exclusively male. The defective males from this first generation were reborn as women. If still defective after this life as a woman they are reborn as 'some animal suitable to his particular kind of wrongdoing.'[11] Evil is continuously retributed at the atomized level of each living creature through the descent and ascent of souls. Just as a sufficiently energized atom may spit out a photon, so the occasional soul, perfectly purified by arduous ascetic practice, may whizz out the top of the spiral. This contrasts with the one-off comprehensive, retrospective moral rectification of the whole of specifically human history (animals are not included) in the Apocalypse. It would be difficult to invent two more polarized schemes for the resolution of evil. Referring back to Weber's classification we have encountered in Platonism the system of *karma*, the most stable of the various schemes for the resolution of evil.

In order fully to illustrate the clash of religions that results from the meeting of the Platonists with the Christians it is necessary first to characterize historically the House of Platonism. This is best done by tracing its religious origin and subsequent evolution. Some indication of that origin can be given in anticipation because it is already discernible in the above. The wheel of birth is an idea intuitive to the observation of nature. It represents the continuous cycle of the seasons and the continuous cycle of birth and death. The idea of transmigration of souls is intuitive to the observation that animals participate in the same animating consciousness, or soul, shared with humans but at a level that is not as advanced. Platonism/panentheism is a religion of nature worship which the House of the Christians is not.

The outline of the development of Plato's thought which follows is traceable through several stages of evolution from the nature worship festivals of ancient Greece, through the immigrant religion of Dionysus/Bacchus, through the spiritual-izing reform of this religion by Orpheus, through the number mysticism of Pythagoras (c570-500 BCE), to the philosophizing of Pythagoras by Plato (427-347 BCE) and finally to the Neoplatonism of Plotinus (205-270 CE). Plotinus condenses the polytheism into a more distinctively singular Absolute. It is this final stage resting with Plotinus that cements the encounter with the Christians.

2.2. The Religious Origin of Plato's Forms

Jane Ellen Harrison (1850-1928), fellow of Newnham College

Cambridge, is our authority on the early history of Greek religion. Her work the *Prolegomena to the Study of Greek Religion*, published in 1903, is a phenomenal piece of scholarly investigation and was a revolution in understanding of the Greeks.[12] Before Harrison there had been a tendency in classical studies, under the influence of narcissistic admiration for the antecedents of our western enlightenment, to romanticize the Greeks as being exempt from the normal development of early societies. Their rationalism and philosophy was imagined to spring pristine from an exceptional intellectual competence the expression of which was there to be discovered in the literary record. Harrison was an anthropologist and more realistic. She went back to archaeological evidence and pieced together pictorial illustrations from pottery and coins, written inscriptions from tablets and tombs, and citations in the literary sources where, as common currency of the day, religious practices were satirized or entered into conversational repartee. Her findings traced the development of many early rites and provided a history of religious currents up to the time of Pythagoras. Harrison produced an outline of the structural developments leading to Platonism comparable to that of Charles' outline of development leading to the Apocalypse.

Harrison's starting point is the spring, summer and autumn festivals of Anthesteria, Thargelia and Thesmophoria. The ritual of Anthesteria, sacred to Dionysus, consisted of the placation of ghosts, rites of aversion practiced in the spring to promote fertility and the purgation of evil influences. The ritual of Thargelia in the summer, dedicated to Apollo, was a first fruits harvest festival preliminary to the main ingathering. It included a ceremonial sacrifice of physical and moral purgation to promote and conserve fertility. In the autumn sowing festival of Thesmophoria the women carried magical *sacra* imbued with the power of direct compulsion of nature. Harrison summed up the subject and practical end of these rites as follows:

In connection with these *sacra* of the Thesmophoria the subject of the 'mysteries' falls to be examined. The gist of all primitive mysteries is found to be handling or tasting of certain *sacra* after elaborate purification. The *sacra* are conceived as having magical, i.e. divine, properties. Contact with them is contact with superhuman potency, which is taboo to the unpurified.[13]

Harrison is not concerned with Plato who is long outside the time span of her study but what is noticeable at this fetal stage are the outlines of some of the main features of Plato's philosophized nature religion. The purification as preparation and facilitation for contact with divine properties prefigures Plato's philosophical purification in preparation for the spiritual ascent. The taboo of the unpurified prefigures Plato's exclusion of the material and the untutored from escape from the earthly cycle. The superhuman potency, in its sense of a higher or hidden reality, prefigures Plato's other world of the perfect forms.

Onto this scene of indigenous nature festivals and the panoply of the Olympian Gods enters, around the seventh century BCE, Dionysus, an immigrant God from the mountains of Northern Thrace. Dionysus was known by several other names but most familiar to us as Bacchus. Dionysus introduced a new element into religious rituals. He is in some aspects a nature God, as Harrison puts it, a God of vegetation, who comes and goes with the seasons but combined with this is the Spirit of Intoxication. The function of the early sacra was contact with the higher power but now the new element of enthusiasm is introduced. This is the possibility of passing from the human to the divine, of actually being possessed by the God through the altered state of intoxication. As Harrison sums up 'intoxication is of the essence of the god Dionysus.'[14] Looking ahead again, this time to Plotinus, in this ecstatic intoxicated experience of union with God the precursor of spiritual/mystical union is prefigured.

For the purpose of the account of religious evolution toward

Plato, the harvest festivals and the God Dionysus are preliminaries compared to the religion of Orpheus which is where the
connections really begin to be made. The sun-gazing Orpheus
with his lyre, song and quiet contemplation, is something of an
intangible mythical figure. Harrison showed that he was a real
person who she relates as a reformer of religion, a dissenter.
Some hard evidence is available. Diodorus wrote that, 'Orpheus,
being a man gifted by nature and highly trained above all others,
made many modifications to the orgiastic rites: hence they call
the rites that took their rise from Dionysus, Orphic.'[15] Another
writer, Conon, gives credence to the myth that Orpheus was torn
to pieces and made a martyr by the Maenads, the wild women
ecstatic priestesses of the Dionysian rites. Harrison discerned the
plausibility of a true story of resentment against this immigrant
prophet from Crete who made reforms in contempt of the
accepted priestly rites. For Harrison, Orpheus was no myth but a
real man. He was a mighty singer, a prophet and a teacher
bringing with him a new religion, seeking to reform an old one.
He was martyred and after his death his tomb became a mantic
shrine.

Harrison, who is herself a true follower of the Nature God,
has let her heart go out to Orpheus. She speaks of a 'new
spiritual flame.'[16]

> Always about him there is this aloof air, this remoteness, not
> only of the self-sufficing artist, who is and must be always
> alone, but of the unscrupulous moralist and reformer; yet
> withal and through all he is human, a man, who Socrates-like
> draws men and repels them, not by persuading their reason,
> still less by inflaming their passions, but by sheer magic of
> personality. It is this mesmeric charm that makes it hard even
> nowadays to think soberly of Orpheus.[17]

The basis of this admiration is that Orpheus spiritualized the

religion of Dionysus. Orpheus produced from Dionysian wine-
induced ecstatic intoxication a religion of spiritual intoxication
attained through spiritual asceticism. He combined two Gods,
one the worship of Dionysus but additionally the new God Eros,
the source of all things. Eros is the embodiment of the old
divinity of generation.[18] Eros supplanted the Kers, representatives of the life impulse and of fertility.[19] In a charming pottery
tableau that Harrison discovered, Eros is depicted watering the
flowers and thus encapsulates this life impulse.[20] Other evidence
came from the writings of Euripides particularly *The Bacchae*. In
this Eros and Dionysus are both represented as 'spirits of Life
and of Life's ecstasy.'[21] Harrison summed up highlighting the
difference between the impersonal religion of potencies and the
personal Gods of theism. 'The Religion of Orpheus *is* religious in
the sense that it is the worship of the real mysteries of life, of
worship of life itself, of potencies rather than personal gods,
theoi; it is the worship of life itself in the supreme mysteries of
ecstasy and love.'[22] This personal/impersonal distinction is
reinforced with a quotation from Gilbert Murray the scholar of
Greek literature, 'These things are... Things which Are, things
utterly non-human and non-moral which bring man bliss or tear
his life to shreds without a break in their own severity.'[23]

Orphism introduced some distinctive new elements that bear
directly on Plato. The resolution of evil in Orphism is, according
to Herodotus, borrowed from the Egyptians, and is effected via
the wheel of life, the endless cycle of rebirth and the possibility of
escape through purgation.[24] As Harrison noted, Plato, together
with Euripides, was haunted by the notion of escape from the
Wheel and from the tomb of the body.[25]

Orphism reinforced the possibility of immortality. The
concept of perfect purity issuing in the attainment of divinity
implies immortality because the divine is conceived of as
immortal. In this, Orphism took another step toward Plato. This
prefigures Plato's immortality of the soul and its philosophical

ascent. As Harrison noted, Plato's mind was charged with Orphism.[26] His dialogue *Phaedrus* which discussed the fallen soul, is 'thoroughly Orphic.'[27] The Orphic cosmic scheme also prefigured Plato. The adopted symbol of the universe was the World Egg, the image of the universe in perfect spherical form and symbol of that which gives birth to all things and in itself contains all things. This World Egg prefigures Plato's spherical astrolabe model of the universe set out in *Timaeus*. The universe is spherical because a sphere is perfect and likewise must be the universe. The World Egg gives birth to Eros the creator of all. Plato avoids mention of the World Egg in *The Timaeus* but we have it in the interpretation of Proclus in his commentary on *The Timaeus* that the 'being' of Plato would be the same as the Orphic Egg. In the springing of Eros from the Egg there is prefigured the model of Plato's plurality proceeding from unity and in much later existentialist theology's becoming and letting be proceeding from being.[28]

To conclude this outline of Orphism it is well to note that what has been presented is the high spiritual aspect. Like many religions it encompassed simultaneously the unreformed rites and tendencies of its inheritance, aspects of which are mocked by Plato and by Clement in his Christian polemic, the *Exhortation to the Greeks*.

The next step of development toward Plato, and this is the crucial step, is the influence of Pythagoras. The fame of Pythagoras as the mathematical theorist of the triangle and of the mathematics of musical harmony has tended to obscure the fact that he was equally the founder of an esoteric religious brotherhood into which his mathematical mysticism was incorporated. Part of the difficulty with ascertaining the thought of Pythagoras is that he wrote nothing and left nothing directly to posterity. The brotherhood was exclusive, with an inner and outer echelon and there are only the reports of his later followers to go on. The fame of Pythagoras was such that his memory

gathered embellishments to the extent that the lives of
Pythagoras composed by Iamblicus and Porphyry are little more
than compilations of fanciful tales. Added to this difficulty the
philosophical fame of Pythagoras in Rome ensured that his name
sold books. Almost anything claiming to be the spiritual
guidance of Pythagoras was ensured of a market. Kitty Ferguson
has devoted a whole work to the attempt to disentangle the real
Pythagoras from the mythical.[29]

Pythagoras, like Orpheus before him, is generally considered
to have been a reformer of religion and can be said to have rationalized or intellectualized Orphism. In this reform we make the
final approach to Plato. Plato was impressed by Pythagoras and
by the good influence that he had exercised on the government of
the town of Croton. The conditions of good government were an
abiding interest of Plato's. At the age of thirty-eight, Plato went in
search of followers of Pythagoras to Croton, part of Magna Grecia
in the heel of Italy, where Pythagoras had had his base.

It can be said that Plato was not just impressed by Pythagoras
but adopted his philosophy wholesale. So similar is the thought
of Plato to the thought of Pythagoras that Bertrand Russell
considered the two identical and went so far as to state that,
'what appears as Platonism is when analyzed found to be in
essence Pythagoreanism.'[30] Ferguson concurs with this view. 'No
one for centuries would make a distinction between Platonism
and Pythagoreanism at all. Almost without exception, everyone
would accept what Plato taught in his Timaeus and his "oral
doctrine"... as the teaching of the early Pythagoras. In the eyes of
the educated world, Plato was Pythagoras.'[31]

This apparent equivalence, however, misses the astonishingly
significant step that Plato made in his transformation of
Pythagoras. On the contrary, it is misleading to say either that
Platonism is Pythagoreanism or that Pythagoras rationalized
Orphism. These are questions which must be deferred for the
moment but which it is hoped to clarify after presenting first the

innovation that Pythagoras wrought.

Pythagoras is the discoverer of the rational universe that underlies the apparent universe. He is the discoverer of mathematical pattern in the seemingly random. He discovered in numbers the key to the understanding of triangles and to musical harmony. These findings had several implications for the understanding of nature. The discovery of these two items alone opened the possibility that the whole of the universe might turn out to be ordered by relations reducible to number. This added a profound dimension to the primitive sense of higher dimensions or higher powers of existence. It heightened the sense of disparity between appearance and reality suggesting a comprehensively hidden higher order not discoverable by ordinary physical perception. It raised the possibility that the whole universe was the product of design by some ordering intelligence and that the reality of existence was a deep harmony and not the random chaos of distinct elements that mere appearance seemed to show. It opened the possibility that the deepest mysteries made perfect sense and were ideally perfect in contrast to observed imperfections of sense experience reality. It opened the door to a vast region of hidden knowledge. It opened a route to discovering that knowledge through dedication to philosophical learning. This proffered the means to an esoteric escape, through trained mental contemplation, from mundane imperfection to the higher perfect spiritual world. All of this is pure Plato.

The question arises, if Platonism is Pythagoreanism, why is it that it is the name of Plato that is deemed to enter Christianity and carries forward to the devotees of the twentieth century? Why did Whitehead famously describe European philosophical tradition as 'a series of footnotes to Plato' and not footnotes to Pythagoras?[32]

The clue to this lies in the restricted appeal of Pythagoras' mysticism of numbers. Bertrand Russell describes it as a peculiar mathematical mysticism with a belief in a super sensible world of exact truth.[33] Numbers themselves have become the objects of worship. They represent the perfect, the real and the eternal order in contrast to the imperfect and temporary world of sense. This fails as a philosophy with general appeal. Numbers for the average person, who is not a mathematically gifted aficionado, are simply tools of life. They are the everyday means by which we divide a cake into eight, ascertain the next rent day and quantify money in the bank. They are as much a common tool as a spade and a fork and as such they are unsuited as objects of spiritual experience. Besides which the numerical mysticism of Pythagoras led down some peculiar avenues. The number three, for instance, was the number of perfection because it is the first number with a beginning, middle and end. The number ten was another perfect number so that the solar system was obliged to consist of ten bodies, the sun, moon, earth and planets orbiting a central fire. There is in Pythagoreanism altogether too much of an exclusive demand for a particular temperamental inclination and a requirement for esoteric initiation. For this reason the religion was unlikely to become more universally taken up and that is how it remained as a self-limiting and restricted brotherhood of carefully vetted initiates.

Plato's step was to philosophize the number mysticism into a more universally inspiring, non mathematics-based format with appeal to a wider range of intellects. Plato's formulation of the ideal, real, unified everlasting perfect world of the forms in contrast to the unreal, imperfect, temporary, pluralistic world of material sense experience generalizes the Pythagorean distinction between singular numerical order and chaos, between higher and lower levels of reality. Plato took an odd number theology with restricted prospects and transformed it in such a way that it has withstood the test of time. It has since appealed to generations of self-respecting intellectuals and to the moderns of each generation. Those people throughout the ages who might feel embarrassment at waving the thyrsos at a Bacchanalian rite or chanting with the druid priests at the solstice, were enabled by Plato to enjoy the same religion, shorn of its gross public cult, in the serenity of their own minds. Plato took the religion of a coterie of mathematicians and made it into the religion of the Academy. He took a provincial religion from the foot of Italy and made it the religion of Europe.

Plato's initiative proved to be a triumph of product development, the psychological potency of which is unmatched except for the Christian progression of the Apocalypse. Platonism stands with the Apocalypse as one of the greatest religious inspirations of all time. Platonism is Pythagoreanism except in this all-important master stroke of a new orientation of the material.

2.3 The Religious Character of Platonism

There is incongruity in the fact that the Apocalypse, which was described as the engine room of the House of the Christians, has been universally despised as a religious force in the twentieth century whereas the Platonist engine room of the Forms meets with universal acclaim. Platonism might just as well be met with a barrage of objection were anyone so inclined.

On the face of the matter it is a peculiar logical proposition that Plato offers which, were it not for the emotional sway of its insatiable edification, might quickly be pricked as a philosophical bubble. Plato offers an argument that has an appeal similar to a snake charmer's ability to mesmerize. The proposition that there must be an essence of The Equal as the essence of things that are equal and The Bed as the essence of all particular beds is a brainteaser and logical conundrum known to philosophers as the problem of universals. To construct as a resolution to this problem a whole parallel universe split into life in an unreal temporary world of imperfect specific examples of beds and an eternal real world of perfect Bed, perfect Equal and perfect Good, of which the unreal world is but a defective template, is intuitively nonsense. This must arise from some defect in our linguistic or conceptual usage but which no ordinary person and indeed no philosophers for a long time had the means to unravel.[34*]

Plato makes the assumption that The Ideal is also The Good. Beauty, Truth and Goodness become the watchwords of Platonist aspiration. But there must equally exist in the real eternal world ideally perfect essences of The Evil, Ugliness and Lies so that the ideal real world comprises not a better world but an exaggerated mirror image equally of both what is bad and good. That is to say that it is perfect in quality but not in content as to what we would normally expect of the good. Given this, it is not clear why we should aspire to the ideal world that we do not live in and despise this world. Nor is it clear why to strive to live by ideals should need these props and stays of an alternative higher world when they must be worth striving for on their own terms. It is difficult also to envisage how we can cross over into that ideal world and to 'live' in it or to sit in its essential Chairs when we are irrevocably not part of it. Lastly, there is a problem with the subject of change. If the real world is eternal and unchangeable then it must contain in advance all the possible artefacts of human ingenuity. Alongside the form of the Bed must be the form of the Mobile Phone and the Satellite Dish. Perhaps by some amazing condition this is in fact the case?

My intention in these objections is neither to try for a logical decision on Plato's proposal nor to interrogate it for convincing logic. It is a mistake to consider that its value is ever to be assessed with logic because it is truly *a vision* disguised as a logical proposition. The motivational power derives from its encapsulation, in entrancing, ethereal and romantic form, aspirations to moral elevation. It is a rendition of the vision of a perfect world that naturally haunts human experience from the consideration of what is and what might be. The vision of the ideal in the House of the Platonists is equivalent to the vision of the

Kingdom of God in the House of the Christians. Just as the Apocalypse is the visionary inspiration of the Christians so the Forms are the visionary inspiration of the Platonists. The workings and articulations of neither are to be subjected to the brutalization of a cold shower of logic.

Such enterprise is an unfruitful approach to either religion because it mistakes the nature of the inspiration that moves the believers. The religious impetus is visionary. Logical dissection has unfortunately been all too evident in the revisioning campaign against the Community God which exposes to disbelief the articulations of resurrection, incarnation and atonement. If religions were perfectly logical they would be perfectly dull and thus defeat the possibility of their existence.

It is incontrovertible that Plato's proposition has indeed commanded visionary attraction for generations of educated minds. Sir Richard Livingstone, one time President of Corpus Christi College Oxford, can be taken to exemplify the admiration:

> The 'Idea' of a chair is more perfectly a chair than any concrete chair. The 'Idea' of Beauty is more completely Beauty than any beautiful sight or person. But if the 'Ideas' are more perfect than any particulars, they are more important. Their world is the real world, beside which the world of senses is a shadow... Clearly the task of man, with these two worlds before him, is to live as far as possible in the higher, the real, perfect eternal world... This was Plato's master work... He created a closely reasoned philosophy of the supremacy of the spiritual life... the greatest statement of the belief that the things that are seen are temporal, but the things that are unseen are eternal. Here is the theory of natural religion; here is the threshold of Christianity.[35]

Livingstone completes the answer to the deferred question as to why Platonism is not Pythagorianism. To return to the other deferred question, did Pythagoras rationalize Orphism? There is a distinction to be made here which is easily lost but which is worth retaining because it offers a key to the next two and a half thousand years of Nature God worship.

Pythagoras rationalized nature not Orphism. The distinction is crucial. The discovery that the universe could be expressed in mathematical relations added a new dimension to the original festivals of Anthesteria, Thargelia and Thesmophoria. It added a profound new dimension to the sun worship of Helios and to the Gods of mother earth. The thought of Pythagoras provided a wealth of new material to expand the original materials of nature worship. Pythagoras philosophized nature and in doing so produced expanded conceptual materials for nature worship.

But this is not a rationalization of Orphism. Nature worship is founded on the mystery of existence. No amount of additional information about the universe has any effect on that mystery which is a question of why more than a question of how? Instead of rationalizing the mystery Pythagoras compounded the mystery of the mystery.

What untold new territories of expression for the mystery were opened up. The philosophical material for the worship of the Nature God was expanded a thousand fold. The difference between the perceived sound of the lyre and its hidden cause in the fractional divisions of the strings, the difference between appearance and reality, introduced a fabulous new dimension to the original distinction between the temporal and the higher powers. It gave a new dimension to the distinction between mind and body. It gave a new importance to consciousness. It gave a sense of the omnipotence of reasoning by seeming to show that truth about nature could be established by mere thinking. Pythagoras opened up to contemplation of the mystery the philosophy of consciousness, the philosophy of knowledge, the philosophy of mind. Nature mysticism, which originally is primarily a sensual experience of existence, is compounded into realms of intellectual sensation.

Some agreed vocabulary would be useful at this point. Although the Forms have been identified as the engine room of Platonism these do not characterize the general type of religion that Platonism represents. The history of development shows that the Platonist Forms are a variation of the Pythagorean mathematical scheme which in turn is a variation of the nature worship of Orpheus. Nature is the common substrate of these religions. Prior to and prompting nature worship is the mystery of the fact of human existence in the world. I propose to take this mystery, the existence mystery, 'that there is something and not nothing', the mystery of nature, the mystery of the universe, 'The Existence Mystery', as the engine room of this type of religion. Plato's Forms are viewed as one specific articulation of the Existence Mystery. The discernment of different articulations is important because although the Nature God enters Christianity by succession from Plato it is not necessarily an exact Platonism that continues through the history. What continues and links all the variations is the Existence Mystery. The names Platonism or panentheism often serve as the general term for variants of this religion which do not specifically rely on the Forms. For example, Whitehead's process theology, though specifically relating to Plato, has the Existence Mystery as its hard core. Likewise Tillich's existentialism, though it has relations to Plato and may be named panentheism, has the Existence Mystery of 'being itself' as its core. A great focus of interest in contemporary theology is the mystical tradition. This may be termed Platonism but we are on more certain and better explanatory ground if we refer to the Existence Mystery and its companion the Nature God.

Pythagoras expanded the articulatory possibilities for the Existence Mystery. The irony of this is that no matter what volumes are written about the Existence Mystery it remains always an indescribable, insoluble mystery. It should be made explicit at the outset that nothing that has ever been said about the Existence Mystery has increased our understanding of it. It has only stated it in endlessly varied form through a vast amount of contemplation.

Elizabeth Johnson provides an illustration of this partnership between the Existence Mystery about which nothing can be said and the ever expanding quantity of words that can be said about it. In discussing the system of affirmation and negation worked by Aquinas, Johnson notes his complaint of the 'poverty of our vocabulary.' Aquinas, nevertheless, reveals that 'an unspeakably rich and vivifying reality is intuited while God remains incomprehensible.'[36] The underlying dialectic of this partnership is expansive without limit. The Existence Mystery about which nothing can be said is necessarily the Existence Mystery about which anything can be said.

Here are some examples of these expanded philosophical realms as they appear in later Platonism taken from Inge discussing Plotinus, Bradley, Spinoza, and Inge giving his own view:

> We shall not understand Plotinus unless we realize in the first place that *ousia* [being] corresponds nearly to what in Mr Bradley's philosophy is called reality as opposed to appearance, and, secondly that this reality is neither thought nor thing, but the indissoluble union of thought and thing, which reciprocally imply each other.[37]
>
> Our mind so far as it understands, is an eternal mode of thought.[38]
>
> Spirit exercises its power from itself and out of itself, which implies that it *is* what it knows.[39]
>
> Our minds travel quite freely over time and space, they are

not confined to the present... in every thought we imply that Reality is supertemporal.[40]

The new power of mind discovered by Pythagoras begins this move to the centrality of consciousness as part of the mystery of existence. This shift in emphasis to consciousness as a dimension of nature and as the supreme product of nature marks a distinct characteristic running through Nature God worship. Consciousness is sometimes looked upon as a peak phase of evolution which will take charge of or supersede biological existence.[41] Consciousness itself seems on occasion to become the focus of worship.[42*] In an anthropocentric transference, God may be equated with the human aspiration to universal power of mind.

Continuing the subject of the incapacity of increases in scientific knowledge to progress the Existence Mystery, a recent example may be taken from the theories of Richard Dawkins. Dawkins' account of the origins of human existence in *The Selfish Gene* and *The Ancestor's Tale* presents a picture of humans as a random event in a morally indifferent universe. Conscious life in this account is exclusively a vehicle to survival of genetic information. This consciousness is cleverly adapted but by this measure of survival no more or less advanced a vehicle than any bacterial life. A large amount of information has been accumulated to reach Dawkins' position and today we know much more about human history and biological make up but the Existence Mystery attached to humans remains wholly untouched by this. It is still not one bit less a mystery. The counter intuitive weirdness of the facts promotes more mystery. It is still absolutely a mystery. So whether it is the expressive form of Bacchus, Orpheus, Pythagoras, Plato or Plotinus that is used to contemplate the Existence Mystery or, to run ahead, the mystical Christian language of Dionysius, the fanciful rational edifice of Aquinas, Newton's mechanics, Einstein's relativity, Tillich's existentialism, or Cupitt's cosmic consciousness, it is still always and forever: the Existence Mystery. Plato's gene for permanent metamorphosis is this combination of the permanent mystery and its transient cultural articulations. This is Plato's secret of eternal youth.

This unchangeableness means that we should expect to find stasis, not progression, in Nature God worship. An example of this is the exchange of Pythagoras for Einstein. The number mysticism of Pythagoras was at the time the very latest, the fashionable and the most compelling advance in science. It was bound to attract enquiring young men such as Plato. Two and a half thousand years later Einstein's theory of relativity appeared as the very latest and compelling advance of science. It was inevitable that a new knowledge of the construction of the universe should be taken up into Nature God worship. That task fell to Whitehead, the mathematician turned philosopher. Whitehead's process theology, which he described as the 'Philosophy of Organism,'[43] which is a riff on relativity/interrelation, is based on the substitution of Einstein for Pythagoras. Whitehead explicitly states his mission as an adoption of Plato and as a reworking of *Timaeus* with minimum changes.[44] He substitutes relativity and change for the fixed mechanics of Plato's astrolabe and Newton's gravitational order. This inserts an advancement of scientific knowledge about the workings of the universe into the articulatory context of the Nature God. It effects no change whatsoever to the underlying mystery of the Existence Mystery.

The great attraction that process theology has exercised in recent revisioning is due to the gift of ammunition against the Community God. Relativity negates command. By a subtle parallelism the physics of interchangeable form between matter and energy is transferred to the supportive relationship of the earth to humans and the emotional reliance of humans on each other.

The great works of Nature God worship in the twentieth

century continue the flux of displacement and substitution of different materials for contemplating the Existence Mystery. Tillich's *Systematic Theology* and Macquarrie's *Principles of Christian Theology* for instance, adopted the fashion of existentialist interpretation of the mystery of being. A recent addition to the panoply of process theology is Catherine Keller's *On the Mystery*. Keller's 'theology of becoming in relation' is a mixture of Einstein's relativity, via Whitehead, some existentialism via Macquarrie and Tillich and some evolutionary theory. But at the end of it all we are, as inevitable, back to the Existence Mystery. As Keller sums up, 'Divinity is surely a mystery,'[45] it is the 'paradox of speech about the unspeakable.'[46] 'What we call "God" is literally-not.'[47]

The prime feature of worship of the Nature God over two and a half thousand years is this flux of different material stating the Existence Mystery that remains without answer. The philosophical number mysticism of Pythagoras is no different in its object than that of the hypothetical first human mother who looked with wonder on the miracle of her new baby and was conscious of herself as the sun rose. It is the grounding in this obstinate fact that gives the sense, when reading for instance the *Divine Names* of Dionysius or the *Summa* of Aquinas, that these works are mantras of contemplation and not the logical expositions that they may be mistaken for. In view of this it is no surprise that despite the endless philosophical variations of Nature God worship the simple nature rapture of Wordsworth still stands as the favored model.[48*] This absence of progression substantiates the observation of William James that 'mystical classics have neither birthday nor native land.'[49] It also substantiates the observation of Inge that mystical ideas are impossible to date by internal evidence as they change so little.[50]

To sum up, Pythagoras and Plato did not philosophize Orphism. The Mystery is permanently immune to such. But the easy elision that they did do this founds the preference for

Platonism as 'natural religion' or 'rational religion.' Religion is derived from nature in contrast to revelation which is the method used by the Community God. There is a particular sense in which 'rational religion' is used as derogatory to apocalyptic. The Apocalypse of the House of the Christians requires structural articulation. These articulations become the target of accusation as irrational. In contrast, The Existence Mystery cannot support an articulatory structure. All articulations, as Keller effectively stated, are invalid articulations. They are self-collapsing structures. The Existence Mystery will always and inherently escape this pitfall of 'rational.' It is this superb 'blank canvas' feature that has given it the decisive advantage for contemporary revisioning.

To draw a concluding perspective on Platonism, the many great historic expressions of this religion are at bottom celebrations of the Anthesteria, Thargelia and Thesmophoria: they are celebrations of the harvest festival.

2.4. Two into one won't go: The Alexandrian Synthesis

The whole of this part one, A Tale of Two Religions, aims to show the clash of two incompatible religions and the reverberation of this clash in the present choices for the future. I hope that enough of a portrait has been given at this stage to show that we have examined two different religions. Each has a long historical development. Each one is visionary. Each is part of a strong cultural background. Each has its own literature and centers of learning. Each is self-sufficient. They are both strong personalities. They have distinctive psychological dynamics. Except for convergence of their ethical result they have no common ground. On the contrary they display fundamental dissimilarities. In view of this the mere suggestion that they could be synthesized is preposterous. The actual attempt to synthesize them is foolhardy. But that synthesis is what the House of the Christians attempted to achieve and supposedly succeeded in doing. Why would anyone wish to prove such an unnecessary synthesis? That is a question of the politics of religion. It is a political struggle between operating programs.

The question of how to overcome the resistance to the Christian message by educated Greeks arose from the moment that Saint Paul was laughed out of Athens.[51] It is a cultural clash that can well be imagined by reversing the situation. Imagine the reception of a foreigner proclaiming a new religion in the precincts of the temple at Jerusalem.

The writings of the early fathers of the church in the three ante-Nicene centuries are imbued with this mission to overcome the resistance of Platonic philosophy. Justin Martyr's *Hortatory Address to the Greeks* is a sustained disparagement of Greek philosophy. Tatian's *Address to the Greeks*, begins, 'Be not, O Greeks, so very hostilely disposed to the Barbarians, nor look with ill will on their opinions.'[52] Theophilus composed a long letter to his friend Autolycus to explain the Christian God against the contempt of the philosophers. Athenagoras in his *Plea for the Christians*, sought to counter the injustices and to show the superiority of revelation over the self-learning of the philosophers.

The matter came to a head in Alexandria where the two heavyweights, Clement of Alexandria (153-217 CE) and his pupil Origen (c184-253 CE), brought the House of the Platonists and the House of the Christians into apparent synthesis. Alexandria was the natural center for the intellectual fusion. It was a cosmopolitan city which, together with the Egyptian hinterland, contained one million Jews.[53] It was in Alexandria that Pantaenus founded his school of catechism, the embryo of the first Christian university. Clement was one of his pupils.

The desire of the Christians to make their Jewish inheritance presentable to the Greek philosophy was not new. The pressure had arisen long before in this major Jewish colony which was culturally separated from Jerusalem to the extent that Greek and not Hebrew was the common language. Symbolic of the cultural dualism faced in Alexandria is the use by this community of the Septuagint, the translation into Greek of the Hebrew Bible, by legend sponsored by Ptolemy with his choice of seventy-two scholars for the work. The Alexandrian Jews were using this translation from about 200 BCE. It was Philo of Alexandria (c20 BCE-50 CE), a Jewish scholar saturated in Greek philosophy, who specifically interpreted the Hebrew Scriptures in terms of Platonism. Philo framed Moses as an original Platonist. His method of reconciling scripture with Platonism was a freeform, creative allegorization.

Philo had already adopted the Greek concept of logos as a key vehicle of synthesis between the two Gods. For the purposes of fusion, logos is conveniently multifaceted and has two meanings that served the case. The philosophical sense is that of reason as a design principle, the rational structure of the universe. In the sense used by the Stoics, the logos spermatikos, it is a generative, animating principle similar to a first cause. It is not difficult to see that this could be interpreted similarly to the God of the Bible. Perhaps taking a lead from Philo, Saint John used logos this time to frame Christ as the 'Word'.

Clement's campaign to fuse the Christian and the Platonist is a six pronged attack.

The first is merciless ridicule of the Greek cults. The second is unreserved praise for Plato. The third is to prove that Plato stole his philosophy from the Hebrew Scriptures. The fourth is to claim that the whole of Greek philosophy was a preparatory culture, a divinely ordained schoolmaster to bring the Greeks to Christ. The fifth is to prove that, therefore, Plato speaks the language of Christ. The sixth is the claim that as there is only one God to both the Platonists and to the Christians that must be the same God.[54*]

Clement is an unabashed pugilist. There is an air of a playground fight about his eight books of *Stromata* (miscella-neous notes): 'My house is bigger than your house.' Jewish institutions are much older than your institutions.[55] Moses was a better legislator than your legislators.[56] The Greeks are children compared to the Hebrews.[57] Faith is superior to philosophical knowledge.[58] Plato is Moses speaking Greek.[59] The Greeks stole their philosophy from the prophets.[60*] As Clement's admiring editor noted 'Like a good nautical combatant, his effort was to "get to windward", and so bear down upon the enemy with heavy-shotted broadsides.'[61] It is by this means that the Platonist and the Stoic alike are taught to 'sit at the feet of Jesus' and that 'we see philosophy yoked to the chariot of Messiah.'[62]

In a different mode, Clement effects synthesis variously between Pythagoras, Plato, Socrates, Moses, Paul, Jesus, the Gospel of John, the Greek playwrights and poets. He has an inexhaustible fluency in Greek philosophy and literature as also the Old and the New Testaments. Here are a few examples of these syntheses which combine the aptitude of the academic with that of the conjurer:

> For the reign of God is hard to attain; which Plato called the region of ideas, having learned from Moses that it was a place which contained all things universally.[63]

> And in general, Pythagoras and Socrates, and Plato say that they hear God's voice in the fabric of the universe, made and preserved unceasingly by God. For they heard Moses say, 'He said, and it was done', describing the word of God as an act.[64]

> For I pass over Plato; he plainly, in the Epistle to Erastus and Corsicus, is seen to exhibit the Father and Son somehow or other from the Hebrew Scriptures... the address in the Timaeus calls the creator, Father, speaking thus: 'Ye gods of gods, of whom I am father; and the creator of your works.' So that when he says 'Around the king of all, all things are, and because of Him are all things; and he is the cause of all good

things; and around the second are the things second in order; and around the third, the third,' I understand nothing less than the Holy Trinity to be meant.[65]

Now the word of God says, 'I am the truth.' The Word is then to be contemplated by the mind... in the *Phaedrus* also, Plato, speaking of the truth shows it as an idea. Now an idea is the conception of God; and this the barbarians [Jews] have termed the word of God. The words are as follow: 'For one must then dare to speak the truth, especially in speaking the truth. For the essence of the soul being colourless, formless and intangible is visible only to God its guide.'[66]

But do you want to hear from the Greeks expressly of one first principle? Timaeus the Locrian, in the work on Nature, shall testify in the following words: 'There is one first principle of all things unoriginated. For were it originated it would no longer be the first principle; but the first principle would be that from which it originated.' For this true opinion was derived from what follows: 'Hear O Israel; the Lord thy God is one, and him only shalt thou serve.'[67]

It is apparent that Clement effects no synthesis whatever between the Platonists and the Christians. His method is a bludgeoning of the texts and a bludgeoning of his audience. At the end of this marathon of paraphrasing, intimations, plain derivation and 'myriads and myriads of examples,'[68] the big boy in the playground sits down on top of the little boy. The result is an unresolved scrap. The little boy will wait his opportunity to get his own back. A reading of the Ante-Nicene fathers as a whole bears testimony to the wearing stalemate of this attempted cultural assassination. To give one more father as example, according to Justin Martyr, Plato took his idea of the forms from the Old Testament instruction to make the tabernacle according to the prescribed pattern.[69] Plato, according to Justin, is really a monotheist but disguises the fact from fear of the polytheists. *Timaeus* is an exact correspondence with what Plato learned from Moses' teaching of God but is, motivated by this fear, filled with studied ambiguity.[70] Here is Justin's verdict on the Greek philosophers. 'A wholly confused and inharmonious opinion has prevailed among them, which only in this one respect appears praiseworthy to those who can form a right judgment, that they have been anxious to convict one another of error and falsehood.'[71]

Only partisanship could see intellectual or religious advance in this cultural assault. As the historian Henry Chadwick described the real nature of the service rendered, 'At Alexandria Clement found a church afraid and on the defensive against Greek philosophy... The method of the *Stromateis*, written with very positive convictions about the truth contained in Greek philosophy... enabled Clement to present his position to the fearful Christian reader in such a way as to diminish his anxieties.'[72]

The anxieties and the cultural clash were not one sided. Many Greeks were dismayed by the threat to their philosophical religion by the unreasoning character of Christian beliefs. This anxiety was exacerbated with the beginnings of the crisis of confidence in the empire beginning around 250 CE. Robert Berchman sums up neatly the attitude of Porphyry, one of the most trenchant opponents of the new religion:

Christians were not simply impious atheists. Their faith was intellectually vacuous and politically dangerous. Their faith *superstitio* challenged the structures of both the divine and human worlds; their religious and political ideas advocated the overthrow of the beneficent gods, ancestral customs, and traditional piety. Their *philosophia* stood *in vacuo* because it demanded belief in propositions for which they were unable to furnish rational proof. These included the elevation of faith over reason, their belief in the incarnation, resurrection, and miracles, and their refusal to accept the eternity of the world and the pre-existence of the soul. That both the world order and its designer follow perfectly rational principles was fundamental to Hellenic doctrine followed by Porphyry. It was the *alogos* character of Christianity that most repelled him.[73]

The two hundred and fifty years of confrontation between Christianity and Platonism was not resolved at the time of Christianity's triumph in 312 CE as the official religion of the empire. The confrontation is incapable of resolution. The symbolic conclusion of the matter was the burning of all copies of Porphyry's *Against the Christians*, by order of the emperor Theodosius in 448. The roundup was so successful that Porphyry's work is known to posterity only by reconstruction through the arguments used to refute him. With power in its grasp, the imperial religion was able to suppress all open opposition for the next one thousand two hundred years until such time as the environment of the enlightenment loosened its grip. That is how two religions were made into one.

There is a Pyrrhic aspect to this triumph of the Christians over the Platonists. Clement had, so it appeared, brought Platonism into synthesis with the Christians. What he in fact did was to understand the Christian symbolism as a veiled Platonism. Clement is a Platonist wearing Christian clothing. Throughout his work he displays himself as a follower of the Nature God. God is ineffable, he shows a mystical tendency, the meaning of scripture is veiled and his favorite point of reference is John's Gospel, the most directly Platonized of the four.[74] The result is a church which, ostensibly absorbing Platonism, is in fact taken over by it at the level of its intellectuals, mystics and theologians.

Platonism did, however, produce in the Neoplatonic thought

of Plotinus (c205-270 CE) a major development that aided the appearance of synthesis with the Christians and which is important to the later mystics. Plotinus is chosen for discussion here because he illustrates the simultaneous plausibility of synthesis and the basic incompatibility.

We are fortunate to know something of Plotinus from the account of his pupil Porphyry who compiled his writings into the *Enneads*, the nine books from which we know his thought. Porphyry writes that Plotinus was a delightful teacher and ecstatic mystic who, in true Platonic style, despised his body as a mere vehicle for his soul. On this account he refused the fashion of having his portrait painted. He never went over any piece of writing a second time and maintained a house full of orphaned young boys and girls whose parents had entrusted to him their education and estates.

Plotinus is acknowledged as the founder of what is today known as Neoplatonism which succeeds the school of Middle Platonism, loosely defined bodies of thought about which it can be said that in the course of six hundred years from the time of Plato there were bound to be accretions to his ideas. The only matter of significance for purposes of this analysis is that Plotinus tidied up the polytheism of Plato. He focused with more singularity on The One. This One, combined with the reflection, taken up from Albinus,[75] that Plato's forms are 'thoughts in the mind of God' is the transition point at which Platonism arrived at the semblance of compatibility with the Christian God.

Here is that doctrine of The One, articulated and described by one of its admirers as 'the keystone in the entire speculative system' of Plotinus.[76] A.H. Armstrong considered that although Plotinus believed that he was simply expounding Plato on this One he actually derives it more from the Jewish Platonist Philo and from a throwback to the number mysticism of Pythagoras than from anything directly inherent in Plato:

First of all, The One is not a number but the measure of

number itself. 'It is the measure and not the measured' (V,5 [32],4)... the One is the source from which the differentiation of unity and plurality proceeds; it is the transcendence of separability rather than the negation of plurality... The One is, statically, the unity by which all number is intelligible, and dynamically, the unity whence and wither all multiplicity moves... Plotinus did not mean 'zero' for zero is within the numerical series and is not the measure of it... The One is not essence either because if it were it would be limited (V, 5 [32],6)... Plotinus would be the first to take exception to our referring to it as a concept. [77]

Plotinus himself wrote,

It would be better not to use the word 'one' at all than use it here in the positive sense, for only confusion would come of that. The word is useful solely in getting the inquiry started aright to the extent that it designates absolute simplicity. But even then this designation must be promptly eliminated, for neither it nor any other designation can be applied to what no sound can convey, what cannot be known on any hearing. Only the contemplative knows it; and even he should he seek a form would know it not (V, 5[32], 6). [78]

It is odd that such a numerical, not-knowable, not-concept should be taken to capture the real meaning of Jehovah, the arbiter on the Day of Judgment, and the destroyer of the world by flood, but this absolutely monist and vaguely monotheistic One is a pivot point around which Platonism is brought into association with the House of the Christians.

The One of Plotinus is not an isolated abstract but heads the integration of a dynamic system of being. From the One emanates *Nous*, translated as Spirit, which is the totality of being, a combination of the divine intellect and the forms. Out of this proceeds

Soul which in its earthly dimension is associated with bodies, the lowest form of existence in the material. The whole is a pulsating flux of emanation, and return, descent and ascent. If Plotinus has produced one God from Plato's polytheism why does the thought not then become dominated by the Apocalypse? The deciding feature that avoids this is that the scheme of Plotinus is not one God omnipotence. It is a system of God. It is a dynamic system of multiplicity stemming from unity and returning back to unity. It is not difficult to notice in this the original philosophization of nature. The flow of emanation and return reproduces the wheel of life, birth and death and the endless cycle of the seasons. The Absolute represents the fundamental mystery of existence with which humans are confronted. It is the essence of being itself distilled from multifarious beings. *Nous* represents the actuality of earth and sun. Soul represents the principle of animation of the living creatures of the earth. A. H. Armstrong brings out the philosophization of nature realized in Plotinus. He describes the spiritual world of Plotinus as 'a place boiling with life' [79] and considers that Plotinus derives this from the dynamic vitalism of the Stoics, 'who saw the universe as a single living organism held together by the Divine Fire which was the fullness both of life and intelligence.'[80] Plotinus may be characterized attractively as a fertile mystic in contrast to the regimental precision of Plato's mechanical universe and his terrible regimented plan for the perfect society.

A cyclical scheme for the resolution of evil is in place with Plotinus. The wheel of life supports Plotinus' adoption of transmigration of souls as the resolution of evil. The antecedent is that Plato adopted this from Orphism and Pythagoras. Plotinus develops it on from Plato. Plato maintained a rough justice equation at rebirth. Bad men may be reborn as women. Bad women may be reborn as dogs. Plotinus refines this into a more reciprocal and educational moral connection whereby, for instance, a murder committed in this life will be reciprocated in the next.[81]

Although the thought of Plotinus disguises the original nature mystery substrate by its philosophical abstraction it is this underlying correspondence with the practical facts of human existence that, even if not articulated, intuitively sustained its popularity and its grip on the imagination.

The God system of Plotinus is inherently inhibited from giving rise to The Apocalypse because the nature on which it is based is cyclical and does not drive toward a conclusive end. Additionally the God system of Plotinus, again corresponding to the Nature Mystery, is an *it* God not a *he* God, it is a God of potencies not a God of intelligent purpose. As Inge insists 'the object of this love is never personalized as in Christianity.'[82] This impersonal determines the method of resolution of evil. The Apocalypse cannot be operated by an impersonal abstract. It is never clear in the system of transmigration who or what it is that decides the correct grade of rebirth. There seems to be a self-adjusting equilibrium built into it rather like those toy wobbly clowns with a weight in the bottom, which, whenever pulled over, always return to upright. To sum up, the thought of Plotinus, despite the tidying up of Plato in the direction of one God, is consistently non apocalyptic on two counts. The One is not omnipotent. An abstract potency cannot preside over a day of judgment.

These two factors, lack of omnipotence and agency, have so far omitted the feature of the perfect goodness of God that was posited as a further necessary precondition of apocalyptic. In some measure evil can be incorporated in the Nature God, a proposition abhorrent to devotees of the Community God. Michael Brierley notes the prevalence of two disputed positions on evil in relation to the Nature God.[83] In the weak version the Nature God is considered to be present in the cosmos which is itself both good and evil so that evil is detached from God. In the strong version the Nature God is considered identical with the cosmos so that evil is necessarily included in God. The origin of this conundrum can be understood by referring back to the fundamental harvest festival substrate. Nature is both the source of good and of evil, both the support and the destroyer of life. Recognition of evil in nature is to be expected. If then that nature is envisaged as God, evil must be accommodated in the character of God. The wish by some devotees to protect the Nature God from the inclusion of evil may well derive from the envious comparison with the Community God who is necessarily absolutely good.

To summarize the relationship of the religious system of Plotinus to the House of the Christians, however much the One has been wishfully synthesized with Jehovah, the different resolutions of evil that these two comprise remain incompatible. The religion of Plotinus is wholly non apocalyptic. To state the objection from the side of the apocalyptic party, in the opinion of that great heresy hunter Irenaeus, 'the transmigration of souls is absurd.'[84]

To complete the overview of incompatibility the religion of nature remains to be thrown into relief by the light of alternative religious substrates. If nature is one pillar of the primary support of human existence the tribe is the other. Nature and Community provide equally important but separate substrates. Compared to other animals, human beings are peculiarly deficient in the adaptation of their biology to the environment. A human infant, for instance, takes about fifteen years to fledge whereas a new-born Wildebeest is up and running with the herd within minutes of birth. The difference highlights the fact that it is the cultural accumulation of human knowledge fostered in the environment of the social group that compensates the biological deficiency. It might be said that if animals have one primary environment of existence human beings have two. It would be difficult to assign priority to either of these. It is nature that ripens the harvest but it is other humans who may rob us of that harvest or drive us off the land. This provides the potential for kinship and the tribe to be the focus of religious rites every bit as strongly and as likely as nature.

When Durkheim came out with his celebrated 'collective representations' as the basis of religious worship it was the tribe that he identified as the substrate. For him the aboriginal totem worship on which his conclusion was based was a self-reflexive worship of the tribe. Here are his words in which he gives a sense of the potent religious forces surging in community:

> Religion is something pre-eminently social. Religious *representations* are collective *representations* which are an expression of collective realities[85]. ...A religion is a unified system of beliefs... which unite into one single moral community... all those who adhere to them[86] ...We cannot but feel that this *moral quality* is dependent on an external cause... but we are not aware of this cause or of what it is. Consequently we usually imagine it to be in the form of a moral force which whilst being immanent in us, is at the same time representative in us of something which the majority of men have never been able to visualize without religious symbols.[87] He cannot, therefore, escape the feeling that outside him there are active causes... and benevolent forces which are there to help him, protect him, and ensure him an advantageous destiny. He necessarily has to confer on these forces a dignity commensurate with the great value of the benefits which he attributes to them.[88] All these facts give some indication of how clan can arouse in its members the idea that forces exist outside them; in short they are religious forces. There is no society in which primitive men are made more directly and more closely dependent on other men. They are immediately conscious of the influence of this group and accordingly it is the same influence which has to be expressed in religious symbols.[89]

Durkheim extrapolated as universal his conclusion from totem worship and effectively identified the clan as the substrate of the Christians. In the Hebrew Bible Yahweh and the earlier named Elohim is the God of the fortunes of the community.

The correction that Platonism has to offer Durkheim is that it is impossible to reduce the classification of religions to one: a minimum of two must be allowed.[90*] It might be suggested against this that as human community is part of nature then the two may be subsumed within one whole but any attempt at such a synthesis obscures the feature that the two religions stem from different sources which originate different structures. It is more beneficial to our understanding to bring out the differences.

2.5. A Classification of the Nature God

The Nature God appears in many guises and it is useful to be in possession of a taxonomy of its features so that it can more easily be recognised wherever it is encountered.

The conventional distinction between the Nature and the Community God is that of God 'in' the world or 'separate' from the world. The 'decisive difference between classical theism and panentheism is the latter's insistence on mutuality or interdependence, in the relationship between God and cosmos.' [91] It has already been objected that this trivializes the distinction. It is as though these two doctrines of God are on offer like a choice between two flavors of ice cream. The distinction reflects a perception in Christianity that the two are variations of the same one God. It could be said that this perception is really a propaganda that derives from the necessity not to admit that this great monotheism has two Gods. It is, however, necessary to be wary of similar names and appearances which might be disadvantageous were we to rely on them. The Sweet potato, for instance, is not a species of potato and will not grow in the same conditions. Likewise the Community God is not a species of Nature God and only misunderstanding has arisen from its treatment as such. It is useful to be able readily to distinguish the two.

Brierley has produced a set of characteristics useful for recognizing the Nature God. Amongst others; the cosmos as God's body; language of 'In and Through'; the cosmos as sacrament; language of inextricable intertwining; God's dependence on the cosmos and the intrinsic positive value of the cosmos.[92] In building a sound sense of the Nature God, Brierley's characteristics can be extended to include both a broader vocabulary of phrases by which it can be recognized and an additional theological class which would incorporate the many species of Nature God that he identifies.

The primary substrate of the Nature God is the mystery of existence. It is the Existence Mystery as defined above. This is named in several stock phrases; ultimate reality; being itself, the ground of being; being above being; being beyond being; the mystery of being; the god beyond god; the one; the absolute; that there is something and not nothing; the depths of existence; cosmic consciousness; the infinite; any terms demonstrating nature rapture hypostasized as God along the lines of William Wordsworth or Waldo Emerson and any terms which hypostasize as God some animating force in the universe.

Contemplation of the Existence Mystery is accompanied by a purposive sense of animation from a hidden force, movement, power, progression, guidance, sheltering, protection or moral purpose in the universe. This was felt by Pythagoras in his mystical numerical ordering. It was felt by Plato in his 'defective template' model of the universe produced by a craftsman. The purposive sense continues in modern times with religious interpretations of Newton's mechanics of the universe, of Einstein's relativity and of Darwin's evolutionary process. All these senses of moral or design purpose inherent in the universe I refer to as The World Soul. Cosmic Soul would serve as well. The taxonomy of the class Nature God then has two primary factors. The object of the Nature God is the Existence Mystery. The resolution of the

Existence Mystery is the World Soul.

The efficacy of this twin condition can be demonstrated by presenting it with a test case to discriminate. I may be as impressed as anybody by the Existence Mystery but I discount the idea that the universe has any significance for human existence or that any moral purpose can be made out in it. I cannot, therefore, be classified as a follower of the Nature God.

It is also useful to classify the Nature God by the taxonomy of its resolution of evil in its comparative aspect to other religions. This is to add a preceding layer to Brierley's classification of panentheism as one of three doctrines of God alongside pantheism and theism. This antecedent layer cites the Nature God as a distinct religion not just a different doctrine of God. Reference is made back to Weber's three classifications that were introduced to gain a perspective on the apocalyptic resolution of evil; the cyclical/ascending; the permanently dualistic irresolution; and the apocalyptic. The Nature God features the stable cyclical resolution. The companion religion to the Nature God is Buddhism and the Orphism in which it has its roots. Cyclical resolution of evil is thus the third taxonomic feature. To present this again with a test case to discriminate: I do not believe that there is any resolution of evil either cyclical or apocalyptic and so I can be neither a follower of the Nature God nor for that matter of the Community God.

Basic to this different resolution of evil is the fact that the Nature God is an impersonal force and not the intelligent agency that is the Community God. This provides the fourth feature in the taxonomy. This feature of impersonal forces has been incorrigibly obfuscated by poetic license and the long intertwining with the language of the Community God. It is natural that in the course of eighteen hundred years of association the conjunction of the Nature and Community God should have produced an intertwining such that they have exercised gravitational influences on each other in the most confusing and inseparable manner. It has to be allowed that the result in Christianity is a spectrum of interpretation of God between two poles of abstraction and personalization. Many followers of the Nature God at one end of the spectrum may understand God as feeling and doing, in contrast to Inge, Harrison and Murray who, in the course of the present discussion, have been encountered as insisting that their religion is based on impersonal potentialities. About this potentiality it could only be poetic license to say that it suffers, plans, or does anything, beautifully expressive though this may be. Keller provides an example of the tendency to this confusing language. She advocates speaking of the 'impersonal infinity' in the personal language of the biblical God.[93] Even making allowance for this licentious trait, it is still disconcerting to find Whitehead, for instance, describing the processes of the universe as God's 'infinite patience.'[94]

In view of this spectrum the variable personality of God on offer in Christianity may be compared to an ellipse. Although in tracing the outline of the ellipse it is difficult to ascertain the influence of one center over the other the whole is nevertheless undoubtedly the product of two centers which remain discrete. At the two equinoxes can be found the extremes of the abstract God and the personal God. In between there is every possible degree of mixture. For the purposes of the taxonomy here the character of the Nature God is determined as impersonal/ abstract. This is because of this feature's explanatory power in support of the religion's resolution of evil and the many thinkers who specifically own abstraction such as Tillich.

As a last taxonomic measure, a thesaurus of Nature God statements is a useful aid to identification. A small selection will have to suffice here. A fine compilation is already available elsewhere:[95]

God is conceived as that reality working through the actual humanizing and relativizing cosmic and historical powers which give us our humanity.[96]

The essence and power of that vision lies in its all-embracing unifying character; it unites religion and science, mathematics and music, medicine and cosmology, body, mind and spirit in an inspired, luminous synthesis. In the Pythagorean vision all component parts interlock.[97]

In the realm of true Being all distinctions cease to exist. I felt myself in tune with the universe.[98]

Having elaborated this identificatory scheme there turn out to be two shortcuts to recognition. Wherever religion and science are mentioned together the Nature God is the subject of discussion. This is the home territory of the Nature God and a large literature is now devoted to it. Nature God books usually have a picture of the milky way on the cover, while Community God books have pictures of people.

To conclude with a summary of the distinctions between The House of the Christians and the House of the Platonists; One holds to God as intelligent agent, the other to God as an abstract potentiality. One resolves evil through a one off comprehensive adjustment of the whole of history. The other resolves evil at the individual level through a continuous spiral of ascent or descent. One is a nature religion the other a community religion. Platonism is the religion of sun worship, the Christian the religion of the clan. Or if the primitive connotation seems derogatory, one is the religion of Mother Earth the other the religion of Mother Community. When the two religions encountered each other in Alexandria the scene was set for a seismic clash. It is like the meeting of two tectonic plates the grinding of which, together with the occasional eruption, still shakes the academy today.

2.6. The Intellectual Caste Division of Christianity

The clash between the tectonic plates of the two religions that occurred in Alexandria was hidden at the official level because it was Clement's purpose to present a synthesis smoothly achieved by the employment of allegory. Thus was born the new religion of Christianity which I define as the character of the conjugal relationship between the House of the Christians and the House of the Platonists. The words offspring or product of this relationship are deliberately avoided because the marriage was sterile from the outset. Both parties were self-sufficient characters who had no need of a partner to make their lives complete.

It was inevitable, however, that the underlying fissure papered over by allegory should produce some symptom. This was immediately apparent in the establishment of an intellectual caste system headed by the initiated, intellectual, 'spiritual' elite. These understood their Christianity in terms of Platonic higher understanding of what they considered the myths accepted by the uninitiated who took the Gospel at its face value. Although Clement had the admirable purpose of demonstrating, in the face of scathing attacks, that the Christian religion was not lacking intellectual satisfactions, this fusion inevitably tended toward a hierarchy of understanding and a class division of believers. Clement formulated this as the contrast between faith and knowledge but his pupil, Origen, went further to contrast an esoteric mystery religion for the educated to the mythical religion of the vulgar. Philosophical religion thus arrived at the conceit of a higher understanding that subsumed the Christian. Charles Bigg remarked the new 'immoral doctrine of reserve'[99] which resulted from the use of allegory as a method of synthesizing the two incompatibles. 'The belief of the enlightened Christian becomes a mystery that may not be revealed to the simpler brother for whom the letter is enough.'[100]

In this Bigg saw the reproduction of Plato's 'medicinal lie', alternatively known as the noble lie or pious fiction posited in

The Republic.[101] This was a myth, particularly in regard to religion, for the good order of society, which was promoted to the auxiliaries and the workers but understood as false by the elite. Bigg observed,

> It is possible to defend the practice of Reserve if it be taken to represent the method by which a skilful teacher will not confuse the learner with principles beyond his comprehension. This however is by no means what the Alexandrines intended. With them it is the screen of esoteric belief. They held that the mass of men will necessarily accept the symbol for the idea, will, that is, be more or less superstitious... This is a necessary corollary of the new compromise between the Church and the world. Freedom remains but it is the freedom of the elite.[102]

John Macquarrie, in discussing Clement, also regrets this 'strong tendency to a two tier Christianity.'[103] The history of the Greek philosophical God within Christianity is a history of repetition of this intellectual superiority complex. Karen Armstrong, for instance, in praising the tradition of negative not-saying about the Mystery refers to the 'theologically less skilled than others [who] interpreted the truths of religion in a prosaic, factual manner.'[104] Inge claimed that 'the fundamentals of mystical religion are now very widely accepted, and are, especially with educated people, avowedly the main ground of belief.'[105] Hick stated that 'all *thoughtful believers* in God, even whilst each think of God in their own way, also insist that God is... the ultimate reality.'[106] C.E. Rolt, an early translator of the crucially influential Neoplatonist text *The Divine Names* by Dionysius the Aeropagite considered that,

> The first stage of religion is anthropomorphic. God is conceived as a magnified Man with an outward form. This

notion contains some low degree of truth, but it must be spiritualized. And in casting away the materialistic details of the conception we begin to enter on a *Via Negativa*. All educated Christians enter on this path.[107]

Scotty McLennan, framing his six stage progression of the religious path, claims the God of the Christians is appropriate to childhood between the ages of two and twelve.[108] Panentheism, for McLennan, is the highest level of ascent.[109] Julian Huxley in his great survey of Platonism, which he titled the Perennial Philosophy, claimed that, 'the lower forms of religion... are never to be accepted as final.'[110] 'Christianity's departure from the norm of Perennial Philosophy would seem to be philosophically unjustifiable... the pure Perennial Philosophy has, now more, now less, been overlaid with idolatrous pre-occupation with events and things in time.'[111] Thomas Merton recounted the revolutionary moment when, reading Etienne Gilson's scholastic philosophy, he gave up God 'this fatuous emotional thing'[112] in favour of the 'deep, precise simple and accurate... aseity of God – God as being *per se*.'[113] It is from a Platonist standpoint that Rowan Williams is able to dismiss the 'ignorance' of John Spong's portrait of Christianity. Williams claimed the 'adult recovery of the tradition' and noted that 'the language of a good many ordinary religious practitioners bears no relation at all to what any serious theologian... actually says about God.'[114]

Rolt, in quoting the German scholar Christlieb discussing Erigena, the ninth-century rediscoverer and translator of Dionysius, elicited the underlying reason for this superiority complex. He noted the end result of Erigena's vacillation between the Community God and the Nature God. 'His attempted reconciliation of Theology with Philosophy ends in the supremacy of the latter... an abolition of Christian revelation.'[115] Inge was frank about the character of the second order interpretation applied to the House of the Christians. 'Christian theology is just

Platonism applied to the interpretation of the beliefs of the first Christians.'[116] Maurice Wiles gave voice to the philosophical superiority complex with the analogy that as relativity is truer than Newtonian physics so God as Spirit is truer than God as Creator.[117] Wiles' book would be more accurately titled *Reason Not to Believe* so much is it a suppression of the House of the Christians by the House of the Platonists. Marcus Borg hopes, in his advocacy of the deeper level of panentheist understanding, that it is possible to speak of 'popular-level Christianity' without implying anything negative.[118] But it is a vain hope. Christian belief has integrity as it stands. Its doctrines are not metaphors for something else. No such deeper understanding is required and none such can escape being supercilious.

The Christians, with a sure instinct for the usurpation represented, have returned the compliment of this supercilious understanding by antipathy to all varieties of the Nature God. This is evidenced in the long list of the condemned, persecuted or forgotten: Origen, Eckhart, Hildegard, Aquinas, Mechtild, Eriugena, Teresa of Avila, John of the Cross, Loyola and the Cambridge Platonists, to name only a selection. It is on the basis of this history that Matthew Fox refers to the denial of the mystic as 'a deep and enduring scandal.'[119] Inge felt the same and set out his plea to vindicate the 'third tradition... in theological life' (having divided Christians into Catholic and Protestant).[120] Franz Overbeck (1837-1905), Professor of New Testament Exegesis at Basel and roommate of Nietzsche, summed up the stand-off between the original faith and its newly acquired philosophy. 'In acceding to power under Constantine the Church enjoyed the fruit of the audacious theological architecture of its first theologians but thereafter condemned Origen and his kind as the worst heretics.'[121]

2.7. Two Symptoms of Structural Friction

This class struggle set up within Christianity is the outcome of the structural incompatibilities of the two religions and their mutual struggle for supremacy. Two examples can be given to illustrate the two prime incompatibilities. These are the Platonist refusal of the Apocalypse and the Platonist dissolution in principle of all dogmatic statement.

The vaporization of the Christian Apocalypse by the Platonic resolution of the problem of evil can be seen in action in Macquarrie's revisioning project. His *Principles of Christian Theology* was a comprehensive attempt to promote the existentialist impersonal God of Being and to follow this through correlatively as the real object of the Christian supposed metaphors. Macquarrie schematizes the God system of Plotinus into a sequence of Being, being becoming, being letting be, being conferring being, being as presence, etcetera, and correlates these with the Christian attributes of God.[122*] All goes plausibly to begin with but the sticking point comes with eschatology where Macquarrie can make no correlation and objects to a 'mythological mentality that we do not and indeed cannot share.'[123] He proceeds with a philosophical re-interpretation of the Apocalypse as continuous consummation in a world without end, a cyclical 'destiny not of death but of new creativity'[124] and a progression toward a 'vaster synthesis of Being.'[125] This is a perfect rendition of Orphic resolution of evil. It does not qualify as an interpretation of the Apocalypse. It is the suppression of one religion by another. Macquarrie commits a theological murder.

In this Macquarrie proves the point made by A.H. Armstrong. 'The fact that orthodox Christians, from St Augustine... to our own times have been able to find a very great deal in Plotinus that has been valuable to them should not prevent us from realizing that his system is... incompatible with Christianity and belongs to a different type of religion.'[126] Keith Ward also specifies this aspect of incompatibility between the apocalyptic and cyclical resolutions of evil found in the different world religions.[127]

The previous chapter outlined the history of apocalyptic rejection framed in terms of cultural alienation and simple incomprehension but a couple of examples illustrate the specifically Platonist rejection in current theology. The scheme to reject Fall Redemption religion in favor of Creation Centered religion, the 'Copernican revolution in religion'[128] that frames the project of Fox, is another way to frame Apocalyptic versus Nature religion.[129] McLennan repeats the same altercation in different words. 'God doesn't have "a plan" for anyone or anything beyond the magnificent natural order of the universe.'[130]

The inbuilt necessity for Platonism to dissolve all Christian dogma is the second structural incompatibility to be illustrated. Taking Platonism back to its substrate in nature worship, the reason for this dissolution has already been highlighted. The Mystery of human existence is a mystery, is a mystery, is a mystery. It is, as John Hick names it, the fifth dimension. Into this no amount of thought and no formulation can ever progress however many thousands of reams of text are devoted to it. In accordance with this statements of the Nature God are always at root negative attributes stating what God is not. Even when they are not categorically framed as negative they will usually claim somewhere the standard over rider of nature mystical experience that nothing can be said. In Keller's phrase 'God *is not* or *does not*.' [131]

Platonism then is not just incidentally supercilious to all dogmatic statements it is impelled to reject them. It can tolerate them only on the basis that they are the trespass of other people's inadequate formulations on the mystery that is in Platonic guardianship. As Inge put it, 'the foundation of all religious symbolism is the attempt to realize Divine immanence in Nature.'[132]

This dissolution of all dogma takes many forms. Strauss, in discussing the personal Hebrew Christian God and the Greek

Philosophical Absolute identified that for philosophy all personal attributes for God are offensive because personality is a limit on deity. Hick held Dionysius to be self-contradictory in the statement that the ineffable One 'has told us about itself in the holy words of scripture.' It is for Hick contradictory to accept symbolic as literal truths, 'for a system of ideas which includes both the absolute ineffability of the ultimately real, and also a set of specifically Christian beliefs about reality, is clearly fatally inconsistent.'[133] Altizer really spells out the Platonist attitude to dogma. For Altizer the new, Platonist religionless Christianity will 'abandon the whole religious body of Christianity even if that body should prove to comprehend very nearly everything which Christianity once knew as faith.'[134] In *The Death of God* Altizer stated the Platonist imperative, 'our situation calls upon us to negate the religious forms of Christendom.'[135] Spong means the same thing from the same standpoint when he calls for a reassessment of Christianity so complete that 'the reformation needed today must be so total that it will by comparison make the Reformation of the sixteenth century look like a child's tea party.'[136] There can be no mistaking the fact that the Platonists are prepared to sack the whole of Christian doctrine without regret. There is a Stalinesque air to this enterprise. Stalin was apt to airbrush out of old photos members of the politbureau once he had eliminated them. Karen Armstrong is prepared to photoshop the whole Judaic tradition claiming the nature mystical negative way as the mainstream: theism was an invention of enlightenment rationalism. [137]

2.8. Jesus the Follower of Plato

When the early Christians first began to formalize their understanding of Jesus they mined the Hebrew Bible for connections announcing Jesus and amongst other matters concluded that he had to be from the House of David. When Philo sought to frame the Old Scriptures in compatibility with the Greek Philosophy he went back to frame Moses as the founder of the Platonist dynasty. It would be unnatural to expect the present generation of Platonists not to want to frame Jesus in terms of their own lineage and claim him for the House of Plato even though Inge lets slip the wishful thinking involved in this endeavor. 'We may venture to call it [the Platonic tradition] the true heir to the original Gospel while admitting that no direct Hellenic influence can be traced in our Lord's teaching.'[138] The Platonist Jesus is characterized by a prime feature easily overlooked because it is a negative feature. The one thing that the Platonist Jesus does not do is the first thing that Mark tells us Jesus did do. 'Jesus came to Galilee, proclaiming the good news of God, and saying, "The time is fulfilled, and the kingdom of God has come near, repent and believe in the good news".'[139]

Borg has it on the authority of recent scholarship that Buddha rejected the notion of a personal God and thinks that Jesus had the same enlightening experience. Jesus experienced Tillich's God beyond God, an experience of 'the way things really are.'[140] For Borg the similarity of the moral teaching of Buddha and Jesus is proof of their identical understanding of God. For Spong, Jesus was originally a nontheistic 'spirit person' before his experience was rationally interpreted and distorted by the theist takeover of an originally panentheist Jesus.[141] Saint Paul is suggested to have picked up this sense from Jesus. Paul is a follower of Tillich's depth dimension of human life and he is struggling to find the nontheistic definition of God that he had encountered in Christ. McLennan, whose Unitarian Universalism is a version of Platonism, adopts Crossan and Borg's Jesus as a mystical ecstatic spirit person and understands that Jesus had 'intense mystical experiences in which he felt the presence of *what he would call* God.'[142]

Foundational to current Platonic interpretations of Jesus is Schleiermacher's formulation of the exceptional God-consciousness of Jesus.[143] This was a masterstroke in that it prioritized mystical experience over apocalyptic. Although the apocalyptic discussion had not arisen at the time of Schleiermacher it is a boon to Jesus the follower of Plato. Exceptional God-consciousness accommodates ambiguity of the experience of God between abstract and personal conceptions allowing further inclination toward the Platonic. The subject of Jesusology in alliance with Platonism comes up in more detail in chapter four, so no more will be said about it here.

2.9. Fifty Years of Platonist 'Radical' Theology

A brief account of Platonist landmarks in the past fifty years, partly set out in the introduction, will bring the project of the House of Platonism up to date. Paul Tillich is the giant Platonist who straddles the twentieth century and has proved the unchallenged figurehead of today's disciples. Tillich's famous statement, 'it is as atheistic to affirm the existence of God as it is to deny it. God is being-itself, not a being'[144] dominates the religion in its various formulations of ground of being, ultimate concern, ultimate reality, infinite depth and God beyond God. Altizer and Hamilton dedicated their book in memory of Tillich,[145] 'the modern father of radical theology... who made possible a way to a truly contemporary theology.'[146] Borg cites Tillich as 'very appealing and authoritative.'[147] McLennan considers Tillich 'the greatest theologian of the twentieth century.'[148] Lloyd Geering considers Tillich 'the most creative theologian of the twentieth century.'[149] Tillich's stock phrases have so much entered common parlance that they are often encountered without need for acknowledgement. Armstrong's uses 'God is not a being.'[150] Hampson adopts ground of being and ultimate reality.[151] Gordon Kaufman investigates Ultimate Reality.[152]

Tillich's existentialist language gave his thought the disguise of something new and fashionable so that he is not immediately identified as a Platonist. These credentials ought to be stated. For all his saturation in Schelling and Fichte, Tillich could have lifted his famous statement of God straight from Plato's *Republic*, the Good which surpasses being and is way beyond human comprehension.[153] The key to Tillich, as flagged in the introduction, is that for all the diversion of his dense philosophizing he is a mystic. Tillich rarely makes clear that 'ultimate concern' is a mystical experience but he did make this explicit on one occasion late in his life in dialogue with students at the University of California.[154*] It is direct experience of The Existence Mystery tracing back through Schleiermacher and leapfrogging back through the mystical and philosophical tradition that connects Tillich to Platonism. Being itself is a version of Plato's Absolute, the One or the Good, the first principle from which all other existence proceeds.[155*]

Altizer's Death of God trumpeted in his *Gospel of Christian Atheism* [156] proposed a new God under the auspices of Tillich. Altizer adopted a Hegelian dialectic to the effect that the death of one God makes way for the affirmation of another. Altizer kills off the institutional, repressive, guilt producing Community God objected to by Nietzsche and Blake and radicalizes Tillich to the extent that Tillich was too old-fashioned to take the final step of jettisoning the whole Christian framework. The new God with which Altizer confronts the old as a 'higher expression', is Oriental mysticism. Oriental is the key companion to Orphism and thus a roundabout appeal to Platonism.

Existentialism today is yesterday's news and postmodernism is now the fashion. Platonism has no trouble with riding the change. A recent work, *After the Death of* God, [157] belies its promise of progress and delivers more Platonist Death of *a* God theology. The work demonstrates the remarkable facility of Platonism, chameleon like, to take on the complexion of the cultural environment. It took the color of romantic nature mysticism with Wordsworth, existentialism with Tillich and here postmodernism. Under the auspices of Jacques Derrida, to whom the book is dedicated, Tillich's 'unconditional'[158] is re-phrased as 'the theology of the event'[159] and transferred to the language of deconstruction as the one undeconstructible event.[160] 'The event is irreducible; indeed... the very form of irreducibility itself.'[161] With this as a definition it is impossible to disagree with the statement: God is an 'inaccessible mystery.'[162] The theme tunes of Death of *a* God theology are repeated. The theist ogre is rejected.[163] Altizer's Hegelian dialectic is repeated: the secular gives space for the rise of real religion.[164]

There is a sense of endless repetition in this perennial dissolution of the Community God by Platonic ideas in different disguises. David Strauss, in 1874, discussing the situation of his day in *The Old Faith and the New,* noted how the one personal God had resolved himself into the 'impersonal but person shaping All' and the 'Cosmic conception.'[165] These two ideas return almost verbatim in Don Cupitt's 'It All' and 'cosmic emotion.'[166]

The glowing coals of Platonism have burst into the current conflagration fueled by the auspicious environment of the late twentieth century which handed it the strategic advantage over the Community God and made it seem like the cure-all for the modern troubles of religion. It is put forward as a resolution to the problem of unique revelation in the face of pluralism, seeming to offer a great ecumenical principle. Platonism offers rebuttal to the atheists who, like Celsus, can be said to hold primitive ideas of God.[167*] On all counts Platonism is the favored vehicle for re-thinking Christianity to address the twenty-first century.

To draw this portrait of The House of Platonism to a conclusion, three different perspectives are useful in gaining an overview of the Platonism of today's intellectual vanguard.

Joseph Hoffmann, the commentator on Porphyry, described the persecution and intellectual standoff with the Christians as 'Rome's Vietnam',[168] 'a last gasp attempt to save the old religious order.'[169] Today the situation is reversed. The Platonist attack is the Vietnam of the Christians. Porphyry of Tyre is the true founder of biblical criticism[170]* suppressed for twelve hundred years until Reimarus then gathering increasing momentum until the Platonist culmination in today's Jesus Seminar. Tyre is the birthplace of the Westar Institute at Santa Rosa. Porphyry and his confederates, Celsus, Hierocles and Julian are the founders of the 1960s' attempt of radical theology to suppress the Community God with the Platonist. The arguments are unchanged. All that changes is the context from a waxing to waning of the fortunes of the House of the Christians. The little boy has been rewarded at last with his opportunity to get even with Clement.

Platonism may be thought of as a repressed religion of Western Buddhism whose proper flourishing was blocked by its sublimation within a successful Christianity. This helps explain the current flow of Christian Buddhism as proposed by Don Cupitt[171] and the welter of books that associate Buddhism and Christianity.[172]

The third perspective is that Platonism and Christianity live in an unhappy marriage that has for so long been locked into its quarrel that the parties fail to see that a simple annulment would be the best solution. Any marriage counselor would spot immediately that the Christian could never be the right partner for Platonism and that Platonism's attempt to prove that the Christian really is the perfect wife, if only she would shed her veil, is an abusive character assassination that should be put a stop to forthwith.

That completes the account of the House of the Platonists. It would be possible at this point to move on to an assessment of that dynasty's claim to inherit liberal Christianity and to vitalize it for the twenty-first century. But there are two other important schools within Christianity that need to be included: The Christian Mystics and the Jesusologists. The intention of the following two chapters is to show that although four main schools can be identified, the appearance of variety is deceptive.

The choice really comes down to two. The Christian Mystics and the Jesusologists are naturally in alliance with the Platonists. Once that point is reached, having framed Christianity as offering only two Gods, we will be ready to move on to assess the claim of one of those Gods to superior relevance for the future – and to propose a third God.

3

The Christian Mystics

The House of the Christians and the House of the Platonists have been presented as two incompatible religions. Is it possible that they could be held together in perfect coalescence? Could they be fused and annealed so that all tension between them is dissipated? This seems to be the achievement of the Christian Mystics who speak Platonism using the language of Christ. The emphasis in that sentence is 'seems' to be. To indicate the direction of this chapter there is a great deal of tension between the Christian Mystics and the House of the Christians. Beneath the language of the Christians lies the Nature God. The situation is something like the relation of the English to the Americans. Although the Americans speak English it is unsafe to assume that they share the same mentality. The Christian Mystics speak the language of the House of the Christians but display the character of the House of the Platonists.

The situation for the purposes of analysis is made difficult by the fact that for the mystics the tension between these two religions, if it is felt at all, is never clearly formulated. Indeed every effort is made not to formulate any such split but to present mysticism as supportive of Christianity. It is taboo for Christianity to be known as a religion of two conflicting Gods. The suppressed fissure can only show up then in subtle ways. It has made itself apparent in terms of conflict between theism and panentheism which has been presented here as a suppressed conflict between two Gods. The difficulty of analysis is compounded by the fact that mysticism is deep water. This chapter is then something of an attempt to fathom the unfathomable, a weakness that will inevitably hang over any result that tries to be decisive.

In proposing the Christian Mystics as a category distinct from the Platonists, I might seem to be suggesting the impossible task of distinguishing mysticism from Platonic philosophy. The intertwining of the two is such that they are perfectly unravellable. On one side Inge defines the essential thought of Platonism as an invisible, unseen eternal world behind our world as immediately experienced. On the other side Louis Bouyer, who is concerned to claim Christian mysticism for the House of the Christians and to deny Greek influence, describes mysticism as the experience of an invisible objective world.[1] On one side Inge described Plato as the father of Christian Mysticism.[2] On the other Charles Bigg described Clement as the founder of Christian Mysticism.[3] With Clement, a thoroughly rehearsed Platonist, the influences are mutually intertwined. There is no point at which the end of a thread can be picked up to start unraveling.

The purpose of discussing the Christian Mystics as a category is not to attempt such separation but to highlight the special world that results from fusing the understanding of God as a volitional agent with God as an abstract potential. What I hope to illustrate is that that special world inevitably inclines toward allegiance with the House of the Platonists. In the interests of establishing an analytic framework I somewhat arbitrarily and with exaggerated decisiveness designate the Christian Mystics as those who understand God as a volitional agent. This seems fair because they speak the language of the Christians and the Community God is such an agent. The Platonists like to contradict this by synthesizing Yahweh with their Nature God of 'being itself' and as proof pick out the enigmatic name of God spoken in Exodus 3.14, 'I am who I am.'[4] This isolated phrase, however, is not sufficient evidence against the overwhelming anthropomorphism of the Old Testament. Even the delivery of the words confirms the anthropomorphism. I want to hold fast therefore to the God of the Christian Mystics as an intelligent agent.

The Platonists are designated as those who understand God as an impersonal force. This is likewise qualified with the proviso of the difficulty of clarity that was stated in the foregoing chapter using the ellipse as representation of the polarities. Although Platonism has been taken here decisively to concern itself with an impersonal force there is an element of ambiguity, notable in Plotinus, sufficient to facilitate its identification with the Christian personal force. A.H. Armstrong noted a peculiarity confronting the translator of Plotinus that while the One and the Good, *to hen* and *to agathon*, are neuter, Plotinus slips naturally into using masculine pronouns.[5] This together with Plotinus' interpretative development of Plato in his conception of the Forms as existing in the 'mind of God' as 'God's thoughts' constitutes the great point of modulation facilitating the elision of Platonist abstract potentiality with the Christian agent.

It is often difficult to discern, in the case of any individual case taken for examination, which alternative has been taken up. The maintenance of the diplomatic *double entendre* has been a necessary survival tactic in the face of church authority. Poetic license also clouds the issue together with what might be the indifference of equanimity or a polite wish not to give offense. Tillich, for instance, as noted in the introduction, was frank about the diplomatically equivocal language used to address his abstract potentiality to his target audience of people in a 'situation of doubt' without giving offense to those content with the traditional symbols of God as agent.

A further complication is the midway theist position that might be called sophisticated anthropomorphism. In this belief God is not a person with the emotions associated with personhood but a disembodied mind or intelligence. This is the position that Ward uses in his complaint that Cupitt has taken leave of an anthropomorphic God that is not really the Christian God.[6] This sophisticated anthropomorphism lies on the boundary where a touch of poetic license may tip the balance from God as intelligent agent to God as impersonal force. Nature or 'Being' can be poetically spoken of in terms of volition or intelligence supporting or caring for us.

Thomas Merton is an example of the perplexity for interpretation that results from these factors. God understood as the impersonal force of 'being itself' is nevertheless spoken of in extravagantly anthropomorphic language.[7] In the absence of clear self-definition given by the thinker it is the theological content that must provide the clue to identification.

Despite this entire proviso I want to hold to the personal/abstract separation on the grounds that this determines the choice of resolution of evil between apocalyptic and cyclical. The mystical focus on the personal union with God gives the clue to the decidedly unapocalyptic nature of the experience. The mystic's spiritual union with God anticipates the Apocalypse, displaces the Apocalypse and renders it redundant. While regular non mystical Christians await their union with God, the mystics have raced on ahead. The Christian mystical experience is on this basis much closer to the Platonist ascent and union than it is to the Christian. Even though God may be thought of as an agent the apocalyptic consequence has been discounted in the union. There is an element of hybridization between the two religions.

This hybridization is indicative that mysticism is able to draw from many sources materials which it converts into its own religion. Despite many languages of expression there is general agreement that there is a static, timeless quality to mystical content which does not evolve over time or display the chronological development that is traceable in many Christian doctrines. It is on this basis, for instance, that Bernard McGinn arranges his book on mysticism thematically instead of chronologically.[8]

Whatever degree to which the end result of mystical contemplation is convergent it is necessary to allow for different source materials. These similar end results should not discount the different sources from which they may be derived. Jewish Mysticism is an example of a source independent of Platonism. It had its own schools and practices and was a discipline in which it has been proposed that Saint Paul may have been schooled.[9]

This different source of mysticism, determining our idea of what mysticism is, may help account for the oddity that Plato himself can be described preferably as a philosopher and 'hardly himself a mystic.'[10] Bertrand Russell detected in Plato a logical or mathematical mysticism which he identified as the influence of Parmenides. This influence is an inclination to logic that continues through all the great metaphysical mystics down to Hegel and his modern disciples.[11] The One as a logical necessity of first cause and the principle of form, number, measure, order and limit can readily be appreciated as a source of rarefied intellectual satisfaction. This is a different type from sensual, ecstatic mysticism exhibited by the many mystics who show no trace of philosophical logic. Matthew Fox can be taken as an example of a fertile mysticism of 'natural ecstasies'[12] experienced playing football, [13] reading Shakespeare, [14] in his own nothingness [15] and in sweat lodges and native dancing.[16]

It is not intended to make much of these different types and traditions except to highlight the potential that disparate or incongruous sources may become fused in mystical practice once culturally associated. The I am who I am interpretation is just such a case of the association of two traditions where the anthropomorphic Yahweh becomes retrospectively interpreted as mystical ultimate reality. The particular importance of this 'bilingual' potential, and this is the focal point of this chapter, is that these mystics are able to adopt elements of the Christian apocalyptic framework and potentially hold these in sincere fusion with Platonic elements. At the level of doctrinal statement Platonism is allergic to apocalyptic articulations and vice versa but at the level of mystical experience the allergy seems to be cured. The mystics have the facility to adopt for mystical consciousness elements derived from the apocalyptic scheme, such as Christ, or from rationally developed elements of dogma such as the Trinity which have no place in Platonism. Fox, for example has produced a lavishly extended contemplation of Christ in his work *The Coming of the Cosmic Christ*.[17] In this work Christ, the apocalyptic articulation, is transformed into Christ the cosmological Nature God. Fox considers that eschatology as a whole is an invitation to mysticism.[18] Michael Hampson takes up the Trinity as a logical conundrum designed to be an exercise that is mystically productive.[19]

This shows that although mystical contemplation might be supposed to be generated by the content of the Existence Mystery itself it is in fact able to absorb structural elements of thought that are generated from sources independent of the mystery. This may be an example of the blank canvas aspect of the Existence Mystery and the dialectic noted earlier that while nothing can be said of it anything can be said of it.

John Hick can be taken as an example of the fusion of the Nature God and the Community God displayed in a Christian Mystic. It was noted above that Hick considered the Apocalypse an absolute requirement of religion. At the same time he was an advocate of ultimate reality as a synthesizing principle for all religions.[20] Hick, therefore, held together the specific Christian doctrine with a more diffuse Platonic element. Hick held definitively to his Christian standpoint[21] but his Day of Judgment has been creatively dissolved into Orphism and a universalist salvation of spiritual ascension consisting of a series of lives that may be lived on planets other than earth.[22]

Yet still Hick illustrates the extreme complexity of discerning the mystical position. The contradiction apparent from my analytic categories may in fact be a genuine hybridization. Spiritual progress through a series of lives is not altogether incompatible as a modern freeform interpretation of the Day of Judgment and that is clearly how Hick envisaged the matter. What he did was take up a part Orphic scenario. He took up the transmigration of souls but discarded the continuous forwards and backwards alternation of the cyclical resolution of evil. He gave to transmigration a Christian unidirectional élan thus uniting an apocalyptic end with an Orphic cycle.

As to the Community God, perhaps Hick reverses the usual mystical tendency to understand the Nature God as the superior understanding of Community God and understands the Community God as the superior understanding of an adolescent Nature God. But would any mystic be able or willing to make or communicate that distinction in a mystical experience that is renowned to be ineffable and non-rational? It seems that Hick must be a follower of the Community God because an incredible intelligence and power is necessary to arrange, as he envisaged, the comprehensive adjusting and apportioned fulfillment of lives that were not fulfilled. If not anthropomorphic there must at least be a universal mind at work controlling the system. I wish Hick were still here to enlighten us on these questions.

There is no intention to claim that Hick is either wrong or confused. The point to be made is that the speaking of the language of Christian concepts is no guarantee of Christian content. Hick was able to forge for himself a satisfying religious understanding from a selection of religious parts. The observation that this has contradictory elements and is not altogether satisfactory would be an observation naturally absorbed by the mystics who relish contradiction as an aid to contemplation. Their singular goal, in comparison to which all rationalism is nothing, is the direct experience of God, which is acknowledged to be an ineffable experience not explicable in rational terms and for which the deliberate cultivation of obvious contradictions is sometimes taken up as an aid to deeper understanding of that non-rational experience.

The fact of Christian language being no guarantee of Christian content is illustrated by Meister Eckhart (c1260-1327) who, alongside Plotinus and Dionysius the Aeropagite, may be counted the greatest influence on European mysticism. In Eckhart there is an intoxicating mixture of poetry, creative imagination and allegory which is able to effect perfect metamorphosis of the originating materials. The Platonist Nature God may speak the language of the Christian Community God with seamless ease.

Eckhart was the mystic who Daisetz Suzuki chose for his comparative study of Christian and Buddhist mysticism. It was the writings of Eckhart which convinced Suzuki that Christianity was essentially Buddhism. For Suzuki, Eckhart redeems Christianity of its 'irrational elements' its 'mythological paraphernalia' its 'unnecessary historical appendix'[23] and the painful figure of the crucified Christ. Christ is painful to Buddhists because it highlights the gap between the West and the East. The religious impetus of Eastern mysticism is that there is no self. There is, therefore, no self to crucify with which to base a religion upon. In the foundry of Eckhart's writings fundamentally different psychological and dynamic characters of different religions are in the melting pot. Here is Suzuki's statement of faith in Eckhart:

> When I first read… a little book containing a few of Meister Eckhart's sermons, they impressed me profoundly, for I never expected that any Christian thinker ancient or modern could or would wish to cherish such daring thoughts… The ideas expounded there closely approached Buddhist thoughts, so closely indeed that one could definitely stamp them as coming

out of Buddhist speculations. As far as I can judge, Eckhart
seems to be an extraordinary 'Christian'... Eckhart's
Christianity is unique... he stands on his own experiences
which emerged from a rich, deep, religious personality. He
attempts to reconcile them with the historical type of
Christianity modelled after legends and mythology...
Eckhart's experiences are deeply, basically, abundantly rooted
in God as Being which is at once being and not being...It is
when I encounter such statements as these that I grow firmly
convinced that the Christian experiences are not after all
different from those of the Buddhist. Terminology is all that
divides us.[24]

The focus on God as Being is the clue to Eckhart's attachment to
the Nature God which underlies the surface expression of
Christian language.

Christian Mystics wish to be supportive of Christian doctrine
and may be said to enrich it. This is in contrast to the Platonists
who are prepared to ditch those doctrines and admit outright to
higher understanding. Tarjei Park for instance in his introduction
to a selection of English mystics writes,

The English mystics... are united in their emphatic advocacy
of the teachings and practices of the Church. They would not
in any way see their writings as countering traditional,
creedal Christianity, rather they see themselves as teachers
who are bringing out the latent mystical truths of the religion.
Their writings were not offered as alternative theologies, but
as texts that revealed the innermost truths of the Christian
tradition.[25]

This enrichment is the basis of Bernard McGinn's definition of
mysticism as not a religion in itself but an interaction with its
companion religious complex.[26]

This well-meaning desire to play a supportive role glosses over the antagonistic and dismissive aspects of the mystics which are shared with Platonism. It is naïve in regard to the consequence of 'bringing out the latent mystical truths.' This ineluctably repeats the supercilious two-tier understanding of Platonism's higher philosophical explanation. There is really no difference between the Platonist project and the mystical project. Oliver Davies, a recent translator of Eckhart, confirms this. He describes Eckhart as 'one of the great speculative mystics of Western Europe, who sought to reconcile the traditional Christian belief with the transcendental metaphysics of Neoplatonism.'[27]

The New Testament presents its message in vivid and completely understandable fashion. It is a celebration of the good news of God's action. That is intended to be taken literally and has in literal manner served generations of Christians with complete conviction. It does not need to have 'latent' or 'innermost' truths elicited from it. Any attempt at second order reflection, be it in the form of theology or philosophy introduces a superior attitude that is subversive of the sufficiency of the structure of the belief. In particular the claim to direct union with God is subversive of all dogma and of ecclesiastical authority. Just as Platonism was analyzed as inherently incapable of supporting dogma so are the Christian Mystics.

I summarize mysticism here as a religion in its own right which sails across the boundaries of specific cultural languages. On this basis the Christian Mystics may have more in common with the Sufis than either of these parties has in common with their apocalyptic hosts. McGinn's estimate of mysticism as an interaction with its companion religion needs to be qualified by the adjective 'apparent' interaction. The real situation is well identified by Hans Lewy in his understanding of Philo of Alexandria.[28] It is useful to have a comparative example from this scholar of Judaism. Lewy is an observer of mysticism outside the

Christian tradition where the recent major works tend to be written by appreciators who are unconcerned with analyzing the sorts of distinctions under review here and treat it as a magnificent body of contemplation in its own terms.

The comparative differences between Philo and the Christian Mystics are singular. Philo's Greek mysticism came as a shock to an already well-framed Jewish mystical tradition so that the Greek philosophical influence is thrown into relief. This was a different situation from Christianity. That new religion was in process of formation so that the philosophical element could be more imperceptibly incorporated. In contrast the spiritual leaders of Judaism cut Philo out of the stock of Jewish tradition.[29] This was partly because of the appeal of Philo's Hellenizing to the developing rival Christianity. The influence of Philo was strongly in the background of Clement and Origen. Philo's bi-cultural education as a Jewish and as a Greek philosopher was one-sided. His supreme erudition in Greek scholarship was matched by a partial learning of the Jewish. Lewy notes that Philo did not know Hebrew; had little knowledge of the Rabbinical interpretation of Law (Halakah) and Bible narrative (Haggadah). Philo's form of biblical interpretation (Midrash) was that of the already part-Hellenized style developing amongst the Alexandrian Jews.

Despite these differences Philo's enterprise as a Jew in Alexandria was parallel to that of the later Christian Alexandrians, Clement and Origen, in the wish to reconcile two different cultures. Influenced by the powerful appeal of Greek philosophy, Philo wished to demonstrate to his co-religionists the identity of their holy tradition with Hellenic wisdom. Lewy is perceptive of the situation that results. As he observes of Philo,

Scripture is, formally, the sole authority which he acknowledges. Yet, as he could, through a symbolic explanation, disengage himself from that obligation at any moment he

wished, he was as a matter of fact, dependent only on Greek
philosophy. Philo ascribes all the doctrines he had, in reality,
derived from Greek sources, to the Old Testament.[30]

Lewy notes that the result is neither Greek nor Jewish but a new
religious movement giving a particular expression to mystical
religion:

> It is, strictly speaking, not a doctrine at all, but a kind of
> atmosphere, the theoretical index of a mystical religion... this
> new body of thoughts was not a definite system but the
> spontaneous expression of a new sense of reality, it possesses
> neither a distinctive native country nor a genealogical tree; it
> has only representatives who try to give expression to this
> common mysticism. Philo of Alexandria is one of its earliest
> spokesmen.[31]

For Lewy the distinctive mark of this mystical amalgam is that it
theologizes philosophy. In using theological language he gives
philosophy meaning quite different to that intended by its originators. 'He populates the realm of the Eternal Forms... with the
Jewish circle of Divine Virtues: Creative Goodness, and Majesty,
Justice and Mercy.'[32] At the same time the amalgam creates a
philosophical allegorization of scripture equally not intended by
its originators:

> He... was unaware of the incompatibility of his method with
> the original intention of the Biblical author... They are no
> longer accounts of the historical development of the Chosen
> People, but images of moral and metaphysical truths[33] ...The
> whole Torah is transformed into a mystic philosophy.[34] This
> results in the combination of contradictory ideas of God. The
> First Cause of the metaphysicians is blended with the Lord of
> the Bible who becomes 'simultaneously abstract and

personal.'[35]

Lewy states, in relation to Philo's use of allegory, what seems the true situation of the Christian Mystic's relation to the Christians: 'instead of an organic combination of the two elements we are presented with a large set of correlations.'[36] This can be restated in my preferred analogy: oil and water cannot be mixed together but if the two elements are sufficiently atomized it is possible to produce the stable mixture known as an emulsion.

Allegory is the key tool with which Philo produces his transformation of the literal into the symbolic. This is a method, in the hands of a master, notoriously able to make almost any material mean something else.

McGinn, despite eliciting a complementary interaction, nevertheless notes that the history of tension with mysticism is not accidental but is rooted in 'explosive tendencies' in the relation to religious authority.[37] This antagonism to religious authority is rooted in this fundamental dissolution of dogma.

There is another aspect to this in the mystical generation of positively oppositional doctrines. Macquarrie's introduction to Christian Mysticism amply illustrates the tension. Macquarrie states frankly that he approaches mysticism with a divided mind.[38] He is wary of 'a shadow haunting the mystics', the pantheistic danger of 'confusing God with ourselves'[39] and the impossibility of reconciling the One with the God of Christian belief.[40] Macquarrie reveals the true attitude of an ecclesiastical mind that requires mysticism to be subordinated to reason.[41] But to ask for a rational mysticism is to destroy the very essence of mysticism. Mystics are free spirits and nothing can constrain their visions of God.

What conclusion is to be drawn from these confusing currents in Christian Mysticism with regard to its potential allegiances with the Community God or the Nature God? A definitive fact confronts the issue: Christian Mysticism in all its history and variety is the bastion of today's Nature God vote for the future of Christianity. My attempt to force a distinction between Platonism and Christian Mysticism, between Nature God mysticism and Community God mysticism must in the end fail when faced with the independence of such as Eckhart, the Nature God leanings of mysticism and the ambiguity toward the House of the Christians. On this basis Louis Boyer's attempt to distinguish monist mysticism from theist mysticism and to prove a Christian Mysticism definitively in Christ and therefore independent of Platonism must fail. So much is the language liable to be adapted to different concepts that Boyer's test of historical word usage is an unreliable guide. Only the actual conceptual content can be used as a test.[42] Mysticism cannot be so divided into classes and needs to be treated as a religion in its own right. The conceptual framework allies itself with Orphism/Platonism, Buddhism and Sufism but not with its apocalyptic host. So to sum up I treat Christian Mysticism, for the purposes of the present discussion within Christianity, as wedded to the House of the Platonists.

4

The Jesusologists

It is necessary before embarking on this chapter to make a distinction between the Followers of Jesus and Jesusology. Jesus retains an astonishing capacity to unite people of all faiths and none. His teaching unites all the four schools of Christianity under discussion here. His teaching can often be found as the religion of people who consider that they do not have a religion. This is evidenced in the study of working-class Southwark and the First World War army that is considered in chapter six. Jesus even wins the admiration of atheists. He received the approval of Richard Dawkins in *The God Delusion*. Who could not be won over by such wonderful parables and the uncompromising command to love? The special factor in this is that Jesus is the authority against all religions. His message is that religion is what is done, not what is believed. It is a message that pierces the charade of any form which belies content. It is a message that religious beliefs themselves can be an impediment to religion. It is a message that is simple and obvious yet permanently opposed by the fractious structures of thought that we erect to program religion. It represents the permanent opposition of the purpose of religion to the side effects of its operating programs. There is always a sense when confronted with Jesus that our incorrigible penchant for division over beliefs is a squalid travesty of what the religious impulse should be. The Followers of Jesus implement a Red Cross style rescue mission in the disaster areas of religious fissure. This is the heartfelt religion of the Followers of Jesus.

The Followers of Jesus are not the subject of this chapter. Jesusology is a different religion that has been forged in opposition to the House of the Christians largely by discontented intellectuals in the academy. It is a concerted liberal proposal to re-think Christianity. The primary motive is distaste for the Apocalypse. In accordance with this Jesus and Christianity must be washed clean of the Apocalypse. Jesusology is the religion that emerges from that wash.

Jesusology is the religion about the human Jesus without a divine nature. This distances the religion from the House of the Christians. It is the House of the Christian Humanists. As one representative states this, Jesus is the greatest and original humanist. The 'divinity' of Jesus is only a disguised way to point, as Jesus did, to the infinite progressive possibilities of human nature. [1] In order to make humans the focus of the divine Jesusology reverses the sense of the incarnation. Incarnation is taken as a reflexive symbol pointing to humanity as the object of divinity. This attaches Jesusology to Feuerbach's deconstruction of God as reflexive of an ideal humanity. For Walter Wink *'divinity is fully realized humanity.'* [2] The Son of Man is the archetype of wholeness of 'HumanBeing.' For Lloyd Geering today's secular world is the logical conclusion of incarnation and the continuation of Christianity.[3] For Don Cupitt the incarnation sanctifies the world.[4] For John Knox, a precursor of the seventies breakout over the 'myth of God incarnate', incarnation is really social change. It is a social force that emanates from Jesus and takes place in communal reality.[5*] For Altizer the redemption effected by Christ's pouring himself out really means the birth of a new humanity.[6]

The implementation of this vision of a progressive humanity developing toward perfection would necessitate dramatic political change. Accordingly there is a strong political element in Jesusology. This stems from the socialist inclinations of some of its prominent representatives. Dominic Crossan's egalitarianism marks him as a good old-fashioned communist.[7] Marcus Borg, who is not so far to the left, is insistent that Jesus is 'deeply spiritual and deeply political.'[8] His manifesto *Jesus: A New Vision* bears the trace of Herbert Marcuse the hero of the late sixties' student riots and associate of the Frankfurt School of attenuated Marxism. Marcuse represents a Marxism that has run out of steam. Borg parallels this with a political Jesus that has run out of steam. Marxism lost its direct object in the twentieth century as the proletariat became bourgeois, workers' pension funds became the new capitalists and the state took over socialism. Marcuse proposed a vaguely directed 'great refusal' in order to revive the original revolutionary fervor. The parallel of Marxism with the political Jesus is that attempts to prove that Jesus was a political revolutionary likewise failed in the sixties. Borg follows in the wake of this discussion and proposes a Jesus who is political by innuendo, a general 'refuser' and critic of culture.

Dominic Crossan has achieved status as the prime visionary of the Jesus suitable for Jesusology.[9*] The success of Crossan's portrait is due to the fact that Jesusology requires a Jesus who points the finger at the political and social organization of society today. Crossan's egalitarian cynic sage renders Jesus sufficiently critical to interpret as political but not directly as such. This sage is sufficiently non-specific to history to be appropriated as political director for today. This sage fulfills Borg's requirement to replace the apocalyptic Jesus who is a 'bit shocking and irrelevant' with a 'persuasive and compelling alternative image' that is of 'extraordinary relevance to contemporary culture and church.'[10] This project by late-century attenuated Marxist Christians to show that Jesus was the original attenuated Marxist suggests that the 1980s' Jesusology inherits the earlier project by Christian Marxists to claim a Marxist Jesus.[11*] With the 1980s' demise of communism the already remaindered Marxism in Jesusology now wanes necessarily into a blander socialism.

Jesusology has been given a great recent boost by studies of Galilee which have expanded our knowledge of the markets, economic circumstances, taxation and social structure of the region. Social science models are used to extrapolate the data. Knowledge of the cultural background of Judaism, such as language, medicine and healing has also been expanded. There is greater recognition of the different religious parties such as Pharisaism and the Essenes. There has over the past fifty years been a festival of extended context. This seems to suggest better possibilities of understanding Jesus and the prospect, at last, of a more authoritative statement about him. But results from this extended context are illusory. They tell us no more than the assumptions brought to them. William Herzog states the assumption. Herzog outlines the 'third quest' for the historical Jesus, as it has come to be known, and the consensus which drives it. This consensus is 'the effort to read Jesus as a political figure.'[12] It is in this light that 'informed guesswork' and judicious gap filling of missing information gives a 'probable idea of what was happening.'[13] A political Jesus fed in to one end of the social studies machine produces a political Jesus fed out of the delivery end.

Jesusology is determinedly anti-apocalyptic. The one thing Jesus does not do is declare the arrival of the Kingdom of God. He certainly does not associate with the obviously apocalyptic John the Baptist. The tar of apocalyptic that swirls dangerously around the Jewish cultural background of Jesus, his relation to John the Baptist and his portrait by the four Evangelists is a worry to Jesusology which must preserve Jesus pristine from its contamination. A subtle gambit is used to render Jesus non-stick to apocalyptic. Chronological imminence is substituted by intensity of vision. According to Robert Funk, '[For Jesus], the future was fused together with the past in the intensity of the present moment to such a degree that he experienced the confluence of tenses in his vision. He stood there in Galilee, back at the moment of creation, so to speak, and, at the same time, he was also there at the end of time in his vision of God's imperial rule.'[14] The disciples were too dumb to understand Jesus' sophisticated notion of time and as they were originally followers of John steeped in apocalyptic they naturally reverted to this understanding after the death of Jesus.[15] From this point on the equally perverse Evangelists completed the damage.

The New Testament portrait of a Jesus who declared the imminent arrival of the Kingdom of God and the New Testament declaration of Jesus as Christ is an outrage for Jesusology. Funk calls for the end of 'canonical imperialism.'[16] Jesusology has accordingly adopted its own canon of texts to situate its own Jesus. The criterion for admission to this canon is that the text should not be apocalyptic. A new canon has been put together incorporating the hypothetical Q gospel source, various other gospels discovered at Nag Hammadi[17] and the Wisdom tradition of the Old Testament.

Accordingly Jesusology holds to a Kingdom of God to be fully realized by human agency. The theoretical grounding for this takes advantage of the puzzle in the New Testament which presents a Kingdom that Jesus declares somehow to be present but also yet to come. This is the subject of the last chapter of this book so will not be expounded here. Suffice it to say that Jesusology adopts the various solutions to the puzzle which resolve it by discounting the future apocalyptic sense. For Dominic Crossan, Jesus declared a sapiential kingdom here and now.[18] Sapiential here means the wisdom of living the power of God's rule eternally present and available to all. This sapiential Kingdom effectively repeats Harnack's version of the Kingdom as the rule of God in men's hearts. Crossan's Kingdom represents the liberal Kingdom of the nineteenth century that sailed untroubled into the twentieth century by means of metamorphosis into the Socialist Kingdom.

In rejecting the Apocalypse Jesusology relinquishes a natural

explanation of many aspects of the case. The Apocalypse explains
the theological inspiration of Jesus. It explains the way in which
he is connected to but different from John. Jesus imminentizes
John's message. It explains how he could win his group of
adherents from a ready-made pool that would be sympathetically
attuned to it.[19*] It explains, through the presence of the
Apocalypse as a factor in the religious background, the possibility of an enthusiastic but at the same time restricted
constituency of potential supporters. It explains the direction of
developments after the death of Jesus. It might be said that Jesus
through the Apocalypse harnessed forces that were stronger than
himself and which did in fact overpower him. In rubbing the
Aladdin's lamp of the Apocalypse he summoned up a genie that
threw over his declaration of the Kingdom of God and substituted his own person as the Apocalypse.

As the Jesusologists discount any connection of Jesus with the
Apocalypse they are left in the situation of needing an alternative
to explain why he became the most famous person of all time.
Jesusology adopts exceptional God consciousness as the factor
that launched him to fame. This adopts Schleiermacher's gift, as
noted in the chapter two discussion of Jesus the follower of Plato.
For Maurice Wiles Jesus had overriding God-consciousness.[20] For
Hick the whole life of Jesus was dominated by consciousness of
God.[21] He was a truly God-filled mystic.[22] This was the basis on
which Jesus lays claim to be a charismatic prophet and healer
who made God real to others. For Matthew Fox Jesus, 'both in his
person and his proclamation', is a sorely neglected mystic [23] who
was motivated by a deep god consciousness.[24] For Marcus Borg,
Jesus is a 'spirit filled mediator'[25] a charismatic religious personality type, healer sage and prophet[26] on a level with Lao Tzu and
Buddha.[27] This is for Borg the best way we can understand Jesus
historically.

Where does the allegiance of Jesusology lie with regard to the
Platonists and the Christians? Jesusology is embarrassed by the

Community God and has taken to heart every secular and theological critique of it. For Geering, placing the doctrine of incarnation at the focal center is a means of rejecting the Community God.[28] As he puts it, 'Theism does not properly belong to Christianity.'[29] Likewise Spong's humanist mission is to rescue Jesus from theism.[30] Thomas Altizer takes the position to its extremity. 'To say that "God is Jesus" is to say that... God has become the Incarnate Word, he becomes fully incarnate, thereby ceasing to exist.'[31]

There is an air of a refugee camp about Jesusology. It is a house that gives shelter to refugees from the other schools of Christianity. Mystical experience of God is not granted to everyone. Those with a pragmatic spirituality are temperamentally immune to mysticism. Nor are the intellectual satisfactions of Platonist contemplation suitable for all temperaments. Some people have lost belief in a supernatural deity but remain attracted to the ethical grounds of Christianity which are especially embodied in the teaching of Jesus. Others have succumbed to the accusations of irrationalism directed to the apocalyptic articulations; Christ, incarnation, resurrection, atonement, judgment and life after death. For these people focus on the human personality of Jesus, his parables and his ethical teaching is a way to circumvent the apparatus by getting back to the original Jesus who pre-dates it. Attachment to Jesus is a natural and attractive way to retain companionship with the church of Christianity despite having given up on the Community God. The Christians, no less than the Jesusologists, are admiring of the human personality of their intimate guide and intercessor so the basis of companionship is mutual. The ethical teaching provides uncontentious common ground. The Christians cannot really dispute this aspect of Jesusology because it takes up their own claim that Jesus was fully human as well as God.

There is, however, in Jesusology a strong coalescence against the House of the Christians. Jesusology dissolves all dogmatic statement. The ground for this is that if the religion of Jesus is Humanist then it is open to dispute in the same way that all human arguments are disputable. There is no privileged ground. This dissolution of dogma allies with the Platonists and the Christian Mystics. To a degree it is Platonist exiles who found Jesusology. Marcus Borg in his leave taking from the Community God is a leading example of Jesusology wedded to the Nature God.[32]

A couple of examples are useful to demonstrate the exit route from dogma provided by Jesusology. John Hick's *Metaphor of God Incarnate* provides a summary of the failure of dogmas. Hick's mission is to end the 'cognitive dissonance' brought on by the apocalyptic doctrine of incarnation.[33] For Hick the doctrine of two natures and two minds of Christ is incapable of explanation and every attempt to do so has had to be repudiated.[34] The self-emptying of God into Jesus is likewise incapable of explanation and ends in dubious appeal to mystery.[35] The claim to divinity generates the impossible conundrum of the trinity. The atonement by the blood of Jesus is morally repugnant.[36] The claim to divinity creates the anti-ecumenical scandal of restricted access to salvation.[37] Hick proceeds to treat all these items not as articulations of the Apocalypse but as metaphors. In so doing he finds humanist correspondences for them.

The American, Leroy Waterman, provided another microcosm of the dissolution of doctrine through Jesusology. Waterman's *Religion of Jesus*, written in 1952, stole a march on Hick and the present generation.[38] Waterman's subtitle is *Christianity's Unclaimed Heritage of Prophetic Religion*. This is a version of 'ethical teaching trumps apocalyptic' that was illustrated by Dobschütz in chapter one. In Waterman's reading Jesus was a wholly ethical prophet who tried to free his countrymen from the nationalist apocalyptic hopes of the false prophets and rescue them from the depravity of the chosen-people idea. Christianity got it wrong about Jesus and it is a great miracle that he was able to stamp his mission on untrained fishermen, steeped in legalistic nationalism, sufficiently strongly that it should be possible for us now to rectify the fact of his intentions after an eclipse of two millennia.[39] For Waterman the religion of Jesus dissolves all dogma. It specifically dissolves baptism, the trinity, the Lord's Supper and blood sacrifice.

Jesusology has a second affinity with Platonism. Catherine Keller demonstrates how the inversion of incarnation can be specifically harnessed to the Nature God. 'The core doctrine of Christianity, the incarnation, celebrates the embodiment of God in the world... This is the implication of Wesley's return to the mystical Christian sense that God is the spirit of the world, the *anima mundi*. God is in all things.'[40] Michael Brierley notes that belief in a human Jesus who is divine by degree as an exceptional human, not by absolute quality, is one of the distinguishing marks of the followers of the Nature God.[41*]

A third factor linking Jesusology to Platonism is the prospect of ecumenical outreach. For Hick Jesusology universalizes a non-exclusive Christianity. Salvation is redefined in pluralist terms as 'becoming fully human.' Jesus is a model of perfect human.[42] The super God-consciousness of Jesus' experience of ultimate reality unites with other religions. The conclusion from these factors is that Jesusology is firmly in allegiance with the House of the Platonists.

The origin of Jesusology can be dated to 1774-1778 when the series of tracts known as the Wolfenbüttel Fragments appeared.[43] The name refers to the Duke of Brunswick's great library where the papers had been deposited anonymously. They were published by the poet, critic and religious freethinker Gotthold Lessing (1729-1781). The author turned out to be Hermann Reimarus (1694-1768) who did not risk the certainty of dismissal from his career with the open statement of his opinions during his lifetime. Reimarus was a respected scholar, rector and professor of Hebrew and Oriental languages. Reimarus can be credited with placing on the agenda of scholarship the question of the human Jesus and his relation to Christ. He did so in electrifying fashion with the suggestion that Jesus was possibly a common political rebel and that his followers stole his body to create their story about his resurrection.

Although Jesusology claims value as a revisioning of Christianity for the future the relationship to Christianity has been questionable from the outset. The House of the Christians cannot permit a distinction between the human Jesus and Christ. From the moment that Reimarus first prompted the possibility that there could be a religion of the human Jesus without a divine nature, distinct from a religion about Christ the tension has been high. David Strauss felt that Jesusology, proposed originally by Lessing, was an appeasement by half-measure. 'To turn with contempt from what but yesterday was the object of reverence produced unendurable contradiction, the result rationalism a compromise between the church and the negative result. Lessing's religion of Jesus is extraordinarily problematic.'[44] Franz Overbeck was more decisive:

> Lessing's concept of a 'religion of Christ' ...takes Christianity as a religion off its hinges. Lessing knew very well that whoever speaks of this religion places himself outside the religion of Christianity... the conception... is based on the discovery of the human being of Christ, that is on the discovery that even in the first moment of Christianity's emergence as a universal religion it lifted Christ to the status of a divine being... it nevertheless projected this conception of him back into the origins of history and especially without justification based its idea of him as a divine being on his witness to himself. It is obvious that the critical significance of this discovery lies in opposition to the whole Christian religion, and it is just as obvious that it is not useable for the

reconstruction of Christianity, because only the projection of Christ as a divine being into the origins of history made the universal religion that we call Christianity.[45]

To put Overbeck's objection into shorthand, Christianity is a religion that is primarily about what God has done through Jesus, not about Jesus himself. Of course it is about Jesus, but the incarnation which elevates Jesus is God's work toward the eventual revelation of his justice.

None of the analysis of the present tributaries flowing in Christianity is done here in the spirit that doctrines should be unchangeable and not be reinterpreted for beneficial use today. I do not, therefore, make any weight out of this awkward mix of disjunction and conjunction between Jesusology and Christianity. I wish, as with the followers of the Nature God, to leave the Jesusologists to the unquestioned enjoyment of their visionary inspiration. This vision undoubtedly serves the motivational inspiration necessary to the heart of any religion. My doubt concerns the capacity of Jesusology to fulfill the conditions for a new vision of God for the twenty-first century. Is this really the second Christianity as Hick proposes? Or Jesus for the new millennium as Funk proposes?

Although the Jesusologists describe themselves as Christian Humanists there can be no such thing as Christian Humanism. Humanism is a different type of religion from either of those reviewed so far. The capital letter is intentional. It is another visionary faith. Its God is Reason. Its faith is that Reason has the capacity to bring about perfect human relations. Humanism is, therefore, compelled to be optimistic about human nature. Were it not invested with optimism, reason could not carry the necessary visionary role. The strength of its God would be sapped. This is not the place to give examples of the extravagance of Humanist optimism. Consideration of that is due in chapter twelve. But the Jesusologists display the optimistic feature in ample measure. John Hick believed that there was 'no limit to the development of the valuable aspects of human nature.'[46] Humans are part of a vast creative process leading to unlimited good.[47*] The 'new being' becomes the symbol for perfect humanity. The person of Jesus becomes the representative model of the perfect human. For John de Gruchy, the South African theologian, Jesus is the fully human being, genuine human being.[48] These are modest humanist ambitions in comparison to the crescendo of humanist perfectionism and the evolutionary ecstasy of Teilhard de Chardin. Chardin was endorsed by the senior humanist, Julian Huxley, which demonstrates the close affinity of religious and secular Humanism.[49] Chardin displays the heady mix of harnessing evolution to a humanist interpreted apocalyptic endpoint. Chardin marries the authority of an acknowledged expert in paleontology with the optimism of humanist theology. In his scheme the development of consciousness, which he terms the *noosphere*, initiated a second stage in evolution where psychosocial transcends biological evolution. In Chardin's language, consciousness becoming consciousness of itself cephalizes evolution. Consciousness will now take over the evolutionary drive and synthesize human cooperation into hyperpersonal organization. It will in due course arrive at the 'omega point' where biological necessity is superseded.[50] This theory bears the stamp of anthropocentric worship of human consciousness that was encountered in the discussion of Platonism.

My objection to Humanism is to this reckless fantasy about human nature and human society which the maturity of the twenty-first century will not wear. If there is one aspect of humanity that has been demonstrated in the hundred years since the First World War it is the permanent presence of barbarity just below the surface of civilization. We have become aware of the fragile nature even of basic order and functioning in society. This fantasy of progress to a perfect human nature cannot be predicated on a new God to serve this century. It seems doubtful that Jesus can be credited with spreading belief in these 'infinite progressive possibilities of human nature.' It seems a foolish thing for a wise man to suggest and one calculated to lose credibility with all but suggestible followers. The place of forgiveness suggests rather the assumption that we are regularly likely to fail and that a means of coping with that holds an important place in religion. This optimism with no bounds is a distinctive vice of Humanism. It is not a mistake made by the realism of the Christians, the Platonists or the Mystics who all allow for the deficient aspects of human nature.

Christian Humanism is caught in a double bind. Christianity is not Humanism and Humanism does not need Jesus. Humanism is a religion self-sufficient in its own terms. The reverse incarnation is superfluous to it. A question mark hangs over the credibility of the construction of Jesusology. It has elements of a feedback loop. It refuses all association with the Apocalypse. At the same time it founds itself on the two apocalyptic articulations, incarnation and the Kingdom of God which catapulted Jesus to fame. It was the inspiration of the Apocalypse that made Jesus into God and the divine perfect human that is now taken as the model for a perfected humanity. The additional feedback peculiarity is that the humanist optimism is itself quasi-apocalyptic. It presupposes an overall purpose to human existence and so adopts an apocalyptic end. 'What is the ultimate objective of the human odyssey?' [51] asks Thomas Sheehan. A religion that rejects the Apocalypse turns out to be indebted to it for its basic precepts.

In addition, Jesusology is too much of a male interest project to make an inclusive appeal. It inherits the tendency of what I call 'Empire Christianity.' The advance toward the perfection of society has to be undertaken by political organization. Politics is still largely a male preserve and swarms with masculine nouns; opposition, accusation, organization, agendas, resolutions, committees, campaigns and progress. Could the new God for the twenty-first century not be a big noise God? Could the new God perhaps be a quiet and slightly feminine God? Could that God be content with the repeated cycle of lives lived to their best? Could the new God perhaps dispense with the self-important ambition to orchestrate the direction of the universe? The relation of the political to the religious domain is the subject of the last chapter so the matter must be deferred for the time being.

5

Can Liberal Theology Save Religion for the Twenty-First Century?

5.1. The Problem of Ecumenical Imperialism

5.2. The Problem of the Ethic

5.3. The Problem of Authority

5.4. The Problem of Esoteric Elitism

5.5. The Mark of Protestant Trauma

5.6. Conclusion to Part One: A Tale of Two Religions

5.1 The Problem of Ecumenical Imperialism

One of the hopes invested in the Nature God is the prospect of reaching out to other religions on the basis that it is a universalizing principle that would synthesize all religions. This is a response to the agonizing tension introduced to the liberal mind by the pluralist religious exposure. The exclusive claims of Christianity become a scandal. Every device has been clutched at to resolve the exclusivity, although none has proved satisfactory. One of the devices is to ascribe to people of other religions honorary Christian citizenship. Through their good spirit they may be taken as Christians in fact though they know nothing of the Christian story. In this scheme it is assumed that God has a plan for them which it is none of our business to know. Although this honor is extended in the best goodwill it retains an element of condescension. The device that seems to be the better plan is to claim that all religions are the same.

The grand figure of this synergizing enterprise is Wilfred

Cantwell Smith (1916-2000) who was for some time director of the Harvard Center for the Study of World Religions and director of the Institute of Islamic Studies at McGill University. His book *Towards a World Theology* espoused the prospects of Nature God synergy. With the extensive comparative knowledge drawn from his official positions, Smith was too much aware of the difficulties to be too outright confident about the proposal. His 'Interim Conclusion' is tentative and subtle. At the same time the temptation of his own 'Neo-Platonist tendencies'[1] seems to have been too much for him not to plunge into the proposal and to take it to heart. The prospect of universalization is ready made in Neo-Platonism. As has been discussed, the seed of universalization originates in the specific context of a higher understanding of the literalisms of Christianity. Why should this not transfer to a higher understanding of the literalisms of all other religions? Smith made the generalizing leap in his distinction between faith as the higher principle and belief as the literalist variations that express faith.[2] For Smith the mystic, God is a reality that explicitly transcends conception. To this mystery all religious history is a response. For Smith, anthropomorphism is inadmissible and it is necessary to end religion as a set of propositional tenets. Religion *'at its best'* (my emphasis) is a response to the surpassingly great other and is a product of the need to interpret the 'cosmic significance' of human life.[3] Smith never quite says that Tillich is behind this suspension of religious beliefs but his stated preference for what he refers to as the modern term transcendence, the euphemism for God, suggests that influence.[4]

Smith has been influential and naturally so because his voice so suitably supports the liberal change of allegiance to the Nature God and its ambitions. Smith was mentor to John Hick's *The Interpretation of Religion*. In this work Smith's early tentative proposal was rendered definite. Hick wanted to produce a religious interpretation of religion. He envisaged a field theory of religion that would account for 'the religious experience and thought of the whole human race.'[5] Beneath the 'bewildering plurality of forms'[6] Hick imagined the singular expression of the one transcendent reality.

Another follower of Smith is Scotty McLennan. McLennan's 'world process of religious convergence' is specifically a response to Smith's call for a world theology.[7] His Unitarian Universalist denomination draws from all world religions framing Jesus, Krishna and Buddha as the central avatars[8] and taking up the Baha'i belief that we are undergoing progressive revelation that has not yet been completed. The Unitarian Universalist inclinations are revealed in their sponsorship of the pagan Native Nature God, [9] the parent of the Philosophized Nature God. The Community God is relegated by McLennan to an infantile stage of religious belief. McLennan is also influenced by Carl Jung's mystical mountain top exhilaration.[10] This is another instance of Nature God mysticism. Jung employed this in his theory of archetypes to bring all religions of the world together. McLennan adopts the mountain metaphor and makes the condescension explicit. The spiritual mountain converges at the very top as mystics of all religions have told us.

Of equal influence to Smith is Tillich's Ground of being which on account of its diffuse statement of the Existence Mystery has been adopted as a useful synthesizing principle. Spong states that God as the 'Ground of All Being', cannot be contained in any religious system and must supersede tribal deities.[11] This principle it is hoped will 'reach across the once insuperable boundaries' and unite Judaism, Islam, Hinduism and Buddhism.[12] Spong takes up ground of being to synthesize Moses, Mohammed, Buddha, Krishna and Jesus.[13] Michael Hampson has similar hopes for the ground of all being to replace the 'many arbitrary and ultimately trivial images of God.'[14] Altizer picked up Tillich's 'ultimate reality' to frame equivalence with Brahman and Tao.[15] For Altizer, this moves Christianity on to a universal form away from the scandal of particularity.[16] John

Macquarrie proposed his 'holy being' version of 'being itself' as present in all religions.[17] Maurice Wiles used direct experience of ultimate mystery to synthesize all religions in different cultures.[18] Marcus Borg posits a cross cultural approach that does not depend on religious belief and does not privilege any particular religious tradition.[19] The synthesizing principle in play is panentheism, the Christian tradition 'understood at a deeper level.'[20] This produces a 'more authentic contemporary faith beyond dogmatic religion.' Matthew Fox takes the mystic experience of the universal Cosmic Christ as a specific equation of Nature God with deep ecumenism.[21] For Karen Armstrong, the mystical tradition is a synoptic understanding that God, Nirvana, Brahman and Dao are all names for ultimate reality.[22] These are also names for 'speech-less "nothingness",'[23] which 'could solve many of our current religious problems.'[24] This is a covert reference to demolition of disliked dogmatic statements.

This group of Nature God advocates represents a resurfacing of the supercilious Alexandrian solution to the junction of the Platonists and the Christians. This time around the solution is universalized out of the Christian context and is ambitious to be comprehensive of all religions.

The temptation of this line of thought is great. In taking a critical approach, I risk seeming to disparage genuine and generous inter-faith motivations. There are, however, authoritative voices warning against the temptation. Ironically Tillich, who has been so much appealed to by the synthesizers, was against any such attempt. Tillich, in his journey to Japan and search for a possible universal principle was struck by the separate and integral nature of the different traditions. 'A mixture of religions destroys in each of them the concreteness which gives it its dynamic power.'[25] Alan Watts is another voice warning against synthesis. He presented the irreconcilably different fundamental bases of Christianity and Tao. A way of liberation that comes not by means of revolution, and a philosophy that holds to the higher knowledge of the mutual interdependence of opposites, cannot be reconciled with a religion that seeks the revolutionary resolution of all evil in favor of the good.[26] Nor is the busy moral endeavor of Christianity the same as the *wu-wei*, not action, of Tao.[27] Nor is completely unsentimental compassion for suffering compatible with Christianity's strenuous emotional compassion.[28]

A giant question mark sits over the claim that all mystical experience is the same. Stephen Katz has brought out the strong differences between Zen and Jewish Kabbalah. *Nirvana* is an experience of no-self, the self being an illusion and the source of suffering. There is no encounter with 'something.' In contrast *devekuth* is not a loss of self. The word means 'cleaving to' God. The goal is a loving intimacy with God who is a distinct entity.[29] In contrast again, Jewish experience is not the absorption experienced by Eckhart. As Eckhart explains, 'If I am to know God directly, I must become completely he and I: so that this he and I become and are one I.'[30] Such a result is forbidden in the Jewish theological structure and therefore it is not an experience of mystical practice.

This project to synthesize all religions is neither good theology nor good sociology. It is driven by liberal embarrassment. Katz observes that the ecumenical overtones come 'primarily from non-mystics of recent vintage for their own purposes.'[31] It is an unconscious theological imperialism driven by goodwill combined with embarrassment at the exclusive claims of the past. The ecumenism is orchestrated by one type of religion facilitated by the debilitated identity inflicted on its suppressed companion tradition. The recipients of this embrace have too strongly developed traditions to originate it. Far from synthesizing all religions the ecumenism is the self-promotion of a distinctive variety of Western nature mysticism. It is a religion of the Christian discontented intellectuals. The irony of the Nature God ecumenism is that it is itself the product of incompatibility. It sets out to extend the hand of friendship to other religions on the basis of a quarrel at home. There is an alternative logic available which is formally to affiliate to Buddhism. In this will be found a congenial and well-developed environment free of the unhappiness of association with the Christians.

There is not one principle synthetic of all religions. The theory that there should be one is a projection of the Platonist ownership of a single metaphysical truth. Within Christianity alone two principles have to be allowed for and worldwide there may be many more. On this basis the mission to synthesize is a misguided way forward into the twenty-first century. The sufficient principle of harmony for the time being is respect and joint charitable works. The analogy is with different software programs. It has to be acknowledged that different religions are incompatible in the same way that different software programs are incompatible. It is misguided to think that a new world standard program can come from a patch that will make them all run together. A new world religion will come from a new software package that will be adopted by new generations of users and gradually take over from the old traditions. If the theological and sociological tasks have been properly done there will be a cherished perspective on these heritages and not a suppressive denial of their character.

5.2 The Problem of the Ethic

The Community God has a certain economy with regard to its ethic in that it is a direct command to human relations. Moses took down the Ten Commandments from the dictation of Yahweh. Jesus/God gives the Sermon on the Mount and in his parables enjoins exemplary behavior. The Community God is directly reflexive. The love that God wants to be offered is the love that we offer one another. 'Truly I tell you just as you did not do it to one of the least of these, you did not do it to me' (Matthew 25:45). If God is defined by intention or by intended effect it can be deduced that the Community God *is* a representation of the ideal potential of human relations. The Community God is an ethical command.

It is a contrasting feature of the Nature God that it does not prescribe directly for human relations but introduces the ethic by indirect means. This is a reflection of the nature substrate. Nature is equivocal to the benefit of humans.

Considering this equivocation in the Native Nature God first, the Sun, for instance, ripens the crops but it may also shrivel them up and promote skin cancer. Mother Earth is the support of human existence but also the source of uncertainty and disasters. Mother Nature, in the form of human biology, is the source of the wonder of consciousness but also the source of unexpected death, viruses and cleft palates. Taking second the equivocation of the Philosophized Nature God, the Existence Mystery is neutral or plain bad in its implication for the conditions of human existence. 'Being itself' in the hands of Heidegger or Tillich is the source of permanent existential anxiety about death. Both Native and Philosophized Nature Gods must have an ethic inserted into them because at root a mystery based on a substrate that is ethically equivocal and cannot be described cannot be a set of rules about human conduct.

Raphael Demos picked up on the point that ethical value cannot be derived from being in a review of Tillich's great Nature God work *Systematic Theology*:

Being as such is innocent... The conception of God as being-itself lacks whatever is necessary to make such a concept available for religion and so for theology. It is possible to be so philosophical in one's theology as to cut it off from its roots in religious experience, and that is a charge which can fairly be made against the Tillich-Thomistic definition of God exclusively in terms of being and with no reference whatever to *value*.[32]

Gabriel Vahanian understood the problematic ethical result of swapping the Community God for the Nature God. He sums up, 'conjectures thrown upon the blank screen of being that is said to be ultimate... means God has become a datum not a living mandatum, little remains of vital significance for human affairs.'[33]

David Jenkins also picked up on this feature in his discussion of John Robinson's Tillich inspired *Honest to God*. For Jenkins 'Being Itself' is an inanimate, impersonal, 'something,' that has no agency or volition so there is a leap to be made to harness it to any system of moral values. Jenkins points out that a second assumption must be put in place.[34] Jenkins has elicited the essential dual 'fact plus value' qualification of Nature God worship. It is contemplation of nature *combined with* the assumption that nature is good.

This dual feature is readily apparent in *Timaeus* the canonical creation story of Nature God worship. Plato simply equates nature and the good. He thus inserts good into the cosmos. The world is the fairest of all things and he is the best of causes. The universe is imbued with moral significance from the start. The primitive chaos of being, space and becoming is brought to a state of the greatest perfection. The physiology of humans equally exhibits divine purpose. The universe itself becomes a blessed God. 'His creation, then, for all these reasons, was a blessed God.'[35] The divine form he made mostly of fire so that it would be bright and beautiful to look at and spherical. Plato's universe is not just a universe it is a representation of perfection.

Bertrand Russell identified the mix up of morals and physics in Plato. 'Physics as it appears in Plato's Timaeus is full of ethical notions. It is an essential part of its purpose to show that the earth is worthy of admiration.'[36] The objection to philosophy that is also edification may be counted a theme tune of Russell's *History of Western Philosophy*:

Philosophy, throughout its history, has consisted of two parts inharmoniously blended: on the one hand a theory as to the nature of the world, on the other an ethical or political doctrine as to the best way of living. The failure to separate these two with sufficient clarity has been the source of much confused thinking. Philosophers from Plato to William James have allowed their opinions as to the constitution of the universe to be influenced by the desire for edification.[37]

In this edifying intention of Plato it is possible to see the reflection of the ethical insertion by Pythagoras into his number mysticism. Ten is the perfect number so ten bodies were created for the universe and the bodies must move in a circle as the circle is the model of perfection.

Taking the lead from Plato, subsequent formulations of the Nature God are obliged to add the assumption of value to the fact. Jenkins identified this second assumption in Tillich as stemming from Schleiermacher. Jenkins named Schleiermacher's 'pious feeling' as the device which makes the leap from the Existence Mystery to the ethics of human relations. 'It is assumed that this feeling or awareness has built into it... an all-embracing awareness of value, unity and fulfilment... it is this twofold assumption which allows Schleiermacher to associate, indeed identify, this immediate self-consciousness with, or substitute it for, knowledge of God and which allows Tillich to make his characteristic use of the notions of ground of being.'[38]

Tillich was too astute a philosopher not to be aware of the necessity for this twofold assumption. He provides for it as a necessary conjunction of the mystical and the ethical, a simple identity between is and ought:

Like all religions, both grow out of a sacramental basis, out of the experience of the holy as present here and now... The sacramental basis cannot disappear. It can however be broken and transcended. This happens in two directions, the mystical and the ethical, according to the two elements of the experience of the holy the experience of the holy as being and the experience of the holy, as what ought to be. There is no holiness and therefore no religion without both elements.[39]

Here are some further examples of the fact plus value maneuver, the injection of the ethical into the Existence Mystery. For John de Gruchy awe before the majesty of the universe, demands justice in the face of oppression.[40] For John Macquarrie the mysterium always includes a response to the mysterium.[41] Macquarrie names his type of theology existential-ontological. The very name embodies the conflation of fact and value. Ontological refers to being. Existential refers to *faith* in being. It is this that allows what would otherwise be Macquarrie's non-sequitur of a leap from God as Being to God as Holy Being. For Marcus Borg, mystical experience always has an intrinsic connection to compassion.[42] Matthew Fox has been particularly troubled by the question of how mysticism relates to social justice.[43] He resolves this in his formulation 'Whee! We Wee.'[44] This embodies the transition from the individual mystical experience to community relations. 'Whee!' represents the individual ecstasy. 'We' represents the turn in symbolic consciousness from I to we. To this Fox adds the third condition 'Wee' which for him represents the prophetic struggle. Fox has effectively recreated Tillich's conjunction of is and ought by means of a conjunction of mystical and prophetic traditions. The prophetic is taken up as the tradition of social accusation by the prophets. For Keith Ward, reality unfolds values of intrinsic worth.[45] The mystical non-verbally expressed has built in a response of total commitment.[46] For Scotty McLennan 'devotion to the source of all life... leads naturally to wanting to serve others.'[47] For Catherine Keller the goodness of creation... is non-negotiable.[48] For John Hick, the starting point of any religion must be the serendipitous character of the universe.[49] There is an act of faith involved in this. As Inge states, 'the vitally important thing is that we should *believe* (my emphasis) Goodness Truth and Beauty to be the source and goal of the whole cosmic process.'[50]

I make no suggestion that there is anything to be disdained in a religion that imbues the cosmos with moral purpose directed at humans. It has recently proved an inspiration to eco theologies. I only wish to query the claim that this ancient insertion of moral purpose into the cosmos can be a religion that addresses human relations in the twenty-first century. The cosmos from another viewpoint is downright hostile to the ideal potential of human relations. It is, for instance, hostile to the realization of human equality because it is our biological necessity to win food and shelter from the earth that leads to economic domination of one human over another. I take the twenty-first century understanding to be that the universe is morally indifferent to human existence. That existence and the nature of humans are an accidental production which is by no means unequivocally good. A new God for the twenty-first century may well occupy a containment role to assist humans to create meaning in the face of this indifference.

The insertion of cosmic purpose seems to be the product of a massive anthropocentrism. The universe is good because it has produced humans. David Pailin gives voice to this. For him 'the human is the highest mode of being of which we are aware.'[51] From this it follows that we should not take as a slight on God Feuerbach's claim that God has been invested with human qualities. Pailin's magnificent worship of human consciousness culminates in extreme form in Teilhard de Chardin, considered in the previous chapter. Chardin's omega point of pure psychosocial consciousness that supersedes biological development, itself becomes a sort of divinity. The parturition of this divinity will be a validation of the existence of the universe. It is a Pythagorean rapture of the power of mind.

There is an underlying difficulty of deriving an ethic from the

Existence Mystery. Even though the cosmos is taken to be good it does not prescribe the details needed to govern human relationships. The symptom of this difficulty is the peculiar maneuver of sympathetic vibration to which Nature God theology is driven. For instance, Einstein's theory of relativity which demonstrates the interchangeability of energy and matter has nothing to prescribe for the conditions of human relations. Yet for Nature God theology relativity is forced to serve. This is achieved by parallelism, a form of sympathetic magic by wordplay on relativity and relations or play on the word harmony.

Just as a struck tuning fork may set up sympathetic vibration in the undamped strings of a piano so aspects of physics are supposed to set off regulatory aspects of human relationships. Pythagoras' harmony of the spheres, for instance, is made to be suggestive of harmony in human relations although emotions and physics have nothing in common. Keller expounds a similar sympathetic vibration as the basis of process theology. In summing up Whitehead's incorporation of the theory of relativity into the Nature God this updated view of the universe is taken to connect to our sense of value in human relations. Keller's theology of relation in becoming is built on this vibration of physics with the ethical. Einstein's theory of relativity vibrates open-ended interactivity as the basis of human relations.[52] A similar device operates for Fox. The unitive experience of the mystical 'unity with' vibrates compassion as 'unitive model for' human relations. Fox reads this as the circular divine energy where compassion becomes justice.[53] So, for Fox the human relationship to nature is taken to vibrate relations between humans. As he puts it: 'relationship as ontological first principle.'[54]

At the end of this procedure we are still left with nature in its goodness, harmony or relativity, as a bare suggestive mimic. The full content of what these might mean to human relations remains unfleshed. It remains to flesh this out from other resources which are transparently our own reasoned resources in relation to which the 'authority of nature' transmitted through our scientific knowledge is reduced to a token.

The direct and detailed command to human conduct was something that the old Community God did very well.

5.3 The Problem of Authority

The practical difficulties of ascertaining an ethic from the Existence Mystery suggests that its real function is to establish a higher authority. That is one important basis of attraction that it has held. Schleiermacher, still the seminal figure in attempts to reconcile religion to modern circumstances, feared that a rational explanation of God would destroy both God and religion. His mission was to steer a path between skepticism and rationalism to find unassailable territory for religion. This territory he found in pre-rational intuitive feelings. It is this formulation that built the impregnable keep of today's Nature God. It is a tenet of Nature God mysticism that God cannot be rationally stated.

Here is a selection of statements which insist on the inadequacy of words to name God and which refuse all rational description. 'God is that which by definition lies outside the capacity of the human mind.'[55] 'No definition of God is to be equated with God.'[56] 'God can never be enclosed by propositional statements.'[57] 'The whole of Western theology had been characterized by an inappropriate reliance on reason alone.'[58] 'Reason alone can produce only attenuated deism... ultimately incredible.'[59] 'God is experiences that exceed our conceptual grasp.'[60] 'We should have no illusions about human reason which is incapable.'[61] 'God... the ineffable one in whom we live and move and have our being, is beyond all of our concepts.'[62] 'God is infinitely incomprehensible.'[63] 'No idea can represent God... we should not be so satisfied.'[64] 'Language of necessity is indirect... the faintest glimmer of understanding.'[65] 'Being cannot be transcended into propositions like those of the

sciences.'[66] 'Symbols are the only way we can attain insight
into and talk about being.'[67] 'The vital thing is the supreme
mysteriousness of talking about God.'[68] The refusal of reason is
so marked that for Macquarrie it is the chief criticism of
mysticism.[69]

The integrity of the subject of theology has been under
suspicion in the university since the enlightenment. Related
studies, such as comparative religion, ecclesiastical history and
biblical studies are safe but theology itself stands out for marginalization and has felt itself to be a subject under siege. Keller
states the prime worry of rationalism: 'A 1950s style reduction of
life to the interplay of chance and natural law is a theological
conversation stopper.'[70] George Pattison observes that theology is
tolerated in the modern university on the same basis as any other
humanistic discipline... but is defining itself out of existence.[71]

It is not certain that the reliance on the non-rational as a basis
for theology is a conscious attempt to preserve the discipline but
it certainly serves as a protective adjunct. Keith Ward states the
preservation of the subject that is maintained by the obscurity of
the ineffable. 'Religion stands as an autonomous activity... it is
sui generis... untranslatable.'[72] The Nature God seems to offer a
brilliant combination of absence of dogmatic apparatus which
renders the outworks unassailable by rational attack, together
with a keep that is itself not approachable through rational
territory. Theology retrenches in the Nature God. The non-
rational serves admirably as the unassailable territory that
Schleiermacher sought.

The refusal of the rational as a basis for authority has so far
been taken at face value. But the face value hides a contradiction.
By the refusal of the rational Mysticism is obliged to inflict upon
itself the defeat of its own proposed source of authority. This is
because what qualifies as mystical experience *is adjudicated by
rational ethical criteria.* The mystical experience, supposedly the
source of the ethics, is in fact determined by the ethics. The origin

of this contradiction is that in positing a mystical experience that is incommunicable and self-certified the mystics have presented themselves with a problem insoluble within its own terms of reference. It is necessary to discriminate genuine mystical experience from pseudo mystical experience, from charlatan money making mystical gurus and from frontal lobe epilepsy. It is a notable feature of mystics that some wish to deny the validity of the mystical experience of others. Matthew Fox is concerned that his Creation Spirituality should not be mistaken for the debased New Age spirituality.[73] His Nature God should not associate with the pagan Nature God. Fox sets up 21 definitional tests to discriminate 'bogus from authentic mysticism.'[74] Otto, it was noted in the introduction, complained that Schleiermacher was wrong about the nature of his mystical experience. Dean Inge had strong views on the subject of what counted as true mysticism. He was concerned about the mysticism of 'ridiculous fables' which for him constituted the debased supernaturalism which usurps the name of mysticism in Roman Catholic countries.[75] He was concerned to protect true from false symbolism and to protect the legitimate mode of intuition from frivolous amusement.[76] He is against the dabblers in occultism and the beggarly elements of later Neo-Platonism.[77] Inge is even prepared to scorn the negative not saying mysticism of Dionysius and Gregory of Nyssa which are much admired in contemporary theology. For this austere Platonist the *via negativa* is a great accident of Christian mysticism. It is an old jargon,[78] an Asiatic leaven and a refuge of men who have lost faith in civilization but will not give up belief in God.[79] Inge wants to distinguish between mystical experiences and visions, dreams and hallucinations many of which are pathological.[80] It is also necessary to discriminate medical conditions. Karen Armstrong's sometimes terrifying mystical experiences were eventually diagnosed as the result of frontal lobe epilepsy and cured by medication.[81]

Yet if the mystical experience is truly ineffable and not communicable as the mystics insist, who is to say that one person's mystical experience is true but another's is invalid? A surprising possibility arises. Perhaps people like myself who consider themselves temperamentally incapable of mystical experience and who do not feel a need for it to validate our religious feelings are having mystical experiences all the time? Perhaps because these experiences are not accompanied by the conventional props of fifth dimension interpretation, mountain tops, moonlit beaches and J. S. Bach we do not recognize them as such? Perhaps life itself is the mystical experience? Perhaps it is the moment a child comes home from school? Perhaps it is the experience of a family sitting down for dinner? Perhaps it is the loss of self-consciousness in the engagement of a creative task? The testimony of Jeanne Warren is to the point. An avowed nontheist she nevertheless had what she considered a definitive religious experience. On a cold winter's night she walked past a poster appealing for blankets to be sent to China. She had a revelation that 'touched bottom.' People should not be left unprotected against the cold.[82] Yet because the experience seemed everyday and fell outside the standard expectation it was discounted by her friends. Nothing, however, apart from a convention in the definition of the indefinable, is able to gainsay this proposition that life itself is the mystical experience.

In view of these equivocations, a device is required that will subordinate self-certification of mystical experiences so that they can be discriminated by those who wish to discriminate them. The device that has been adopted by the mystics is evidence of the transforming ethical behavior that flows from the experience. Only those experiences that transform behavior are true mystical experiences. That is to say that mystical experience is defined by ethics. It is defined by rational criteria. Hick is explicit that the criteria of authenticity do not lie in the character of the experience. The criterion is transformation.[83] Rufus Jones (1863-

1948), a great original researcher into the mystical tradition, is in agreement. 'These physical phenomena however are as spiritually unimportant and as devoid of religious significance as are the normal bodily resonances... the significant features of the experience are the consciousness of fresh springs of life.'[84] Fox similarly sets the test of genuine mysticism as compassion.[85] Macquarrie commends Eriugena whose importance is 'to provide mysticism with a sound intellectual basis that safeguards against emotionalism and sentimentalism.'[86] The consequence of this, taken to its conclusion, is something awful. The validity of a person's mystical experience can only be decided by a committee of moral policemen. This qualification by the rational seems to confirm Harnack's opinion that it is 'nothing else than rationalism applied to the sphere above reason.'[87]

Although the ineffable is claimed as the keep of the authority of this religious experience the real keep is ethics. This seems to be the natural result of Plato's maneuver. 'The good' is inserted into the cosmos as the starting point. The mystical experience then discovers that good. That is the rationalism of mysticism. Mystical experience holds great religious authority for some people. But the question mark over its validity as the authority of religion does not fulfill quality number four necessary to a God to lead the twenty-first century: the ability to stand up to any interrogation.

5.4. The Problem of Esoteric Elitism

Mystical experience is not given to all. Michael Goulder, the biblical scholar who resigned his priesthood, regretted that the experience had never been granted to him not for lack of effort or desire.[88] He described his own 'spiritual tone-deafness'[89] and stated that the experience was rare and limited to a few people. Most clergy and laity of his acquaintance had never had it.[90] John Hick confirmed that probably only one-third of people have the experience and even then perhaps briefly and only once.[91] John Hick had a single foundational mystical experience of 'existing in the unseen presence of God.' This came to him unexpectedly during his student days while on a bus in the middle of the city of Hull.[92] As Don Cupitt explains 'many people are completely blind to religious feeling and experience.'[93] According to Marcus Borg 'most of us have cataracts in our second lens' and do not perceive the world of spirit.[94] According to McLennan 'most of us don't make it completely to the 6th and highest stage, the domain of the mystics.'[95] The experience is rare and of short duration maybe only a few minutes.[96] McLennan relates his few mystical experiences of nature rapture at a Shinto shrine in Japan,[97] hearing organ music as the essence of spirituality[98] and in a hyperaware sense of another dimension during a moonlit beach experience.'[99] Mystical experience is by these accounts permanently exclusive by temperament. It is only available to a select band. This seems to have been a feature of the religion since the time of Orpheus. In the common understanding of the time 'Many are the wand bearers but few are the Bacchoi.' In other words many are the supplicants but there will be few who achieve the ecstatic union with the God.

Hick nevertheless insisted that those without this experience should defer to those who have. They should defer to 'worldwide experience[100] and reserve judgment in face of the weight of tradition.[101] That is to say that people who consider themselves temperamentally incapable of mystic experience are placed in an outsider position. The religion has hierarchy built into it.

Examples of the superiority complex of the religion were given under the heading The Intellectual Caste Division of Christianity in section 2.6. A few more examples may serve here. Karen Armstrong implies this hierarchy in her use of the words, 'the *greatest* spiritual masters'[102] and the '*best* theologians and teachers'[103] (my emphasis). In Armstrong's scheme the second rank of theologians and teachers are suitable for the Community

God. Aldous Huxley is a vicious example that it is a little unfair to quote, except that he only exaggerates the inclination. Huxley spoke of the 'nice, ordinary, unregenerate people' whose theology carries little conviction and who are doomed to 'perpetual stultification' in their efforts to achieve direct awareness.[104] 'The earnestly respectable... don't in fact have any direct acquaintance with that for which the sacramental activity really stands.'[105] The divine reality can only be apprehended by people who have chosen to fulfill certain conditions.[106] 'It is folly to recommend the worship of the God without form to those only able to understand the personal.'[107] According to Albert Einstein, 'The most beautiful and deepest experience a man can have is the sense of the mysterious. It is the underlying principle of religion as well as all serious endeavor in art and science. He who never had this experience seems to me, if not dead, then at least blind.'[108]

This superiority is an intellectual superiority which is connected with education. Inge, already quoted, confirmed this. 'The mystical is the main ground of belief for educated people.'[109] This is to say then that the mystical is exclusive both by temperament and by education. In the context of our society today it probably means a division between those who do and those who do not have a university education.

There is a further element of exclusion by leisure, age and wealth. It is part of the Buddhist tradition that enlightenment is to be sought by those who have completed their family obligations or through monastic dedication. The ascetic and devotional practices are not easily fitted in by working mothers and fathers. Western practice is different but displays similar attributes. The new spirituality of holistic practices which is the subject of current vogue in the sociology of religion is an occupation for those with both the leisure and the money to pay for the classes.

These elements of exclusion have never been a fault of the Community God. No God to serve the twenty-first century can qualify if not freely accessible to all.

5.5. The Mark of Protestant Trauma

Although the rejection of the Community God by the revisioners is supposedly driven by a response to the incredulity of the modern mind [110] there is an element of rejection that arises from an aspect internal to Protestantism. A wrathful ogre has driven the turn to the Nature God. Don Cupitt described passionately the guilt and suppression of creative energy produced by his religious upbringing:

> The aim was sin-reduction. You sought to make yourself as passively-conforming and perfectly inoffensive as possible... Christians have sought, they can understand humility, self-denial, obscurity, resignation, impotence and reliance on faith, but they scarcely know what to do with creative energy. I can personally testify that the old, terroristic, corrupt cosmic-protection-racket Christianity was still flourishing in the 1950s, because I was raised in it.[111]

Cupitt cites John Calvin as the originator of this 'paralysing anxiety' and 'masochistic avoidance-behaviour.'[112] Alan Watts, the nineteen sixties' inspiration to the beat generation, who renounced his priesthood, was similarly motivated by unhappy feelings about Christianity. Watts rejected all guilt ridden religion.[113] David Boulton is a less regretful product of the Plymouth Brethren, [114] the dour aspect of which sect Edmund Gosse has given a striking portrait.[115] Michael Hampson is in retreat from the 'wrathful king.'[116] Marcus Borg is driven by reaction to the monarchical model which for him originates in Martin Luther's religious experience and 'is the classic Lutheran and more broadly Protestant approach.' [117*] For Thomas Altizer, taking a lead from William Blake and Nietzsche, God himself is the repressive enemy of human creativity.[118] God has degenerated into a contradiction of human life.[119] God is the deepest embodiment of man's self-hatred.[120] Blake perceived God, sometime before Nietzsche, as a denial of the life force and vividly portrayed God as Satan.[121]

The result of this trauma is a need to despatch this Protestant monster. One method of effecting this is illustrated by Borg's artificial polarization of the 'monarchical performance model' of God and the 'spirit relational model.'[122] Borg sets up a straw God by investing the monarchical model with all things repressive and controlling; 'the policeman who never sleeps', judgment, distant power, emphasis on sin, guilt, the punitive debilitating superego, domination of women and, in its domination of Nature, 'the primary cause of the contemporary environmental crisis.'[123] In contrast the spirit model is invested with all things beautiful; God as Mother, Intimate Father, Wisdom, Lover, Journey Companion, dialogical relation, connectedness to creation, and human self-worth.[124]

From the point of view of an upbringing in a sunny Catholicism in which God was presented as an inexhaustibly encouraging friend who invites us to engage our talents in his overwhelmingly beneficial design for humanity,[125] I can only look with dismay on this disaster of Protestantism. It is not the now despised theist God that needs to be put on trial but the mindset that prioritized judgment over forgiveness. Christianity has been, should only ever have been, an exciting energization of the present.

It is saddening to listen to Cupitt's constant refrain that we must live life now instead of negating it in preparation for the life to come. It is saddening also that he feels the need to 'create a Christian ethic, almost as if for the first time.'[126] Cupitt is convinced that Christianity is a world denying religion. We learn from him that there is an anti-life mentality. Ordinary life has been asset-stripped to enrich the supernatural. Traditional theism, affirming our miserable comparison against the perfect

God, requires anchorist rejection of the world.[127] 'Traditional Western spirituality... shrinks from life.'[128] Church Christianity was anti-life.[129] Consequently Cupitt's project is proposed in antithesis as an affirmation of life. Turning to life is now the new religious object.[130] 'The Fountain', 'Fire' and 'Life' are to be deployed as metaphors that reconcile us to life.[131] We should no longer orientate ourselves to eternity but to love life now.

Cupitt has taken leave of this punishing God of Protestantism and it is possible to view the whole of his theological project as an attempt to exorcise this demon. It is the need to demolish the authority of this God that explains Cupitt's adoption of postmodernism which is good for laughing in the face of all authority. Cupitt's method of exorcism is different from Borg's. With the right hook of postmodernism Cupitt brings down the Protestant God. Following with the left he gathers up an ethic from a medley of sources; Nietzsche's affirmation of life,[132] Kant's cure for disabling intellectual anxieties that threaten happiness,[133] Wittgenstein's cognitive behavior therapy,[134] Spinoza's active and passive emotions,[135] Tolstoy,[136] and 'the philosophy of art central to our understanding of ourselves.'[137] Cupitt lays hands on anything but the resources available within the Christian tradition of God except for the occasional nod toward Jesus who is co-opted as an original 'solar', that is proto Buddhist, personality.[138] With this traumatic Protestant God as its background the current adoption of the Nature God has the character of scar tissue: however well healed and serviceable it bears the mark of this self-inflicted wound.

This Protestant trauma is not a fault inherent to the Community God. It is a circumstantial cultural artefact. It was produced by a few unfortunately overwrought personalities, who, jealous of their own authority, employed God in their service. The consequence has been the turn to the Nature God but this is not an inevitable deduction from the premise. The cure for the trauma can be recognition of the fact that the Community

God has been abused by charismatic personalities and ecclesiastical hijack.

It is understandable that Catherine Keller and Elizabeth Johnson should consider that negation is crucial to the challenge to masculine God images.[139] For these two, omnipotence should be challenged by the incomprehensible nature of God. But the image of a loving God the father has served generations of Christians and the cure for the patriarchal hijack is frank recognition that it was a hijack. There is no impediment to framing God as loving mother. Daphne Hampson is one of the few revisioners who has not jumped ship for the Nature God. Hampson's rejection of the Christian apparatus of father and son because it is indelibly masculine does not mean that Hampson is driven to adopt the Nature God. She holds to a revised image of the Community God arising directly from the conditions of human relationships.[140] Keller's scheme of a God who works by lure not domination is by no means a quality exclusive to the Nature God that she adopts.[141]

The title of this book is intended to state the mission to rehabilitate the Community God that has been abandoned by the liberals due to its traumatizing past. It is not certain that the image of mother would serve any better than has the image of father. Our images of mother and father are culturally determined in many objectionable ways and cannot serve without a degree of romancing. There is nothing unequivocally ideal about actual mothers and fathers many of whom can be abusive and exercise the power to ruin their children's lives.

The new God to be proposed will frankly be an 'it' God that cannot be the genderized agent of trauma.

5.6. Conclusion to Part One: A Tale of Two Religions
The survey of the orthodox and the three liberal positions in Christianity is now complete. It seems prodigal to have spent nearly half of a book merely to arrive at a position to begin to

discuss what one really wants to put forward. The hiatus, however, has served a valuable purpose. It is a support to the confidence of any enterprise to know which alternatives are not being pursued and to be secure in the reasons for this.

The conclusion from the foregoing survey is that none of the three liberal positions offer the four qualities needed of a God for the twenty-first century. Quality number one is freedom from historical and cultural limitation. What is on offer in the liberal position is a brand of Greek philosophical mysticism. Cultural limitation is not an objection specific to Christianity. It hangs today as a cloud over all the traditional religions. What is needed, or at least must be attempted whether successful or not, is a religion with potential to unite the new international generation of those alienated from their religious traditions. Quality number two is a concept of God believable by atheists. Primary to this basis of believability is the end of indirect appeal to the good via the ancient metaphysics of a fifth dimension. The liberal alternative within Christianity, for all its departure from the orthodox, is rooted in the same fifth dimensionalism. Quality number three is continuity with the old God. A sound relationship with our ancestry, however questioning that may be, is necessary to the peace of mind of any new culture. It is hard for any child to go out into the world with a broken relationship to its parents. The liberal position is unfortunately imperialist to this ancestry. It swaps traditions and seeks to ditch the God of the Bible. The combination of discard and repetition in the liberal offering shows that it has not done its marketing homework. All good new product developments work by putting a new aspect on what is already established. Platonism and Christianity are two of the greatest examples of such product developments. Quality number four is open appraisal. The mystical element in the liberal position places the authority of God in the same reserved space as the orthodox. A source of authority hypostasized to a non-rational sense of a fifth dimension is not open to free appraisal.

To take an overview on this situation what is occurring is that the liberal positions are governed by an incestuous argument within Christianity. They are not outgoing in the way that they must be if they are to address the new century. The second part of this book leaves all that behind. It seeks to work backward from a sense of what 'secular' religion is today, at work in the culture, outside of the Christian jurisdiction. It then seeks to forge continuity by exposing the connections with what the Christian tradition has been.

The next chapter begins the outward bound process with another preliminary. It asks whether the sociology of religion has any different ideas about what religion might be. To anticipate the result of that chapter the answer is no. It turns out that sociology, naturally saturated with liberal intellectuals from the Christian tradition, speaks liberal theology in disguise.

There is, however, some benefit in surveying the sociological attempts to spot 'secular' religion today that has migrated outside of Christianity. The survey throws up one or two fertile ideas that can be taken forward.

At this halfway stage a further signpost to the mission would be a useful pointer. The overarching aim of the second part of this book is to overturn the conventional understanding of the division between the subject matter of theology and sociology. It is the platform of Social Theology that God derives directly from the conditions of existence of the human person in relation to others. Theology means talk about God. Sociology means talk about human relationships. My conviction is that all talk about God is an indirect way to talk about human relationships. Theology is a department of sociology. It expresses some profoundly important aspects of the ideal possibilities of human relationships in a profound manner. The search is on, at last as promised in the preface, for that real thing that God represents. Having established this point I want to go on to show that theology is not absorbed into sociology but forms a distinctive subject matter within sociology. It effectively retains its independence. It will take until the end of the book to illustrate this but that is the direction in which the remaining chapters are headed.

Part Two. A New Vision of God for the Twenty-First Century

6

The Sociology of Religion is the Puppet of Plato

6.1 Introduction

Readers who are not sociologists of religion and who have to date viewed the discipline only from afar can be excused for imagining that it operates with a more sophisticated understanding of God than they themselves possess. I can give the assurance that the reader's own understanding of what God means to one's self is at least as sophisticated as anything so far produced by the social scientists. Liberal theology, for instance, is in a privileged position by comparison to sociology. It unanimously presents a single idea of God that is valid for a great number of people and thereby attains an impressive coherence. By contrast sociology displays the dissipation of a hundred different ideas of God, which, by their mutual refutation add up to a value on the negative side of zero. The subject is a black hole fed by a continuous stream of books.

There is an aura of distress that surrounds the discipline. Linda Woodhead's survey *Five Concepts of Religion*, for instance, is an attempt to rescue from dispatch the very word religion. It responds to criticisms of the concept of religion without 'abandoning the term.'[1] Even her five concepts, culture, identity, relationship, practice and power do not tell us anything about what religion is. They would be more appropriately described as aspects of the social effects of religion. As such they are not exclusive to discussion of religion. They could equally well be applied to football, nationalism or sailing clubs. Woodhead pinpoints the result of this distress over the subject matter. Sociology feels most comfortable discussing institutions and the doctrinal beliefs that differentiate them. This type of discussion 'has dominated much sociology of religion.'[2] But the safe ground of measurable things, membership statistics, class composition and attendance rates are a severely restricted dimension of religion which ducks the main issue of interest. What is God? By analogy the sociology of religion is like a study that tells us exhaustively about the rituals and history of teatime, but has no idea what is cake.

It can be argued that sociology does not need to know what God is. It takes people's belief in God at face value. Its focus of attention is the social effects of those beliefs as expressed in institutional and culture structures. There are, however, two sides to this. Sociology has never in fact so restricted its focus. Sociologists of religion have been inveterate theologians. Driven by irresistible fascination the subject proliferates theories of God for use in its internal conversation. With regard to the people it studies sociology adopts the different measure of an understanding of what God means to them. Sociology cannot avoid the need to know what God is. For at least the past fifty years it has been fixated on the exercise to tell us whether religion is on the increase or decrease. To analyze this it uses this subject's own understanding of God. In a situation that clearly involves seismic changes, sociology risks a trivial answer in either direction if it restricts itself to the old convention of what God is. It risks beaching like a piece of driftwood left high and dry after the tide has gone out. My conviction is that this risk has materialized because today's society is integrally religious and sociology cannot see how this is so. New conceptual capital, however, is needed to demonstrate the fact. Sociology contains much untapped potential with which to produce this capital. In this chapter I would like to illustrate some dimensions of the case, some dead ends, and most importantly some new starting points for the conceptual capital developed in the chapters which follow.

The sociology of religion is in deep conceptual trouble. The root of this trouble is that sociology, without recognizing the fact, has adopted Christian definition for its understanding of religion. It, therefore, suffers unconscious dictatorship of Christian concepts of what religion is. Much of what passes for the sociology of religion today is liberal theology in disguise speaking sociology. It is in effect a Christian sociology of religion. This means that sociology is caught in a tautological loop. It can tell us about religion today only what Christianity will permit it to say. It tells us what Christianity considers obvious: belief in God has declined, therefore, religion has declined; Christianity is on the wane, therefore, we live in a secular society that no longer has a religious basis. Although sociology proudly states its 'methodological agnosticism,' or in different words its 'professional reluctance to endorse the truth claims that religious organisations make,'[3] it has in fact swallowed whole the fundamental theological truth claim. That truth claim is that religion is constituted by fifth dimensionalism. What counts as religion is defined by this particular metaphysical framework. Sociology needs to recognize that it deludes itself with the claim to 'methodological agnosticism.' Under the terms of the conceptual framework of fifth dimensionalism nothing else is permitted to count as religion. Holistic practices, for instance, which do not incorporate fifth dimensionalism, but which seem to be not exactly 'secular' are placed in the convenient newly developing rag bag category spirituality.[4]

The situation is full of irony. Theology has always been alarmed by the sociological claim to the privilege of an independent higher viewpoint. But theology has all along been spooked by none other than its own ghost. The character of that ghost is by now well known to the reader. It is the Nature God. The reason for sociology adopting the Nature God as a basis for theorizing religion is evident from the chapter two discussion: it purports to be the higher understanding of religion. The Nature God is the representative of natural or rational theology. It, therefore, appears to be the sociological explanation of religion in preference to revealed religion which is the basis of the Community God. Sociology brackets the propositional claims of the apocalyptic Community God. It looks upon them with a skeptical eye. It thinks that it knows better. It thinks that these claims are really trying to express something else. In this it follows exactly the script of Platonism. Sociology repeats the 'higher understanding' of religion that founds the House of the Platonists. Sociology parrots liberal theology. The sociology of religion is the puppet of Plato.

The Nature God, however, is not a sociological understanding of religion. That is to say that it does not understand religion to arise from an aspect of the conditions of human relationships. Its source of religion is metaphysics. I call this definition of religion exclusively by reference to a particular metaphysics the 'metaphysical remnant.' The import of this is that sociology has adopted a perfectly unsociological definition of religion. It cannot look for religion in the social reality of human relationships. It cannot admit religion to arise solely from within the parameters of those human relationships; any practical, non-mystical ethic which is concerned with the ideal potential of human relationships, but which is unconcerned to add to that extra dimension, 'an attempt to grasp reality as a whole'[5] is barred from qualification as religious.

This sociology sets up a parallel universe of ethical behavior. Two identical ethical actions performed by different persons are allocated to two different universes. One action is religious if the person performing it thinks of it in an ethical/metaphysical frame. The same action is not religious if the person performing it thinks of it in an ethical frame. There is little wonder in that case that sociology is blinded to any solution to the most intriguing question that haunted a few theologians and sociologists in the twentieth century. That question was the possibility of, and the problem of recognizing, emerging new forms of religion that have dispensed with the metaphysical umbrella. This metaphysical remnant bars the way to any conceptual progress. The sociology of religion needs to be liberated from it. Because this remnant originates in theology, it is a concept from which liberal theology also needs to be liberated if there is to be any progress in that department. That is the subject of the next chapter.

It will take a few steps to illustrate this 'theology speaking sociology'. First I would like to demonstrate that sociology is fully aware that it has a problem conceptualizing religion but does not know what the nature of that problem is. After that some examples of theology speaking sociology can be presented. But as a preliminary to these examples it is necessary to state a relationship to Emile Durkheim. Durkheim is the key witness to both sociological and unsociological definitions of religion. He is the key source of the confusion between the two. As I will be making extensive use of him to analyze the situation some presentation of Durkheim's understanding of religion is needed.

The relationship to Durkheim is doubly important because I will be making use of some logical developments from his understanding to lead the way out of the tautological loop of sociology speaking Christianity. The liberating escape from that loop is the subject of the last three sections of the chapter.

6.2. Conceptual Anxiety in the Sociology of Religion

Leading practitioners have been complaining about inadequate conceptual capital for the past fifty years. Edward Evans-Pritchard (1902-1973), professor of social anthropology at Oxford, was distinctly doubtful about the psychological and illusion based theories of his predecessors Edward Tylor (1832-1917) and James Frazer (1851-1941). These two brought to religion the smugness of civilized Victorian self-congratulation. They held pre-conceived notions that 'primitive ideas' would give way to the march of science. This effectively adopted the assumption of evolutionary intellectual progression proposed by Auguste Comte (1798-1857). Comte's scheme of cultural evolution from the theological to the metaphysical then to the scientific stages may be considered the foundation of the sociology of religion.

On the other hand this purported foundation of a discipline is too high a claim for what is really a dose of enlightenment hubris. Frazer, the armchair anthropologist, sat in his room in Cambridge collecting from all over the world hearsay reports of native rituals gathered randomly by untrained travelers. He wove these into his best-selling *Golden Bough*, a book of fables that fed and entertained the civilized superiority complex of a generation of late Victorians and Edwardians. Frazer held the stage with a wealth of curious detail but his twentieth-century assumption was no advance on the nineteenth. Frazer was convinced that silly religious ideas would give way to science.

Evans-Pritchard, in contrast, pioneered close field study and did his doctoral research living among the Azande people of the Nile. His later research continued with the Nuer people of the

Southern Sudan. His conclusion was that theorizers rarely got inside the worldview of their subjects. What he discovered was neither simplistic nor primitive but a rather sophisticated worldview. His book, *Theories of Primitive Religion*, reviewed with sustained disappointment the sociological approaches to religion to date. He stated, 'for the most part the theories we have been discussing are, for anthropologists at least, as dead as mutton.'[6] In his summing up of Nuer religion he remarked, 'the insufficiencies of the theories of primitive religions I have mentioned are apparent to all students today, but little has been put in their place.'[7]

Clifford Geertz (1926-2006) was equally doubtful and noted:

Two characteristics of anthropological work on religion accomplished since the Second World War strike me as curious when such work is placed against that carried out just before and just after the first. One is that it has made no theoretical advances of major importance. It is living off the conceptual capital of its ancestors adding very little save a certain empirical enrichment to it. The second is that it draws what concepts it does use from a very narrowly defined intellectual tradition. There is Durkheim, Weber, Freud, or Malinowski, and in any particular work the approach of one or two of these transcendent figures is followed.[8]

Thomas Luckmann remarked even a step backwards from earlier insights:

Scrutinizing the publications in the recent sociology of religion one finds a rapidly increasing number of studies in parish sociology, the demography of the churches, statistics in participation in church activities... a flourishing enterprise, characterized not only by large quantities of studies but also by a proliferation of specialized journals, conferences, symposia and institutes. Unfortunately, one is disappointed in trying to find theoretical significance... The external flourishing of the discipline was not accompanied by theoretical progress. On the contrary, compared to Weber's and Durkheim's view of religion as the key to the understanding of society the state of theory in the recent sociology of religion is, in the main, regressive. The classical positions were largely abandoned and the sociology of religion became increasingly narrow and trivial.[9]

Thirty years later Malcolm Hamilton, writing his textbook, finds no better comfort:

It has to be acknowledged, however, that in this field, as in so many in what is still a relatively novel subject like sociology, we remain at a rudimentary state of knowledge and understanding, especially with regard to religion which has tended to be treated as rather a peripheral area failing to attract many to specialise in it.[10]

Grace Davie trumps all these reservations for skepticism. Davie is an advocate of the theory that religion is not so much disappearing as mutating but she doubts the chances of making sense of her analysis:

In many ways the conceptual framework within which to describe the nature of belief in contemporary Britain still seems to be lacking... How should the sociologist proceed? For almost at once the argument discloses the complexities of contemporary society, so much so that the standard frameworks simply do not apply. The data demand a new start, an altogether more constructive frame of reference. Is it possible then to rework, if not a fully-fledged theoretical framework for the sociology of religion then at least some ground rules?[11]

Nearly fifteen years later, following the embarrassment of the discipline over its darling theory of the inevitability of secularization, Davie still has to repeat the call. She cites Peter Berger's about turn to a view of the world 'as furiously religious as ever' and exhorts, 'There is an equally urgent need to devise tools and concepts appropriate to the task.'[12]

A recent collective work comprising five individual voices is 'born of frustration at conventional analyses' and strikes out for 'A new set of navigational tools.'[13]

Don Cupitt sums up the root of the problem:

> The whole architecture of 'traditional' religious beliefs is *philosophically* ruined... modern knowledge... has exposed all the old metaphysical assumptions... and we simply *cannot* think like that any more. But that means we no longer have the vocabulary in which we can state clearly what God is, or was once, supposed to be.[14] All forms of religious belief in modern society appear to be in an intellectual mess.[15]

Davie does not name as strongly as I would the dire effect of this conceptual poverty which is visible, for example, in the work of Steve Bruce the champion of the secularization thesis that religion has been displaced from society. Although the assumption is never made explicit, Bruce understands the supernatural to be fantasy unrelated to any social root. That is to say that a completely unsociological definition of religion is in play as the following passage indicates:

> There is obviously the logical possibility of some religious propositions arising from contemplation of the human situation... Anything can be imagined by someone... strange claims about space travel, the likelihood of life on other planets, and the unlikelihood of people having built the pyramids, marinating these with a large dose of wishful

thinking, and coming up with Bo and Peep's flying saucer cult.[16]

In another section, explaining why football does not count as a substitute for religion, 'Few believe that the world was created by the directors of Scumchester City FC or kept in its orbit by the club groundsman.'[17]

So, to state the real import of Davie's concern about the dearth of conceptual capital, if this methodology can be accepted by the discipline without a cry of protest then the sociology of religion is bankrupt. It has regressed, as Luckmann saw, pre-Durkheim, to its infancy in Tylor and Frazer. It has given up a social basis for religion and reverted to febrile theories of psychology and illusion. There has been no progress in the two hundred years since Comte 'founded' the subject and framed secularization as a self-fulfilling prophecy.

6.3. A Perspective on Durkheim

To generate some fresh capital I will be making concerted use of Durkheim. Durkheim is the key to both the sociological and the unsociological understanding of religion. A clear perception of these two different understandings is the precondition of escape from the present tautological loop. As there is something of a settled assessment of his sociology of religion that I want to depart from, my perspective on Durkheim needs to be stated as a preliminary.

6.3.1 The Distinction between Durkheim's Method and his Conclusion

Durkheim is honored by enshrinement in the canon as one of the three founding fathers of the sociology of religion.[18] He never fails to achieve a mention in any course or textbook. At the same time Durkheim has been dishonored by neglect in development of his method. His is a barren entombment of ossification rather than a shrine of fertile productivity. The source of this paradoxical honor with dishonor is to be found in the failure to distinguish between Durkheim's method and the particular conclusion that he drew from his method.

Durkheim's method may be named the 'reflexive principle.' Religion is an expression of a social reality that it attempts to articulate. All talk of God, therefore, is really talk about something arising from the conditions of human existence. The implication of this is that all religion, however fantastic might seem some of its aspects, cannot be dismissed as fiction disconnected from human relations. The job of the social scientist is to discover the reality that religion tries to express. This reflexive principle was a valuable advance in the sociology of religion. It was the first sociological theory of religion. It departed from the preceding theories tinged with the self-congratulatory element of the enlightenment. The reflexive principle is grounded in Durkheim's early experience of religion within the intensely community focused Jewish religion. He was the offspring of three generations of Rabbis. Unlike his companion workers Weber, who was self-confessed 'religiously unmusical', and the similarly inclined Marx and Freud, Durkheim understood that the powerful emotions experienced in religion derived from the community experience. Such emotions could never arise from or be sustained exclusively by the form of expression. They had to be based in something real. The conclusion of this is necessarily reflexive: the emotional substrate is connected to but independent of the form of its conceptual articulation.

The reflexive principle contains a challenge to identify the social substrate. Durkheim implied it and drew his particular conclusion. This was that religion is a communal representation. It represents the supportive forces of community. The focus on the representation of the group is summed up in his statement 'the species that designates the clan collectively is called its *totem*... it is an emblem, a virtual coat of arms.'[19] In this conclusion, however, the great problem with Durkheim arises. The problem is that his particular conclusion can be attributed nothing like the same universal status as his method. The conclusion is, for instance, readily repudiated by Christianity. It is difficult to frame Christianity as a celebration of collective representations because it is dissatisfied with them. It is critical of the social order and looks to another. Nor is it easy to frame it as a tribal religion. Its very origin was the transgression of a self-sufficient cultural boundary and a mission of appeal to all mankind. Durkheim's conclusion is altogether too close to the appropriation of nationalism as religion. As his translator understands the matter, the totem is a sacred flag. It is this sense of deification of the nation to which Evans-Pritchard objected. 'It was Durkheim and not the savage who made society into a god.'[20] Although there is a type of Christianity that is a national religion and in America a national identity,[21] its true spirit cuts across nationalisms.

In Durkheim's inadmissible leap from Aboriginal totem worship to the apocalyptic religion of Christianity can be seen the tendency of two primary faults of the sociological enterprise. Firstly it displays the over ambition of sociology to explain all religions in one theory. Durkheim's one 'well-defined experiment' which was his intention for *The Elementary Forms of the Religious Life,* was a great advance from 'summary generalizations... without relying on the analysis of any one religion in particular,'[22] but his 'universally valid... essence of religion,' is laughable. Secondly Durkheim's leap demonstrates a lack of close investigation of particular religions. For instance, collective representation is the opposite of the individualism of the Platonic escape and ascent of the soul. For another example, the Apocalypse represents not the collective representation of unity but a division of the community. Sociology must be prepared to engage theology closely if it is to gather material by which to gauge the theories that it wishes to put forward.

In view of these objections Durkheim's conclusion has limited value. The unfortunate aspect of his enshrinement is that the conclusion and the method are taken as one. Durkheim is taken to be collective representations end of story. In the adopted shorthand Durkheim said that God is society. Collective representations are endlessly repeated as incantations around Durkheim's shrine. The reflexive principle which produced this result is by comparison neglected. It is discounted by association with the weakness of the specific conclusion. The true honor accorded to any thinker is the continued fertile application of their theories. In Durkheim's case only limited attempts at development have sprung from the reflexive principle. This is the meaning of the paradox of honor with dishonor.

The de facto closure on the sociological definition embodied in the reflexive principle is premature. Any amount of adjustment, development and more appropriate limitation of scope can be made to collective representations. Durkheim's seminal statement of method is repeated here in full as a reminder that the endeavor to identify the social reality to which Christianity gives expression is as yet wholly open-ended as to its outcome:

> It is a fundamental postulate of sociology that a human institution cannot be based on error or falsehood, otherwise it could not have lasted. If it did not have its roots in the very nature of things, it would have encountered opposition to things which it could not overcome. Consequently, we approach the study of religions secure in the knowledge that they are the products of a reality of which they are the expression.[23]

In developing new capital from Durkheim's reflexive principle I will be holding fast to collective representations as a conclusion that is essentially headed in the right direction but in need of much refinement. Those supportive forces of community that were quoted in section 2.2 are fruitful as an embryonic understanding of the Community God. There are, however, more specific things to be said about those supportive forces if they are to be properly characterized and to be thrown into relief as the basis of today's 'secular' religion. The task of redirection and expansion of Durkheim's conclusion is taken as pivotal and the rest of this book is concerned with trying to say those more specific things.

This is not necessarily a simple task. One of the reasons that the Community God has served with such tenacity is that the social reality is complex but the Community God somehow encapsulates it simply with vivid dramatic power. The nationalist sense must be rejected but validation of nationalism is only one interpretation of 'communal effervescence.' The rejection does not negate the open-ended sense in which, as Steven Lukes puts it *représentations collectives... are in some sense "about" society.'*[24] The more fruitful open-ended sense in which this should be taken up is that of William Robertson Smith (1846-1894), the Scottish Old Testament scholar and specialist in the comparative religion of the Semitic tribes. Smith was Durkheim's inspiration and is the original spark of the reflexive social reality of religion.[25*] As Smith put the matter, 'Religion... is a relation of all the members of a community to the power that has the good of the community at heart.'[26]

With regard to scope there is a lesson to be learned from Durkheim's over ambition. The enterprise of this book has a restricted arena. Although it uses the word religion as if in the sense of religions in general this is to relieve the monotony of the vocabulary and the five syllable mouthful Christianity. It does not refer to religions in general. Christianity is the sole subject under discussion. Even the name Christianity encompasses too much. Within that religion two Gods have been identified. This work takes up only the Community God and seeks to discover the social reality represented by that particular God.[27*]

From another perspective, in holding fast to the reflexive principle I am not adopting Durkheim. It is just that his proposition resonates with my feeling that human relations are inalienably religious regardless of the cultural forms used to render this. The statement 'I am not religious' that has become a standard badge today I discount as meaning only the rejection of broken forms and morally repugnant associations. Durkheim's reflexive principle is a means to analyze and display this. I owe him nevertheless a debt of gratitude because it was in a flash one day going to church that what I had read of his and taken up as a merely theoretical proposition became vital. This flash was that *God is Us*. This led to an obsessive quest to work out *what Us is*. The whole of this book may be taken as the attempt to state that Us.

6.3.2. The Maverick Sacred and Profane

Simultaneous with his reflexive definition Durkheim introduced a second definition which contradicted it. This has ever since wrought havoc with sociology's adoption of Durkheim. This contradiction defined religion by the distinction between the sacred and the profane:

All known religious beliefs... present a common quality: they presuppose a classification of things... into two classes, two opposite kinds... the *profane* and *sacred*. The division of the world into two comprehensive domains, one sacred the other profane, is the hallmark of religious belief.'[28] 'The sacred and the profane have always and everywhere been conceived by the human mind as separate genera, as two worlds that have nothing in common.'[29] 'Because man's notion of the sacred is always and everywhere separated from his notion of the profane by a logical gulf between the two, the mind radically rejects any mingling or even contact between the things that correspond to these realms.[30]

This portrait of two absolutely heterogeneous worlds is not original to Durkheim. It is pure Plato. It is an objective metaphysical definition of religion not a social definition. It is an unsociological definition which contradicts Durkheim's sociological reflexive principle. It is by this means that Plato has been inserted into the subsequent sociology of religion. Plato now runs wild in today's sociology. What happened is that the authority of Durkheim allowed subsequent sociologists of religion to indulge their natural Platonist inclinations.

Looking at the matter from another perspective Durkheim, probably inadvertently, escaped one Christian definition of religion only to jump into the arms of another. He roundly rejected any definition of religion as belief in supernatural beings. [31] He identified that the totem as a representation of the clan did not enjoy supernatural powers. In this he broke away from the programmatic monopoly of Christianity. The illustrative example that he chose was the sacred, but non-supernatural, Four Noble Truths of Buddhism.[32] In this he inclined toward the attenuated supernatural fifth dimensionalism of Platonism.

There are two ironies in the sociological stampede to Platonism that Durkheim set off. The first is that it was one of the penetrating criticisms by other anthropologists that the aboriginal culture held no distinction between the sacred and the profane.[33] There are good grounds to suspect the integrity of Durkheim's definition. Although it was presented as the result of investigation of the Arunta it was transparently a conclusion matured long before. It represented a Christian interjection into the anthropological data. Christianity is deeply imbued with the distinction between the sacred and the profane, between the religious and the secular, on account of its political status. Once accepted as a partner in government it had to define its relationship with political authority. The Platonist division is an ideal basis for the religious secular distinction. W.E Stanner, Professor of Social Anthropology at the Australian National University, himself a fieldworker, voiced the objections of many. Stanner recounted his personal difficulty with the 'established force' of sacred profane division. 'I blamed myself for incompetence when the facts would not fit it.'[34] For Stanner 'the Aboriginal universe of "all that exists" is not in fact, and should therefore not be divided in theory, into two classes.'[35] 'The dichotomy itself is unusable except at the cost of undue interference with the facts of observation.'[36] 'As far as *The Elementary Forms* is concerned, the utility of one bequest – the strained, static categories – has long been used up.'[37]

The second irony is that Durkheim understood perfectly well that this distinction was not an objective metaphysical reality as Platonism proposes, but that it was reflexive of moral dimensions of a social reality. He thus subordinated the unsociological characteristic that he identified to his sociological definition. The Platonist objective unsociological interpretation is incompatible with Durkheim's consistently stated understanding, which runs through his earlier works *The Division of Labour* and *Suicide*, that religious conceptions are a project of the social milieu. The hyper spiritual reality posited in the sacred is a product of the complex moral reality. Should that basic fact of Durkheim's orientation need reinforcing here is another categorical statement which Stanner quotes from one of Durkheim's articles:

> I know of only one being that possesses a richer and more complex reality than our own and that is collective being. I am mistaken; there is another being which could play some part, and that is Divinity. Between God and society lies the choice. I shall not examine here the reasons that may be advanced in favour of either solution, both of which are coherent. I can only add that myself I am quite indifferent to this choice, since I see in Divinity only society transfigured

and symbolically expressed.[38]

Crowning this refusal of Platonism Durkheim rejected the Nature God as a possible explanation of religion (See note 90 chapter 2). He well understood that this was a non-sociological basis for God that would undermine his whole theory were he to admit its validity.

The corralling of Durkheim by the sociological branch of the House of Platonism is an arrest which rides roughshod over the thought of a theorist who does not belong there.

6.4. Liberal Theology Speaking Sociology

Durkheim's adoption of the sacred profane distinction became the vehicle through which sociology bypassed his reflexive socio-logical theory while claiming that it had absorbed his thought. The claim to allegiance disguises repudiation. The old illusionist theories which he had done so much to counter were indeed abandoned but they were now replaced by a *theological* definition of religion. The catalyst for this was the influential Mircea Eliade. The reagent turned out to be Rudolf Otto, that member of the powerful Platonist twentieth-century Triumvirate cited in the introduction. Eliade's book *The Sacred and the Profane* [39*] took up Durkheim and illustrates the new theological treatise that now appeared under the guise of sociology. Eliade builds on Rudolf Otto's *The Feeling of the Holy*, that is, the sacred is the non-rational experience of a different order of reality, 'a reality that does not belong to this world.'[40] Eliade has taken up an individualist, psychic, philosophical, Platonist explanation of religion. Linda Woodhead has no hesitation in disclaiming the value to sociology of Otto's experiential basis for God. 'It falls outside the scope of this discussion, given that it is resolutely non-sociological.'[41] Yet Otto courses through twentieth-century sociology of religion and his Platonism determines the whole perception of so great a figure as Robert Bellah.

Eliade had a huge influence on a generation of sociologists of religion. Peter Berger is an example of an influential sociologist whose theological beliefs were such that he was overpowered by the need to come out as a theologian. His book *The Social Reality of Religion*, took up Rudolph Otto as its basis for a humanist understanding of religion that bracketed out truth claims.[42] This was followed by *A Rumour of Angels*, in which Otto was again taken up this time as the representative of 'signals of transcendence' which confirmed Berger's belief in the supernatural.[43] The vaunted 'humanistic approach in sociology'[44] turns out to be another case of the Platonist higher understanding.

An example of theology speaking sociology for the past fifty years is the voice of Robert Bellah. This can be illustrated by the detective puzzling of my own effort to discover the conceptual framework in his magnum opus *Religion in Human Evolution*.[45] Without knowing the fact at the beginning I was hampered by the assumption that sociology has something different to say from theology. I was also hampered by the fact of unfamiliarity with the cultural, psychological and anthropological authorities that Bellah's erudition brings into play. Their concepts seemed as though they must be different from the theological cohort with which I was more familiar. It was only gradually that I realized that Bellah has enlisted all these sources to the service of theology. So, after a first reading I was at a loss. It was only on going through a second time that I was able to piece together the clues. The detective process went as follows.

Bellah presents a distinctive evolutionary scheme which begins way back in pre-history before humans developed speech and ends in the 'axial age' well before Christianity begins. In making use of the axial age Bellah relies on and greatly develops Karl Jaspers' proposal of this great intercontinental turning point around 700 BCE when prophetic social criticism began to question the legitimacy of monarchical rule. In Bellah's scheme this is the third, and for the purposes of today still current, evolutionary stage of religion. He names it the theoretic stage. The first evolutionary stage, pre-language was mimetic. Mimed gestures and dance gave form to a religious reality. The second stage was the mythic when mythical narratives and ritual gave form to religion in the deification and legitimation of rulers.

What struck me in Bellah's preface was his opposition to the suggestion that we are in a second axial age with a new cultural form emerging. 'Maybe I am blind, but I don't see it. What I think we have is a crisis of coherence.'[46] Bearing in mind that I feel we do have a new emerging form that is fully coherent, I was intrigued to discover what he meant by incoherence and looked forward to the promised revisit of the matter in his conclusion. But nothing transpired in the conclusion so I had to fall back on the idea that by incoherence he is referring to the customary idea of secularization and breakdown of the traditional religious framework.

For me, on the contrary, Bellah's own evolutionary analysis provided the basis to identify the new coherence. Development through mimetic to mythic to theoretic begged for completion in a fourth stage. The prophetic axial turn sited religion as the critique, the alternative imagining, a different legitimation to the reality of government by King. What we have today is what might be called an axial zig-zag. Present society, following the logic of that alternative imagining, has invested government/municipality with responsibility for implementing the alternative imagining. Today's government in so far as it is mandated to work toward the alternative reality is, therefore, religious.

Why should our collective enterprise exercised through the state not qualify as religious? Southampton hospital offers a week's palliative radiotherapy to a terminal cancer patient from the Isle of Wight and pays transport and hotel accommodation for an accompanying spouse. Oxfordshire council runs a campaign to prevent old people from being financially abused by carers responsible for their allowances. A young person is rescued from a life disabled by psoriatic arthritis by free drugs that cost ten thousand pounds a year. All of us, as a community, have chipped in, and willingly do so to provide this. These are religious actions directed to enablement and fulfillment of the person. These actions are qualitative extensions of the same principle of mutual care practised by the friendship groups that comprised Paul's churches. They are an extension in direct line from what the Lambeth churches were also doing before their religious function was embodied in municipalization.[47] They are the sequence to Bellah's theoretic stage of religion.

The question that posed itself was why is Bellah blind to this new religious basis of society which to me is so obvious? Why are the same actions which once qualified as religious now disqualified as religious?

It struck me that the answer was that I had misinterpreted Bellah's evolutionary scheme. I had understood the theoretic stage to be a qualitatively different religion from the two predecessors. In this qualitative change religion becomes a vision of a new social order which the mythic and mimetic stages are not. Where I went wrong is that for Bellah there is no such qualitative difference. All three stages are variations of the same thing. The *metaphysical framework* is determinative. The three variations of expression are subordinate to it. For Bellah it is the Nature God which founds all three. At the basic level there is no evolution in religion.

I had had clues along the line that this was the case but had not been able to connect them on first reading. Bellah mentions in the acknowledgments his great debt to Tillich and to Wilfred Cantwell Smith a follower of Tillich. Bellah's, contra Dawkins, insistence that there is meaning in evolution is an echo of the world soul of the Nature God. Bellah's abandonment of 'propositional truth claims' [48] as an approach to religion is the trigger sign in theology that the Community God is being trumped by the Nature God.

However, Bellah does not make his use of Tillich's mystical ultimate reality explicit in the book. He employs an alternative panoply to say the same thing. He makes use of Geertz, general order of existence; Alfred Shutz, multiple realities which contrast with everyday life; Abraham Maslow's being cognition and deficiency cognition; biologists' use of online and offline and his own vocabulary on Durkheim's sacred as non-ordinary life. Bellah summarizes the whole group as defining 'a clear contrast between the world of daily life and the world of religion.'[49] This is the sacred and the profane appearing in a different form of words.

I pinpointed at last confirmation of Bellah's overall conceptual scheme in his adoption of the theologian George Lindbeck's 'experiential-expressive approach.' This experiential-expressive is Schleiermacher's. The Triumvirate is speaking through Lindbeck. Bellah is using the words 'a clear contrast between the world of daily life and the world of religion' to name reality versus mystical/ecstatic experience. We are in the world of Platonist fifth dimensionalism. Bellah reinvests this into his preferred vocabulary of Maslow's Being cognition. He then uses this to synthesize all religious history.

Bellah never exactly states the assumption that religion is defined by fifth dimension metaphysics in this book but in an earlier essay there is an explicit statement that religion for him is exclusively defined by the presence of a metaphysical framework and that nothing outside this could count as religious. 'The danger here as elsewhere is that post-critical religion can become purely utilitarian. This can happen if one fails to see that any religious symbol or practice, however relative or partial, is an effort to attain the truth about ultimate reality. If such symbols and practices become mere techniques of "self-realization", then once again we see utilitarian individualism reborn from its ashes.'[50]

I was at last able to place the conceptual framework of *Religion in Human Evolution*. It is Schleiermacher speaking sociology. The Nature God appears in the clothing of sociology. Bellah is a liberal theologian. His methodology that synthesizes the whole of religious history repeats that of Cantwell Smith's *Toward a World Theology* and John Hick's *Interpretation of Religion*. In a piece of Platonist imperialism that was objected to in section 5.1 ultimate reality is proposed to synthesize all religions. To sum up, Bellah's conceptual framework is a case of Christianity in the guise of Platonist fifth dimensionalism dictating the analytic framework of the sociology of religion. Although sociology vaunts its methodological agnosticism it has swallowed whole the fundamental theology.

To fix the nature of Bellah's maneuver, although he states in his acknowledgment a great debt to Durkheim and a special closeness to him as a sociologist he absolutely negates the sociological Durkheim. He mistakes the sacred/profane metaphysics, which accords with his personal Platonism, as the essential Durkheim. The profound reorientation effected by this is that religion is no longer viewed as reflexive of a social reality but governed objectively by a supposed metaphysical truth that beams ethics out of the cosmos into human relationships. The ethics does not arise direct from those relationships. This coupling of metaphysics with ethics surfaces in Bellah's visionary plea for a new religious basis of society. A new 'revolutionary culture would have a firm commitment to the quest for ultimate reality.' This metaphysical adoption should bring fundamental ethical change, social and structural. Bellah here speaks the same insertion of ethics into the cosmos as Plato's edifying philosophy. It is the same language as the Platonist liberal theology of the past fifty years. Bellah, in the disguise of a sociologist, turns out to be a liberal theological campaigner.

The result of Plato's dictation to both theology and sociology is devastating. So long as Plato is in charge *both subjects are conceptually immunized against recognizing the new forms of religion that arise directly out of human relationships.* For example my approaching proposal that the 'authority of no authority' is the new form of an old religion Bellah could never recognize as religion because under his conceptual scheme it is 'purely utilitarian.' No natural religion based on a one dimension metaphysic can be admitted to the fold of religions. Plato's dictatorship is totalitarian. Even the viewpoint of an atheist sociologist cannot escape its control. What counts as atheist is defined by Plato. Atheism is refusal of fifth dimension dualism.

The extent to which the sociology of religion is hamstrung, blindfolded and devastated by the metaphysical remnant is displayed in a recent work which undertook to examine the question of why women are more religious than men.[51] The work applies a rigid framework of fifth dimensionalism as the qualification of what is religious. In the attempt to answer the question a number of artful explanations are passed under the spotlight with no result; male irreligion may express a form of risk taking whereas women might be more conformist and less involved in delinquent activity; women may be more concerned about bodily appearance and therefore the afterlife; perhaps women are credulous and men more rational. The blindfold on the undertaking is that the work categorically refuses any definition of religion by the social reality of what is done. It uses the unsociological definition of religion, not the sociological definition of religion. It specifically disclaims that religion could be about caring for others and that this may attract women to it:

> We feel somewhat uneasy with this argument and suspect that our discomfort is explained by a professional reluctance to endorse the truth claims that religious organisations make... the social scientist adopts the posture of methodological agnosticism... To accept that love and compassion (rather than, for example, authoritarianism and fear) are prevailing

features of Christianity... and to use that as part of an explanation of some aspect of human behaviour feels a little like
buying a religion's PR spiel. It seems more like religious
propaganda than social science explanation.[52] That one
spends time caring for others will not make one religious
(either in reality or by definition).[53]

At a stroke the work amputates, with its unconscious methodological dogmatism, the one fundamental aspect of religion that
might make women especially inclined to it. In this Bruce relinquishes, by one-sided metaphysical interpretation, the value of
his own two sided definition of religion. 'Beliefs, actions and
institutions which assume the existence of supernatural
entities... *possessed of moral purpose*'[54] (my emphasis). A sociological methodology understands that the metaphysical entity is
reflexive of the moral purpose. There is only one place that moral
purpose can arise. It is from within the parameters of human
relationships. The metaphysical entities *have no existence outside
their reflected moral purpose*. Religion is precisely about the moral
purpose of caring for others.

The result of denial of this is a wholly unsociological
treatment of women's response to religion. It defines religious
participation by its peripheral programmatic paraphernalia,
ornaments of ritual observance, by church attendance and
lighting candles. The pictorial representation on the front cover
encapsulates the methodological bias. Instead of religion being
represented by a deed, such as, for instance, a picture of Ruth
standing by her widowed mother, or perhaps the Quaker peace
activist Ellen Moxley throwing Trident submarine computers
into the Clyde, it is represented by a picture of rosary beads and
a silver crucifix. The work is an exercise in the trinketology of
religion.

That is the result of Plato pulling the strings. It illustrates the
danger of adopting 'largely common-sensical conceptualization

of religion'[55] when what has become common sense through monopoly usage was originally defined by an ancient Greek philosopher. It illustrates that most subtle of methodological traps flagged in the introduction: an assumption so embedded in thought that it is not recognized as an assumption.

6.5. The Distinction between Religious Purpose and the Operating Program

What is the way out of this conceptual impasse of the metaphysical remnant? In view of its totalitarianism no compromise will work. It is necessary to break free completely from the jurisdiction. I want to propose two exit routes. In this section the distinction between purpose and operating program. In the next section the proposal is to abandon the sacred/profane distinction.

The distinction which permits the departure from metaphysical thraldom is the distinction between purpose and operating program. The subject was flagged in the introduction section 1.4 with the analogy of the purpose of accountancy and the operating programs. To illustrate this with an additional analogy the discipline of political theory is useful. Imagine a political theory that was defined exclusively by democracy. This would define politics as the exercise of democratic elections. With this definition the fading out of elections in favor of monarchical rule would determine that the changed society was not a political society. Likewise dictatorships and oligarchies would be excluded as political forms.

Political theory, however, does not make this elementary mistake of confusing purpose and operating program. Politics is defined as the exercise of power. The exercise of power is the purpose of politics. Political ideologies such as socialism, communism, fascism, monarchy, oligarchy, autocracy and democracy are all alike defined as operating programs which articulate the purpose of exercising power. That purpose is integral to all societies. It is an inevitable requirement of society. It is inconceivable that any society should not incorporate the controlled exercise of power. The conceptual possibility that the requirement of exercising power could disappear from society in the same way that religion is envisaged as doing so, can never arise. If a situation arose in which the exercise of power seemed to have disappeared then political scientists would, from their position of methodological security, refuse the very possibility and not rest until they had relocated the operation of power. That is what Marx did when he saw through the status of a divinely ordained order of society.

In framing its conceptual apparatus, political theory has been better assisted than the sociology of religion by the sequence of events. Democracy has gained its ascendancy only over the last few centuries so it has been easy to frame it conceptually as a new operating program for an old purpose. But imagine a situation where for the past seventeen hundred years democracy had been the exclusive universal format for politics. The thought framework would tend to compound purpose and program as one. If there was then a change in one country to monarchy it might well be theorized that politics had disappeared.

That seventeen hundred year monopoly by Christianity incorporating both purpose and program is the situation faced by the sociology of religion. The conceptual difficulty of distinguishing the two is compounded by the fact that the politics of Christianity, literally its power, depends on the refusal of the distinction between purpose and program. The program must be presented as the purpose otherwise this would admit the validity of other programs. The implied separation of the two aspects is the reason for the outrage to Christianity caused by Durkheim's reflexive principle. But this outrage is not just a cynical ploy. It is in the nature of religious programs that to work they must be exclusive. The analogy with accountancy provides a perspective on this. While Quickbooks or Sage will individually produce accounts the attempt to run both together would defeat their purpose.

Some terms of definition would be useful before going any further. I intend to discard the term 'religious belief' in favor of 'religious operating program.' This is in order to avoid ambiguity. The discussion of purpose is a subject distinct from the discussion of the program but theories about the nature of the purpose could as well be described as religious beliefs as beliefs about the programming. The intention of rejecting the term 'religious beliefs' is to highlight also the fact that most of what sociology discusses as religion is in fact constituted by discussion of programming. When someone is asked what is their religious belief both the question and the reply are always framed in terms of programming. In contradiction to this I want to define religion by its purpose. Religion is the purpose that religious operating programs articulate. Religion is what is done not what is professed. This new vocabulary, discarding all reference to belief, frames the matter of religion in two questions: What is religion? What is your religious operating program?

The distinction in practice between purpose and operating program is amply illustrated in the intuitive religious intelligence of the working class people of Southwark and of the First World War Army. This population was studied by Sarah Williams.[56] The religious programming of these people has been variously described as folk religion, popular religion, inarticulate Christianity and 'diffusive Christianity.'[57] There is a palpable air of condescension in this by the comparison with the standard of the real thing defined by the institution. Williams' project in this work was to refuse institutional definition and validate this folk programming.

Williams conducted a series of oral interviews with elderly inhabitants of the Borough and supplemented this with autobiographies and recollections of the time, annual reports from the parish churches, Charles Booth's comprehensive survey of laboring people, [58] and a YMCA sponsored report on religion in the First World War Army. Williams does not explicitly bring out the distinction between purpose and program. She notes in passing the distinction of morality versus religiosity.[59] In this the distinction between purpose and program is implicit but otherwise it passes under her radar and I have interpolated it into the work in what follows.

Williams identifies the popular idea of the 'true believer' and the 'genuine Christian' which the people of this culture held in contrast to people who made formal profession of Christianity. This innocent idea is a revolutionary breach of the institutional boundaries. The distinction between purpose and program contained in this is brilliantly exhibited in the emphatic answer of Lucy McLelland to the question of whether her mother went to church on Sunday. 'No, no, no, she never got to church, cos she was a Christian woman you know, in her way.'[60]

Williams identifies the fact that there was a strong sense of the purpose of religion independent of the program. One of the reasons for the absence of formal profession of the Christian program was a sense that it was difficult to live up to the purpose and a desire to avoid the hypocrisy that this would involve. The profession of the program required a distinct behavior of not drinking, swearing, smoking or gambling.[61] The annual report of All Saints Surrey noted this combination of modesty and avoidance of hypocrisy:

> To be a churchgoer will not square with certain habits and practices which as yet they do not feel equal to giving up. They could not live up to what the definite practice of religion means. They have their ideal; they respect even admire it but doubt their ability to at all realise it. So any outward profession of religion is not for them.[62]

As Revd W. Thompson stated 'Church going implies a much

higher standard of consent among the lower class. They will not be hypocrites.'[63] There was a great popular awareness of the hypocrisy. One chaplain in the Army and Religion Inquiry noted that, 'constant reference is made to the inconsistency of the lives of professing Christians with the faith they say they believe.' One such example, recorded by Walter Southgate in his autobiography, was the hated employer Mr Dale. Dale refused to grant a day's pay to a man for stopping away from work to look after his sick father; 'the indignation which spread throughout the courts around Lant Street centred in part on the fact that the employer was churchwarden and Sunday school teacher at Hornsey and that such action was a corruption of good Christian practice.'[64]

Williams sums up the matter:

> Mere abstention from vice, the wearing of a frock-coat, possession of a bible, discipline in work and attendance at church services on the part of those who formally allied themselves with the church were seen as worthless in so far as they were substitutes for 'genuine belief' expressed through acts of humanitarian kindness.[65]

This genuine belief which names the purpose of religion was, in the culture, nowhere defined by programming but by action. 'Above all neighbourliness and brotherliness'[66] and 'the practicalities of communal relationship.'[67] As Stanley Barrow stressed, 'treating people kindly is my religion, to make a big show of it, I don't believe in all that show and that kind of thing in front of people.'[68] An example of this was the woman who lent her clothes to her lodger so that she could go out to work, even though she was thereby confined to stay in bed until her friend returned.[69] As Miriam Moore described her mum 'to me she was a Christian, cause you didn't have to go to church to be a Christian.' As an example of this, 'It didn't matter if the neighbour was out of work ur... Mum would make, if she had it, she'd make extra food and give it over to them and say, "I wasn't thinking, I made too much" and give it to the kids... as I said to you a little while ago my mother to me and I am sure to God, she was a true Christian.'[70]

A particular aspect of the separation of purpose and operating program was the separation of the teachings of Jesus from the teachings of the church. Jesus was effectively seen as the exemplar of religion in action. 'They distinguish him from the churches, which they criticise without stint.' Williams sums up the evidence: 'Jesus was seen as the model for a pattern of morality which was determined above all by the practicalities of communal relationship. The attainment of heaven or the 'hereafter' and the definition of sin were subject to what was regarded as the quintessence of religion, notably "doing good to one's fellow man".'

The intellectual result of this intuitive sense of the distinction between purpose and program is the categorical refusal by this culture of the exclusive claim by the Christian program to police access to heaven. The fulfillment of a set of ethical criteria was considered sufficient title to the status of true believer. It was title to a claim on heaven independently of the program. As counterpart to this the culture displayed a decisive undenominationalism whose charity was well in advance of the inter-Christian programmatic disputes. For instance, in the prevalent practice of sending children to Sunday schools there was indifference to the denomination.[71] As the vicar of St Jude's Church knew, 'the vast majority of them are ignorant of the differences of standpoint and would not care two pence about them if they did know.'[72] F.T. Bullen discovered in his contact with working-class sailors that religious instinct was combined with perfect discount even of the basic Christian programming:

As to the plan of salvation they knew next to nothing. Dim and hazy ideas of the vicarious sacrifice of Christ for man

were somewhat timidly hazarded but of the great fundamental truth of Christianity summed up in the words 'God
was in Christ reconciling the world to himself', they had not
the shadow of an idea.[73]

One symptom of the undenominationalism was the universal
attendance at church for baptism, churching after childbirth,
marriage and funerals side by side with the refusal of confirmation. Confirmation was considered to enter too much into
programmatic distinctions.[74]

Williams' subjects were ordinary people. A contrasting voyage
by a philosopher that arrives at the same distinction between
purpose and operating program can be found in the autobiographical sketch *The Search for Reality in Religion*[75] by John
Macmurray (1891-1976). Like Williams, Macmurray does not
name the distinction in my terminology. He uses the contrast
reality and form. The word reality in the title represents the same
attempt to distinguish something essential about purpose that
underlies variable programming.

Macmurray recounted the inception of his feeling for the
distinction. He was brought up in the traditional Calvinism of the
Scottish Church which he described as 'perhaps the most intellectual of the Christian traditions with the central stress falling
upon soundness of doctrine.'[76] At school, in the heat of the
revivalist fervor of Torrie and Alexander's campaign, he formed
a bible group and took part in evangelistic activities. Looking
back, at the age of seventy-four, this is what he has to say:

I think that all this religious activity was second-hand and
somewhat priggish. It was the result of the teaching of others,
absorbed and elaborated by a quick and busy mind rather
than the expression of a personal religious experience. In spite
of its seriousness and conviction it was religiously unreal.
From this I learned, in the end, how easy it is for religious

convictions, in spite of the sincerity and passion with which they are entertained and expressed, to be imitative and imaginary, the products of a romantic sentimentality or the symbols of pressures on oneself that are not themselves religious. At the same time I found myself unable to question the reality of the religious experience of my parents, even when the forms of its expression, particularly in doctrine and belief, became more and more incredible to me. It was a long time before I was able to draw the full conclusion from this... It is this. The dichotomy which governs religious experience is one between real and unreal... it is possible for us to have a real religious experience coupled with religious beliefs and practices which are fallacious and undesirable... with no reality to sustain them... I might say this. I was convinced that religion had its own reality, so firmly that I have never afterwards been able to question it for a moment. This came from the quality of the religious life of my parents; and is the most valuable thing that they gave to me.[77]

Macmurray goes on to describe the key stages in his religious progress at university. The next stage was a mistrust of theological dogma. In preparation for conducting a class for young men at Glasgow Mission Hall he undertook to study Paul's Epistle to the Romans on the basis that this was the taproot of Christian theology. The result of this study was startling. 'I discovered, after checking and re-checking my work that these great doctrines of the Christian faith just were not there... this did not result in a rejection of theology far less of religion itself. But it made theology questionable and destroyed its dogmatic claims.'[78] 'I should never again fall into the gross mistake of *identifying* religion with theology or with any system of beliefs. ...Religion... is not primarily a matter of beliefs. The beliefs, so far as they are real, are derivative.'[79]

A critical turning point came when, on sick leave from the

Somme battlefield, Macmurray was invited to preach in uniform at a church in North London. He had found in the trenches that the soldiers had sympathy for their opposite numbers. 'We were sharing the same spurious obscene life, no doubt with the same feelings. They had been dumped into war as we had, so we had fellow feelings for our enemies, which showed itself in odd little ways.'[80] Macmurray was shocked on this visit to civilian life at the spirit of 'ignorant and superstitious hatred of the Germans, and equally ignorant and unreal glorification of us in the trenches.'[81] He was shocked to the extent that he was glad to get back to the trenches which offered companionship of the real pacifists. For his sermon he took the opportunity,

> to advise the church and Christians in it, to guard against this war-mentality, and to keep themselves, so far as possible, aloof from the quarrel, so that they would be in a position – and of a temper – to undertake their proper task as Christians when the war was over of reconciliation. The congregation took it badly; I could feel a cold hostility menacing me; and no one spoke to me after the service was over. It was after this service that I decided, on Christian grounds, that I should never become a member of any Christian church... I spoke and wrote thereafter in defence of religion and of Christianity, but I thought of the churches as the various national religions of Europe.[82]

The later philosophical works of Macmurray display a lifelong concern to theorize religion as a necessary ideal of human existence independent of programming. In this he is a rare non fifth-dimensionalist theologian. His thought on the subject is considered in chapter eight but to summarize for the time being he demonstrates, just as the people of Southwark, the knowledge that religion is defined by actions not by beliefs. Religion is defined by what is done not by what is professed. Religion is doing not believing. The distinctive difference between Macmurray and the people of Southwark is the comparative difficulty for an intellectual formed in a strong programming environment to spot the purpose and shed the programming. In the Southwark population the intuitive religious intelligence made the distinction easy because it had built the understanding into the culture.

The question left hanging so far is what is the purpose of religion? The people of Southwark and Macmurray have already defined this handsomely. It is communal relationship, neigh-bourliness, brotherliness, humanitarian kindness, transgressing through personal relationship the murderous political relations that are imposed on people, generosity to people in need, doing good to one's fellow man and, using our time and material resources, caring for other people. To summarize this, the purpose of religion is the exercise of the ideal potential of human relationships. I take this 'ideal potential of human relationships' to be the substantive definition of religion. This is the escape route from the Platonist dictatorship.

There is a result to be had for sociological understanding from separating purpose and program. To define religion by the program can yield only a trivial result. By this definition Hitler was a religious person. His Catholic upbringing brought him into the Christian quarrel with Judaism that has been pervasive in the Christian program. But Hitler's extermination of the Jews cannot be a religious act, it was a programmatic act. It resulted from the incompatibility politics of the religious software programs. Likewise, to fly a plane into a skyscraper under the influence of hate cannot be a religious act. It is a programmatic act. It results from the natural clash of software programs compounded by cultural hijack.

It is the tragedy of religious operating programs that while their purpose is to articulate the ideal potential of human existence, to articulate the unity of humanity through equality, freedom, sisterhood and brotherhood they have, in the mere articulation of the function, been the source of the most vicious division.

Why ever would it come about that religion should be determined by what a person believes and not by what a person does? The change of perspective that I am asking for will prove the sticking point of my whole mission because it demands a comprehensive change of focus. Sight operated with a daylight filter will see quite different things to sight operated with an infrared filter. The switch proposed will be for the institutions of religion as bad as upsetting the tables in the temple. John Macmurray tackled the origin of the artificial priority of belief over action in a major philosophical review in his Gifford Lectures.[83] Macmurray finds that origin in the whole direction of the Western philosophical tradition. Who does he identify behind this? It is Plato.

6.6. Three New Conceptual Assumptions for a Future Sociology of Religion

The capital that is being developed in these two proposals to distinguish between purpose and program and to dissolve the sacred profane distinction is in fact an application of Durkheim's reflexive principle. This principle can be made use of to develop from a theoretical perspective what Macmurray and the Southwark culture develop from experience. Three logical corollaries from the reflexive principle can be stated.

Firstly, if religion embodies a social reality to which it gives expression it follows that *religion is not exclusively defined by its metaphysical expression*. The adoption of this axiom means that if investigation is able to locate the social reality that is expressed in the metaphysic it will turn out to be *equally religious* regardless of the fact that it is stated in what are presently known as secular terms.

It is the duty of good sociology not to take the obvious at face value. Metaphysics is not a fact which founds the ethical impetus of religion. Metaphysics is the means by which religion *establishes the authority* of the ethics. The intuitive religious intelligence of today's culture perfectly understands that and rejects it. No God that will serve the twenty-first century can pull off the metaphysical trick as a basis for its authority.

Secondly although the supernatural expression of religion may be in decline because of changed scientific knowledge about the universe there is no reason to suppose that this factor affects the social reality which religion expresses. The religious basis of society can, therefore, be understood as a constant, the supernatural expression of which is a dependent variable. The proposition then arises that *human relations are integrally religious.* Religion on this basis is not something that can be optionally added to or subtracted from human relationships; this accords with the evidence of the universal presence of religion. There is no analysis, other than the self-congratulation of enlightenment hubris, which has shown why our modern society should be the exception to the fact that all previous societies have been religious.

Thirdly the logic of the reflexive principle is that the religious social reality remains there to be discovered *even though it is not currently presented in formal articulation.* That seems to be the case with the situation faced today in a society where the old religious programming has broken down and nothing apparent has been put in its place. The assumption to be taken forward is that a new religious program must be in operation. Our problem is only that our preconceptions about what it should look like have prevented us from spotting it.

These three propositions are the platform of Social Theology. They found my belief that secularization is an illusion brought about by our present conceptual framework. They found the attempt to discover the new programming of religion that operates the purpose of religion in today's society.

7

By What Authority? Is this the End of Theology?

7.1 By what Authority? Is this the End of Theology?
7.2 The End of Artefactual Theology
7.3 Where is God Hidden in Today's 'Secular' Culture?

7.1 By What Authority? Is this the End of Theology?
Under the laws which govern the present conceptual regime any proposed theology which does not take up fifth dimensionalism as its basis of authority stands to be ejected from theological citizenship. It stands to be scorned by theologians and sociologists alike. In the words of Robert Bellah 'purely utilitarian,' of Don Cupitt 'empty radical humanism.' Linda Woodhead cites such a move as tending to a 'post-theological theology... a form of radically democratised and egalitarian theology, which by virtue of that fact perhaps ceases to be theology altogether.'[1] The natural reaction in conventional terms is that any such theology *cannot be theology*. It would be shallow or lacking in depth. The ethical principles are not of themselves credited with sufficient authority. The whole bias of the regime is encapsulated in the disparagement of materialism by idealism. The proposed 'no fifth dimension' Social Theology is intended to register protest against and get out from under the Platonist totalitarianism which in defining itself presumes to define its opposite.

Our new methodology, using the reflexive principle, states that the subject matter of Social Theology is the same as the subject matter of revealed or natural theology. It is just as religious. It is just as profound. It is just as vitally important to human relationships. The reflexive principle predicts that there cannot be an end to theology. Like energy it is permanent. It is never used up but merely transfers from one medium into another. That is the transfer that the reflexive principle effects. The concept of God is transferred back into the substrate of human relationships from which it arises. It is a validation of the concept of God. Social Theology and revealed theology are talking about the same thing.

These accusations, utilitarian, shallowness, lack of depth, are all directed to one thing. It is the question of authority. They do not attack the ethical substance nor could they. The ethical result of Humanism, Platonism and the House of the Christians is convergent. The different programs represent *different sources of authority*. That is the essential point that distinguishes them. For Platonists the ideal world beams ethical commands to us. For the Christians God directly commands us. The accusation then is that Social Theology has no authoritative basis of authority. It is merely human authority, which, in the nature of humans is endlessly contentious. It is only the fifth dimension that provides a certificate of guarantee. Where is the authority of a Social Theology to come from? This question of authority is the critical aspect of the fourth quality necessary for a God to serve the twenty-first century so the question is worth considering. The authority of God must be open to any quantity of free interrogation. It must not be hypostasized to a privileged zone where it cannot be questioned and by the same token cannot be believed.

Linda Woodhead displays the symptom of the current conceptual chains. Her conceptual frame can be taken as an example. For her it is the external source of authority that defines what religion is. 'A... defining mark of theology is the theologian's appeal to special authority.'[2] Any theology that accepts that each individual has supreme authority for deciding

for themself where truth is has ceased to be theology. 'If it takes
this option, theology must abandon its claims to speak for God.'[3]
In this framework any way of life that does not posit a source of
authority external to human relations is relegated to a quasi-
religious zone. In Woodhead's conceptual framework it qualifies
in the half religious category spirituality.

Woodhead uses the distinction heteronomy and autonomy to
set up the difference between religion and spirituality. Religion is
defined as 'life-as'. This is life lived in accordance with external
expectations. 'The key value of the mode of life-as is conformity
to external authority.'[4] It subordinates life to 'the "higher
authority" of transcendent meaning.' In contrast spirituality is
defined by 'subjective-life'. This consists of attention to one's own
inner sentiments as a source of authority in order to 'become
truly who I am.'[5] 'The key value for the mode of subjective-life is
authentic connection with the inner depths of one's unique life-
in-relation.'[6] This scheme has absorbed Charles Taylor's 'subjec-
tivization thesis' which attempts to explain the decline of religion
by the discarding of traditional authorities. It is an exercise
within the boundaries of the current secularization debate and its
task is to ascertain whether spirituality is taking over from
religion.

Woodhead's scheme is attractive but the question of authority
is more complicated. It is doubtful that it can bear the burden of
the analytic expectations loaded upon it. To pose the subject of
authority from a different angle, for instance, leads to the
conclusion of this book that spirituality, especially in its determinative aspect of feminine focus on relationship to other persons,
'life-in-relation', is as fully a religious endeavor as any. Indeed it
is the essence of religion.

Religious authority is equivocal to heteronomy. Heteronomy
is the imposition of rules by an external authority. The aspect of
imposition states that we have to obey that rule whether we like
it or not. The further implication of imposition is that there will

be a penalty for disobedience. These are the facts of life about driving or stealing. The peculiar feature of religious authority is that it is a self-imposed authority. The individual voluntarily accepts it because it has value to themself. That is to say that it contains within it principles of value that are judged to be self-sufficient by the standards which the person uses to judge them. Religious authority is not then the heteronomous imposition that it appears at face value.

In addition there is no sanction for disobedience to religious authority. Religious authority has barely a shred of consistency available to be obeyed. In accepting any one religious authority we have made the decision to disobey hundreds of others. We are all free to join any church as we wish. In doing so we have a free choice of a spectrum that ranges from the most doctrinal Calvinism, through the wonderful broad church that is Anglicanism, in which everyone may, only half surreptitiously, believe anything that they wish, through to the Society of Friends where even the suggestion that there may be any authority other than our own light is denied.

There is a fundamental dynamic operating in religion that, as Thomas Hobbes pointed out, subverts anything but the authority of the individual believer. Hobbes insisted, to the horror of some of his countrymen that in the interests of national cohesion, there had to be a single national religion. This was to be chosen by the monarch. It was to be the law and in obedience to it every person was to be obliged to conform. In response to objections Hobbes pointed out that his proposal implied no change from the current position. Everyone believed exactly what they wished and would continue to believe what they wished. Imposed conformity in religion could only ever be an outward observance of forms. No power could enforce or even discover what each person believed in the sanctuary of their own mind.

Hobbes further outraged his time with a comment on the source of religious authority. He pointed out the fact that the authority of the bible is hearsay. Its authority rests on what one person tells another is authoritative. In this, and especially in the critical matter of the interpretation of what that authority implies, we each of us exercise our personal discretionary judgment. That is to say that the authority of the bible is subject to a source of authority that is not the bible. In this Hobbes merely followed the logic of the Protestant reformation. The priesthood of all believers, the interpretation of the individual themself, is the real authority of *sola scriptura*. Ecclesiastical jealousy over authority runs deep. For pointing out these transparent facts Hobbes had to defend himself against accusations of atheism.[7]

It might be objected to this that 'life-as' is determined by the power of cultural imposition. It was the case, for instance, fifty years ago, that there was a general cultural expectation that women and men should live out their lives in conformity to predefined roles of housewife and breadwinner. There were indeed sanctions to this. Women who went out to work were subjected to accusations that they were neglecting their children. Against this it can be said that the current cultural climate in which we are all encouraged to find ourselves and to forge our own path in life is just as much a cultural imposition as the previous culture. There is no change in the authoritative role of culture. It is just that in this age the culture enjoins something different. In obeying either culture without inputting our personal appraisal we act as cultural automatons.

The factors involved in this question of heteronomy versus autonomy are too complex for the distinction to serve as an analytic tool. Heteronomy must be understood as the proposed but not the actual authority of religion. The individual may propose that their religious viewpoint should be binding on others. Their church may make the same proposition. But the individual themself chooses to make that authority authoritative. It is not imposed upon them. In her recent research Woodhead confirms 'it's striking how few people take any guidance from religious leadership even so-called "followers." Amongst Anglicans the figure is 2%, Catholics 4% and Jews 6%... as previous pages have shown, a majority of Christians today disagree with their churches' teaching on a range of issues.'[8] It would be preferable to understand the difference between heteronomy and autonomy not as a cultural change but as a more timeless matter of temperament. There are some people who are terrified at the prospect of relying on their own worldview. They are happy in the adopted security of one that is ready made. What is authoritative to them and what is institutionally supported provides a necessary comfort. On the other hand there are people who relish uncertainty. David Jenkins, former Bishop of Durham, may serve as an example. Jenkins' temperament is that of an irrepressible lover of uncertainty. For Jenkins the voyage of open-ended adventure, the permanent wrestling with questions about God, is the very essence of what God is. Jenkins' temperament is so much inclined in this direction that he was quite incapable of understanding the mentality of the 'certainty-wallahs.'[9]

The mention of certainty-wallahs is a reminder of the great distortion that needs to be factored into the equation. This is the institutional abuse of religious authority. Ever since Christianity joined the Roman Empire and became Empire Christianity we have become so used to religion as institution, worldly power and authority that we have become blind to the fact that religion is the sole possession of the person. An institution cannot have religion. It cannot experience religion. The name religious institution is a contradiction in terms. The purpose of the institution is to assist the personal experience. But it is in this very purpose that it is open to abuse. It is part of the tragic conflict between the purpose of religion and its operating programs that personal experience has to find expression in communal and cultural language. The poison of institutional power in religion can only be countered by a strong theological antidote. It is an antidote that sociology is not qualified to minister; hence the continued necessity of theology.

A brief recapitulation of the powerful authority heritage from which we need to recover may be helpful. It will assist a perspective on the ingrained nature of the problem and the immensity of the task to turn around our concept of what religion is. Constantine well understood that the exercise of power demands certainty. It needs the authority of 'Truth'. Under his direction the Church immediately began the process of hammering out its Regime of Truth with the instruments of banishment, sinecure and book burning. What had been a multitude of small Christian communities each practicing their religious instincts with their own understandings was welded into the One Truth. Likewise the state gave licence to eliminate the plethora of antecedent Greek and Roman religions. The very names 'cult' 'superstition' and 'pagan' are defined by Not Truth. The symbolic culmination of this consolidation of political power, which has nothing to do with religion except that it uses religion to gain power, is the burning of all Not Truth books by order of Theodosius in 448AD. It is the irony of the Reformation that those who broke the Roman monopoly in the name of free conscience repeated the monopoly. The vaunted priesthood of all believers which states the democratic dissipation of authority in religion soon fell by the wayside. Luther, Calvin and Knox were overwrought characters with the same Roman conviction that their truth was The Truth. This was a tragedy which was also a necessity. Power can only be overthrown by power and the reformers rose to the occasion. We are a long way yet from recovering from this trauma of Protestant and Roman authority. Fifteen hundred years of cudgeling is a lengthy beating that it is taking more than the past fifty years to recover from. Some indications of the current therapeutic recovery process were given in The Mark of Protestant Trauma, section 5.5. Woodhead's conviction that theology is by definition a presentation of Truth is a symptom of the continuing damage of that trauma.

This paradoxical feature of religion that the source of authority is proposed to reside outside the individual but is in fact sourced from within the individual has relevance to the question of the basis of authority in Social Theology. Social Theology frankly recognizes that the source of authority resides in the ethical principles of human relationships which the individual will find compelling or not according to their own light. It recognizes that religion comes from the bottom up not from the top down. Experience of God arises from something in the experience of every person in relation to other persons. The reflexive principle states that the idea of God represents an attempt both to embody those principles and to crystallize them as commanding authority because they are authoritative in the sense of their power to win consent.

Social Theology confirms a respect for the traditional concept of God that cannot be underestimated. The concept embodies in a powerfully condensed and attractive way some vital feature of the conditions of human relationships that would otherwise be difficult to formulate, would perhaps be dull to communicate, and could never exercise the vivid motivational presentation that God achieves. The task of Social Theology is to seek that something in the social reality which is experienced as authoritative for human relationships and which is embodied in God. The grounds have already been stated for partial agreement and partial disagreement with Durkheim's conclusion that it is the supportive forces of community that deliver the inspiration and emotional sustenance experienced as God. The task undertaken in the following chapters is to refine this.

The task is to elicit some ethical principles of community that stand the possibility of universal appeal and are also to be found embodied in the concept of God. The first of these principles has already been established. It is that religion consists of what is done not what is believed. The second principle to be demonstrated is the Authority of No Authority in human relationships. The proposed universal appeal of this proposition is that any basis of social organization that is founded on the principle that some people can legitimately be subordinated to other people has to be admitted, by those who propose it, to be a recipe for permanent war over who should be the subordinators. The Authority of No Authority is the first and foremost religious principle available to govern human relations.

7.2 The End of Artefactual Theology

There is one aspect of theology, however, that will find no place in Social Theology. This is artefactual theology. Although the reflexive principle understands God to be reflection of a social reality it has to be reckoned that a great part of theology does not represent any social reality. This is because it is a secondary structure. It is derivative from the original reflection and does not directly relate to the social reality. Once God is thought of as a person a whole raft of questions about that person and their intentions come in to play. This gives rise to the traditional list of the attributes of God: aseity, immanence, immutability, impeccability, incomprehensibility, infinity, omnipotence, omniscience, omnipresence and a dozen others. Artefactual theology comprises the largest part of that great aspiration of theologians the magnum opus of a systematic theology. These works seem to have dried up in any case. Tillich's was the last of any note and it is significant that his was a product on the cusp of a modernism that could not quite break free from the edifice of the tradition. His system of correlation made the mistake of taking artefacts as having real referents outside of their internal relations. He elaborately attempted to correlate the artefacts with what he saw as existential reality. Systematic theologies are today being replaced by the new style poetries of the Existence Mystery.

The Apocalypse is a feature that illustrates the erection of secondary structure. It arises only on the precondition of one God omnipotence. The question, does God exist? and the vast literature wasted upon it, is likewise an artefact. The real question is what does God represent? A vivid example of an argument arising not from the social reality but from secondary structure is the supralapsarian dispute. This arose within Calvinism as a controversy between the two professors of theology at the University of Leiden, Francis Gomarus (1563-1641) and Jacob Arminius (1569-1609). Calvin himself wisely ducked out of elaborating the horrible character of God which results from his doctrine of pre-destination. He did not expound on the arbitrary nature of the divinity who randomly with complete indifference to merit, chose to save some and condemn others and knew all this before humans were even created. Calvin covered the divine purpose in inscrutable mystery. His successor at Geneva, Theodore Beza (1519-1605), was not so diplomatic. Beza delved into the question at which point in time God decided to elect some and not others. Was this before the fall of Adam or after the fall? The latter seeming a slight softening of God's callousness because at least at this stage man had done something wrong to be taken into account. Gomarus, following Beza, pressed the hard option. He insisted on the pre-fall decision as it was the only way to protect the absolute sovereignty of God over his creation. This sovereignty, according to Gomarus, would be compromised if there were any glimmer of human influence on God's decision. The result of this interpretation for God's moral character is atrocious. Someone had to challenge this portrait of God as tyrant and executioner. It was Arminius who took up the controversy against Gomarus.

The argument gripped the Dutch nation for a period of about ten years and divided the society into two. Many of the soft option mollifiers were jailed pending the verdict of the Synod of Dort. The outcome was that the mollifiers were condemned as heretics. Some three hundred people were dismissed from their churches, exiled or imprisoned. The Synod confirmed the official doctrine of the Dutch Reformed Church, known as the TULIP doctrine; 'T' the total depravity of humans; 'U' unconditional election of some humans regardless of merit at God's discretion; 'L' limited atonement, Jesus did not die for everyone only the predestined; 'I' irresistible grace; 'P' perseverance of the elect regardless of their own effort.

It is a giddy, whirligig argument that throws off conundrums at every turn. To put in my own pennyworth as must have done every thinking person in Holland, why would Jesus, who is also God and party to this, waste his breath telling people to love their enemies when actions make no difference to your salvation? We might today be tempted to dismiss the subject as the aberration of theological fever but it cannot be brushed aside. On its own terms of reference it demands an answer. In its own terms of reference there must be an answer and the question must remain today a live, though perhaps suppressed, issue in Calvinist churches as it was in the seventeenth century.

Supralapsarianism is secondary structural theology generated by the premise of God as an intelligent agent. It demonstrates the incredible power of confectionary ideas to plunge a whole society into conflict. We cannot congratulate ourselves that we are free of such potential today. For the purposes of discussing God in Social Theology this artefactual theology will come to an end. None of the attributes of a supernatural intelligence that generate artefactual theology can be predicated to an impersonal social reality, except by metaphor or poetic license. On this basis whole shelves worth of books need to be consigned to the museum of religious operating programs. Theology needs to be liberated from the artefactual edifice that has comprised historically so much of its staple talk. Although the transference of God to its location in a social reality does not end talk of God it will be talk to which much of the previous architecture of discussion will no longer apply.

With regard to ascertaining those subjects worth interrogating for the social reality and those which are not there is bound to be some difficulty in separating primary personification from secondary structure. This is not a matter to go into here but an indication of the parameters may be useful. The means to discriminate secondary structure is not always apparent. Christ, for instance, as an articulation of the Apocalypse, seems to be a clear case of secondary structure for which God is the primary reference. I have, therefore, in what follows, not placed any reliance on Christ as expressing a social reality but have focused on God. On the other hand Christ/Jesus also represents God directly. In the Southwark evidence Jesus was adopted to represent the purpose of religion and so has plenty to say about the social reality. In the same vein I take Paul's sensation of being 'in Christ' to express the harmony of being in tune with the function of peace and love for one's fellow humans. Christ could on this count just as well be taken to represent the social reality instead of a secondary structure.

A similar difficulty attends the evaluation of the Kingdom of God. This visionary element may be taken to be a secondary structure which serves to articulate another secondary structure, the Apocalypse, and therefore not worth investigation. On the other hand the Kingdom of God seems vividly related to something social by way of contrast. The indication that this vision is based in a social reality is that it also arises independently of the apocalyptic secondary framework. The example that confirms this is the Humanist and Anarchist visions of society which turn out to be identical to the Kingdom. I have, therefore, treated the Kingdom of God as a primary statement of a social reality.

At the same time that the presence of secondary structure complicates the issue it also simplifies it. The assumption predicts that there is no point in trying to locate a different social reality for each programmatic division within the church. These divisions are secondary structural disputes and not fundamental variations in the social reality. Protestantism, for instance, arises as an argument over who possesses God's authority. This is a case of secondary structure. No attempt is made here to sort out these gray areas. The subject is raised only to indicate that the investigative task is not necessarily straightforward, will be subject to decoys and remains a great venture for theology.

7.3. Where is God Hidden in Today's 'Secular' Culture?

The remaining chapters of this book seek to identify the social reality of God as it has come to be hidden in today's culture. The method is that of cross-referencing secular ideas with the same ideas embedded in religious practice and in the concept of God. The sequence of the investigation is first to look at the minority group of theologians who have already moved in the direction of God discovered to arise directly from the dynamic of the human person. These see God neither as the metaphysical reality of the Community God nor the Existence Mystery reality of the Nature God. They see God directly in the conditions of human relationships. This marginalized social theology is the subject of chapter eight. Chapter nine takes up the sociological counterpart of this. The chapter examines the work of a minority group of sociologists who have sought to identify religion in today's culture. Building on both the theological and the sociological enterprises I identify respect for autonomous fulfillment of the person as the 'Super Ethic' of our culture. Under current conceptual terms this is considered a secular ethic and is refused status as religious. I seek to prove that it is a religious ethic because it can be demonstrated to be embodied in religious practice and in the concept of God. Chapter ten begins this demonstration of correspondence by joining both this Super Ethic of our culture with its expression in the Christian practice of 'the Religion of the Authority of No Authority.' Chapter eleven returns to another correspondence by analyzing the peculiar case of the religion of political anarchism.

All the authorities on political anarchism are agreed that this represents a religious ideal and not a political ideology. The final result of this cross-referencing between the religious and the secular examples of the same function is a formulation of the social reality represented by God which is present unarticulated in contemporary culture. This is named 'The Religion of the Authority of No Authority.'

The final task undertaken in chapter twelve is to define the distinction between the religious and the political domains of human existence. The purpose of this is to replace the conceptual apparatus that defines religion by reference to the sacred and the profane or what is the same thing, the religious and the secular. The proposition is that the fundamental division in human life is between the religious and the political domains. This new conceptual frame is constructed by way of a biblical study. The timing of the arrival of the Kingdom of God, as it is presented to us in the New Testament, is a puzzle that has baffled scholarship. Like all puzzles it is a gift and a challenge to analysis. In this case it proves a handsome return for the time invested in considering it.

8

God Derived from the Dynamic of
the Person

8.1. A New Concept: Psychosymbiosis: The Creative Power of
All Persons in Relation to Each Other
8.2. Theologians of the Person as the Origin of God
8.3. Psychosymbiosis Correlated with God
8.4. Psychosymbiosis Correlated with the Sacraments of the
Church

8.1. A New Concept: Psychosymbiosis: The Creative Power of All Persons in Relation to Each Other

It is a testimony to the occasional enslavement of academic disciplines to patently wrong ideas that it took a generation of rebels in psychology and some horrible experiments on monkeys to establish what every mother already knows.[1*] Independent socially confident children are produced by the encouragement of secure affection and stimulating playful adventure. In contrast to this, expert advice on the upbringing of American children through the 1920-50s promoted separation from the mother's love. The psychology of the time was dominated by an alliance between Freudian behaviorism and hygiene. The stimulus/response focus of behaviorism claimed the child's attachment to the mother as a function of the gratification of milk. It discounted affection and personality as sources of attachment. It was the era of the belief that genes determine intelligence. It was the era in which advocacy of eugenics to raise the quality of the population took hold.

Professional recommendations for bringing up children centered around aseptic conditions and a belief that touching and holding infants was sentimental foolishness. John Watson, president of the American Psychological Association ran a crusade against the dangers of affection. 'When you are tempted to pet your child remember that mother love is a dangerous instrument.' For Watson too much mother love produced invalidism. Cuddling parents were destined to end up with dependent failures. Correct child care required disciplined parents. 'Don't pick them up when they cry, don't hold them for pleasure.' Children should be pushed into independence from the day of birth. After a while 'you'll be utterly ashamed of the mawkish, sentimental way you've been handling your child.' The same message from Luther Holt ran through fifteen editions of his book *The Care and Feeding of Children*. As advisor to the government, Holt's message found its way into three million copies of official Infant Care publications. 'Never kiss a baby, especially on the mouth. Do you want to spread germs and look immoral? The rule that parents should not play with the baby may seem hard, but it is without doubt a safe one.'

This madness was epitomized in arch behaviorist Frederick Skinner's baby box which he constructed for his daughter and hoped would be widely adopted. The air in the box was filtered and humidified, the sound-proofing prevented disturbance from telephones, doorbells and parental voices. The safety glass comprising one side permitted communication by waving and smiling.

Other psychological researchers were, however, well aware of the damaging effects of isolation on personality and health. There was overwhelming evidence that orphanages were baby killers. The New York physician Henry Chapin's survey of ten foundling homes reported that in all but one of the homes every child admitted was dead by the age of two.[2] William Goldfarb working for the foster homes of the Jewish Family Services noted that food and cleanliness were impotent against the damaging impoverishment of relationships. Loretta Bender of the child psychiatric unit at Bellevue hospital identified that a high proportion of her clients came from orphanages and were completely confused about human relationships. Her colleague Harry Bakwin named the damage of the lonely child syndrome as 'hospitalism.' David Levy theorized a deficiency disease of the emotional life comparable to the effects of nutritional deficiency. Rene Spitz produced a film graphically to demonstrate his knowledge that absence of any mother and isolation from human touch and affection in hospitals destroyed children's ability to fight infection. *Grief: A Peril in Infancy* recorded the arrival of children at his foundling home and the process of their withdrawal and decline under the influence of emotional deprivation. James Robertson produced a film with the same message, *A Two Year Old Goes to Hospital.*

The psychological profession felt insulted and betrayed by these films which it considered sentimental. Nothing could shift the Freudian insistence that our autonomous fantasy lives are a more important influence on personality than real events. It took the pioneers John Bowlby and Harry Harlow to change the direction of thinking. Bowlby was a pioneer of the value of taking account of real trauma as an explanatory factor in behavior. He was struck by the privation and loss which had been suffered by many of his patients.[3] His World Health Organization report in 1951 established emotional trauma as a cause of neurosis and gave birth to Attachment Theory. Harlow ruthlessly forged a reputation for himself on the basis of this challenge to the establishment. He engaged in a series of experiments on monkeys at the University of Wisconsin and famously demonstrated the importance of physical contact using substitute wire and cloth mothers.

To cut a long story short, in the late sixties Harlow decided to go to the extreme in demonstrating the devastating effects of emotional deprivation. The aim was to breed an emotionally deprived monkey from an emotionally deprived monkey. Baby monkeys were taken from their mothers and raised in solitary confinement. It was discovered that after a month or two of this treatment some monkeys would refuse food and starve themselves to death. In order to keep the monkeys alive for the one year needed to reach sexual maturity they were force fed. This produced a semi-paralyzed animal that did not explore, barely moved and appeared alive only by the beating of its heart. These creatures could not engage in normal sexual intercourse so a forced mating rig was designed to produce pregnancy. The fate met by most of the babies was that they were simply ignored. One mother held her infant's face to the floor and chewed off its feet and fingers. Another crushed the baby's head in its mouth.[4] Harlow had proved the point that it is happy creative social interaction that perpetuates happy creative social interaction.

In the normal course of childhood this process of social inter-action producing socially intelligent adults able to continue the cycle happens so naturally that our absolute dependence on it is hardly noticed. In this respect it is an unremarked force compa-rable to our reliance on gravity. Without gravity tea would not pour into a cup and we would fly off the face of the earth. We tend to be unappreciative then of the paradox of human existence that although we are physically independent beings we are psychologically dependent. The psychological dependence is absolute. Even our physical functioning which might seem biologically given is dependent on our emotional, interactive capital that starts building from the moment of birth.

There is a patriarchal factor also which tends to discount this psychological dependence. It is part of the process of gender-ization that the masculine personality is encouraged to think of itself as independent. The exaggerated perception of masculine independence to which genderization tends is epitomized in

Rousseau's description of his noble savage. The magnificent, pre-civilization, self-satisfied male individual struts his territory without it would seem any parents, wife, children or relatives. It is a vision of pure self-sufficient, self-centeredness that Rousseau managed to live out in his own life by, amongst other matters, consigning his children, in succession of their arrival, to the orphanage. Aristotle is another patriarchal influence. He considered that the magnanimous man does not like to recognize his need for help and consolation from others. He is ashamed to receive benefits because it is the mark of the superior to confer them.

The fallacy in this patriarchal vision is that it discounts the process of upbringing and socialization that produced that autonomous individual. The dedicated input that produced autonomy is discounted. There is no noble savage without a noble mother. The goods that are prized by masculinity are not the same goods that perpetuate those goods from one generation to another. It is only by means of our psychological dependencies that we are able to become psychologically independent. The paradox of this process of psychological dependence is that in order to contribute to the successful creative exchange of dependencies, which is what life is all about, we have first to become autonomously creative individuals. The production of mental clones would be as damaging to healthy succession as the result of physical inbreeding.

To say that humans are dependent on each other is apt to be an understatement the extent of which is not fully appreciated. Compared to animals ours is a psychologically interdependent existence in the extreme. The correct functioning of these dependencies is, therefore, the supreme important creative factor in human existence. In the words of the psychoanalyst Joan Rivière:

There is no such thing as a single human being, pure and simple, unmixed with other human beings. Each personality is a world in himself, a company of many. That self... is a composite structure...formed out of countless never-ending influences between ourselves and others. The other persons are in fact part of ourselves... we are members of one another.[5]

This process of dependency on creative interaction does not cease with the transition to adulthood. It is a permanent necessity of human life which is faced with complex decision making. The successful progress through life for humans is an endeavor that continuously negotiates different courses of action and prioritizes different goals in the light of an imagined future. The process is fraught with potential disaster and needs reasoned assessment in order to steer the best course of action. In so many situations decisions are needed which may turn out beneficial or disastrous, yet situations in which we ourselves are not necessarily the best judges. Self-knowledge is necessary but is usually a shared achievement. We need to seek, to be offered and to weigh the opinions of other people. The progress of a human life is a maze of choice requiring careful reason. The list of these occasions is endless: the choice of apprenticeship; choice of course for university; choice of career; ending a relationship; moving home; changing jobs; recognizing the limitations and possibilities of illness, disability or old age; coping with abuse, coping with a bad boss. None of these decisions in a well-flourishing family, friendship network or community should have to be taken alone. To be human is to be a creative power in relation to other humans. In applying our intellectual, emotional and physical resources to the benefit of others we create each other's lives daily in thousands of small ways right down to the warm welcome home at the end of a day's work.

The philosopher Alasdair MacIntyre took up the same subject. He made it his mission to make good the deficiency of moral philosophy which has in its tradition ignored the part played by the dependencies of human life and its vulnerability to physical and mental damage. He counter posed the recognition of human animal dependence by Aquinas to the self-sufficiency of Aristotle. MacIntyre was struck by the difference between these two when reading a prayer of Aquinas in which he asks God to grant that he may happily share with those in need what he has, while humbly asking for what he needs from those who have.[6]

MacIntyre developed the theme of dependency and creative interaction that this discussion has been following. He had some distinctive ways to explain the matter. For MacIntyre the one essential constituent of human flourishing is the ability for 'independent, practical reasoning.'[7] The salient feature of this is that it is highly susceptible to disruption. This ability is never self-sufficient or innate. In its development it is socially produced by practice and guidance. In its mature exercise it is characterized by gathering the opinions of others. In this sense the precondition of independent reasoning is acknowledgement of dependency:

> We may at any point go astray in our practical reasoning because of intellectual error: perhaps we happen to be insufficiently well-informed about the particulars of our situation; or we have gone beyond the evidence in a way that has misled us; or we have relied too heavily on some unsubstantiated generalization. But we may also go astray because of moral error: we have been over-influenced by our dislike of someone; we have projected on to a situation some phantasy in whose grip we are; we are insufficiently sensitive to someone else's suffering. And our intellectual errors are often, although not always rooted in our moral errors. From both types of mistake the best protections are friendship and collegiality... There is no point then in our development towards and in the exercise of independent practical reasoning at which we cease altogether to be dependent on particular others.[8]

MacIntyre sums up with an echo of Rivière in stating the condition of the human self. 'I can be said truly to know who and what I am, only because there are others who can be said to know who and what I am.'[9]

MacIntyre develops a moral argument from this analysis. It is clear that human beings cannot pursue their goods except in cooperation with each other. The character of this cooperation must be unconditional commitment. We never know when or what assistance we ourselves will need. Consequently our participation in this relationship must be an uncalculated giving and receiving. MacIntyre quotes the charming Lakota expression 'Wantantognaka.' This is the virtue of individuals who engage the recognition of participation in extravagant ceremonial acts of uncalculated giving and conferring honor. 'Wantantognaka names a generosity that I owe to all those others who also owe it to me.'[10]

MacIntyre's argument had a target that he disliked. It was the liberal contract theory of society which enjoyed a renewed vogue in the seventies and eighties.[11] This theory assumes that a fair society can be achieved by a distribution of material goods and opportunities. The flaw in this contract is that the most important goods of human existence, those of well-adjusted creative individuals, are not there for the taking. Nor are they there on a contractual basis. This greatest of goods is created freely by spontaneous giving. I would like to add to MacIntyre's conclusion something that he was hinting at but did not put into so many words. He illustrated the religious basis of community.

This power that operates between us needs to be given a name and although it is often described, half-adequately, as love this does not really convey the qualities involved. Harlow's experiments, for instance, were presented as investigations into the nature of love but the word love in this case had a political implication. Harlow was a great self-publicist. Love was the word he needed to stake his territory, engage popular sentiment and provoke the behaviorists. The energy and power under consideration in this name 'love' is really that of creative interaction. Sure the mother loves the child but there is a joyous productive engagement. It is an exciting open-ended creative project. It is also a job. It has the satisfaction of a good job in that it makes full use of a person's creative talents. The mother creates the child's life and the child creates the mother's life. This creative power does not stop at the boundary of parenthood or the boundary of extended kinship. It is a project which community makes provision to be extended and given a safety net by means of paid professionals such as teachers and care workers who do not necessarily love their charges.

This reciprocal creative process, the psychological interdependence of human beings I name *psychosymbiosis*. This is a fact of the human person the importance of which may be understood by its more common counterpart physical symbiosis. Nature provides a number of examples of physical symbiosis which demonstrate survival achieved by mutual support where one organism alone could not exist. The bacteria which accomplish digestion in the human gut is the example closest to home. Lichen is a good example of the great advantage of symbiosis. Lichen is composed of two organisms, fungus and algae. The fungus encloses a number of algae. These algae photosynthesize nutrients for the fungus which it cannot produce itself. The fungus in turn provides the necessary physical shelter for the algae. Lichen is a successful species that colonizes the most inhospitable parts of our planet like the windswept tops of mountains and the stonework on church towers. The only nutrition available is rainwater and a few minerals washed out of the stone. Neither organism alone would be able to survive such a condition. Human beings have achieved this pervasive colonization too but they have done this by their psychic interdependencies, through culture, language and social cooperation. Psychosymbiosis is the creative power of psychic reciprocity and it is the essential condition of successful human existence.

I want to propose that it is this power that is the social reality represented by religion. To qualify that slightly it is the *ideal potential and ideal workings* of this power that is the subject matter of religion. The power is not in itself good or bad. It may be put to bad use. It may be abused. It may operate partially or defectively. It may not be put to use at all. We hold the ability to apply this power to damage each other irrevocably. The realization of the ideal is a constant effort of willingness, application, vigilance, prognostication, adjustment and correction. That constitutes the role of religion. Psychosymbiosis better identifies, certainly as far as Christianity is concerned, the communal representations posited by Durkheim. Durkheim's presentation tends to associate the representations with tribe or nation. Psychosymbiosis locates to prior levels in personal relationships. Rivière's words 'we are members of one another' were long predated by Saint Paul's refrain 'we are members one of another.'[12] The sentiment is repeated in the communion offering 'The body of Christ.' It is this social reality of interdependence that is celebrated by Christians in every act of Holy Communion.

I propose that the ideal potential of psychosymbiosis corresponds to God. This very complex, subtle, not easily identified power, unique as a property of human existence, is what is expressed in brilliantly condensed and compelling format in the concept of God. It is a power that is in us and yet transcends us. It is a power that we can sense but is not obviously sensible. It is a power that is of ultimate value in human existence and therefore authoritative. It is a power that it is no abuse or mistaken projection to personify as a caring and guiding super personality because it is indeed personal and super personal. It is Us.

An atheist standpoint may object, why call this God? The response is that it is a feature of existence and so must have a name. This ideal potential is also a singularly important value.

What the concept of God tries to do is to represent this to us. By analogy with physics it has the quality of a vector. In physics any force must also have a direction in which it acts. There is, for instance, no wind that is not also a North, South, East or West wind. The human person is a creative force and any action of a person cannot help but act in a particular moral direction. A vector is needed to make sense of the creative existence of a person. A vector is necessary to realize creativity. God is such a vector that directs the creative energy of a life.

8.2. Theologians of the Person as the Origin of God

A few theologians during the course of the twentieth century identified that God derives directly from the dynamics of human relationships. Their common ground is an understanding of the human person as a relationship. Put at its simplest there is no I without You. These theologians are effectively working around, but without naming it, our new concept of psychosymbiosis. They are, therefore, useful to deepen the sense of the concept. The theologians concerned span two generations. The first includes Martin Buber, John Wren-Lewis, John Macmurray and John Robinson. The second includes Daphne Hampson, Anthony Freeman and, taking up an illuminating African tribal concept, Desmond Tutu with his Ubuntu theology.[13]

Robinson frankly disavowed the traditional anthropomorphic God 'out there.' At the same time he refused any suggestion that this put an end to God. 'That is not an attractive proposition: inevitably it feels like being orphaned.'[14] Robinson had the same experience of convincement that affected Macmurray. Despite abandoning the 'incredible' beliefs of the Scottish Calvinism that he was brought up in he says 'I was convinced that religion had its own reality, so firmly that I have never afterwards been able to question it for a moment.'[15] Robinson's search for the development of what he called a 'genuinely lay theology'[16] outside the world of the professional theologians is another way to state the search to translate the supernatural God into its social reality. These theologians are distinct in being liberal theologians who are not at the same time advocates of the Nature God. The distinction of their method is that they do not first identify God as a general creative potentiality of the universe then derive from this an ethic for human relations. For these theologians it is the parameters of human relations themselves that generate the ethic: God.

These few voices in theology, too uncoordinated to name either as a movement or even group, have had little influence in comparison to the overwhelming liberal migration to the Nature God. They are not followers of Plato. Their marginalization is due largely to their speaking a Platonist disparaged 'secular' theology. Marginalization is partly due to the situation of four of them on the periphery of Christian theology. Buber was Jewish. Wren-Lewis was a scientist and lay theologian. Macmurray, although he gave the prestigious Gifford Lectures in 1952-4, was by profession a philosopher. Hampson has given up on Christianity as irredeemably male. Gerald Priestland should not be forgotten. As a journalist he is never cited amongst the ranks of the theologians. But let's take the grand aura away from the title. Anyone who sets themselves to thinking about what God might be is doing theology. As religious correspondent to the BBC, Priestland did theology live. He was a people's theologian. He interviewed the whole spectrum of leading figures, ministers and ordinary people and asked questions about every doctrine. Priestland had no certainties[17] but every answer was put through the lens of his firm sense that God is something in the everyday encounters between people. He discovered and spoke for what he called 'the Great Anonymous Church of the Unchurched'[18] which anticipated by fifteen years the current sociological tool of 'believing not belonging.'[19]

This marginalization was compounded by the fact that the theology never achieved its mature expression. It was an incipient theology that was revolutionary only in potential. That revolution never came to fruition because it was diverted by Robinson into the wrong channel. Robinson mistook his allegiance: he presented a non-metaphysical theology under the auspices of Tillich's thoroughly metaphysical Nature God. Robinson's theology was grounded in a Social Community God. His primary influences were Buber, Wren-Lewis and Macmurray. They were not the Teutonic voices that he mixed this group with and which are included in his book. Robinson had worked out a fully-fledged theology of God derived from human relationships from his own temperament, reinforced by Buber, Wren-Lewis and Macmurray, before he encountered Tillich. Robinson had no need of Tillich to express himself but for some reason hitched his theology to Tillich's Nature God of being itself. Tillich proved an advantageous vehicle for presentation because his theology had some popularity and his heavyweight intellectualizing as back up.

But the deference to Tillich was detrimental to a true understanding of Robinson's theology. Robinson threw himself and his three companion theologians under the umbrella of the Nature God where they do not belong. At the same time Robinson's appropriation of Tillich was paradoxical. It was a complete subversion of the Nature God, who, in Robinson's hands, is metamorphosed into a Social Community God. Tillich's mystical ultimate concern was made into what it had never been: the rational statement God is Love. On account of these confusing aspects, to this day Robinson's understanding of God easily mistakes the reader. In the ostensible transmission of Tillich, Robinson deceived even himself. [20] Something of a retrieval is needed then to rescue this branch of theology which lost its way and has lacked a strong advocate because its best candidate mistook his mission.

Robinson praised Wren-Lewis whom he spoke of as coming to the same conclusions as himself.[21] He cited a number of passages from Wren-Lewis to illustrate his own views. Wren-Lewis is taken up here as spokesman for the group because he states so eloquently his sense of God in human relationships. Wren-Lewis is a greatly overlooked voice in theology.[22*] He was a later life convert to Anglicanism who, as he said of himself, 'rebelled against the whole oppressive atmosphere of conventional religion at the age of twelve' and declared himself an anti-theist.[23] He later rediscovered his faith under the tutelage of someone he names as an enlightened Anglican clergyman. Wren-Lewis came to prominence through his series of lunchtime lectures on the meaning of the word God given at the liberal St Margaret's Church near the Bank of England. The lectures were published by Modern Churchmen's Union in 1956 as a booklet titled *Return to the Roots. A study of the meaning of the word God.* This largely anticipated Robinson's book but met the fate of oblivion. Here are the words in which Wren-Lewis recounted his re-conversion:

> I accepted from him the general notion that the real meaning of theistic assertions has to do with the relationships between persons and, moreover with those distinctly personal relationships in which persons *become* persons rather than relationships of mere social cooperation.[24] ...the human body does indeed seem to be dependent for its integration or disintegration upon such personal factors as psychological health, which in practice means openness to personal relationship[25] ...For me the positive discovery of Christianity became possible primarily through the discovery in experience of the religious character of personal relationships[26] ...But it is one thing to say that religious propositions can be referred to the common experience of the creative character of personal relationships: it would be quite another to say that people commonly *recognize* their experience of personal relationships for what it is – an encounter with the transcendent. Clearly

they do not, or there would be no need for religious apologetics – and what was special about the group of people I met
through this Anglican clergyman was that he had led them to
be aware of the full religious significance of their relations
with one another[27] ...I cannot emphasize too strongly that
acceptance of the Christian faith became possible for me only
because I found that I did not have to go back on my
wholesale rejection of the superstitious beliefs that had
hitherto surrounded me.[28]

In his lecture series from which the following three quotations
are taken Wren-Lewis expounded aspects of God as the creative
power in human relationships. The italicised emphases are all
original to Wren-Lewis:

Our very being as persons in fact, comes from our encounters
with each other – and since this is true for each of us then
there must be something between us which is there before us
and is bigger than all of us. Here, in fact, at the heart of
personal life, we have an actual *experience* of creation – not just
an idea of the Universe being made by somebody, but direct
knowledge of ourselves being created by a Power 'between
man and man.' It is this knowledge, upon which all religion is
grounded, the knowledge which St John summed up when he
said that 'God *is* love.'[29]

To say that the Controlling Intelligence behind the scenes of the
Universe ought to be imagined as like a father is superstitious
nonsense, but that is not what the Fatherhood of God means. The
genuine doctrine, like all doctrines about God, is *a descriptive
statement about the Creative Power which we experience directly in our
relations with one another*. Those who have made the great
discovery 'that love can love and be loved' know that love is a
personally reactive Reality which (or Who) works continually

towards our growth into personal maturity-in-relationship: love, in fact, exercises towards us a Fatherhood of which ordinary fatherhood is a pale and distorted expression:[30]

> The importance of the Jews in human history... consists primarily in the fact that as a people they have never wholly lost this sense of the Universe as first and foremost an encounter with persons... The Jewish rabbis taught that the *skeckinah*, the presence of the glory of God, lay between the husband and wife in marriage, and Jesus said... 'The realm of God is *between* you.'[31]

John Robinson summed up his own viewpoint as follows. 'To believe in God as love means to believe that in pure personal relationship we encounter not merely what ought to be, but what is, the deepest veriest truth about the structure of reality.'[32]

Wren-Lewis explains the matter well but before moving on to Macmurray a few more examples of God experienced as the creative power in human relationships will help illustrate the case. A lady who wrote in sympathy to Robinson described her experience working on an adult literacy program in a hospital in Africa:

> We worked mostly in the surgical wards and during the hottest time of the day. It was extremely tiring, and often the wards smelled awful. But I found myself going as though to a party and coming away exhilarated as if I'd had a good stiff drink. I've never met such wonderful people; patient, enduring, cheerful, eager to learn, and incredibly brave. Their love was an honour and a benediction and again I felt I walked with God, even though I rejected the image of somebody 'up there' putting out a hand to me. I used to look for god when I was miserable. I didn't find him because he wasn't there and when I was too busy to think and worry

about myself, there he seemed to be.[33]

Don Cupitt brings out a particular aspect of this creative power in human relationship. This is the essential and sometimes gratuitous validation of the human person by other people. He describes a moving experience from his days as a young priest in Salford:

> I think I was at that time approaching the view that religion does not explain the causes of events in the world, and religion does not offer an auxiliary technology to be introduced when science has failed. Religious things must be done for their own sakes and entirely disinterestedly. I came nearest to this conclusion one night at 3 am, after I had left a deathbed. The patient had been quite unconscious and no relatives had come to sit by him as he died. I did not hold the magical view that giving him the last rites would actually alter his eternal destiny from what it would otherwise have been. So nobody knew I had been there and even I did not think that I had achieved anything measurable; and yet I still thought it had been worthwhile. Why? My Thought was mythological. I said, 'On the Day of Judgment it will be the case that somebody cared, somebody turned up. I hope somebody else does the same for me when my time comes, and that is all there is to it.' Mythological thinking is not clear thinking, but that was the best that I could do at that moment. Now I can put it a little more plainly and say that a religious act, like praying has to be done for its own sake and because it is intrinsically good to do it, and not for the sake of some kind of subsequent pay-off. Religion is a way of responding to life, shaping life, giving ultimate meaning and value to life.[34]

Cupitt's experience sums up in a poignant example the religiously significant content of countless minor acts of validation that we perform for each other every day. We value each other using our creative power, freely given, not necessarily requited, reciprocal, or even noticed, with no expectation of return in the knowledge that that act is an expression of our essential human nature. The accumulation of such acts is the vital life giving support and dependency of all human flourishing. It can be called God's will, religious feeling, Christianity, psychosymbiosis, humanism or in today's colloquial speak 'a nice one', the motive and the value are all the same.

John Macmurray is the heavyweight philosophical theoretician of God derived from the dynamics of human relationships. Where Wren-Lewis and Robinson arrive intuitively at the understanding that this is the substrate of religion, as does Macmurray, Macmurray knew that for this understanding to be accepted it was necessary to challenge the prevailing framework of Western philosophy. It was this challenge that he took up in his 1953 Gifford lectures *The Form of the Personal*.[35] Macmurray's immediate target is the course of modern philosophy from the time of Kant and Descartes. He charges this with the double complaint that it is theoretical and egocentric. Macmurray was concerned that this work could not be made popular because it was very serious and very difficult.[36]

It is not necessary, however, to follow every step of Macmurray's detailed argument in the history of philosophy to grasp what he is against and to take the benefit of his result. Macmurray is against the Platonist understanding of the person or soul as 'a thing'. This is known as the organic view of the self. For Macmurray the person is a relationship. 'The Self is neither substance nor an organism but a person.'[37] The self is exclusively a person in relation. 'The self exists only in dynamic relation to the Other. ...it has its being in its relationship... this relationship is necessarily personal.'[38] The egocentric 'I think' self of philosophy makes it 'formally impossible to do justice to religious experience.'[39] The organic view of the self makes others objects to be known rather than to be in relationship with.

Because this self cannot theorize relationship and religion is exclusively about relationship then this philosophy is inherently atheist.

Macmurray states a credo of psychosymbiosis as emphatic as anything I have managed to say so far. The human being is born into a condition of absolute dependence and can survive only through other people in a dynamic of communication:[40]

> This complete and unlimited dependence of each of us upon the others is the central fact of personal existence. Individual independence is an illusion... In ourselves we are nothing... it is only in relation to others that we exist as persons; we are invested with significance by others who have need of us; and borrow our reality from those who care for us. We live and move and have our being not in ourselves but in one another... Here is the basic fact of our human condition... since our knowledge of one another conditions all our activities, both practical and reflective, we find here the ultimate condition of all our knowing and of all our action. This is the field of religion.[41]

Macmurray champions the fact that religion is what is done not what is believed. We saw earlier how he came to this conviction through his Calvinist and wartime experience. In his philosophical project he investigated how 'I think' came to have primacy over 'I do.' For Macmurray the nineteenth-century philosophers reinforced the Greek tradition that the real life is reflection not action. This transfers the focus to speculation and therefore the irrelevance of religion. 'Religion [in Kant] appears as a kind of justifiable mythology, concerned wholly with another life and another world; as a sop to the weakness of human nature.'[42] Religion, which is essentially empirical practice, is falsified by dogmatic and speculative apparatus.[43]

Murray, therefore, mounts an attack on metaphysical dualism

which he sees as a decisive contributor to the modern view that religion is irrelevant. In a reflexive move worthy of Durkheim he identifies the ideal not as the real but as the product of the real. Macmurray is adamant in his conclusion. 'Any dualistic mode of thinking is incompatible with religion.'[44]

For Macmurray the prime certainty of existence is 'I do' not 'I think.' The primacy of 'I do' transfers the center of reference to action and to the body and becomes personal and relational. It is this experience of community as personal relationship that founds God. 'What is generalized... in the religious use of the term God is a matter of empirical experience. It is our experience of personal relationship with one another.'[45] The problem of making a symbolic representation of community is how to make a representation of the universal personal relationships which found it. God for Macmurray is this necessary symbolic relation which he explains as follows:

> How can a universal mutuality of intentional and active relationship be represented symbolically? Only through the ideal of a personal Other who stands in the same mutual relation to every member of the community. Without the idea of such a universal and personal Other it is impossible to represent the unity of a community of persons, each in personal fellowship with all others... The universal Other must be represented as a universal Agent, whose action unifies the actions of every member of the community... The necessity is... for a ritual head... so that each member can think his membership of the community through his relation to this person, who represents and embodies the intention which constitutes the general fellowship. In its full development, the idea of a universal personal Other is the idea of God.[46]

The result of Macmurray's philosophical rearrangement was

expressed in simple practical terms in his Terry Lectures at Yale University given in 1936 *The Structure of Religious Experience*. This slim forgotten volume deserves to stand as the introductory core text for students of the sociology of religion as a companion to *The Elementary Forms of the Religious Life*. Macmurray does three things in these lectures. He sites religion as integral to human relations. 'Religion is an inseparable component of human life and always must be. To say that religion belongs to the early stages of human life and is destined to be superseded as human development goes on is to talk foolishness.'[47] He outlines in this work everything that needs to be expanded and reoriented in Durkheim's collective representations to remove them from the unfortunate nationalist association. This is done by bringing the collective strata right down to the interpersonal strata. Finally he abandons the Plato/Durkheim metaphysical dualism of the sacred/profane. The sacred is the act of reflection on community. Here is the passage which says this:

> The task of religion is the maintenance and extension of human community... the mainspring of human life is the activity in which we relate ourselves to one another. It is this that is the 'given' for religious reflection... The primary activity of religious reflection is the mutual expression of the experience of mutual relationship. If two people, or a group of people who share a common life, have their experience of common life brought into the focus of their consciousness, their mutual consciousness of community demands an expression for itself. Such an expression must be something that they do together to express consciousness of a common life. It will therefore be at once part of their common life, and yet a symbol of it, and so transcending it. It must be a common activity set apart from all other common activities and so invested with special significance. They may dance together, or sing together, or simply eat together; but because they are

doing such things to express the consciousness of their common life, the dance will not be an ordinary dance, but a sacred dance; the song will be a sacred song, the meal a sacred meal... on ordinary occasions they do these things together. On these special occasions they do the same things together to express the fact that they always are together in doing things; so that these things become celebrations of their consciousness of belonging to one another in common life... it is not merely the experience of a common life, but rather the experience of its precariousness that lies at the root of religious reflection...it expresses at once the sense of community and the fear of its failure; and in so doing it strengthens and sustains the unity that it expresses.[48]

I have quoted Macmurray extensively because he is the great and the greatly overlooked religious thinker of the twentieth century. He is at one and the same time both a theological and a sociological thinker. In his thought the boundaries of the two disciplines are dissolved. He is an unacknowledged Durkheim for whom all theology is sociology. Yet in doing that sociology he identifies the independent territory of theology and makes the profoundest validation of the meaning of God. He succeeds, as I am trying to do here, in forging the vital link between what we had in the past and the way we can have that same thing for the future. He provides for that quality number three for a God for the twenty-first century: A God which is new, but not at all new. He is much the greater theologian than Durkheim. He makes a penetrating and convincing presentation of the same subject matter that Durkheim hit upon as collective representations. Without ever using the name, Macmurray is a great feminist Community God theologian. His thought is a prompt for a revolution in our conceptual apparatus for religion that has been incipient for the past fifty years.

8.3. Psychosymbiosis Correlated with God

The proposition that the ideal potential of psychosymbiosis is the social reality that is embodied in the concept of God can be illustrated by a number of correspondences between the characteristics of God and the characteristics of psychosymbiosis. Daphne Hampson provided a template for the character of God which is useful for this correlation.

The pivotal concern in Hampson's work *After Christianity* is with 'the nature of personhood.' Hampson is a great advocate of understanding God as the self-in-relation. Many of her remarks indicate this. 'The way in which I am conceiving of God suggests that God is involved in the process of persons coming to themselves.'[49] 'We may well think of God as being present within the communication which takes place between oneself and another person.'[50] Hampson quotes as 'profoundly parallel to what I also wish to say' a passage from the feminist theologian Linell Cady:

> It has often been noted that our conceptions of the human person and of God are dialectical, each being mirror images of the other... The vision of human being and the moral life sketched out above does not lend support to traditional theism with its focus on an independent transcendent divine being. I have been using love as a primary metaphor for depicting the orientation of human life that most facilitates the emergence of greater being and value. Incarnating this spirit is analogous to what traditionally has been understood as love and relationship to God. However, important differences render the latter expression misleading. Most basically, the self does not relate to an independent divine being but embodies the spirit of the divine. Nor should this be understood as the creative work of God operating in human life, insofar as that formulation suggests the activity of an independent agent operating on or through humans... From

[the] perspective [which she is advocating] the self is no substantial entity, complete and defined, but a reality always in the process of being created through the dynamic of love, which continually alters boundaries and identity.[51]

It is to our benefit that Hampson has given up on the patriarchal formulation of God and aims to start afresh from what God means to her. Working from this basis Hampson explores the qualities of God necessary for a 'future theism,'[52] and sets a specification. Hampson, unfortunately, defers her understanding of God to that of Schleiermacher. 'He advanced the thesis that the self exists in an immediate interconnectedness to that which is more than itself. I am in agreement with Schleiermacher that the question of that membrane between the self and that which exceeds the self must form the kernel of theology.'[53] Schleiermacher's formulation is in fact ambiguous between the self in relation to the traditional anthropomorphic Community God, the self in relation to the Nature God and God actually as representing the self-in-relation to other people that Hampson expounds. I prefer to rely on Hampson's own interpretation which stands happily independent of Schleiermacher, is not ambiguous and not tinged with Platonism.

Hampson's starting points are the enlightenment paradigm shift to a new ethic of equality. This rejects heteronomous authority and therefore necessarily the Community God. 'As long as religion is considered to be revealed – and Christianity is necessarily a religion of revelation – there must be a God who is other than the world towards whom Christians will exercise a relationship which is in essence heteronomous.'[54] Bi-polarity is built into Western religion: humanity representing the 'other' and female pole in relation to the 'male' God... the only way forward is to break the paradigm open, so that its bi-polarity gives way to what we may call a heterogeneity, in which there is no longer that which is the One and consequently the 'other' to it.[55]

Hampson is an inadvertent exponent of Durkheim. 'The basis for theology (in an age in which the concept of a particular revelation is no longer viable) must surely be that experience of a dimension of reality which humans then name God.'[56] The very paradigms of inter-relationality which notably women are fostering may prove useful in the attempt to conceptualize what it is that God may be. God, so I believe, must be understood... as that through which we come to be most fully ourselves.'[57]

Hampson has a clear idea of what that reality is. 'God must be understood to complete what it is to be a human being and not be conceived as set over against humans.'[58]

Hampson cites as a profound influence an article by E. Haney which 'comes as close as could be to describing what is also my ideal for what it is to be a human being.'[59] Haney counters the Christian understanding of love as self-giving *agape* with a feminist understanding of friendship, *philia*, a love between centered selves who are essentially equals:

To make friendship central is both to transform the power relations that most often hold between individuals, groups, people and the earth... Friendship is a relation of mutuality, respect, fidelity, confidence and affection. It is... therefore a rejection of most competitive patterns... and paternalistic patterns of relating... In the effort to name that way of being that is both independent and responsible and yet related and interdependent, I and some other feminists use the term *centring*. That seems to come closest to describing a way of being that is neither autonomous, nor dependent, nor, somehow both. ...the centring self lives on her own terms, out of her own roots, in tune with the reasons of her heart and head, competent and capable of shaping, in concert with others, our individual and corporate lives... I wish to [suggest] that a feminist ethic... is on the one hand a critique of, and indeed contradiction to, the emphasis on self-sacrifice and centring in God characteristic of Christian ethics because it places the self in a position of importance and authority. From that perspective, centring in one's self smacks of egotism... Yet on the other hand, self-centring is precisely that movement of one's personal existence that brings women into an at-homeness with the universe. It is one pole in a graceful relationship with all that is, it is one extremely important step in a process of coming into congruence with others, of becoming whole.[60]

Hampson proceeds to set out her understanding of the qualities of God as a basis for discovering what God is. This specification is not set out in so many words or in one section, so I have gathered together this list of required qualities:

1. God should be illuminating not comfortless.

Though I believe that it is imperative for us to overcome anthropomorphic metaphors which suggest a 'being' separate from what we are... We may understand God as that which gives us illumination, which allows us to heal in ourselves and which passes between us and those whom we love. God is both that which connects me to the greater whole and that which enables me to be my true self. What this model of God rules out are such attitudinal stances as those of worship and obedience.[61]

2. Relationship with God must be conceived of as dialogue.[62]
3. God cannot be heteronomous or a hierarchical God of worship and obedience.
4. God must perform a transcendental function.[63] God cannot be just me but must be different in kind from me.[64]
5. God must be actively present.[65]
6. God must be a dimension of reality which is present to every age, which is for us to discern.[66]

7. God must follow from feeling, and not be predicated on conformity to dogma.

How peculiarly masculinist it strikes me as being that theology should be tied to purportedly 'objective' creeds, so that it is largely divorced from the worlds of experience and spirituality.[67]

8. God must express the power of good and faith in the power of good.[68]

To this list can be added three attributes of my own.

9. God must be demanding. It must continually demand of us the engagement of our creative power in the service of others.
10. God must allocate a subordinate value to material goods in comparison to the spiritual goods of human relationships.
11. In expressing the power of good, God must also name the practical moral rule that would realize that good.

The following correlations can be noted between the ideal potential of psychosymbiosis and these attributes required of God.

1. Illumination and comfort.

An understanding of the power of Psychosymbiosis is illuminating in that it states the supremely important factor in human relations, something that is easily discounted for being unremarked. It is comforting because it is part of our own power and a power that we are able to command by reciprocity. It is a supportive power on which we can depend for help freely given to us by others.

2. Dialogue.

The ideal potential of psychosymbiosis dictates nothing. It is an invitation that is specifically mutual.

3. Not heteronomous or hierarchical.

There is no authority in the ideal potential of psychosymbiosis except the inspirational value which we ourselves accord it. It relates us to others on the basis of a power that derives from us all and contrary to imposing any hierarchy presupposes the equal value of every member of the group. Obedience is not required.

4. Transcendental.

Psychosymbiosis is my self but also outside myself.

Father Harry Williams of the community of the resurrection at Mirfield expresses this as an interpretation of the key theological doctrine that God is both immanent and transcendent, 'God is from one point of view infinitely other and infinitely greater than I am. From another point of view he is my deepest self; he is what I am.'[69]

5. Actively present.

Psychosymbiosis is part of every day of our lives. It is our life. In the words of Gerald Priestland, 'It is an old Quaker cliché that the whole of life is sacramental.'[70]

6. Present to every age.

Psychosymbiosis has applied universally to all humans in all ages and is available, as Hampson wishes, for discernment and cultural formulation for our own age.

7.   Follow from feeling not dogma.

The practice of psychosymbiosis derives from our own feelings. It is not predicated on any externally opposed dogma but relies for its strength on an appeal to our acceptance solely through the value it demonstrates to us. Any masculinity of dogma as a precondition, which Hampson objects to, is absent.

8.   Express faith in the power of good.

The ideal potential of psychosymbiosis is our supreme good because it is the essential basis for our flourishing. John Spong states the correspondence in a number of phrases. 'God is mystical presence in which all personhood could flourish.'[71] 'The God experience is like swimming in an eternal ocean of love.'[72] 'God is the source of that power that nurtures personhood.'[73]

9.   Demand the use of our creative power.

Psychosymbiosis depends for its successful operation on the use of our creative power of reason in combination with the directional power of love. It asks of everybody the commitment of their own particular talents as a valuable addition to the whole. Matthew Fox comes close to saying this. He considers that the 'Word' in John's gospel mistranslates the Hebrew *dabhar:* the creative energy of God.[74]

10. The superiority of the emotional over the material.

The ideal potential of psychosymbiosis recognizes that the flourishing of our psychological relationships is a precondition to any enjoyment of material well-being.

11. The moral rule of conduct.

Any ethic, which 'the ideal potential of psychosymbiosis' is, must have a corresponding moral rule which would implement it. That moral rule is the subject of chapters ten and eleven. For the time being the moral rule can be stated as friendship. This names mutual equality as the basis for relationship.

8.4. Psychosymbiosis Correlated with the Sacraments of the Church

A further pointer to psychosymbiosis as the social reality of religion is its correspondence with the sacraments of the church. There are traditionally seven of these; baptism, confirmation, communion, matrimony, penance, holy orders, and the last rites before death. Some allowance must be made for artifice in this list. Seven is the desirable number. Holy orders, because it cannot be generally applicable, looks like the ecclesiastical makeweight. The correspondence of the sacraments with pyschosymbiosis is that they mark the key articulatory points of our psychosymbiotic relations. Birth marks the arrival of a new dimension. Confirmation marks the transition to adulthood and the change from a fledgling to a valued contributor to those relations. Marriage is a double transition celebrating both a personal change and the joining of two sets of families pledged to support that relationship. Communion is the necessary regular reminder and renewal of our commitments to one another. Penance, I would prefer to state, the sincere request for forgiveness, is the necessary mending of relationships when they have gone wrong and without which relationships are destined to permanent fracture. Holy Orders can be taken to represent the key decision of a choice of career. Death is the end of psychosymbiotic relations which the last rites and funeral help us adjust to.

The sacraments represent the social reality of key articulatory stages in our psychosymbiotic relations. The language of sacrament and grace used in religious talk can be deciphered as an indirect, reflexive way of stating this reality. In religious language sacraments are defined as ordinances, mediated through the church, which have an essentially social structure. They are the means whereby the union of God and man consequent on the incarnation is perpetuated in Christ's mystical body of His Church, its members incorporated in him and through Him united to one another.[75] A sacrament was defined by Augustine as 'a sign of a sacred thing.' It has also been described as a mystery 'the mystery of Christ.' Holy Communion, the Eucharist, is considered to be the 'sacrament of sacraments' and the 'food of eternal life.'[76] Most importantly the function of sacraments is to convey grace. According to the catechism, 'Sacraments are symbols which produce feeling in the recipients which enable them to receive grace.' Grace is variously theorized. The dictionary definition is 'the supernatural assistance of God bestowed upon a rational being with a view to his sanctification.' Tertullian considered grace to be divine energy.[77] Augustine taught grace as the gift of the Holy Spirit. In alternative words, 'the most comprehensive blessing that can be invoked includes "the grace of our Lord Jesus Christ." '[78]

To decipher this reflexive religious language, a sacrament is the occasion of emotional food. That food is derived from the celebration, reminder and renewal of our psychosymbiotic dependencies. The sacrament is the particular occasion of taking the emotional meal. Grace is the energy and emotional sustenance derived from that occasion. The mystery of Christ serves to state the mystery of these unseen but potent psychic forces. The grace, in the grace of our Lord Jesus Christ, the comprehensive blessing, serves to state the inspiration and energizing power of working for the ideal potential of those forces. The 'supernatural assistance' represents the unformulated potencies of the psychosymbiotic power that is being celebrated. 'Our Lord Jesus

Christ' represents the source of the inspiration, the ideal potential itself. To employ our reflexive understanding, Christ in the usage above represents the ideal potential of human psychosymbiotic relations: that is to say that the ideal potential of human relations is God.

9

God Hidden in the Invisible Religion of Today's Culture

9.1. The Search for Religion Disguised in Popular Culture
9.2. The Super Ethic of Popular Culture
9.3. The Religious Character of the Super Ethic

9.1 The Search for Religion Disguised in Popular Culture

A minority sociological enterprise has been underway to detect a new form of religion hidden in today's society. A number of thinkers have been on the track of religion mutated out of Christianity and vanished into the camouflage of our popular culture. Their conversations are not connected and this unifying assumption is not always explicit so that these thinkers can hardly be called a group. They are nevertheless all pioneers of the possibility that religion is not necessarily defined by the ecclesiastical forms which police the definition of religion as belief in the supernatural. They are pioneers of mutation of religion in the true sense of mutation: the same substance will be discovered in different form. This is an application of Durkheim's reflexive principle although he is not the acknowledged inspiration. The source of inspiration seems to be a sense of plain disbelief that people or society can have undergone such a fundamental change. It is a sense that the ecclesiastical frame has played a trick on us. It is a sense, as illustrated in chapter six, that our conceptual apparatus itself is causing the blockage. It is a sense that the nuggets of religion are there waiting to be dug out if only investigation could locate them. It is on this fruitful line of thought that this chapter builds. A brief acknowledgment is needed of the work of Thomas Luckmann,[1] Sarah Williams,[2] Charles Taylor,[3] Don Cupitt,[4] Geoffrey Ahern and Grace Davie,[5] and Paul Heelas and Linda Woodhead.[6] The common enterprise may be summed up as the attempt to discover what is 'everyday religion' outside the jurisdiction of the churches. The aim of the following review is to illustrate that this project represents a great bid for freedom from theological paralysis that never quite manages to break free.

Luckmann takes historical precedence. He accepted Talcott Parsons' social differentiation thesis about secularization. This states that religion has been displaced out of the public sphere to the private sphere due to the takeover by the state of many functions that were previously under church auspices. The study by Jeffrey Cox of the churches in Lambeth around the turn of the nineteenth century illustrates this well.[7] The period was one of great municipal projects for health, water, housing and education. The process culminated in state provision and in the National Health Service. Prior to local government enterprise the church provided education and welfare services. Consequent on this the church was the focus of employment opportunities for many people, particularly women of a particular class, for whom there was little alternative opportunity to exercise their talents. Williams' evidence from Southwark that was encountered in chapter six showed the wealth of voluntary employment opportunities in the work undertaken by the church missions; Sunday schools, free breakfast clubs, crèches, church outings, medical and legal assistance. The reminiscences of Margaret Penn in *Manchester Fourteen Miles*, illustrates the pivotal role of the church in a village community. It was the focus of entertainments even, organizing annual outings, teas, fêtes and the harvest festival.[8] With the transfer of education to local government and later the founding of the National Health Service the focus of activity moved away from the church. Our sources of entertainment have burgeoned magnificently compared to what they were. A notable aspect of these shifts is that they say nothing about decline in belief any more than today's shift from Pub going proves a decline in drinking. The social differentiation thesis states that the economic and social center of gravity moved away from the church.

In accepting the social differentiation argument for banishment from the public to the private sphere Luckmann was nevertheless convinced that something more profound had affected religion in this private haven. The subtitle of his book serves as key to his assumption: *The Transformation of Symbols in Industrial Society*. To analyze this Luckmann went back to the first principles of religion as the relation of the individual to society and its reciprocity. His hunch was that modernity had brought about a profound change in the relation of the individual to society and that if he could work out what this was then he would have the answer to the different form that religion now took. Luckmann made a number of exploratory sallies but was frank about the lack of satisfactory answers to his project.[9]

In retrospect it can be seen that there is an underlying fault of tautology in Luckmann's assumption that has continued to play havoc with the sociology of religion. Modernity is largely defined by freedom from the trammels of religion. That release of society from religion cannot then be analyzed by the concept of modernity without being tautological. Nevertheless 'invisibility' was a gift to sociological analysis. It suggests a chameleon like presence of religion hidden against its cultural background. I hope to demonstrate that Luckmann was closer to a solution than he imagined. He proposed the status of the autonomy of the individual as the new location of the 'sacred cosmos'[10] and the newly emerging religion.[11] Pride of place may be given to his prophetic insight. 'We are observing the emergence of a new social form of religion characterized neither by diffusion of the sacred cosmos through the social structure nor by institutional specialization of religion[12]... the modern sacred cosmos is to be found neither in the churches nor the state nor the economic system.'[13]

Following Luckmann's lead Sarah Williams refused to take the institutional definition of religion as her frame of reference. She noted the prevailing incorporation into sociological work of the 'simplistic identification of religion with institutional church practice.'[14] Despite a certain move in sociology to address this bias she noted that 'it none the less remains the case that a concentration on formal religious behaviour so outweighs a consideration of the more intangible expressions of belief that popular religion continues to elude us as a serious subject of enquiry in its own right.'[15] The context of Williams' work was a counter to the thesis that it was urbanization that destroyed religion. This entailed that popular religion in the city must, therefore, be a hangover from rural and pre-industrial times. Williams protested the simplistic treatment, the neglect of popular culture[16] and the focus on 'formal outward signs' and 'irreligious caricature'[17] ascribed to working families. She sought to identify a transfer of religious feeling to elusive and eclectic dimensions. Williams found that the people were not passive receivers 'they were the makers of their own culture in religion.'[18] Williams concluded that we should appreciate 'popular religion as a distinctive system of belief in its own right.'[19]

To take a view on Williams' work the serious consideration of popular culture as religious is a great advance in sociological sophistication and independence from Christianity. The refusal to take the obvious at face value was a gift to analysis in the tradition of good sociology. At the same time the conceptual apparatus used by Williams does not move forward. Popular religion is defined tautologically as a variety of religion and does not add any more information about what religion is.[20] This means that we are left in effect with another case of the Christian determination of sociology's definition of religion. The work, therefore, only extended the boundaries of religion into the peripheries that surround the Christian keep.

The unspoken assumption that religion has something to do with miraculous happenings and belief in the supernatural led in Williams' work to the inclusion within the boundary of all manner of medical magic, charms against fate, the invocation of luck, manipulation of lovers and the intertwining of these aspects with Christian mascots, crosses, rosaries and sacred hearts. The folklorist, Edward Lovett, devoted his life to recording such practices. His books *Magic in Modern London*, and *Belief in Charms*, thus achieve the status of a religious compendium. They incorporate such items as burning tormenteil root at midnight on Friday to revive waning male affection. To cure a child's cough put the hair of the child's head between two slices of buttered bread and give it to a dog. Williams drew extensively on these folk practices to shape what she saw as the popular religion. The definition of religion employed is, however, not a sociological definition. Religion is defined by magic not by social relations.

Williams' approach founds a body of literature that proposes migration and sees folk religion in football, popular music and the pub. The resistance to her move demonstrates the paralysis of the conceptual apparatus. It has been rejected by the supporters of the secularization argument who claim that it has moved the goalposts.[21] It is also considered conceptually to be too much like shifting sand. As Davie states the worry, 'Once the gold standard, in the form of the supernatural, has been abandoned, it is difficult to draw any precise boundary.'[22] Sociology is only comfortable on firm ground. That, however, is a worry that sociology has to deal with. It is not a defect of religion that it might cross boundaries. The only fault of the mutation and migration investigation to date is its incipient and hesitant nature. It carries with it a lack of conceptual advance to pinpoint what it is about popular culture that constitutes religion. Nancy Ammerman claims the project as teaching us 'new ways to think about religion'[23] but at bottom all those new ways turn out to be still one and the same way. They discover new boundaries but not new qualities. The sociology of religion has reached a dead end which will only be got out of by a theological breakthrough. The new ways to think about religion are not a sufficient antidote to stave off the debility brought on by the conceptual paralysis.

Ahern and Davie in a series of interviews carried out in the working-class district of Tower Hamlets tested out the concept of common or implicit religion, versus conventional religion. The work is interesting chiefly for the conceptual dead end which such investigation meets when equipped with the presupposition that religion is defined by assent to propositions about God. This defines from the outset that common religion will be a patchy and corroded reflection of conventional. The investigation set out with a mixture of suppositions, which, like Williams, extended the boundaries of the institutional territory. The tools of discernment used were the paraphernalia of life after death, baptism, carol singing, horoscopes, Jesus as the Son of God, civil religion, occult and magic and a rating scale for the importance of God. The result of the definitional assumptions is the inevitable conclusion. The work made a distinction between religion and superstition.[24] It found a diffuse theism which fell short of being Christian.[25]

Ahern seems to have been taken aback by the experience and showed a sense of the absurdity of the project. In retrospect he felt that the concept of 'belief' was a privilege of educated articulation inappropriately abstract for the working class. 'My most lasting impression of white working-class Tower Hamlets – and I think it pervades the account of what follows – is of the inappropriateness of the cultural concepts "belief and disbelief."'[26] Ahern was brought up short by the respondent who volunteered, 'I do believe in Christmas.'

Yet a glimpse of the religion of the people of Tower Hamlets was not completely absent from the work if definition by deed is adopted. One glimmer of this was the worry of financial embarrassment at the possibility of a vicar knocking at the door. 'Usually you decide... a collection. People usually haven't got the money to give them but they do, just out of the kindness of their hearts.'[27] The actual religion of these people could only be ascertained by, the probably impossible, means of an intellectual researcher wholly accepted into the community for a couple of years. The method of turning up with a tape recorder and a barrage of questions yielded only a pre-defined result.

Don Cupitt and Charles Taylor develop the same idea about popular culture from the theological and philosophical angles. Cupitt carried out an impromptu research project on everyday speech and discovered that 'Life' and 'It All' commonly substitutes what used to be God. He notes a person-centered religion in place of God centered and the sacralization of life in place of the sacralization of religion.[28] An example is the phrase, spoken in praise of a dead person, 'she loved life.' The phrase that that substitutes, 'she loved God' would today likely meet an embarrassed silence.[29] Cupitt is convinced that common speech has implicit in it a new secular religion and that ordinary language is generations ahead of the theologians.[30] He talks of the 'post ecclesiastical' stage of religion and elicits a series of 'structural resemblances' between the ethics of postmodernity and traditional Christianity.[31] He considers that Christianity has transcended itself into something greater.[32] This is the same claim as that of the Jesusologists, outlined in chapter four, that secularization is a fulfillment of Christianity. Cupitt's linguistic interest, his acute ear and his insistence on listening to our culture in action make his trilogy an escape from wooden presuppositions and a milestone in the advance of sociological investigation of religion.

Charles Taylor's massive and regretful philosophical investigation backs up some of the elements discovered by Cupitt.

Taylor identified humanist belief in self-success as arising out of and in many ways a continuation of Christianity, [33] Christian concepts as it were, without their Christian names. Taylor also spotted the affirmation of ordinary life as one of the greatest changes in outlook. He traced the sanctification of daily tasks originating as far back as the reformation divines and quotes the irresistible William Perkins:

> Now if we compare worke to worke, there is a difference betwixt washing of dishes, and preaching the word of God; but as touching to please God none at all... yea deeds of matrimonie are pure and spiritual... and whatsoever is done with the lawes of God though it be wrought by the body, as the wipings of shoes and such like, howsoever grosse they appeare outwardly yet they are sanctified.[34]

Perkins has effectively stated that the whole of life is religious and that religion is defined by what is done. That is, wiping snotty noses and washing of dishes uses our creative powers in the service of the lives of others. There is no separate sacred domain. Life is the sacred domain.

Taylor also theorized the 'expressivist turn' in the modern self.[35] He observed a new freedom, a 'new power of expressive self-articulation... the power which... leads to an even more radical subjectivism and an internalization of moral sources.'[36] Taylor added to this the new 'primacy of self-fulfillment.'[37] He is a great questioner of the suggestion that industrialization and rationalism is the explanation of 'loss of belief.'[38] Taylor's theorizing is fertile and I read him as a champion of the principle that religion has not disappeared but has metamorphosed. However, Taylor is a mourner for religion who would not go very far with this. He has a sense of the superiority of the lost theism over the replacement humanism[39] and concedes only a compromised validation to anything that might be determined as a new religious form.

Heelas and Woodhead adopt Taylor's subjective turn and confirm it as 'the defining cultural development of western culture.'[40] They make use of it to test the proposition that spirituality is taking over from religion, a project touched on in the preceding chapter. The subjective turn is used to define the difference between religion and spirituality. Being in touch with inward feelings about roles and the self are the new source of authority. On this basis Heelas and Woodhead set out for a fieldwork investigation of the churches and the holistic milieu of Kendal. One of the conclusions is that spirituality is relational orientated: 'many of those active in the milieu understand themselves to be developing the "me" of their lives by way of the "we" of the group and one-to-one encounters.'[41]

There are a number of intriguing aspects of this work. The holistic practitioners are all anarchists. The new dogma is that there is no dogma. 'I certainly don't have a fixed faith or dogma that I adhere to', 'we don't want to be something that we impose on somebody else.' The practice involves 'the client having a conversation with themselves.'[42] All practitioners emphasize serving the participants, helping, guiding, supporting, facilitating.

To take a view on this project it departs productively from the institutional definition of religion but runs into another institution. The holistic milieu may be more freeform and eclectic but it is composed of a variety of disciplines led by experts, a new priesthood of professionals in yoga, shiatsu, acupuncture, reflexology, etcetera. Spirituality is defined by acts of participation. On this basis the work is precluded from theorizing religion for all people. The young do not figure. Under thirties form less than one percent.[43] The clientele is eighty percent women.[44] Men are largely excluded. The working class fall out of the scheme altogether. The clientele is largely educated, has the money to pay for expensive services and the leisure time permitted by departure of children from the home. The authors propose that this may be the first religion organized by women. On the other hand the spirituality seems to be restricted to added value for educated older women. I do not at all wish to imply that this is not religion but only take account that the constituency is so restricted. This limitation of scope provides a useful pointer to the task to discover the social reality of religion. Whatever principle that turns out to be it must be qualified with a more comprehensive basis and freer access than this tiny exclusive world of spirituality.

To sum up, this survey of attempts to discover religion in popular culture all consider the possibility of transformation of the framework of religion and migration from the ecclesiastical umbrella. The conviction is that present day culture somehow comprises religion. That is the valuable conviction to be taken forward here.

I will not, however, be taking up the idea of secularized society as the fulfillment of Christianity. This validates the concept of secularization which I hope to dispose of. It also suggests some sort of completion of the religious task, something which can never be.

Cupitt and Taylor propose that ethics provides the synthesis between religion and today's culture. The purpose of religion does indeed provide ethical convergence and can synthesize the Christians, Platonists, Jesusologists, Christian Mystics, Humanists and other religions. The weakness in purpose as the basis of synthesis is that it is too vague to be informative. Theology well recognizes that the ethical standards of believers and atheists may be indistinguishable but separates the two on the basis of the operating program. What needs to be identified is the new program that operates the religious purpose today and then to prove its qualification as religious even though it appears to be 'secular.' A start on identifying that new operating program is made in the concept of the 'Super Ethic' and continues through the next two chapters.

9.2. The Super Ethic of Popular Culture

A starting point in the detective work to discover the new religious operating program is Durkheim's concept of mechanical solidarity. This has proved one of the lasting contributions to the theory of society. Durkheim proposed that there are two aspects of human relations that hold any society together. One aspect is organic solidarity. This is the division of labor. The theory of organic solidarity states that we have an interest in cooperation because of the beneficial complementarity of different skills. The farmer grows the food, the baker bakes the bread, the schoolteacher educates the children. We all need each other. Everyone benefits from this specialization of tasks. Life is much better than if we had to do everything ourselves. We have an interest in cooperation and that holds society together.

But that cohesive force is not enough. Durkheim proposes that in addition to this all societies are held together by a group identity. Every society has a sense of who it is, some sense of purpose, destiny, ancestral tradition, some sense of 'us', some sense of itself whatever that might be. This common framework of ideas holds the group together. If there is not a common framework, if there are for instance opposed frameworks, then the society will break up into smaller fragments or fight until some new common framework is established. The English and American civil wars are great examples of two competing frameworks of mechanical solidarity coming into violent collision. The partition of India after the departure of the British and the break-up of the Soviet Union with the end of Russian imperialism also illustrate the case. The current rash of civil wars that has broken out after or about the deposition of dictators is a contemporary example of the need for one common framework that everyone, or at least enough people, must believe in for the society to work. The striking feature of the deposition of these dictators is that they turn out to have been suppressing deep divisions and holding together by force societies that do not have mechanical solidarity.

The conclusion from these two forms of solidarity that Durkheim theorizes is that our common consent to what our society is about is the most important thing in holding it together. Of the various frameworks of consent that might serve to produce mechanical solidarity, religion is the one that has been almost exclusive. All early tribal societies have a religious basis. In many modern nations the national and religious bases are made to coincide. The pledge of allegiance to the American flag is an example. 'I pledge allegiance to the Flag of the United States of America and to the republic for which it stands, one nation under God, indivisible with liberty and justice for all.' The fact that religious operating programs are one of the prime sources of the fracture of societies is paradoxically proof of their power to hold them together.

Out of this cohesive feature of religion arises a prime clue to detecting the new religious operating program of our society. It is generally theorized that our society no longer has such a program. The theory goes that old ideas of religion have broken down. This means, if we accept the value of Durkheim's theory, that some other consent or group identity must be holding it together. The thesis that I am going to work with is that if we can identify what the new mechanical solidarity is, then that will turn out to be religious. It will turn out to be the new religious operating program.

There is a further dimension to the case that provides another detective clue. The prevalent analysis held by sociology is that in modern society mechanical solidarity is absent. The theory is that mechanical solidarity cannot work in a pluralist situation and that the society must in fact be being held together by some other means. This originates the 'holding the ring' theory of the state. Political theory tells us that the origin of the modern liberal state is rooted in the necessity to enforce discipline on the murderous rivalry of competing Christianities after the break-up of the Roman Catholic monopoly. The origin of this 'holding the ring' theory of the state can be traced to Luther's appeal to the German Princes for protection against Rome and the adjustment in French government after the Huguenot revolt.[45]

The perception is, therefore, not that the state is an embodiment of mechanical solidarity but that it is the enforcer holding the ring against breakdown. This holding purpose is perceived further to be reinforced by the extended dimension of religious and cultural pluralism that is a feature of today. Complementing this idea of breakdown the religious establishment likes to purvey the view that the collapse of religion brings the collapse of moral values and disintegration of the self. Collapse of standards was the successful formula for Billy Graham's mass conversions and the formula, in more intellectualized format, is still purveyed from the intellectual heights of the Anglican Church. Vernon White states the deconstruction of traditions and the broken consequences: the past is regret, the future is fear and the present is 'specious.'[46]

Bryan Turner is a sociologist proponent of this breakdown of mechanical solidarity. He theorizes a society held together by various controls. Turner's point of view unites social and political theory, the sociology of religion and the Anglican Church. 'Late capitalist societies are neither coherent nor integrated around a system of common values.'[47] Rowan Williams, for instance, adopts Turner and believes that 'Societies that are able to control their populations in such ways do not need the legitimization of "values"; they do not need myth or religion or morality.'[48]

What then are the controls in operation today proposed to hold our society together? Turner's theory is what I call the 'theory of materialist stupefaction.' It is a vaguely anti-capitalist argument that we have been bribed into submission. Capitalist marketing has convinced us that the pursuit of the latest product is the goal of life. Television renders us soporifically indifferent. The barrage of advertising continually pricks anxiety about getting the next new product. The effect of this is to override our cultural differences. The role of the state is that of supporting this capitalist machine.

It is not necessary to be taken in by stupefaction theory for two good reasons. Firstly the history of societies going through a process of fracture shows that material well-being is low in power of cohesion in comparison to the ideas. Where there is a dispute over consent the opposing parties have been prepared to watch the destruction of utilities and the reduction of the population to starvation rather than concede. Were material well-being really the power that stupefaction proposes then there would be no violent disputes. These disputes are always in potential absolutely destructive.

Secondly stupefaction theory is not really sociology. It is another case of theology speaking sociology. The Christian church is once again dictating what sociology is allowed to say. It has made sociology into the mouthpiece for propaganda about its own vision of itself. Stupefaction theory turns out to be the theory of secularization in disguise.

The church is out of touch if it thinks that values have broken down and that as a result people lead lives of meaninglessness and despair. It is religion itself that is in the dock today as the moral pariah. Far from Christianity being the upholder of a morality that has broken down, the situation is reversed. In 1975, with the exemption from the Sex Discrimination Act that it engineered, [49] the Church formalized its placement outside the new and superior ethic of the age. Christianity revealed itself as the backward and restraining influence spouting incomprehensible reasons for its opposition to the good. That judgment on Christianity is made from the position of the values of the society. That means that the society does in fact have in operation a strong set of values. It holds that women should be treated equally with regard to employment. It holds that people outside the heterosexual standard should be allowed to marry and adopt children. It holds that the church is an archaic force in holding out against this. It holds that religion itself is a divisive force and impediment to the realization of better human relations.

It is no great step from this acknowledgement of a strong set of values to pinpoint what the new basis of mechanical solidarity is for our society. The young people that I encounter do indeed have a vital set of values even though the underlying principle tends to be inarticulate. They celebrate each other's individuality and prize this as the contribution to the group. They have a strong sense of creating each other's lives. They have a strong sense of the demands and commitments of friendship and what it is to fail in these. They have an absolute sense of the sanctity of relationships and of what is manipulative and what is supportive in sexual relationships. They are honest, peaceful and purposely engaged in the progress, interest, adventure and excitement of the project of their own lives and those of their friends. They are open to relations with people of any culture and respectful of other people's cultural values. All this is outside the orbit of Christianity with which they do not wish to be associated and about which an impromptu opinion poll will yield a spectrum of viewpoints from polite embarrassment, irrelevance and oddity to positive fears of divisiveness and intolerance.

In working toward defining the inarticulated underlying ethic of these young people the generation must be approached from the perspective of its historical antecedents. In debates over the religious crisis of the sixties, much referral is still made to the ethical revolution of the sixties generation.[50] This is characterized by a group of issues; abortion, divorce, contraception, women's liberation, gay rights, anti-consumerism, anti-parental authority. It is rebellion, freedom, an undermining of the moral authority of the establishment and so by implication that of the church. What characterizes much of this is that it was negative because it was in opposition. It was a challenge to the establishment, a revolt, a counter-cultural freeing from restraint. What it is necessary to realize for a proper perspective on the ethic of today is that this was two generations ago.

Today's ethic is not wholly a continuation of the permissiveness of the sixties and seventies. The ethic has become mainstream. The freedoms battled for in the sixties are handed axiomatically to this generation. The counter-culture has become the culture. In doing so it is transformed into a positive creative injunction. It is no longer a negative revolt. The ethical environment has moved on from a negative sixties demolition of values to a constructive phase. As a further adjustment to our perspective it is also worth reworking the concepts of 'expressive individualism' and the 'subjective turn' that have been used to frame our understanding of post-war culture.[51] These have a tendency in the hands of Charles Taylor, speaking from his religious angle, to be tinged with a derogatory hint of selfishness and to be seen as anti-community. In fact all true individualism is demandingly reciprocal. This is the implication of the concept of psychosymbiosis introduced in the previous chapter.

To characterize the ethic of today it is *respect for the absolute autonomy and self-determined fulfillment of every person*. It is this that underlies the ongoing tornado of gender dissolution. This began as a freedom from gender restriction of women's personality but is now driving to its logical conclusion and cannot be stopped short of same sex marriages, adoption by same sex couples, women bishops, homosexual bishops and the first female and perhaps lesbian Archbishop of Canterbury. This latter would be an example of enlightenment which these young people would applaud. It is the ethic of respect for autonomy that makes Britain and London in particular, the culture that it is and has accelerated its multicultural attraction. It is this ethic that provides the commitment of each individual to the society. It is this ethic that forms the new mechanical solidarity and the basis of political goals. For shorthand reference I name this ethic the *Super Ethic*. 'Super' because it is practiced by these young people as synoptic of the different ancient religions that have traditionally embodied the ethic.

This Super Ethic welds pluralism into a cohesive force. Our commitment to the society is reciprocal. The solidarity is that everyone should be free to fulfill their lives in their own way. This is the new mechanical solidarity of today's society. Pluralism has been taken by sociology to be the cause of breakdown of mechanical solidarity but it has missed the paradox of cohesive commitment to pluralism. Linda Woodhead's research confirms the great extent of this principle. She finds a 'significant liberal consensus.' There is agreement by 90% of the population of Great Britain that 'individuals should be free to make up their own minds how they live their own lives... most people not only believe that when it comes to important decisions about their own life they themselves should be allowed to decide them, rather than some higher authority, but that people should be treated fairly and on the basis of equal human dignity.'[52]

9.3. The Religious Character of the Super Ethic

This Super Ethic is disqualified as a religious principle under the present conceptual apparatus because of the impediment of the metaphysical remnant. The super ethic does not say anything about the universe as a whole. It arises solely from within the conditions of human relationships. It is classed as a secular principle. Robert Bellah, for instance, would describe it as 'purely utilitarian.' To Peter Berger it would be a 'triviality' that needs to be reset within metaphysics if it is to have religious status.[53]

I want to show that the super ethic is a fully religious principle. Respect for the autonomy of other persons is a supremely religious principle that is already embodied in the scripture, in one powerful example of Christian practice and in the concept of God itself. What is afoot in this respect for the autonomy of others is a negation of authority of one person over another. The ethic states that no coercive authority exercised over the individual is legitimate. That is to say that institutional or personal exclusion on the basis of ethnic, sexual, class, physical, linguistic or other discrimination must be eliminated. This extends to cultural restraints over, for instance, marriage partners or careers. It goes further than this and extends to the inequality of resources that underlie the coercive power or advantage of one person over another. Above all it implements the rule that every person is considered to be of equal value in their contributory potential to the society and to the creation of other people's lives. The moral rule that implements this ethic is 'no authority of one person over another.' We already possess the name and reference material for this ideology of the rule of no authority in human relations: it is Anarchism. The principle of the Super Ethic and its binding cultural force is Anarchism. To state the mechanical solidarity of our society in one word it is *Anarchism*. This is the key to the synergy of the religious and the supposedly secular basis of community.

It is an unfortunate fact that, excepting students of political theory, Anarchism as a cohesive social force will seem a contradiction because the name is associated in the general imagination with mindless destruction. There is then a necessary task of habilitating the history of this peaceful philosophy of human relations before its religious identity can be accepted. That task, just as with the Apocalypse, would ideally be based on a full scale work to provide ready reference. But there is no such work on which to rely so it is necessary in the next two chapters to habilitate Anarchism as a religious principle. The reader may be more easily able to bring their mind round to this fact of Anarchism as religion if it is re-named for what it is, the Religion of the Authority of No Authority. The place to begin the demonstration that Anarchism is religious is with the Christians who practice this religion.

10

God in the Christian Practice of the Authority of No Authority

10.1. The Religion of the Authority of No Authority

The assertion that God is a representation of the ideal potential of human relationships needs further exposition to bring out its character as a fully-fledged religion. To begin with the assertion lacks any content that would tell us what that ideal is. We have reached the point of sophistication today when any such statement as 'the ideal potential of human relationships' is automatically met with the question, whose version of the ideal potential? Past history shows that Christianity has been a male defined version of the ideal. The general ethic of our new definition of God needs to be complemented by a specific goal that constitutes that ideal potential. In this we are presented with the task of specifying the ethic and its companion articulation that was rehearsed in the examination of the Apocalypse. What is our definition of the ideal potential of human relationships? What is our definition of God that fulfills qualities number one and two needed for the twenty-first century?: A God without cultural restriction, which is not exclusive and which is a concept believable by atheists? What moral rules would articulate the fulfillment of that ideal?

To anticipate the answers that are in development here the ethical ideal is the *self-chosen self fulfillment* of the person. The moral that articulates this is *respect* for the autonomy of all persons. That is to say that it is not a self-fulfillment governed by the authority of others. This is the fundamental ethical scheme of the Religion of the Authority of No Authority.

This moral of respect for autonomy has already been elicited as the essence of the basis on which persons become persons. It has also been elicited as the basis of today's Super Ethic. So far, under the dominion of the current conceptual scheme, this moral would be considered a secular and not a religious principle. I want to show that it is fully a religious principle by cross-referencing it now with its place in Christian practice and its embodiment in the concept of God.

Some discussion of changing ethics is appropriate at this point. It is a common misconception that ethics have fixed content. The word ethical suffers from the same sort of abuse as the word quality. Quality is a neutral noun that does not of itself inform us whether any particular article is of good or bad quality. Yet adverts of the type that offer 'quality merchandise' make the assumption that quality here refers to good quality and not bad. An ethic is a goal to be achieved. It is not necessarily good or bad. It is, though, always considered to be good *because it is a goal that we have chosen as good.*

However, there is nothing to prevent someone else deciding that our ethic is bad. The ethic of one age, once thought good, may easily be overturned by another age which considers it bad. By way of example, one of the examination questions faced by students of the Hebrew Bible is, does the Hebrew Bible advocate ethical behavior? That is a poser when the book recounts so much rampaging genocide orchestrated by God. The resolution of the problem is that the Hebrew Bible is indeed a model of ethical behavior, *but it is a different ethic from ours today.* The ethic of the Hebrew Bible is that of tribal prosperity. This is measured by fertile lands, perpetuation of male lineage and protection of male honor. The fruition of this ethic is guaranteed by the correct worship of God. This ethic produces different standards of conduct from what we would consider ethical today. As illustration, Onan is struck dead for the failure to inseminate Tamar, his dead brother's wife and thus perpetuate his brother's lineage.[1] Uzza is struck dead for accidentally stumbling against the Ark of the Covenant and endangering the respect due to the deity.[2] Saul is removed from his Kingship for moderating God's murderous instructions in favor of a touch of humanitarian behavior.[3] Saul broke the ethic of tribal leadership which requires unquestioned obedience to the tribal head. The bloody revenge of Dinah's honor by Simeon and Levi is met with Jacob's mild reprimand that they have caused the inconvenience of a bad name for him.[4] Male possession of female honor stands higher than the slaughter of the inhabitants of a whole town. The ethic of the Hebrew Bible is not the same ethic of our society today which is the autonomous self-fulfillment of the individual. We believe that society exists for the benefit of the individual. There is no hint of any of this in the Hebrew Bible.

If the word ethic does not automatically specify the content of the goal to be achieved neither does it automatically inform us how it is best implemented. The discussion of the Apocalypse in chapter one brought out the differences of opinion and the difficulty of ascertaining, what would constitute the eventual revelation of God's justice. It also showed up ethically driven changes to what might be accepted to constitute that revelation. Eternal hellfire was once generally accepted. Today universal salvation is more in favor. That discussion rehearsed the fact that every ethic must be given practical articulation in the set of moral rules that would implement it. The conclusion to be drawn from this with regard to God as 'the ideal potential of human relationships' is that the articulation just as much as the content of the ethic is up for discussion. This is not a God that relies on privilege. It is a God intended to stand up to any interrogation and fulfill quality number four set out in the introduction.

If the identification of the social reality of God is to crystallize in these last three chapters into the full dimensions of a religion, we need to settle the content of the ethic and the means of its articulation. The proposal that 'the ideal potential' of psychosymbiosis represents God needs qualifying to be of service. One disadvantage of this definition is that it is ambiguous to ideal personal relations and to ideal political relations such as socialism. I want to exclude political relationships, which are indirect personal relationships, from the subject matter of the religious domain. The full explanation of this exclusion cannot be achieved till the end of chapter twelve. For the time being I want to emphasize the direct person to person creative enterprise of the religious domain which is what makes it inclusive of all persons. To refine the definition of the ethic with this distinction in mind, God is 'the ideal potential of the psychosymbiotic *creative power of the self-fulfillment of persons in relationship to one another.'*

With that definition as the ethic it is now necessary to state the articulation. I propose that *respect* for the autonomous self-fulfillment of other people, identified in chapter nine as the Super Ethic of our culture, is the articulation. This respect is by no means the whole of the articulation or by any manner its detailed fulfillment. It needs a set of virtues to make the ethical scheme complete. But respect for autonomy is the fundamental precondition of implementing the ethic. For example, mutual respect is the basis of friendship. Within the framework of friendship all manner of creative activity can occur. To state the opposite of this articulation, relationships of domination, exploitation, the exercise of power in the use of one person to the service of another person cannot articulate the ethic.

It is a distinct feature of the Super-Ethic present in today's culture that it operates on an ad hoc basis without theoretical articulation. It is an impromptu cultural movement. It is not theorized as religion. It simply operates as a practical religion. The great good of autonomy is taken to be its ethic. This contradicts my theoretical framework in which autonomy is not the ethic but its articulation. I want, however, to impose that frame because it is helpful to display the structure of the ethical system involved.

The following three-part structure is set in place. The ethic, God, is the ideal potential of psychosymbiotic creative power of persons in relation to one another. The moral rule, the articulation of the ethic, is realized by respect and assistance to the autonomous fulfillment of other persons. The virtue, the actual implementation of the moral rule, the religious practice, is the activity of applying the moral on a daily basis.

Relating this scheme to the bipartite aspect of religion as purpose and operating program what is established in this three-part structure is a program that operates the purpose. The faith of this religion, just as with any religion, is that adherence to the program will yield the beneficial result intended by the purpose. It is indeed an act of faith. There is no guarantee that respect for the autonomy of others will be reciprocated. It is an act of faith in a vision. It is a vision that such behavior can and must be implemented in face of the disastrous negative potential in human relations.

The testimony of Kathleen Lonsdale is an example of witness to that difficult faith:

I have sometimes been asked what were my reasons for deciding on that refusal to register for war duties that sent me to Holloway Jail 22 years ago. I can only answer that my reason told me that I was a fool, that I was risking my job and my career, that an isolated example could do no good, that it was a futile gesture since even if I did register my three small children would exempt me. But reason was fighting a losing battle. I had wrestled in prayer and I knew beyond all doubt that I *must* refuse to register, that those who believed that war was the wrong way to fight evil must stand out against it however much they stood alone.[5]

The engine room of this religion, its vision that serves the same function as the Platonist Forms and the Christian Apocalypse, is respect for the autonomous fulfillment of other persons. The vision and faith of this religion is the 'Authority of No Authority.'

10.2. The Religious Nature of Respect for Autonomy

The connection between pacifism and respect for autonomy is not always made. The testimony of Kathleen Lonsdale may well have puzzled the reader as to its relevance. The relevance is that the refusal to return violence is a strong form of respect for the autonomy of others. Even though those others may wrongly harm us with evil intent, pacifism respects that. Absolute refusal to return violence, to the extent that one is prepared to lose one's life for the principle, is absolute respect for the autonomy of others. Pacifism embodies disdain for one's life if it cannot be lived in accordance with this religious principle. This is the teaching of Jesus. 'Do not fear those who kill the body but cannot kill the soul; rather fear him who can destroy both soul and body in hell' (Matthew 10.28). It is the faithful adherence to this principle that founds admiration for Jesus who gave up his life even though he might at any moment have saved it by calling on violence. Jesus is a great respecter of the autonomy of others. As reported by Matthew 5.38 Jesus commands, 'You have heard it said, "An eye for an eye and a tooth for a tooth." But I say to you, do not resist an evildoer. But if anyone strikes you on the right cheek, turn the other also; and if anyone wants to sue you and take your coat, give your cloak as well; and if anyone forces you to go one mile, go also the second mile.'

Robert Barclay, an early Quaker took up the scriptural basis for the non-violence:

> Whoever can reconcile this, 'resist not evil', with 'resist
> violence by force', again, 'Give also thy other cheek', with
> 'Strike again'; also 'love thine enemies', with 'Spoil them,
> make a prey of them, pursue them with fire and sword', or
> 'pray for those that persecute you, and those that calumniate
> you' with 'persecute them by fines, imprisonments and death
> itself', whoever, I say, can find a means to reconcile these
> things may be supposed also to have found a way to reconcile
> God with the Devil, Christ with Antichrist, Light with
> Darkness and good with evil.[6]

The idea that Jesus meant what he said and that Christianity has
discarded the message was resoundingly proclaimed by Leo
Tolstoy. Tolstoy is the eloquent exponent of the religious basis of
non-violence. His towering literary reputation tends to
overshadow his work as an interpreter of Christianity which he
took up as a serious, almost obsessive, enterprise. After finishing
Anna Karenina, at the age of fifty and at the height of his fame,
Tolstoy suffered a depression and crisis of doubt about the
meaning of his life. To cure this he undertook a thorough investigation, lasting seven years, of the Christianity he had been
brought up in. He re-translated the gospels with commentaries,
and wrote a number of religious works; *An Examination of
Dogmatic Theology, What I Believe, A Confession* and *The Kingdom of
God is Within You*.

Tolstoy considered the doctrine of non-violence the key to the
gospel teaching. He took as his guiding principle the command of
Jesus given in Matthew 10.28. Tolstoy's primary complaint
against the Church is that it has accommodated itself to approve
violence in its support of the state and its armies. The principle of
non-violence has so much disappeared or remains dormant in
Christianity that it is worth recounting Tolstoy's voyage of redis-

covery as a reminder of its centrality to religion. The following shortened passage has been pieced together from the lengthy preface to *The Kingdom of God is Within You*:

> Among the many points in which this doctrine [of the Church] falls short of the doctrine of Christ I pointed out as the principal one the absence of any commandment of non-resistance to evil by force. The perversion of Christ's teaching is more clearly apparent in this than in any other point of difference... I have told why I formerly did not understand Christ's teaching, and how and why I have now understood it.... ... ... It was... an instantaneous illumination by the light of truth. It was an occurrence such as might befall a man who, by the guidance of a wrong drawing, was vainly seeking to reconstruct something from a confused heap of small bits of marble, if he suddenly guessed from the largest piece that it was quite a different statue from what he had supposed, and having started to reconstruct it, instead of the former incoherence of the pieces he saw a confirmation of his belief in every piece... I found the key to Christ's teaching, which revealed to me the truth with a clearness and assurance that excluded all doubt.
>
> This discovery was made thus. Since I first read the Gospels for myself when almost a child, what touched and affected me most of all was Christ's teaching of love, meekness, humility, self-sacrifice, and repayment of good for evil. Such always was for me the essence of Christianity. But... the Church repelled me by the strangeness of her dogmas and her acceptance and approval of persecutions, executions and wars. But what shattered my trust in the Church was just her indifference to what seemed to me the essence of Christ's teaching... Was it possible that the teaching of Christ was such that these contradictions were inevitable? I could not believe it... And so, after many, many, vain seekings and

studyings... ... I understood that Christ says just what he says... it is quite impossible not to admit that Christ said very clearly and definitely just what he meant to say... 'Resist not him that is evil' means 'never resist him that is evil.' ...suddenly, for the first time I understood this verse simply and directly... He says: Do not resist him that is evil, and while doing this know in advance that you may meet people who, having struck you on one cheek and not met resistance, will strike you on another.[7]

This absolute respect for autonomy is a principle exceedingly difficult to implement for anyone but a passionate idealist. It is impossible that human society could be organized on a basis of non-violence. It only takes one person to destroy that basis. It would always result in the wolves eating the sheep. As Machiavelli pointed out it is a dereliction of duty for the Prince not to use violence because that is the requirement of stable government which is the only security against warring bandit fiefdoms. But it is right here in the tension between the visionary and the rational that we encounter the energizing principle essential to religion. Non-violence is both a fabulous ideal for human relations and it is, should we have a mind so to spurn it with a dose of cold logic, fabulously irrational. The religious and visionary status of absolute respect for autonomy is confirmed by the opposition to it of politically accommodated Christianity. Tolstoy was met with stunned disbelief from the commentators. Aylmer Maude, his translator, fought him every inch of the way in a series of footnotes. He calls Tolstoy's belief,

As gross a superstition as any of those he attacks. If his theory be right (and he claims for it Christ's authority) nothing can, and nothing should, save our industrial, political, or national existence from destruction... there is no logical escape from the ultimate conclusion that any Government using force, all compulsory law, all police, and all protection of life or property is immoral. ...Even if Christ meant what Tolstoy says he meant, if this conflicts, as it does, with our reason, conscience and experience of life, it is still our duty to reject it.[8]

T.N. Rogers, introducing the Dover edition of *The Kingdom of God is Within You* explained more mildly, 'For churches and governments and Christians in general, it has been a hard message to stomach; it is much easier to ignore it, or to assume that Jesus didn't really mean it.'[9]

Pacifism is the extreme limit of respect for the autonomy of others. Although it may be fundamental it is called upon exceptionally. It does not constitute the day to day work of respecting the autonomy of other people as expressed in their beliefs, sexual orientation and cultural prejudices. It is this arena that forms the core religious practice of one determined group in Christianity and consideration of the practice of this group is useful to illustrate the dimensions of the religious ideal.

10.3. The Authority of No Authority in Christian Practice

The bravest attempt to implement the authority of no authority in Christian practice has been that of the Religious Society of Friends, popularly known as the Quakers. This is a small part of Christianity but the small sample cannot be taken as evidence of weakness in the practice. The exemplary influence of the Friends should not be underestimated.

The principle of respect for the autonomy of other people has been framed as an articulation derivative from the ethical principle. That principle in the case of Friends is the equal value of all persons. This is an alternative way to state the ideal of the self-chosen, self-fullfillment of every person. It is the equal value of all persons that founds the practice of the Society. That this is the religious ideal principle of human relationships is indicated by the fact that it is the fundamental principle embodied in the concept of the Community God. Equality is encapsulated by the absolute value of every soul, utterly without discrimination, to the God that made it. To God every person is of equal value. The equality is reflexive as given in the statement that we are all made in the image of God. By extension to each other of the relationship to God each one of us must treat every other person as an equal.

The Quaker formula states this reflexive equality in God. There is 'that of God' in every person. To quote from the society's yearbook:

> Do you respect that of God in everyone though it may be expressed in unfamiliar ways or be difficult to discern? Each of us has a particular experience of God and each must find the way to be true to it.[10*] At the centre of Friends' religious experience is the repeatedly and consistently expressed belief in the fundamental equality of all members of the human race. Our common humanity transcends our differences. Friends have worked individually and corporately to give expression to this belief. We aspire not to say or do anything or condone any statements or actions which imply lack of respect for the humanity of any person. We try to free ourselves from assumptions of superiority and from racial prejudice.[11]

To consider human equality for a moment as a fact of human existence instead of a principle of behavior, there is nothing more perfectly equal than the absolute dependence of a selection of new-born babies. There is nothing more perfectly equal than our biological equality before the chance elements of disease, fate and death. How is it that one of those babies might turn out to exploit the others? It is the economic and political structures of human existence that intervene to break this primordial equality.

The practice of the Friends is to refuse the structures and see through them to the equality. There is no more poignant expression of this than the instructions for the erection of gravestones:

> Friends are left at liberty to adopt the use of plain gravestones in any burial grounds; it being distinctly understood that, in all cases, they are to be erected under the direction of the monthly meeting; so that, in each particular burial ground, such uniformity is preserved in respect to the materials, size, form and wording of the stones, as well as in the mode of placing them, as may effectually guard against any distinction being made in that place between rich and poor.[12]

This can be contrasted with the tombs of kings that adorn the cathedrals of the culturally accommodated churches. It can be left to the reader to decide which of these practices represents a true religious spirit.

The bravest and most difficult tenet of Quaker faith in equality and the accompanying respect for autonomy is the commitment to non-violence and refusal of military service. The Quaker Yearbook devotes an extensive section to recording the history of 'Our peace testimony.'

The peace testimony is probably the best known and the best loved of the Quaker testimonies. Its roots lie in the personal experience of the love and power of Christ which marked the founders of the Quaker movement... Friends sought to make the vision real by putting emphasis on Christian practice rather than primarily on any particular dogma or ideological system. Theirs was a spontaneous and practical religion. They recognized the realities of evil and conflict, but it was contrary to the spirit of Christ to use war and violence as a means to deal with them.[13]

Fox recorded the principle in action in an incident in Scarborough Castle:

There were amongst the prisoners, two very bad men, that often sat drinking with the officers and soldiers; and because I would not drink with them too, it made them the worse against me. One time when these two prisoners were drunk, one of them came to me and challenged me to fight with him. Seeing what condition he was in, I got out of his way; and next morning, when he was more sober, showed him how unmanly it was in him to challenge a man to fight, whose principles, he knew, it was not to strike, but if he was stricken on one ear to turn the other. I told him that if he had a mind to fight, he should have challenged some soldiers that could have answered him in his own way. But, however, seeing he had challenged me, I was now come to answer him with my hands in my pockets; and (reaching my head towards him), 'Here', said I, 'here is my hair, here are my cheeks, here is my back.' With this he skipped away and went to another room; at which the soldiers fell a-laughing; and one of the officers said, 'You are a happy man that can bear such things.'[14]

The peaceful principle was formulated in a declaration to Charles II, in 1660:

Our principle is, and our practices have always been, to seek peace, and ensue it, and to follow after righteousness and the knowledge of God, seeking the good and welfare, and doing that which tends to the peace of all. All bloody principles and practices we do utterly deny, and all outward wars, and strife and fightings with outward weapons, for any end, or under any pretence whatsoever, and this is our testimony to the whole world.[15]

The principle was one severely tested in the abuse of Friends by their fellow culturally accommodated Christians:

But it was a time of great sufferings; for, besides imprison-
ments through which many died, our meetings were greatly
disturbed. They have thrown rotten eggs and wild fire into
our meetings, and brought in drums beating, and kettles to
make noises with that the Truth might not be heard; and
among these, the priests were as rude as any, as may be seen
in the book of fighting priests, wherein a list is given of some
priests that had actually beaten and abused friends.[16]

In Bristol, on 7th July 1682,

They dispersed the meeting which then consisted mostly of
children; for the men and women generally being in prison,
the children kept up the meetings regularly and with
remarkable gravity and composure... On the 30th, in the
afternoon, about fifty five were at the meeting, when Helliar,
with twisted whalebone stock, beat many of them unmerci-
fully, striking them violent blows on their heads, necks and
faces, few of them escaping without some marks of his fury.[17]

The great gift of Quaker faith to the investigation of what
religion is, as flagged in the introduction, is that the very specific
social practices inform us exactly what the 'inner light' is. These
social practices are the refusal of 'hat honor', the adoption of
plain dress, and the refusal of the hierarchical form of address
'you' in place of the familiar thee and thou. The common factor
of these practices is that they refuse the structural/cultural
distortions of the biological and spiritual equality of all persons.
The King in this religion is no different a person from the pauper.
The inner light is a vision of the equality of all persons. The fact
that these quite mild samples of rebellion strike at the heart of
the pretensions of society is displayed in the paroxysms of
apoplexy that they provoked in their fellow Christians.

The custom of 'hat honor' formed in seventeenth-century

society a daily acknowledgement of the most intricate gradations of social status. In any encounter each person gauged their personal status in relation to the other and the inferior party had to initiate the acknowledgement by raising their hat. Just as in the Japanese custom of bowing to superiors it was possible to convey, in the manner in which it was done, a variety of attitudes from exaggerated respect to calculated insult but omission was not an option and the formality itself was rigidly observed. George Fox recounted in his journal an incident of the rage which this refusal of hierarchy set off:

> Then... the Judge fell upon us about our hats again, bidding the jailer take them off; which he did, and gave them to us; and we put them on again. Then we asked the Judge and the justices, for what cause we had lain in prison these nine weeks, seeing they now objected to nothing but our hats. And as for putting off our hats, I told them that that was the honour which God would lay in the dust, though they made such ado about it; the honour which is of men, and which men seek from one another, and is a mark of unbelievers. For 'How can ye believe,' saith Christ, 'who receive honour one from another, and seek not the honour that comes from God only?' Christ saith, 'I receive not honour from men'; and all true Christians should be of His mind.[18]

Quakers also negated the conventional hierarchy of address in the refusal to address superiors with the formal 'you' but only the familiar thou or thee. The young Thomas Ellwood reported the trouble that he got into for refusing 'the vain salutations of the world.'

> The sight of my hat upon my head made [my father] presently forget that I was that son of his, whom he had so lately lamented as lost; and his passion of grief turning into anger,

he could not contain himself; but running upon me, with both his hands, first violently snatcht off my hat, and threw it away; then giving me some buffets on my head, he said Sirrah, get you up to your chamber… But whenever I had occasion to speak to my father, though I had no hat now to offend him, yet my language did as much; for I durst not say 'You' to him; but 'Thou' or 'Thee', as the occasion required, and then he would be sure to fall on me with his fists.[19]

Plain dress was another refusal of the displays of social hierarchy to which clothing gives opportunity. Thomas Chalkley recorded his suffering from plain dress:

When between eight and ten years of age, my father and mother sent me near two miles to school, to Richard Scoryer, in the suburbs of London. I went mostly by myself to school; and many and various were the exercises I went through, by beatings and stonings along the streets, being distinguished to the people (by the badge of plain-ness which my parents put upon me) of what profession I was; divers telling me, 'Twas no more sin to kill me, that it was to kill a dog.[20]

To sum up these social practices of the Friends, the program that operates the religious purpose is the equal value of all persons. The Friends do not use my terminology of the authority of no authority, nor do they adopt the name Anarchists but that is what the Friends are. The Society of Friends is the Religion of Anarchism. It is a distinctive feature of this religion, relevant to earlier discussion of the metaphysical remnant, that it is independent of any metaphysics. The principle of the equality of all persons is a self-sufficient religious principle that stands up in its own right. It might be brought in evidence against this under-standing that the Friends adopt the bible and Christian language and are therefore within the metaphysical umbrella. Against this it can be said that the scriptures are subordinated to the principle of equality, the inner light that inspired them. There is for the Friends no authoritative metaphysical text.

Fox tells us this in his account of the outburst to which he was inspired in a church in Nottingham. A priest after giving his sermon,

> Told the people that this was the Scriptures, by which they were to try all doctrines, religions, and opinions. Now the Lord's power was so mighty upon me, and so strong in me, that I could not hold, but was made to cry out and say, 'Oh no; it is not the Scriptures!' and I told them what it was, namely the Holy Spirit, by which the holy men of God gave forth the Scriptures, whereby opinions, religions and judgements were to be tried, for it led into all truth.[21*]

The strict adherence to scriptural anarchism allows the Friends to achieve that most difficult feat, an organization without dogma. The only dogmatic element is that there should be no dogma:

> Remember that we do not seek a majority decision nor even a consensus. As we wait patiently for divine guidance our experience is that the right way will open and we shall be led to unity.[22] Friends call themselves 'seekers after truth.' To whatever she always feels the insufficiency of their understanding and fulfilment of it, and is always striving to a fuller understanding and fulfilment. And therefore, to assert of one's self or any body of men, that one is or they are in possession of perfect understanding and fulfilment of Christ's word, is to renounce the very spirit of Christ's teaching.[23]

Another result of the consistent Anarchism is that it renders religious institution a contradiction in terms. The institution of a church falls within the ambit of human cultural structures which inevitably create the hierarchies that contradict the equality of all persons. There is a strong sense in both Fox and Tolstoy of a religious complaint against religious institution. Fox disdains 'church faith' and refers to 'The apostasy that hath got up since the Apostle's days.'[24] The Friends organize their church on a minimalist basis. There is more to be said on the definition of a church and the tension with its institutional form in chapter twelve.

The result of this consistent Anarchism, scriptural, dogmatic and institutional is that the Society of Friends is a model of the principle that religion is what is done not what is believed. There is in this doing an admirable record in the forefront of the struggle against slavery, in pacifism and in social and humanitarian projects. The Friends have an exemplary understanding that it is the programs of religion that themselves have a tendency, by causing division, to contradict the religious purpose they aim to operate. It is this doing not believing that has caused an ironic difficulty for the Society in its role as member of the World Council of Churches. The irony is an example of program contradicting purpose. The Friends are naturally ecumenical with practical openness to other faiths. The advice given in the Yearbook to Friends living in places where there is no meeting is, 'We do not desire in any way to discourage those from associating in worship with members of other religious denominations.'[25] One verse notes 'the belief that the same God known through Christianity is also present in other faiths. The study of other faith positions is therefore important, not only for its own sake, but as a contribution towards humility before the mystery of faith.'[26] The World Council has an ecumenical purpose. Its method of achieving this is to establish the lowest common denominator agreed statement of doctrine. The Friends cannot agree to the principle that faith can be enshrined in a doctrine.[27] The ironical result of this is that the most ecumenical of churches was excluded from the ecumenical process and offered non-voting associate membership.[28]

It is on account of these non-scriptural, non-dogmatic, non-institutional, non-exclusive, non-metaphysical characteristics that I take the Friends to be the permeable transitional boundary between traditional Christian faith and the Super Ethic of today's culture. The correspondences between today's inarticulate religious culture and the religion of the Friends is such that the Super Ethic may be said to have re-invented Quakerism without recognizing it.

To conclude the point of this chapter, respect for the autonomy of others is not a secular principle. It is the fundamental religious principle enshrined in Christianity.

11

God in the Religious Vision of Political Anarchism

11.1. Introduction
11.2. A Sketch of Political Anarchism
11.3. Political Anarchism is a Religious Vision

11.1. Introduction

The moral of respect for autonomy has so far been elicited in the formation of the human person, in the super ethic of today's culture and in Christian practice. The attempt has been to show how perverse our present conceptual apparatus is to posit the same principle as secular in the first two cases but religious in the third. Consideration of the moral of respect for autonomy continues with the same moral found in Political Anarchism. Here we reach a climax of equivocation between the classification of the moral as secular or religious. The Political Anarchists are enthusiastic atheists. Their self-understanding is that theirs is a secular movement. All commentators, however, consider Political Anarchism to be a religious vision.

The sporadic Anarchism that presents itself today is a faint echo of a once glorious dream. Those smashers of property, those agents provocateur that hijack peaceful demonstrations are the remnant of a movement that came to a categorical end in the Spanish Civil War. Political Anarchism is a lost cause that will never be revived. In practical terms it is impossible. Why would I even ask the reader to consider Political Anarchism?

It is the combination of visionary status with practical impossibility that puts Political Anarchism in the same class as the Kingdom of God and the Platonist Forms. Political Anarchism is a vision. It is not necessary for a religious vision to be rational or practical to have an inspirational driving effect on the creative energies of the believer. In fact I would go so far as to say that any religion *must* be both visionary and impractical. If it were capable of practical fulfillment it would long ago have removed the grounds for its existence. How uninspiring religion would be if it were certain of achieving its goals. Nothing but wonderful visions can evoke the stirring power that is religious belief. Political Anarchism is just such a vision.

Both the Apocalypse and Plato's Forms were described as the engine rooms of their respective religions. At the same time they were both considered 'irrational.' With regard to the Apocalypse, in realistic terms there is not going to be a comprehensive readjustment of the moral deficit of human existence at the end of time. The Kingdom of God is a vision. With regard to the Forms, in realistic terms an alternative perfect world does not exist. The ideal real world is a vision. The engine room of Political Anarchism is a vision of a new society free of oppressive authority. There is, however, a distinction of profound consequence between the Apocalyptic Kingdom of God and the Forms on one hand and Anarchism on the other. With the Apocalypse and the Forms the vision is removed to a different plane of existence, respectively a future plane and a metaphysical plane. Anarchism wishes to implement the vision *here and now*. It is ready to smash the repressive forces that bar the way to the vision. That is where the trouble starts.

I will not be suggesting that we become Political Anarchists. I want to propose that a Religious Anarchism, that is Anarchism in the relationship between persons, the Authority of No Authority, constitutes a religious vision driven by Political Anarchism. I will not fully be able to characterize this until the distinction between the religious and the political domains is drawn in the last chapter. Nor will I till then be able to state why Political Anarchism and the Christians are in exact agreement about the nature of 'evil', the nature of the oppressive structures that they oppose. For the time being suffice it to say that this Religious Anarchism is already constituted as a religion. It was identified in the practice of the Society of Friends and I identify it as the as yet inarticulated religious basis of the Super Ethic of today's culture.

This authority of no authority draws together a fundamental feature of the Community God with the new 'secular' religion of today. It thus provides the necessary element of continuity with the old religion and at the same time states the discontinuity. This continuity fulfills quality number three stated in the introduction that the new God for the twenty-first century must not really be new but must embody something centrally important in the old God. The continuity is that the practical content of this new religion is the same as the practical content of the old. The discontinuity is trivial in comparison with the continuity. The discontinuity is only that the authority of this religion has been transferred from a metaphysical basis to an internal basis. The 'authority of no authority' is a principle self-sufficient in its authority. This is an example of the reflexive principle in operation in Social Theology. An unexpected fact emerges. There is very good reason that the anarchist principle should be personalized and hypostasized in the concept of God. Were the command that there should be no authority between humans to come from a human source it would constitute a self-contradiction. Only an authority external to human relations can make that command. This basis in an internal authority fulfills condition four, stated in the introduction, for a new vision of God for the twenty-first century. That God must freely stand up to any interrogation and not attempt to rest on privileged metaphysical ground.

What I hope to bring out in the following pages is that Political Anarchism and the Christians speak the same language. They speak the same purpose of religion operated by different programs. The stage has come to propose that the identical principles that appear disguised in the three different garments of the Christian, the Political Anarchist and the Super Ethic of today's culture fulfill all four of the qualities required of the new vision of God.

The mere name Anarchism, just as the Apocalypse, is apt to provoke alarm. It is necessary in view of the alarm to retrieve the reputation of Anarchism. This is best done through a brief historical and theoretical presentation which follows. To give an overview in anticipation, the history of communism, of which Anarchism is part, is a history of tragedy. It is tragedy in the true sense of progression to inevitable results that can be foretold from the originating situation. With our hindsight of one hundred and fifty years we know the disaster of state communism. But we have forgotten the counter theme to that tragedy which was revolution from the bottom up instead of revolution from the top down. To understand the nature of that glorious dream it is necessary to make a mind switch back to the years before the Russian revolution. In those years the possible constitution of the new society that would arise from the defeat of capitalist powers was a ferment of visionary excitement. If it were permissible to remove the word from its Christian meaning that ferment was a truly 'apocalyptic' excitement about the friendly possibilities of human nature free of the grinding oppression of property and the capitalist market. A devolved society of local empowerment and spontaneous cooperation was the vision. The two actors in the tragedy knew the score perfectly. Marx knew that without rigorous organization to effect the takeover of state power there would be no revolution. Michael Bakunin knew that any such revolution would be no revolution at all. It would only repeat the structure of a repressive elite running society. So it turned out.

11.2. A Sketch of Political Anarchism

Anarchism in America got a bad name for violence the day that twenty-one-year-old Alexander Berkman (1870-1936) walked into the office of the American steel baron, Henry Frick, intending to kill him. Berkman was a mild mannered, intellectual young man with a burning sense of injustice being done to others, the sort of terrorist that could be fostered in any comfortable home. The date was July 22nd 1892 and the occasion, the strike at the Homestead Steel Works near Pittsburg. Frick, together with his boss, Andrew Carnegie, had completed their maneuvers to monopolize American steel production and were now engaged in breaking the incipient power of organized labor. That organization achieved a new focus during the 1870s with the demand for an eight-hour day. The opposition of the employers was backed by the decisions of the Supreme Court which interpreted the constitution as an absolute right for free enterprise to hire and fire as it pleased. Frick had hired a substitute workforce and hired Pinkerton's private army to break the picket. On July 6th, eleven unarmed working-men were shot dead in an action that roused public indignation against Frick who responded with the declaration that he would rather see every striker killed than concede a single demand.

Berkman's motivation has to be understood in the context of different practical routes to the revolution predicted by Marx. Marx had theorized that the very fact of the overwhelming power of labor had to lead to the recognition of that power. The proletariat was like a sleeping giant that only needed to be woken up. Class consciousness of this power would grow and be forged in union organization and experience. However, this still left the details of the practical implementation to be filled in. Two opposing views emerged over the question: would the revolution be spontaneous? Or would it be organized? Lenin thought that the power of labor would need to be realized through strict leadership and a plan of action to take control of the power of the state when the event came. The Bolshevik party was organized with military discipline. It was as a vanguard to which Lenin imparted the single minded purpose of a general. Bakunin, spokesman for the Anarchists and the counterweight to Marx considered that to take over the power of the state with an elite would only serve to perpetuate the existing structure of repression and privilege. It could not constitute a genuine revolution. For Bakunin, the revolution would be and had to be spontaneous with the workers taking control of production and economic resources thereby making the state redundant.

Berkman was inspired by the Anarchist spontaneous line of thought. When the situation was ripe the sleeping giant could be woken up by a single dramatic act, the *attentat*. This presupposed that oppression was so rife and so resented that all would rise against it at the given signal. With the feelings of the nation running high, the Homestead strike seemed just such an occasion. Although revolutionary fervor had broken out more frequently in Europe, the international scope of Marx's theory could not preclude America as a place to originate the revolution. Emma Goldman, Berkman's girlfriend, recounts the breathless excitement:

> Far away from the impending struggle, in our little ice-cream parlour in the city of Worcester, we eagerly followed developments. To us it sounded the awakening of the American worker and the long-awaited day of his resurrection. The native toiler had risen, he was beginning to feel his mighty strength, he was determined to break the chains that had held him in bondage for so long, we thought. Our hearts were fired with admiration for the men of Homestead… One afternoon a customer came in for an ice-cream, while I was alone in the store. As I set the dish down before him, I caught the large

headlines of his paper: 'LATEST DEVELOPMENTS IN HOMESTEAD – FAMILIES OF STRIKERS EVICTED FROM THE COMPANY HOUSES – WOMAN IN CONFINEMENT CARRIED OUT ONTO STREET BY SHERRIFS.' The inhumanity of Frick towards the evicted mother, inflamed my mind. Indignation swept my whole being... I locked up the store and ran full speed the three blocks to our little flat. Sasha was the first on his feet. 'Homestead!' he exclaimed. 'I must go to Homestead!' I flung my arms around him, crying out his name. I too would go. 'We must go tonight' he said; 'the great moment has come at last!'[1]

It was all a delusion. There was no general uprising. The one-sided interpretation of rights in the land of the free was rectified by gradual amendment. To the dismay of Berkman, who wanted to sacrifice his life for the cause, Frick did not die of his gunshot wounds. Instead of murder, Berkman faced the charge of attempted manslaughter for which he served fourteen years in Allegheny jail. Meanwhile, Anarchist theory had to move on from the *attentat*. The 1890s saw a spate of high profile assassinations; Carnot, the French president in 1894; Canovas, the Spanish prime minister in 1897; Empress Elizabeth of Austria in 1898; King Umberto of Italy in 1900 and the American president McKinley in 1901. These reaped only a hundredfold harvest of imprisonment and repression.

It is a problem of Anarchism that as a creed with no membership qualification and no directing organization it is difficult to dissociate from the nihilist, the criminal and the mentally disturbed. Any bomb can plausibly be traced to the door of the theorists and provide a convenient excuse for wholesale suppression. Berkman came to realize that the *attentat* could achieve nothing. Maturing Anarchist opinion moved to favor anarcho-syndicalism, that is, trade union federalism as an organizational model for the new society and the general strike as the means of revolution. Berkman was eventually deported from America and he went to serve the Russian revolution which from afar seemed the realization of his dreams. These idealist dreams were quickly replaced by bitter disappointment.

Although the *attentat* was the sensational difference between Anarchism and Lenin's Bolsheviks it was not the substantial difference. This difference is the much deeper question: is society going to be organized from the bottom up or from the top down? It is the difference between state communism and Anarchist communism. On this subject the Anarchists have a decided opinion. All central government is evil. It is a source of repression and war whether it be capitalist or socialist. Authority itself is a corruption of human nature. Central government must be swept away if there is to be a real change in society. Anarchism is optimistic about human nature. Left to free initiative without central direction, humans will spontaneously organize to their mutual benefit. Factories will be cooperative ventures run by the workers. Schools, hospitals, health insurance, shops and housing will all be organized mutually at the parish, factory and local community level. Central government is a hindrance to these mutual energies.

Marx himself was the original Anarchist. With impeccable logic he theorized that as the state only existed as a tool of capitalism, then the abolition of capitalism would necessarily mean the disappearance of the state. Communist organization would become local, decentralized and mutual. This was the basis of his famous phrase the 'withering away of the state.' Marx, however, envisaged this as a second, postponed and indefinite stage after the first necessary step which was the hijack of state power. This marked the irreconcilable division of opinion with the Anarchists which became quickly apparent during the first International Workingmen's Congress which met in Geneva in 1866. The argument split the International with Bakunin on one side and Marx on the other. The split ran with increasing acrimony through successive conventions for ten years until the congress itself was dissolved at the Philadelphia congress in 1876. This dissolution was engineered through the machinations of Marx, who preferred to see the International fail rather than see the triumph of the Anarchist viewpoint. Marx moved the International to America in the knowledge that the European Anarchists could not afford to attend and he could win the majority vote.

Bakunin's objections were prophetic. He predicted that a revolution effected by a vanguard takeover of state power would do no more than replicate the same repressive system to which it was ostensibly opposed. He accurately pinpointed the way that adherence to the authority of the state would turn Marxist socialism into a political tyranny. In 1873 he wrote:

That minority [the rulers], the Marxists say, will consist of workers. Yes, of *former* workers. And these, as soon as they become rulers or representatives of the people, will cease to be workers, and will begin to look down upon the entire world of manual workers from the heights of the state. They will no longer represent the people, but themselves and their own pretensions to rule the people. Whoever has any doubts about that does not know human nature. But these selected men will be ardently convinced, and at the same time learned socialists. The term 'scientific socialism', which continually occurs in the works of Lassalle and of the Marxists, proves that the alleged People's state will be nothing else but the despotic rule over the popular masses by a new, and not very numerous aristocracy of real or spurious savants.[2]

Bakunin's instinct was sound. His predictions were fulfilled in the Bolshevik revolution of 1917 and the subsequent development of Stalinist Russia. As Leonard Shapiro prefaces his history of the communist autocracy,

This is the story of how a group of determined men seized power for themselves in Russia in 1917, and kept others from sharing it; and of the consequences which ensued both for themselves and for their political rivals when it became evident that they had but little popular support.[3]

The Bolshevik party, in the interests of keeping its hold on power, granted itself license to kill its subjects at will in the construction of a pervasive totalitarian bureaucracy that made Tsarist Russia look benign in retrospect.

Anarchism bears the same relationship to socialism that Judaism bears to Christianity. It is a parent that became a rival and lost out in a period of vital struggle. The dominant survivor controlled the propaganda against it. 'Left-Wing Communism, an Infantile Disorder' was bruiser Lenin's harangue: 'Supernatural nonsense,' 'Herculean pillars of absurdity,' 'opportunist scum.'[4] Lenin blustered disingenuously,

All the work of the Party is carried on through the Soviets, which embrace the working masses irrespective of occupation. The district congresses of Soviets are *democratic* institutions the like of which even the best of the democratic republics of the bourgeois world has never known; and through these congresses (whose proceedings the Party endeavours to follow with the closest attention), as well as continually appointing class-conscious workers to various posts in the rural districts, the role of the proletariat as leader of the peasantry is exercised, the dictatorship of the urban proletariat is realized... It can be hoped that the reader will realize why the Russian Bolshevik who is acquainted with this mechanism and who for twenty five years has watched it growing out of small, illegal, underground circles, cannot help regarding all this talk about 'from above' *or* 'from below,' about the dictatorship of leaders *or* the dictatorship of the masses, etc, as ridiculous and childish nonsense, something like discussing whether a man's left leg or his right arm is more useful to him.[5]

Lenin was right that only a disciplined party could seize power. Even his success was in the balance for the first three years. The weakness of Anarchism was demonstrated finally in the Spanish Civil War where the strongest of European Anarchist traditions was defeated and it became clear that Anarchist spontaneity can never be a match for the organizational discipline necessary to win a war. On the other hand the Anarchists were right that the seizure of power constitutes a political, not a social, revolution. It is a token revolution. The communists won the propaganda battle and eliminated the Anarchist. Today, with the heat of the original issues long gone cold, there is left only the residue of simple prejudice.

Some illustrations of the Anarchist spirit in action need to be put forward. Decentralization, devolution, federalism, the end of nationalism, the cooperative movement, self-help, self-sufficiency, mutualism, the socialism of craft guilds can all be counted as aspirations of the Anarchist but these are general concepts. The real character of Anarchy in action needs to be brought to life. The resistance to Bolshevik domination that arose in St Petersburg and its associated naval base of Kronstadt, during the first three or four years of the Bolshevik consolidation of power provides a good case. A first-hand record of these events has been left by the Anarchist Vsevolodm Voline, a law student in St Petersburg who, on graduating from college, started up educational classes for the workers.

Voline recounts the origin of the first soviet (council) of workers delegates to coordinate strike action between the various factories. The occasion was a strike in St Petersburg in 1905 during which there were offers of food and money from well to do sympathizers. The question arose as to how these offerings should be distributed. Delegates to a coordinating committee were elected from each factory and the young Voline was offered the direction of this body. Voline turned this down. His motives express the Anarchist principle of self-help:

> Moved by the trust the workers expressed in me, I nevertheless turned down their offer. I told my friends: 'You're *workers*. You want to create an organism that will deal with your interests as *workers*. Learn, then, from the very beginning, to deal with your problems *yourselves*. Don't commit your destiny to someone who is not one of you. Don't set new masters over yourselves; they'll end up dominating or betraying you. I am convinced that in everything that has to do with your struggles and your liberation, only you yourselves will be able to reach real results. *For* you, *above* you, *in place* of you yourselves, no one will ever do anything. You should find your president, your secretary, and the members of your administrative commission *from among yourselves*... If you need intellectual or moral advice which presupposes a certain amount of education, then you can turn to intellectuals, to educated people, who should be happy, not to lead you as masters, but to give you their help without interfering in your organisations.'[6]

The workers did not heed Voline's advice. The post was accepted by his acquaintance, a legal clerk by the name of Nossar. It is not surprising that people who felt the disadvantage of illiteracy should want to engage the power of those who could read and write.

Soon after its formation Leon Trotsky became the president of the St Petersburg soviet. This began the Bolshevik realization of the political value of the soviets. Trotsky organized the infiltration of Bolshevik candidates and the manipulation of elections. Once the soviets around the country were safely in the pocket of the Bolsheviks, Lenin launched his famous platform for revolution 'all power to the soviets.'

Voline's exhortation to self-determination can also be found in the campaign of the Anarchist Nestor Makhno who spearheaded the revolution in Southern Ukraine, south of Kiev and Kharkov. The region is about a thousand miles from St Petersburg and had, until consolidation, a degree of independence from Bolshevik control. Makhno led a peasant army effecting the appropriation of the land and fighting the counter revolutionary Tsarist generals supported by the monarchies of Europe. The motto under the black flag was 'Liberty or Death, Land for the Peasants, Factories for the Workers.'

> In all towns captured notices were posted up to inform the inhabitants that the place was, for the time being, occupied by the Makhnovite Insurgent Revolutionary Army, a force in the service of no government, no political party and no dictatorship. The army's sole aim was to protect the liberty of the toilers against all. The liberty of the toilers was their own possession and subject to no restriction whatever. It was for the peasants and workers to organize themselves as the wished. The army was willing to help and advise, but would not govern and would not give orders.[7]

Makhno met Lenin on one occasion and the following conversation is reported:

> Lenin asked what the Ukrainian peasants made of the slogan 'All power to the Soviets.' Makhno replied that they took it literally – assuming that they were to have complete control of all affairs affecting them, and added, when Lenin asked him, that he himself felt this was the correct interpretation. *Lenin,* 'Then the peasants are infected with anarchism.' *Makhno,* 'Do you think that is bad?' *Lenin,* 'I did not say that;

it may be to the good if it speeds up the victory of communism.'[8]

The young Makhno was disillusioned with his visit to Moscow which appeared to him as 'the capital of the paper revolution, a vast factory turning out empty resolutions and slogans while one political party, by means of force and fraud, elevated itself into the position of the ruling class.'[9]

For the Anarchists any expression of local initiative was to be welcomed, but for the Bolsheviks any action not under their tutelage was denounced as counter-revolutionary. When, in May 1919 the Revolutionary Military Soviet at Makhno's headquarters called the Fourth Congress of Peasants', Workers' and Insurgents' Representatives the Bolsheviks tried to suppress it. 'Order 1824, signed by Trotsky at Kharkov on June 4th forbade the holding of the Congress, declared that any participation amounted to high treason against the Soviet State and ordered the arrest of all delegates and all concerned with the distribution of the invitations.'[10]

Voline reports a number of examples of the suppression of local initiatives:

> In the beginning of 1918, the working population of Kronstadt, after debating the subject at many meetings, decided to proceed to socialize all dwelling places. It was a question, first of all, of obtaining the agreement of the local Soviet, then of creating a competent organisation to carry out a census and examination of buildings and an equitable distribution of dwellings... Horrible hovels were discovered in which the unfortunate lived, sometimes several families together. On the other hand, there were comfortable apartments of ten or fifteen rooms which were occupied by only a few persons. For example the director of the Engineering School, a bachelor, occupied himself a luxurious apartment of

twenty rooms... Soon all those who filled the unhealthy
shacks and garrets and the filthy cellars were lodged in
somewhat cleaner and more comfortable places... Later on,
the Bolshevik government destroyed this organisation and
wiped out its constructive beginnings. The management of
buildings passed to a purely bureaucratic institution, the Real
Estate and Buildings Centre, which was organised from
above... This Centre installed in every building, district and
borough an official, or to be more accurate, a *policeman*, whose
main function was to supervise activities in the houses, to
keep track of the movements of the inhabitants in each
district, to report infractions of lodging and visa regulations,
to denounce 'suspects' etc.[11]

Voline recounts the struggle between local and centralized
initiative over closure of the St Petersburg oil refinery:

One evening near the end of 1917, in Petrograd, two or three
workers from the former Nobel oil refinery (it had employed
about 4000) came to the meeting place of our union and told
us the following: The refinery having been abandoned by its
owners, the workers had decided... to operate it collectively... But the Commissariat of the People at Work informed
them that... 'the Government had decided to close all these
establishments and to lay off the workers, giving them two or
three months wages, and to wait for better times.' The
workers would not accept this decision and the government
proposed a general meeting of the whole plant, for whom
Voline was chosen as spokesman to be attended by
Shlyapnikov, Commissar of the People at Work. 'He spoke
first. In a dry official tone he repeated the terms of the
Government's decision. He ended by declaring that the
decision was positive, irrevocable, without appeal, and that, if
they opposed it, the workers would commit a serious breach

of discipline.' Voline then tells of an excited meeting at which the workers express their confidence at being able to overcome the imagined raw material and distribution problems and make a successful contribution to the economy. 'A thunder of applause ensued... on all sides the audience acclaimed our joint conclusion. Then Shlyapnikov spoke again. Coldly, although visibly angry... he asserted that... the decision of the Government to close the refinery was final. 'You yourselves put us in power' Shlyapnikov said. 'You voluntarily, freely entrusted us with the destinies of the country... You the working class of the country, wished us to take care of your interests. So it's for us to know them, to understand them, to watch out for them... In any event, I must warn the workers of this plant and also the Anarchist gentlemen, those professional wreckers, that the Government can change nothing of its carefully considered decisions; one way or another it will make them respected. If the workers resist, so much the worse for them! They will simply be laid off by force without indemnity... as to the Anarchist gentlemen, let them take care! The Government cannot tolerate their mixing in the affairs that are none of their business, inciting honest workers to disobedience... The Government will know how to penalize them, and will not hesitate. Consider it said![12]

The domineering Bolshevik methods became more and more resented in St Petersburg. The city of two and a half million had been reduced to seven hundred thousand through starvation and chaos but roadblocks were set up to confiscate all produce gleaned from the countryside by parties sent out from the factories, on the grounds that it should have been delivered to the state. The system of thirty-three different levels of rations caused resentment. Most hated were the political supervision of the factory floor, political supervision of elections and the Labour

Army of 'volunteers' from the Red Guards which Trotsky sent into factories as strike breakers.

The culmination of this, on March 1st 1921 was the historic Resolution of the General Meeting of the 1st and 2nd Squadrons of the Baltic fleet. This was a list of fifteen demands calling for free elections by secret ballot and the abolition of political pressure and privilege. This was to lead to the most traumatic event of the revolution. Lenin fully understood that this democratic challenge was more dangerous to the power of the Bolsheviks than the combined power of the White counter-revolutionary armies. He determined to crush it. Trotsky issued an ultimatum to submit to the authority of the Soviet Republic and made preparations for a military attack.

Some background is needed to understand the awful betrayal involved in this decision. Kronstadt is an island at the bottom of the Gulf of Finland that guards the approach to St Petersburg. The port was the base for the Baltic fleet staffed by some twenty-five thousand sailors and soldiers. The town had played a pivotal part in the revolution of February 1917. The sailors, with their high levels of skill and their exposure to foreign countries, were a politically aware and organized group. In the uprising they killed the commanding officer and admiral of the fleet, executed two hundred of the officers that were disliked and elected their own council as governing authority. It was a few shots from the cruiser *Avrova* in support of the people of St Petersburg that had decided the fall of the Kerensky government. Trotsky gave the Baltic fleet the accolade, 'the pride and glory of the revolution.' The historian George Katkov described the sailors as the *sans-culottes* of the Russian Revolution, the guardians of the revolutionary conscience who had been active on every front in the civil war. This 'pride and glory of the revolution' was now the subject of Trotsky's threat 'I will shoot you like partridges.'[13]

It was not easy to get the Red army to attack its renowned comrades. The lie was spread that Kronstadt was being led in rebellion by a tsarist general. A news blackout was imposed. Units from afar, not familiar with the local situation were brought in. The island was subjected to a bombardment from the shore batteries and an invasion over the ice, in a bloody battle that lasted five days. White shrouded troops coming over the ice were machine-gunned and many drowned where the ice was breaking up for the season. The attack ended with bitter street fighting in the town and wholesale massacres. Kronstadt was the end of autonomous initiative and symbolized the end of Anarchist participation in the revolution. Bolshevik intentions were nakedly displayed. Meanwhile, on the Southern front, once the alliance with Makhno had fulfilled its purpose of defeating the White general, Wrangel, the Bolsheviks turned their guns on Makhno's peasant army.

To summarize, Anarchism rejects power centralized in state authority in favor of local initiative. This opinion of the positive evil of state coercion is something that we are unsympathetic with today and probably consider far-fetched. Modern democracy saps local initiative and seems to love state regulation in every aspect of people's lives. We look with expectation to state initiative as provider, planner, regulator, setter of all standards and solver of all problems. We have today contentedly accepted regulated capitalism as the compromise that produces a maximization of resources available for taxation and redistribution.

With this modern lack of sympathy to the Anarchist complaint prejudicing our inclination it is necessary to cast the mind back to the conditions of the time in order to appreciate properly the idealism of the movement. A hundred and fifty years ago Russia and Spain were landlord despotisms with peasant populations in a condition of slavery.

Tolstoy, the Anarchist who derives his Political Anarchism from his Christianity, vividly portrayed brute force as the basis of the state. He told of a chance encounter which led to his enlightenment:

> At one of the railway stations my train passed an extra train
> which was taking a troop of soldiers to flog and murder these
> same famishing peasants... And here I saw the spectacle of
> good Russians full of the Christian spirit travelling with guns
> and rods to torture and kill their starving brethren... ... The
> matter in dispute was a fall of water which irrigated the
> peasants' fields and which the landowner wanted to cut off
> and divert to turn his mill. The peasants rebelled against this
> being done... ... the women went to the dykes, overturned the
> carts, and drove the men away. The district commander made
> an order that from every house throughout the village one
> woman was to be taken and put in prison. The order was not
> easily executed. For in every household there were several
> women, and it was impossible to know which one was to be
> arrested... The peasants began to defend their wives and
> mothers and beat the police and their officer. This was a fresh
> and terrible crime: resistance had been offered to the author-
> ities. And so this governor... proceeded to the scene of
> action... ...delivered a prepared harangue and asked for a
> bench...for flogging... the governor ordered the first of the
> twelve culprits pointed out by the landowner as the most
> guilty to come forward. The first was the head of a family, a
> man of forty who had always stood up manfully for the rights
> of his class. He was led to the bench and stripped and then
> ordered to lie down... The convicts spit into their hands,
> brandished the rods and began to flog... The victim's back
> and thighs and even his sides, became more and more
> covered with scars and wheals and at every blow came the
> sound of the deep groans that he could no longer restrain...
> When more than fifty strokes had been given, the peasant
> ceased to shriek and writhe and the doctor... announced to
> the representative of authority that the man undergoing

punishment had lost consciousness, and that to continue the punishment would endanger the victim's life... But.... the flogging was continued up to the seventy strokes. When the seventieth stroke had been reached the governor said 'enough! Next one!' Thus they flogged them up till the twelfth.[14]

Tolstoy went on to explain his revelation:

After my thoughts had for two years been turned in the same direction, fate seemed expressly to have brought me face to face, for the first time in my life, with a fact which showed me absolutely unmistakably in practice what had long been known to me in theory, that the organization of society rests, not as many interested in maintaining the present order of things like to imagine, on certain principles of jurisprudence, but on simple brute force, on the murder and torture of men.[15] All state obligations... are always based on bodily violence or the threat of it.[16]

In identifying the state as resting on brute force, Tolstoy anticipated Max Weber's later definition of the state as 'the monopoly of the legitimate use of violence.'

But this insight is not the concluding point in Tolstoy's perception of the state as evil. For Tolstoy the state is evil because the violence needed to maintain it is achieved by the abrogation of individual conscience. State power is based on the army. This army is only able to get men to shoot their brothers by suspending their personal conscience. 'The whole power of the state is based in reality on this delusive emancipation of men from their duty to God and their conscience, and the substitution of duty to their superior officers.'[17] Tolstoy brings out the real meaning of enlistment at conscription:

'I promise and swear by Almighty God upon his holy Gospel' etc. 'to defend' etc., and that is, to murder anyone I am told to, and to do everything I am told by men I know nothing of, and who care nothing for me except as an instrument for perpetrating the crimes by which they are kept in their position of power, and my brothers in their condition of misery. All the conscripts repeat these ferocious words without thinking then the so-called 'father' goes away with a sense of having correctly and conscientiously done his duty. And all these poor deluded lads believe that these nonsensical and incomprehensible words which they have just uttered set them free for the whole time of their service from their duties as men... And this crime is perpetrated publicly and no one cries out to the deceiving and the deceived: 'Think what you are doing; this is the basest, falsest lie, by which not bodies only, but souls too are destroyed.'[18]

Tolstoy quoted a speech of the German Emperor which said plainly what other rulers take trouble to conceal:

'Conscripts! you have sworn fidelity to *me* before the altar and the minister of God... that means that you are now my soldiers, that you have given yourselves to me body and soul. For you there is but one enemy, my enemy. In these days of socialistic sedition it may come to pass that I command you to fire on your own kindred, your brothers, even your own fathers and mothers... even then you are bound to obey my orders without hesitation.'[19]

Tolstoy was able to explain to himself this puzzling power of the state only by what he called 'the influence of state hypnotism' and the 'metaphysics of hypocrisy' which commands the delegation of personal conscience and its subjugation to official position. 'The substitution of duty to their superior officer for all other duties... This belief is founded on a conscious deception practiced on them by the higher classes.'[20]

From this analysis Tolstoy proceeded to his Anarchist solution, the mass civil disobedience that was so much to influence Gandi. If the state can only be maintained by people in this hypnotized state of suspension then a mass awakening of conscience could bring down the structure. It is through the present awakening to repression that Tolstoy saw the Kingdom of God as imminent and gave a pacifist interpretation to that passage in Matthew:

> The Kingdom of Heaven suffereth violence, and the violent take it by force (Matt. xi. 12). It is this violent effort to rise above external conditions to the recognition and realization of the truth by which the kingdom of heaven is taken, and it is this effort of violence which must be and can be made in our times. Men need only understand this, they need only cease to trouble themselves about the general external conditions in which they are not free, and devote one-hundredth part of the energy they waste on those material things to that in which they are free, to the recognition of the truth which is before them, and to the liberation of themselves and others from deception and hypocrisy, and, without effort or conflict, there would be an end at once of the false organisation of life which makes men miserable, and threatens them with worse calamities in the future. And then the kingdom of God would be realised, or at least that first stage of it for which men are ready now by the degree of development of their conscience. Just a single shock may be sufficient, when a liquid is saturated with some salt, to precipitate it at once in crystals, a slight effort may perhaps be all that is needed now that the truth already revealed to men may gain mastery over hundreds. [21] The time will come, and is inevitably coming when all institutions based on force will disappear through

their uselessness, stupidity and inconvenience becoming obvious to all. . . .The prophecy that the time will come when men will be taught of God, will learn war no more, will beat their swords into ploughshares and their spears into reaping hooks, which means, translating into our language, the fortresses, prisons, barracks, palaces and churches will remain empty, and all the gibbets and cannons will be left unused, is no longer a dream, but the definite new form of life to which mankind is approaching with ever-increasing rapidity. [22]

11.3. Political Anarchism is a Religious Vision

Tolstoy, in the last few paragraphs was speaking his Political Anarchism from the convictions of his Christianity. The Anarchist vision is the same as the vision of the Kingdom of God. All commentators on Anarchism consider that it is a religious and not a political movement. There is a good theoretical foundation to what the commentators find in practice. Anarchism does not figure on the syllabus of political theory.[23] Political theory is concerned with the ways in which power is delegated from the individual to the state, the reasons for its delegation and how the use of that power is accepted as legitimate by the people from whom it is derived and against whom it may be used. Anarchism does not recognize that there can be any legitimate power over the individual. Human relations in anarchist theory are spontaneously cooperative. The only legitimate basis for the organization of society is, therefore, spontaneous cooperation. In Anarchist theory it is the powers of authority and the capitalist market that perverts and prevents this cooperation. With its adherence to these principles, Anarchism does not come within the subject matter of political theory. My tutor would always shake her head woefully at the mention of anarchy. Anarchism shares the honor of this disqualification with Christianity which is another viewpoint that cannot be accommodated by political theory. Christianity adheres to a source of authority, God, which comes from outside the system. The legitimacy of this authority is not open to discussion. Political theory which concerns the way authority is legitimated can handle neither Anarchism nor Christianity. Is it possible that they could be related?

Before moving on to those authorities who think Anarchism is religious, the apparent disqualification of violence needs to be faced. It seems incongruous at first sight to classify a belief that is opposed to violence with a belief that advocates violence. The Anarchists have been responsible for some gory scenes. In 1873, in the Andalusian papermaking town of Alcoy, the workers struck in favor of an eight-hour day. After the police opened fire on them there was a general battle in the town during which the mayor and twelve policemen were shot. Their heads were then cut off and paraded round the streets in triumph. The scene is symbolic. The new Anarchist kingdom can only be given birth through a violent overthrow of the existing structures of oppression.

In this respect, however, the Anarchist kingdom is no different from the Kingdom of God. Why is it that the Kingdom of God is going to come 'with power'? (Mark 9.1). Why is the Son of Man going to come 'with power'? (Matthew 24.30). Why is the Son of Man 'seated at the right hand of power'? (Matthew 26.64). This power is necessary to make the apocalyptic transition. The existing structures of oppression which bar the earthly implementation of the Kingdom must be broken up. The power is going to be used to sort out the accursed who are ordered to 'depart from me into the eternal fire prepared for the devil and his angels' (Matthew 25.41). John the Baptist, Jesus, Paul and the Revelation of John are explicit about the coming violence. 'You brood of vipers! Who warned you to flee from the wrath to come?' cries John, and he warns of one coming after him who will burn the chaff with unquenchable fire (Matthew 3.7–11). Jesus is uncompromising in his threats. 'Woe to you Chorazin! Woe to you Bethsaida! ...And you Capernaum... you will be brought down to Hades... on the day of judgement it will be more tolerable for the land of Sodom than for you' (Matthew 11.21). Paul tells the Corinthians of the battle to be undertaken by Christ during the interim period of his return. 'Then comes the end, when he hands over the kingdom to God the Father, after he has destroyed every ruler, and every authority and power. For he must reign until he has put all his enemies under his feet' (1 Corinthians 15:24). The Revelation of John is specific in the awful details of retribution that give birth to the Kingdom:

> When the thousand years are ended, Satan will be released from his prison and will come out to deceive the nations at the four corners of the earth, Gog and Magog, in order to gather them for battle; they are as numerous as the sands of the sea. They marched up over the breadth of the earth and surrounded the camp of the saints and the beloved city. And fire came down from heaven and consumed them (Revelation 20:7–9).

Anarchism and Christianity are not incompatible on the basis of the violence needed to bring in the new Kingdom. Both envisage that it is necessary as it were to crash through a sound barrier of violence to reach the peace on the other side. The difference is that the Anarchists must actualize the Kingdom with their own hands. They, therefore, provide historical examples of violence in the attempt to do this. Christianity postpones and delegates to God the violence needed to bring in the Kingdom. It can, therefore, appear as the more innocent party. But the New Testament is clear that the actual event will not be different in principle from the parading of severed heads through the streets of Alcoy.

Writers on Anarchism are unanimous in remarking its

religious nature. Franz Borkenau, the Austrian sociologist, who gave an eyewitness account of the Spanish Civil War notes:

> Anarchism *is* a religious movement in a sense that is profoundly different in the sense in which that is true of the labour movements in progressive countries. Anarchism does not believe in the creation of a new world through the improvement of the material conditions of the lower classes, but in the creation of a new world out of the moral resurrection of those classes which have not yet been contaminated by the spirit of mammon and greed.[24]

Borkenau further categorizes Anarchism as a 'half-religious Utopian movement.'[25] James Joll in his survey writes:

> Although anarchism is also a product of the rationalism of the eighteenth century, and anarchist political theory is based on confidence in man's reasonable nature and belief in the possibility of intellectual and moral progress, this is only one of its strands. The other is a tendency which can only be described as religious and which links the anarchist emotionally, if not doctrinally with the extreme heretics of earlier centuries. It is the clash between these two types of temperament, the religious and the rationalist, the apocalyptic and the humanist, which has made so much of anarchist doctrine seem contradictory. It is also this double nature that gives anarchism a wide universal appeal.[26]

George Woodcock noted the world rejecting, non-materialist aspect of the movement:

> The anarchist's cult of the natural, the spontaneous, the individual, sets him against the whole highly organised structure of modern industrial and statist society, which the

Marxist sees as the prelude to his own Utopia. Even efforts to encompass the world by such doctrines as anarcho-syndicalism have been mingled with a revulsion against the world, leading to a mystic vision of the workers as moral regenerators; even the syndicalists could not forsee with equanimity the perpetuation of anything resembling industrial society as it exists at present.[27]

Gerald Brenan is the prime commentator on Spain and he provides the most extensive discussion of the religious aspect of Anarchism:

When one seeks to penetrate into the real meaning of the Spanish Anarchist movement one is struck, I think, by two main aspects that in practice fuse into one. There is first of all the strongly idealistic and moral-religious character. These anarchists are a set of men who are attempting to put into practice their utopia (which is severe and almost ascetic like the old Jewish-Christian utopia) at once and what is significant, by force. Secondly they are Spanish villagers and working men who are trying, though without being consciously aware of it, to reconstruct the primitive agrarian conditions (in this case the collectivist commune) that once prevailed in many parts of Spain and to recover the equality and leisure, and above all the dignity, that, to a greater or lesser extent, they enjoyed in previous centuries... However violent these anarchists may be... they speak the same language of love of liberty, of dependence upon the inner light that Enlightenment once used to do. And they are uncompromising moralists. Every action is either right of wrong; they admit no such thing as expediency.[28]

Brenan goes on to describe Spanish Anarchism as a religious heresy:

There is one sort of heresy... of which both the Catholic and the Protestant Churches have always shown a particular terror. It is that which consists in taking literally the very frequent allusions in the Scriptures to the wickedness and consequent damnation of the rich and the blessedness of the poor. What the authorities could not forgive in [the] sects was the emphasis they laid on the social teaching of the Gospels. And it will be remembered with what almost insane fury Luther urged the destruction by fire and sword of those peasants who were compromising him by taking his teaching on Christian freedom in a literal sense. The reason for this violence is obvious. The Bible, and especially the New Testament, contains enough dynamite to blow up all the existing social systems in Europe, only by force of habit and through the power of beautiful and rhythmical words we have ceased to notice it. An intelligent Chinaman has been more observant. Sun Yat Sen, when he visited Europe, was amazed that a religion which persistently extolled the poor and threatened and condemned the rich should be practised and maintained chiefly by the richest, most selfish and most respectable classes. The political skill and duplicity required for such a feat seemed to him to go far beyond anything that simple Orientals could run to... I would suggest then that the anger of the Spanish Anarchists against the Church is the anger of an intensely religious people who feel that they have been deserted and deceived... When they took up the struggle for the Christian utopia it was therefore against the Church and not with it. It may be thought that I have stressed too much the religious element because Spanish Anarchism is after all a political doctrine. But the aims of the Anarchists were always much wider and their teaching more personal than anything that can be included under the word politics. To individuals they offered a way of life: Anarchism had to be lived as well as worked for. To the community they offered a world founded exclusively on moral principles.[29]

These moral, religious, ascetic, even saintly qualities of anarchists are borne out by the lives of some of the renowned figures of Anarchism. Peter Kropotkin (1842-1921) can serve as an example of the Anarchist saint. Kropotkin was a prince born into an aristocratic Russian family. He served the military apprenticeship compulsory to his class in the Corps of Pages, the elite school that provided personal attendance on the Tsar. It was in his capacity as page to Alexander II that he formed his opinion of that man's passionate but weak personality. The Corps was a stepping stone to the highest positions in army and government. On graduating with honors, Kropotkin was assured of a place in the most illustrious regiment of his choosing, but his interests were scientific and literary:

> That I should not enter a regiment of the Guard, and give my life to parades and court balls, I had settled long before. My dream was to enter the university—to study, to live the student's life. That meant, of course, to break with my father, whose ambitions were quite different, and to rely for my living upon what I might earn by means of lessons. Thousands of Russian students live in that way, and such a life did not frighten me in the least. But – I saw no possibility of providing even the little money which would be required for the modest start.[30]

Instead Kropotkin enlisted in the mounted Cossacks of the Amur, a regiment without court status, in the newly annexed region of Siberia. This offered some freedom from the oppressive atmosphere of St Petersburg. It was only the personal commendation of the Tsar that overcame his father's disgust.

It was in Siberia that Kropotkin encountered the enlightened, but soon to be removed, administration of the thirty-five-year-old general Kukel. In the capacity of aide de camp Kropotkin was set to work reporting on reform of the prisons. This exposure laid the ground for his convictions on the state as a perverted impediment compared to the self-sufficiency and mutual organization of the local peoples. His international reputation as a geographer for his discovery of the geological formation of Siberia stems from this period of extensive travel through the region:

> The five years that I spent in Siberia were for me a genuine education in life and human character. I was brought into contact with men of all description: the best and the worst; those who stood at the very top of society and those who vegetated at the very bottom – the tramps and the so-called incorrigible criminals. I had ample opportunities to watch the ways and habits of the peasants in their daily life, and still more opportunities to appreciate how little the State administration could give to them, even if it were animated by the best intentions. Finally my extensive journeys, during which I travelled over fifty thousand miles in carts, on board steamers, in boats but chiefly on horseback, had a wonderful effecting strengthening my health. They also taught me how little man really needs as soon as he comes out of the enchanted circle of conventional civilisation. With a few pounds of bread and a few ounces of tea in a leather bag, a kettle and a hatchet hanging at the side of the saddle, and under the saddle a blanket, to be spread at the camp fire upon a bed of freshly cut spruce twigs, a man feels wonderfully independent.[31]

Kropotkin became de facto an Anarchist through personal experience. The name and theory he discovered only years later:

> I soon realized the absolute impossibility of doing anything really useful for the masses of the people by means of the administrative machinery. With this illusion I parted forever.

Then I began to understand... the inner springs of the life of human society. The constructive work of the unknown masses... and the importance of that constructive work in the growth of forms of society, appeared before my eyes in a clear light. To witness, for instance, the ways in which the communities of the Dukhobortsky migrated to the Amur region; to see the immense advantages which they got from their semi-communistic brotherly organisation; and to realise what a success their colonisation was, amidst all the failures of State colonisation, was learning something that cannot be learned from books... and was to store up floods of light which illuminated my subsequent reading... I began to understand the difference between acting on the principle of command and discipline and acting on the principle of common understanding. The former works admirably in a military parade, but it is worth nothing where real life is concerned and the aim can only be achieved through the severe effort of many converging wills... I lost in Siberia whatever faith in State discipline I had cherished before. I was prepared to become an anarchist.[32]

It was in Siberia, talking to some of the eleven thousand exiles from the 1863 Polish uprising, sent to their death by hard labor in the mines, that Kropotkin formed two lasting convictions: Revolutions must be made from the bottom up; military service enforces the evil suspension of personal conscience. The Polish uprising went disastrously wrong because it was hijacked by the landed interests. This allowed the Russians, whose serfs had recently been 'freed', to intervene as saviors of the peasants and thus gain their support. This foretaste meant that Kropotkin was wise to the autocratic nature of the 1917 revolution when it came. When some of these Polish exiles made a bid for freedom across Mongolia Kropotkin narrowly escaped being sent to capture them. This brought home the realization that the fundamental nature of his military service was to kill people with whom he had no quarrel, indeed in this case people with whom he had outright sympathy. It was at this point that he vowed to leave the army.

From then on Kropotkin eked out a living from his scientific publications combined with free service to editing and writing Anarchist literature. Although he longed for a secure source of income he turned down the post of secretary to the Geographical Society because he felt that all salaries were bread taken from the mouths of famished peasants. He became involved in self-education and propaganda groups in St Petersburg distributing banned literature. He was arrested for this in 1874 and imprisoned in solitary confinement in the St Peter and Paul fortress. When his health gave out he was transferred to the hospital and from here made a thrilling escape to Hull and did not return to Russia until the revolution. By this time a figure of international repute he was preserved untouched by Lenin as a front while he eliminated the lesser known Anarchists. At his death in February 1921 there was a massive turnout for his funeral and seven comrades, let out from imprisonment for the day, carried his coffin.

This kindly, scholarly man, filled with love for mankind, concerned that his intensive market gardening experiments should bring the benefit of science to feed the peasants, carrying out a worldwide correspondence from Bromley and Brighton, is the antidote to the caricature of the bomb throwing anarchist. In his memoirs Kropotkin states his vision of a coming new society. Allowing for the difference of language that two thousand years must bring, this vision is not dissimilar to that of Jesus:

There is in mankind, a nucleus of social habits which is *not* maintained by coercion and is superior to coercion. Upon it all the progress of mankind is based... We saw that a new form of society is germinating and must take the place of the old one:

a society of equals, who will not be compelled to sell their hands and brains to those who choose to employ them in a haphazard way, but who will be able to apply their knowledge and capacities to production, in an organism so constructed as to combine the efforts for procuring the greatest sum possible of well-being for all, while full, free scope will be left to every individual initiative... no need of government will be felt, because free agreement and federation can take its place in all those functions which governments consider as theirs at the present time.[33]

This visionary nature of Anarchism is presented strongly in the writing of Alexander Berkman. He published an introduction to Anarchism because he felt that the truth of its vision needed to be told to counteract the misrepresentation and uninformed disparagement to which it was subjected.[34] It was published as the *ABC of Anarchism* but its contents would be better described with the title *Berkman's Proclamation of the Kingdom of God*. Berkman sets out a vision of the Kingdom that rivals that of the Sybilline Oracle:

'Anarchism teaches that we can live in a society where there is no compulsion of any kind.'[35] 'It means that all men are brothers, and that they should live like brothers in peace and harmony. That is to say, that there should be no war, no violence used by one set of men against another, no monopoly, and no poverty, no oppression, no taking advantage of your fellow man.'[36] 'Crimes resulting from government, from its oppression and injustice, from inequality and poverty, will disappear under anarchy. These constitute by far the greatest percentage of crime. Certain other crimes will persist for some time, such as those resulting from jealousy, passion. But these will gradually disappear under wholesome conditions with the passing away of the atmosphere that cultivated them.'[37] 'Under anarchism each will have the opportunity for following whatever occupation will appeal to his natural inclinations and aptitude. Work will become a pleasure[38] ...a joyous application of physical effort to the needs of the world.[39] Laziness will be unknown, and the things created by interest and love will be objects of beauty and joy.'[40] 'Most hard toil could be eliminated by the use of modern machinery.'[41] 'The fear of competition would be eliminated with the abolition of private ownership. Every one would have full and unhindered opportunity to live and enjoy life to the utmost of his capacity.'[42] There will be equal pay for all.[43] 'Three hours work a day will suffice when all the unproductive members are put to work once war is abolished, as would of course be the case under anarchy.'[44] 'There will be no buying or selling... money becomes useless... exchange will be free.'[45] 'Science is the wizard who enables man to master all difficulties and overcome all obstacles... bread and wellbeing for all. First bread, then wellbeing and luxury.'[46] 'Our present system of civilisation has... made the belly the centre of the universe. But in a sensible society, with plenty for all... the feelings of human sympathy, of justice and right would have a chance to develop, to be satisfied, to broaden and grow.'[47] 'Living will be an art and a joy... Life will mean the striving for finer cultural values... the attainment of higher truth... Free to exercise the unlimited possibilities of his mind... to soar on the wings of imagination... man will reach his full stature and become man indeed.'[48]

That is a pretty comprehensive vision. If any of us could think of some benefit missing from this ideal society, Berkman would surely incorporate it as a blessing of Anarchism. Christianity and Anarchism produce identical visions of the Kingdom of God.

There are a number of structural parallels between the

Anarchist kingdom and the Kingdom of God. Capitalism takes the place of Satan. 'Government is the worst criminal man has ever known of. It fills the world with violence, with fraud and deceit, with oppression and misery. Its breath is poison, it corrupts everything it touches.'[49] Where Jesus sees 'Satan fall from heaven' (Luke 17.18) Berkman sees 'the ultimate breakdown of government and capitalism.'[50] Where Jesus has faith that the Kingdom of God is coming, Berkman has faith that 'the abolition of capitalism is inevitable.'[51] 'I consider anarchism the most rational and practical conception of a social life in freedom and harmony. I am convinced that its realisation is a certainty in the course of human development.'[52] Jesus' description of this age and the age to come is mirrored by the Anarchist present and future Kingdom. The transitional function of the messiah is mirrored by the transitional function of the revolution. Just as with the messiah the revolution is the hoped for, imminent but not definitely timed event. The present element of the Kingdom consists of preparations to be made now in the same way that the token of earnest is required for God's Kingdom. The revolution is 'not destruction but construction.'[53] The present is a time for preparations. We are to use our time now to get used to the idea that there is no such thing as private ownership. 'No man can create anything by himself, by his own efforts. Now, then, if labor is social, it stands to reason that the results of it, the wealth produced, must also be social, belong to the collectivity. Union activity is a training ground for self-reliance.'[54] We must learn to live without authority and compulsion and free ourselves from narrow conceptions of ownership.[55] Anarchism has the same hypermorality of Jesus. In place of turn the other cheek Berkman commends 'the cure for evil is more liberty.'[56] Christians would describe the Kingdom of God as living in the presence of God. Anarchism parallels with the synonym living out the ideal potential of human existence.

To sum up, Political Anarchism throws up the strongest

parallels with Christianity to the extent that Christianity can rightly be described as Religious Anarchism. They are both wedded to the equality of all persons as their ethic. They are both wedded to respect for the autonomy of all persons as the articulation of that ethic. The Anarchist utopia is the same vision of human relations as the Kingdom of God. Anarchism and Christianity share a disdain for materialism. They are both moral systems prescribing equality and community. It is only a conceptual perversity that could distinguish one of these visions as secular. Political Anarchism is a religious vision. Respect for the autonomy of others is religious.

12

The Distinction between the Religious and the Political Domains – What is the Kingdom of God?

12.1. What is the Domain of Religion?

The question of the relationship between the domain of religion and the domain of the secular or political has been in abeyance since my proposal to abandon the sacred profane distinction and to abandon as an unfortunate construct the word secular that this produces. Political Anarchism turned out to be a misnomer. It is disqualified as a political ideology because it cannot form a political society and its vision is religious. It is really Religious Anarchism in disguise. The difference that provides that disguise is that one variety of Religious Anarchism attempts to actualize the vision right now. The other Religious Anarchism defers actualization. Yet both immediate and deferred Religious

Anarchism are united against the same thing. What is that same thing? My proposal is that that same thing is the domain of the political. The domain of the political is that which is able to form a political society and in relation to which religion is situated in permanent opposition. My proposal is that the fundamental division in human life is that between the religious and the political domain. That distinction replaces the sacred and the profane metaphysics which currently frames the 'secular'.

In order to make this distinction it is necessary to possess not only a definition of religion but a definition of the political. A comparison with Durkheim's delineation of the domain sociology is a good starting point here as it will also form an endpoint. Durkheim rendered to sociology, in lasting manner, the great service of distinguishing its subject matter from that of other disciplines. His definition of a 'social fact' founded the science of sociology. His opening paragraph in *The Rules of Sociological Method* stated the problem of boundaries to the subject which were at the time too diffusive and which he wished clearly to delimit:

> Before enquiring into the method suited to the study of social facts, it is important to know which facts are commonly called 'social.' This information is all the more necessary since the designation 'social' is used with little precision. It is currently employed for practically all phenomena generally diffused within society, however small their social interest. But on that basis, there are, as it were, no human events that may not be called social. Each individual drinks, sleeps, eats, reasons; and it is to society's interest that these functions be exercised in an orderly manner. If, then, all these facts are counted as 'social' facts, sociology would have no subject matter exclusively its own, and its domain would be confused with that of biology and psychology.[1]

Durkheim defines a social fact as a constraint on individual behavior. This constraint precedes the birth of and is outside the control of the individual. As he says 'I am not obliged to speak French to my fellow countrymen, nor to use the local currency, but I cannot possibly do otherwise.'[2]

In contrast to sociology the domain of religion has never been so well defined. In fact its domain remains both contentious and perplexing. In so far as religion is considered to be about the whole of life it can be taken to be in some sense 'about everything.' On the other hand there is a strong sense in the history that the domain of religion is separate from the domain of the political. It is, therefore, not at all about everything. There are presumed to be some matters constituting a whole important aspect of society to which it is indifferent. The church established in power by Constantine allocated separate spheres to the temporal and the heavenly swords. This was perpetuated by Luther at the reformation which continued a division of labor between church and state. There is also an intuitive sense that religion is somehow above politics.

The irrelevance of the political may be said to stem from the famous pronouncement of Jesus 'render unto Caesar that which is Caesar's.' This is a single instance of such an attitude that has been made much of. The statement was made in the circumstances of a test, so it may be considered exceptional. On the other hand Jesus consistently displays a non-political nature. In all his demands he never asks what is the village committee going to do? He always asks what are *you* going to do? The same root of religion in personal action is reproduced in Paul's early churches. These are small groups of friends helping and celebrating their lives together. They did not need to, and could not in any case, have taken on the Roman authority. The issue of the separation of the religious and the political has, however, been greatly contested by twentieth-century Jesusology and liberation theology. These both made strenuous efforts to claim religion as a political force. I discount these efforts however, as indicated in the introduction, on the grounds that this is the surest way to make religion irrelevant and its membership exclusive. These twentieth-century efforts were an attempt to 'make religion relevant' under apparently desperate circumstances of declining influence.

One seemingly obvious solution to the boundary of the religious domain is in the distinction between the sacred and the profane. Religion is concerned with the sacred. The political powers are concerned with the profane. This is another way of stating the division between the spiritual and the material and transposes religion from this world to an other-worldly realm. I have however already rejected this division as displaying the influence of Plato and as a division that is artificial. Religion is wholly about our actions in this world. The other-worldly Platonist or apocalyptic frameworks are in reality reflexive means to focus action in this world. My conceptual framework abandons altogether the distinction between the sacred and the profane except to the extent of the common usage of sacred as 'what is supremely important to us.'

In moving to define the domain of the political the first obstacle is that this is a subject of varying interpretation by political theorists. I will be adopting an understanding of the political that is not conventionally what we refer to as the world of politics. That world consists of macro level policies, parties and personalities. It is party politics. This macro level is not excluded but the principle that it embodies is transferred to embrace a much wider constituency. It is transferred down the scale to the micro level of small organizations and small groups of people. My interpretation extends that of Bernard Crick as expounded in his book *In Defence of Politics*.[3] Crick has a distinctive mission of defense. Politics is about progression through *compromise* between competing interests. Crick's target was types of political ideology that assume the reserved ground of a non-negotiable element. For Crick any such non-negotiable stance is unpolitical. In political progress everything, absolutely everything, is a matter of compromise between competing interests. It is only this that ensures cohesion. Non negotiation is fragmentation and the beginning of war which the exercise of politics is designed to foreclose.

In that word compromise there is a hint of relationship to Durkheim's social fact. Compromise names that which we cannot effect freely as individuals. It states a limitation on personal creative power. Such action can only be effected in concerted action with others. All committees, even a committee of three, involve compromise and act as limitations on our personal creative power. This can be related to the demand of Jesus what are *you* going to do. It is this appeal always to personal creative initiative that is the empowering and inspiring message of Jesus. In this distinction between individual and collective initiative can be found the essential difference between the religious and the political domains. The subject requires illustration to bring out the distinction but as a guide in anticipation I define the religious domain as *the creative power of the person*. This puts religion in relationship to the social fact which is a *constraint* on the creative power of the person. The social fact, or as I have framed it here, the political domain, is in some way the opposite of the religious domain. That is the definition that we are working towards in the following. An analysis of what the New Testament tells us about the Kingdom of God elicits clearly the basis of this relationship.

12.2. The 'Semi-Final' Puzzle in the Arrival of the Kingdom

It is not immediately obvious to the casual reader of the New Testament that there are contradictory indications about the timing of the arrival of the Kingdom of God. In some places Jesus indicates that it is yet to come although it is imminent. In other places he says that it is already here. For both Jesus and John the

Baptist there is no doubt that the Kingdom is on its way. 'Repent, for the kingdom of heaven has come near,' cries John the Baptist (Matthew 3:2). John is echoed after his execution by Jesus; 'Repent, for the kingdom of heaven has come near' (Matthew 4.17). This seems to be a straightforward initiation of the Apocalypse. God is now implementing the eventual revelation of his justice.

However, just what stage this is at or how it is being implemented is uncertain. There seems to be a strong element by which we ourselves are involved in the implementation. The Kingdom is already here and we are ourselves producing it. This puzzle has been the subject of exhausting discussion by scholars with no result. This puzzle is what I call the 'semi-final-puzzle' and it is a great clue to the distinction between the religious and the political domain. The puzzle has divided scholarship into two camps that advocate either present or future interpretation. No interpretation has been able to accommodate the clear sense of a Kingdom which is here but which is not yet here. The resolution is still an open-ended quest which is what makes the subject interesting. No arcane knowledge is required. The information is all there in the Bible. The novice stands in the matter on a level playing field with the scholar.

It would be useful to have fresh before us the evidence of the conflicting statements about timing. While assembling this evidence it would be useful also to gather up the material that tells us what the Kingdom is. In brief it is a vision of a perfect society membership of which is not inclusive of the existing population. Entry to this society is via the condition of judgment and some people will be excluded.

The evidence to be assembled can be marshalled under three headings; the character of the Kingdom as a perfect society; judgment as the condition of entry; the timing of arrival. Once this evidence has been set out we will return to detective work on the semi-final puzzle.

12.3. The New Testament Portrait of the Kingdom of God

12.3.1. The Perfect Society

The character of the Kingdom has never been a contentious issue. It is a vision of a perfect society which the four gospels hold in common. Matthew refers to the Kingdom of God and its synonym the Kingdom of Heaven thirty-seven times. Mark refers to it ten times, Luke twenty-seven times and John twice. These differences are not a measure of their relative interest in the Kingdom. All the gospels are suffused with the idea. John uses the image of family instead of kingdom but the content is the same. The difference between Matthew and Mark is that Matthew is a great information giver, whereas Mark is more off hand. Matthew, for instance, tells nine parables of the Kingdom but Mark, after reporting three of them breaks off, 'With many such parables he spoke the word to them' (4:33). Because of his fuller description Matthew is used here as the main informant on the Kingdom. The other gospels are brought in only for any additional information that they have to offer.

John the Baptist deserves precedence in giving us characterization of the society that needs to be made ready for the Messiah. Some of his message is reported by Luke:

And the crowds asked him, 'What then should we do?' In reply he said to them, 'Whoever has two coats should share with anyone who has none, and whoever has food should do likewise.' Even tax collectors came to be baptized, and they asked him 'Teacher, what should we do?' He said to them, 'Collect no more than the amount prescribed to you.' Soldiers asked him, 'And we, what should we do?' He said to them, 'Do not extort money by threats or false accusation, and be satisfied with your wages' (3:10-14).

These few snippets amount already to an extensive characterization of the Kingdom. People will be generous with their goods toward the needs of others. People in official positions will not use their power to exploit. Everyone will disdain material gain. It is a pity that we have only this fragment of John's teaching. As Joan Taylor, who has championed the retrieval of John the Baptist points out, much more of John's message than he is credited with may be reflected in the gospels, but these are concerned to ensure that John does not upstage Jesus.[4]

Nevertheless there is no shortage of details in characterizing the Kingdom because Matthew handsomely fills out the theme. Those who will inherit the Kingdom are those who give food to the hungry, drink to those who are thirsty, who welcome strangers, clothe the naked, look after the sick and visit people in prison (25:35-36). In chapter five a further shortlist is presented. The Kingdom of heaven is a place where people who are poor in spirit (I take this to mean disheartened) will be comforted, where people who mourn will be comforted, where meek people will not be pushed aside, where people who hunger for righteousness will be satisfied, where merciful people will receive mercy, where people who are pure in heart will see God, where people who work for peace will be welcomed, as also people who have been persecuted for their beliefs. The chapter goes on to describe some rules of conduct that will achieve these goals. You will obey every letter of the Jewish laws. You will not murder anyone. You will reconcile yourself quickly to anyone you have been angry with or have called a fool. You will not be adulterous, you will not seek revenge, you will not perjure yourself, you will give to everyone who begs from you, you will lend to anyone who asks, you will give your coat to anyone who wants to sue you for it. You will not make any show of piety or charitable giving. You will not pray extravagantly with empty phrases but will ask simply for God's Kingdom to come and God's will to be done. You will forgive others. You will show disdain for material possessions. You will not judge others (Matthew chapters 5, 6 and 7).

This already looks like a full picture of ideal human relations, but this is not the whole of Matthew. We learn that, 'unless you change and become like children, you will never enter the kingdom of heaven' (18.3). Whoever becomes humble like this child is the greatest in the kingdom of heaven. It will be easier to enter if we are not rich (19.3). The Kingdom will not be like a typical Gentile princedom where rulers are tyrants. 'It will not be so among you; but whoever wishes to be great among you must be your servant, and whoever wishes to be first among you must be your slave' (20.26). Finally the Kingdom will be inclusive of outcasts, such as the tax collectors and prostitutes who serve as the biblical symbol for those on the fringe of society (20.31).

Some of the parables that Matthew reports extend the characterization. The parable of the King who annuls the debts of his slaves is a vivid illustration of forgiveness and abrogation of legal rights in favor of personal sympathy (18:23). The parable of the pearl of great price and the treasure in a field emphasize the immeasurable value of the Kingdom (13.44-45).

Matthew's portrait has shown that the Kingdom will turn upside down everything we expect of a typical social order. After this comprehensive picture there is little to be added by the other gospels. Luke reinforces the theme of forgiveness in his parable of the prodigal son (15:11). He is also insistent on the priority of spirit over material goods. 'Take care! Be on your guard against all kinds of greed; for one's life does not consist in the abundance of possessions' (12:15). 'Life is more than food, and the body more than clothing' (13.23). Luke takes up the quelling of pride. When invited to a feast always sit down at the lowest place (14:10). John vividly illustrates service to others and absence of pride in the example of Jesus washing the feet of the disciples. 'You call me Teacher and Lord and you are right, for that is what I am. So if I, your lord, have washed your feet, you also ought to wash one another's feet' (13:13-14). John's characterization of the Kingdom is condensed as he is content to distill out the overriding essence; 'I give you a new commandment, that you love one another. Just as I have loved you, you also should love one another' (13:34).

The fact that John mentions the Kingdom of God only twice is no indication of lack of interest. It is just that he uses different images. His preferred term is 'children of God' and 'my Father's house' (14:2). This suggests family, children and household as an alternative model for kingdom and citizenship. He has the high priest prophesy that Jesus will die 'not for the nation only but to gather into one the dispersed children of God' (11:52). He refers to the children of light (12:36). John is imbued with the antithesis of the Kingdom, 'the world' and its ruler Satan. He uses the word walk which suggests a domain. 'Whoever follows me will never walk in darkness but will have the light of life' (8:12). He uses the word conquered which suggests kingdom, 'But take courage; I have conquered the world' (16:33). John tells us three times about the ruler of this world which is Satan's kingdom. 'Because the ruler of this world has been condemned' (16:11). He uses a number of antitheses to express the ideal kingdom and the anti kingdom: Light/darkness, death/eternal life, below/above, truth/freedom versus sin/slavery. John's special focus is that Jesus himself embodies the Kingdom of God. For instance where Luke and Matthew give parables expressing forgiveness John reports Jesus personally acting out the Kingdom in the forgiveness of the woman taken in adultery. John is not alone in variety of terminology used to refer to the Kingdom. Luke uses the phrase 'inherit eternal life' (10:25) which is synonymous. Matthew tells us that 'the road is hard that leads to life' (7:14). He reports a questioner coming to Jesus to ask: 'Teacher, what good deed must I do to have eternal life?'(16:17). He refers to 'the word of the Kingdom' being choked by the cares of the world and the lure of wealth (13:19). Terminology is proliferated further by the ambiguities of translation. The Greek basileia can be translated kingdom or rule. The original Aramaic malkuth can be translated kingship, kingly rule, reign or sovereignty.[5] There is no need to be concerned that this variety of expression implies confusion. There is no dispute about the beautiful society that is referred to.

12.3.2. The Time of Arrival

In contrast to the clear-cut evidence of the character of the Kingdom the timing of its arrival is a subject of varied interpretation of a date anywhere between already present and due in a thousand years. This is not surprising. Anyone presented with the beautiful vision, which contradicts all experience of human nature, must wonder when and by what process the transition could be made. The gospel evidence for the timing of the Kingdom can be summarized under four headings: just begun, here present, near and indefinite future.

Just begun: For Jesus a cosmic event is under way. He tells his disciples: 'I watched Satan fall from heaven like a flash of lightning' (Luke 17:18). This reflects the background in apocalyptic literature of a cosmic battle taking place in heaven which is mirrored on earth. John confirms this understanding of Jesus, in the passage already quoted 'the ruler of this world has been condemned' (16:10). Matthew has this sense of beginning when he reports the response of Jesus to the request of the Pharisees to show them a sign. 'You know how to interpret the appearance of the sky, but you cannot interpret the signs of the times' (Mat 16:3). It is this hyper urgency feeling of events breaking in that may distinguish the message of Jesus from that of John the Baptist, Jesus has radicalized the imminence.

Already present: Jesus is accused by the Pharisees of using the power of the devil to effect his healings. He replies that Satan cannot drive out Satan and therefore he, Jesus, must be using the power of God. 'If it is by the spirit of God that I cast out demons then the kingdom of God has come to you' (12:28). Luke repeats this and illustrates with the example of the strongman whose property is broken into by someone who is stronger. 'When a

strong man fully armed is on guard over his palace, his possessions are safe. But when someone stronger attacks and
overpowers him, he carries off the arms and armour on which the
man had relied and distributes the spoil' (Luke 11:17). The key
passage demonstrating a present Kingdom is reported by Luke.
'Once Jesus was asked by the Pharisees when the kingdom of
God was coming, and he answered, "The kingdom is not coming
with things that can be observed;" nor will they say "Look here it
is!" or "there it is!" For in fact the kingdom of God is amongst
you' (Luke 17:20-21).

Near: That amounts to six passages relating to beginning and
here present but a much greater number refer to near and future.
Chapter 16:28 in Matthew sets a definite time scale of one lifespan
for the expectation. 'Truly I tell you, there are some standing here
who will not taste death before they see the Son of Man coming in
his kingdom.' This is Paul's timescale of expectation. He is faced
with a problem of reassuring the Thessalonians that those who
have died before the arrival of the kingdom will not be excluded
from it, and he advises that on the contrary they will precede the
living. 'For since we believe that Jesus died and rose again, even
so, through Jesus, God will bring with him those who have died.
For this we declare to you by the word of the Lord, that we who
are alive, who are left until the coming of the Lord, will by no
means precede those who have died' (1 Thess. 4:13-18). Joseph of
Arimathea is described by Mark as 'waiting expectantly for the
kingdom of God' (Mark 15:43). There is a sense of near expectation
in Mark's report of Jesus; 'I will never again drink of the fruit of
the vine until that day when I drink it new in the kingdom of
God.' (Mark 14:25). John implies a timescale within one generation when Jesus declares; 'In my Father's house there are many
dwelling places. If it were not so, would I have told you that I go
to prepare a place for you? And if I go and prepare a place for you,
I will come again and will take you to myself' (14:2-3). A fairly
immediate timescale is implied in John's passage, 'Now is the

judgement of this world; now the ruler of this world will be driven out. And I, when I am lifted up from the earth, will draw all people to myself' (12:31-32). The comparison with the fig tree recounted in Matthew repeats the timescale of a generation by analogy with the seasons. 'From the fig tree learn its lesson: as soon as its branch becomes tender and puts out leaves, you know that summer is near. So also, when you see all these things, you know that he is near, at the very gates. Truly I tell you, this generation will not pass away until all these things have taken place' (24:32-35). This passage is combined with the element of unexpected arrival illustrated by the examples of the thief in the night, the flood in the time of Noah, the sudden arrival of the master of the house and the bridesmaids who fell asleep. 'But about that day and hour no one knows' (24:36), 'Therefore you also must be ready, for the Son of Man is coming at an unexpected hour' (24:44). 'Keep awake therefore, for you know neither the day nor the hour' (25:13). Luke has the theme of unexpected arrival. 'Be on your guard so that your hearts are not weighed down with dissipation and drunkenness and the worries of this life, and that day does not catch you like a trap' (21:34). The 'that day' in the passage is clearly an event not a process. Mark describes the 'beginning of the birth pangs' (13:8) when recounting the signs preceding the end. 'When you hear of wars and rumours of wars, do not be alarmed; this must take place, but the end is still to come. For nation will rise against nation and kingdom against kingdom, there will be earthquakes in various places; there will be famines' (13:7-8).

Luke gives a clue that at the time of Jesus there was no consensus on the timing and that there was probably intense discussion about it. He reports Jesus contradicting a crowd who 'supposed that the kingdom of God was to appear immediately' (19:11). He tells the parable of the nobleman who went on a journey giving each of his slaves a pound to trade with while he was away. The moral of this is that there may be a wait for the kingdom but the important thing is good stewardship in the meantime and preparation for the kingdom to come.

We come finally to the statements that portray the kingdom coming in an indefinite future. These turn out to be as numerous as all the other statements put together. They are summarized in the prayer that Christians have prayed from the very beginning at the instigation of Jesus. 'Lord, teach us to pray, as John taught his disciples.' He said to them, "When you pray, say: Father, hallowed by your name. Your kingdom come" (11:1-2). The image of the end of an age and of two separate ages is prevalent. 'Then Peter said, "look we have left our homes and followed you". And he said to them, "truly I tell you, there is no one who has left house or wife or brothers or parents or children, for the sake of the kingdom of God, who will not get back very much more in this age, and in the age to come eternal life"' (Luke 18:28-30). Matthew reports Jesus on the Mount of Olives with his disciples asking him, after he has predicted the ruin of the temple, 'Tell us, when will this be and what will be the sign of your coming and the end of the age?' (24:3). Matthew varies the theme of different ages; 'Truly I tell you, at the renewal of all things, when the Son of Man is seated on the throne of his glory, you who have followed me will also sit on twelve thrones judging the tribes of Israel' (19:28). There is a sense of an event in the indefinite future in the complaint of the Gadarene demoniacs; 'What have you come to do with us, Son of God? Have you come to torment us before the time?' (18:29). There is a sense of lengthy endurance required in the face of persecutions. Mark exhorts his readers; 'but the one who endures to the end will be saved' (13:13). Matthew repeats this verbatim in 10:22 and again at 24:12 with the addition; 'And this good news of the kingdom will be proclaimed throughout the world as a testimony to all nations; and then the end will come.' This proclamation suggests much work to be done before the arrival and increases the indefinite timescale. This is also implicit in Matthew's 'All is accomplished',

'For truly I tell you, until heaven and earth pass away, not one letter, not one stroke of a letter, will pass from the law until all is accomplished' (5:18). Paul gives a sense of a lengthy sequence of events and a hint of continuing battle with Satan, who although fallen from heaven as Jesus saw him, still has some life in him:

> For since death came through a human being, the resurrection of the dead has also come through a human being; for as all die in Adam, so all shall be made alive in Christ. But each in his own order: Christ the first fruits, then at the coming those who belong to Christ. Then comes the end, when he hands over the kingdom to the Father, after he has destroyed every ruler and every authority and power. For he must reign until he has put all his enemies under his feet... when all things are subjected to him, then the Son himself will also be subjected to the one who put all things in subjection under him, so that God may be all in all (1 Cor. 15:20-28).

The Revelation of John gives Paul's scheme a specific timescale of a thousand years, or perhaps we should say a wholly indefinite one. A thousand years can be taken as a poetic symbol for a long time well outside our own possible experience. 'I saw also the souls who had been beheaded for their testimony to Jesus and for the word of God. ...They came to life and reigned with Christ for a thousand years. (The rest of the dead did not come to life till the thousand years were ended.)... When the thousand years are ended Satan will be released from his prison and will come out to deceive the nations at the four corners of the earth, Gog and Magog, in order to gather them for battle...they surrounded the camp of the saints and the beloved city. And fire came down from heaven and consumed them' (20:4-10). Although the timescale is indefinite here, the eventual completion is conclusive.

12.3.3. Judgment: The Condition of Entry to the Kingdom

Judgment, the condition of entry to the Kingdom, is the final aspect to be considered. Although there is uncertainty about the timing of the Kingdom there is complete agreement that there will be judgment. The wheat will be separated from the chaff, the tares will be separated from the wheat, the sheep separated from the goats, the coarse fish separated from the edible, an account must be rendered. Luke's parable of the person who gave a great dinner, only to find many of the guests making excuses not to come expresses the potential but not actual inclusion (14:16). Matthew quotes John the Baptist; 'he will... gather his wheat into his granary; but the chaff he will burn with unquenchable fire' (Matthew 3:12). 'Collect the weeds first and bind them in bundles to be burned, but gather up the wheat into my barn' (Matthew 13:30). 'When the Son of Man comes in his glory, and all the angels with him, then he will sit on the throne of his glory. All the nations will be gathered before him, and he will separate people one from another as a shepherd separates the sheep from the goats, and he will put the sheep at his right hand and the goats at the left' (Matthew 25.31). 'Again, the kingdom of heaven is like a net that was thrown into the sea and caught fish of every kind; when it was full they drew it ashore, sat down, and put the good into baskets but threw out the bad. So it will be at the end of the age. The angels will come out and separate the evil from the righteous and throw them into the furnace of fire where there will be weeping and gnashing of teeth' (Matthew 13:47-50). 'On the day of judgement you will have to give an account for every careless word you utter; for by your words you will be justified and by your words you will be condemned' (Matthew 12:36). John has a different image of exclusion. 'No one can see the kingdom of God without being born from above' (3:3). Mark has a different way of expressing the matter. 'Those who are ashamed of me and of my words in this adulterous generation, of them the Son of Man will also be ashamed when he comes in the glory of his Father' (Mark 8:38). The Day of judgment is not going to be pleasant. 'Woe to you Chorazin! Woe to you Bethsaida! For if the deeds of power done in you had been done in Tyre or Sidon they would have repented long ago in sackcloth and ashes. But I tell you, on the day of judgement it will be more tolerable for Tyre and Sidon than for you' (Matthew 11.20-22).

12.4. Scholarly Attempts to Resolve the 'Semi-Final' Puzzle
To sum up this evidence, the New Testament portrays a Kingdom which is at the same time both here present and yet still future. The problem of interpreting this has produced reams of speculation but the result as it stands today is unsatisfactory. All attempts to resolve the question have been forced resolutions that prioritize one aspect at the expense of the other. There has as yet been no solution that genuinely combines both future and present aspects. That is to say that there has been no interpretation that accepts the Kingdom as an irreducibly two component event one part of which is within reach of humans the other part of which requires the action of God.

The history of interpretation is mired in partisanship because the matter is the battleground of apocalyptic and anti-apocalyptic interpretations of Jesus. If the future timing of the Kingdom can be marginalized or otherwise discounted then Jesus can be framed, in accordance with the Socialist Kingdom, as a non-apocalyptic announcer of a new political order on earth that is just beginning. No twentieth-century liberal liked the exclusionary feature judgment and this maneuver avoided it. On the other hand if the present element could be discounted then Jesus can be framed as an apocalyptic prophet. This polemic aside all three main surveys of the matter have unanimously concluded that neither the one element nor the other can be discounted. This conclusion forms the central theme in Bishop Lundstrom's survey of 1947. Norman Perrin stated it as a conclusion of his 1963 survey and Bruce Chilton confirmed it in his roundup twenty years later.[6] The situation of resolving the semi-final puzzle is a peculiar one. Sociology, with its disdain for close engagement with theology, ignores the matter. Theology, with its embarrassed address to the twentieth century wishes to change the facts.

In a roundup of contributions to the scholarly debate Norman Perrin (1920-1975), one time president of the Society of Biblical Literature, summarized the inconclusive situation at the time as follows:

> It may be said to be established that the Kingdom is both present and future in the teaching of Jesus. The discussion has reached this point; Weiss and Schweitzer were not able to convince the world of scholarship that it was wholly future. Dodd was not able to maintain his original view that it was wholly present and subsequently modified it, and Bultmann's wholly futuristic view was modified at this essential point by his *Schuler*. But to decide that the Kingdom is both present and future raises immediately the question of how we are to understand this tension in the teaching of Jesus.[7]

In an updated survey twenty years later Bruce Chilton recounts the same difficulty of interpretation. 'Just what are we dealing with when we hear of a kingdom which presents itself so flexibly as both future and present?'[8] At this period in the early eighties, however, Chilton senses a movement 'a developing dissatisfaction, or at least unease, with the eschatological consensus.'[9] He finds a new consensus that looks for a replacement framework. The reader has been prepared, in the discussion of the Apocalyptic Resistance, to foretell what that consensus is: nobody will give a home to that embarrassing future bit of the Kingdom.

Today there is no sign of progress toward an answer to that riddle of present and future. The solutions to the riddle still minimize one element at the expense of the other. The Socialist 'realized' Kingdom collapses the future into the present. Chilton's own solution leans in this direction. It relies on the differences of emphasis that arise in the translation of the Hebrew bible into the Aramaic language version, the Targum, which was familiar to Jesus. The Targum uses a number of times the expression Kingdom of God, which is not common in the Hebrew. In the Aramaic, Kingdom of God also has a distinct sense of the 'self-revelation of God.' The Kingdom interpreted as self-revelation has a progressive and diffusive element joined with an indeterminate timetable. This is a gift to apocalyptic resistance. As God is timeless there can be no future element to him and he awaits discovery. 'An exclusivist time scheme focuses so single-mindedly on when sovereignty is mechanically asserted over a territory that it does less than justice to the targumic and dominical insistence that the kingdom is a personal God revealed. When Jesus announced the kingdom, he made nothing less known than that God, who was and is and is to come (Isa. 41:4; Rev. 1:8).'[10]* In this subtle way Chilton manages to subsume the future into the present and joins the Apocalyptic Resistance interpreters.

In the face of the puzzle the solution by the Jesusologists is that the apocalyptic future element has been interpolated, contrary to the wishes of Jesus, by the limited cultural horizon of the gospel writers. We can in this view simply discount all the gospel evidence of a future event. The Jesusologists take the extreme measure of composing their own scriptural canon in order to avoid the facts of the Kingdom.

So much has this puzzle absorbed the attention of scholars yet so much has it defied satisfactory explanation that John Meier, one of the most thoroughgoing authorities on Jesus, is prepared to consider a desperate position of last resort: maybe it is a logical contradiction that Jesus did not realize he was making? Maybe people in those days were not too concerned about this?

Maybe our wish for resolution is an inappropriate demand of the modern mentality? [11]

This is going too far out of desperation. Meier's casting about highlights the fact that theology still lacks a framework that wholeheartedly understands the Kingdom as here present and yet to come. The question of the 'semi-final' puzzle remains a delightfully open-ended challenge to interpretation.

Before moving on to present an interpretation it is worth a pause to set the context of what is to be proposed by illustrating some of the inventive contortions that scholars have put themselves through. Johannes Weiss insisted that a choice had to be made. 'Either the kingdom is here or it is not here yet.'[12] To make his apocalyptic case he had to discount the present aspect. He proposed that the Kingdom was here in the sense of parallelism between events in heaven and on earth. 'In what sense does Jesus speak of a "presence" of the Kingdom of God?... We have to bear in mind that for the Israelites, likewise for Jesus, there existed a twofold world, and thus a twofold occurrence of events. The world of men and history is only the lower floor of the world's structure... what happens on earth has its exact parallel in heaven... thus an event which on earth is only beginning to take place may... be... already enacted in heaven.'[13] Weiss goes on to say that Jesus normally thought of the Kingdom as future and only broke out into talking of the Kingdom as present in the excitement of finding that his own actions were successfully driving out Satan and wishing to 'impress malevolent questioners.'

Schweitzer proposed a similar parallelism using the analogy of a cloud. 'Being still to come, it is at present purely supramundane. It is present only as a cloud may be said to be present which throws its shadow upon the earth; its nearness, that is to say, is recognised by the paralysis of the Kingdom of Satan.'[14] In this way Schweitzer eliminates the two key kingdom present passages noted above (Matthew 12.28 and Luke 17.20). Chilton encapsulates the objection to this apocalyptic solution. It makes the Kingdom a form of tokenism present only by anticipation in the ministry of Jesus.[15]

The device used by C.H. Dodd to discount the future element in favor of the present is that Jesus really spoke of a higher, not a future, reality; it was just that he used apocalyptic language to express it:

> The thought of Jesus passed directly from the immediate situation to the eternal order lying beyond all history, of which he spoke in the language of apocalyptic symbolism. He did not strip history of its value, for he declared that the eternal order was present in the actual situation, and that this situation was the 'harvest' of history that had gone before. His teaching is not therefore rightly described as mystical, if we understand the mystic to be one who seeks to escape from the moving world of things and events.[16]

In a move that places Dodd as grandfather to the Jesusologist school of thought he considered that only later did a literal minded church develop the idea of a second coming along the lines of Jewish apocalyptic.

12.5. Gradual Growth: A Common-sense Solution?

As a last illustration of the difficulties of interpretation a resolution should be considered that is bound to occur to the reader and is equally bound to be dismissed. Surely Jesus saw the Kingdom as a process of development that was present in that it was beginning but future in that it had not reached maturity? This is the homely sense in which the parables of the leaven in the dough, the seed growing secretly and the mustard seed can be interpreted. There is a certain inevitability that, in the absence of any other contender this 'progressive change' solution should turn up as the default position. It can be seen in

John Meier's unconvinced acceptance in the face of a situation that he feels has defeated us.[17*] 'A static kingdom of God understood as a set place or a set state of affairs could not be both present and yet coming. But the kingdom of God as a dynamic mythic drama does allow for the coming in stages, with strategic battles already won, yet final victory still to come.'[18]

Gradualism as a resolution is, however, excluded as an explanation by the fact that the New Testament shows a qualitative change to be necessary before the arrival of the Kingdom. The arrival is not a quantitative progression to completion. There is a certain intuitive realism in this. What evidence of progression is there in our experience of the past two thousand years? This qualitative requirement is Paul's understanding of the matter. In his first letter to the Corinthians he responds to a question about resurrection and tries to explain what bodily form will be taken by those who are resurrected from the dead. It's a delightful passage in which Paul flails around for a suitable analogy then gives up at the impossibility of description with a sigh of relief:

> But someone will ask, 'How are the dead raised? With what kind of body do they come?' Fool! What you sow does not come to life unless it dies. And as for what you sow you do not sow the body that is to be, but the bare seed, perhaps of wheat or some other grain. But God gives it a body he has chosen and to each kind of seed its own body. Not all flesh is alike, but there is one flesh for human beings, another for animals, another for birds, another for fish. There are both heavenly bodies and earthly bodies, but the glory of the heavenly is one thing and the glory of the heavenly another... What I am saying, brothers and sisters is this: flesh and blood cannot inherit the kingdom of God, nor does the perishable inherit the imperishable. Listen, I will tell you a mystery! We will not all die, but we will all be changed, in a moment, in the twinkling of an eye... for this perishable body must put on

imperishability' (1 Corinthians 15:35-54).

Luke confirms the notion of a physical change necessary for the completion of the Kingdom when he answers the silly question from the Sadducees about the woman who is married successively as the widow of seven brothers who die in turn. They want to know whose wife she will be at the resurrection (Luke 20:27-36). Luke reports the answer of Jesus. 'Those who belong to this age marry and are given in marriage; but those who are considered worthy of a place in that age and in the resurrection from the dead neither marry nor are given in marriage. Indeed they cannot die any more, because they are like angels and are children of God.' John also expounds the theme that physical existence must be transformed. For John 'Jesus gave power to become children of God, who were born, not of blood or of the will of the flesh, or of the will of man, but of God' (1:14). 'It is the spirit that gives life; the flesh is useless' (6:63). 'No one can see the kingdom of God without being born from above' (3:3). The conclusion to be drawn from these passages is that however far humans may progress in the formation of the Kingdom it cannot be completed with our existing bodies. The Kingdom requires a qualitative step to the future. The parables using the analogy of growth are not parables of quantitative growth, rather, as Paul's analogies suggest, they are parables of contrast.[19] From the mustard seed you would never guess what the magnificent tree would be like. From the beginnings of the Kingdom on earth you could never imagine the magnificence of the mature Kingdom. A miraculous transformation is to occur.

A qualitative change in human nature that can be imagined but not explained is, therefore, a condition for the completion of the Kingdom. This accords with our understanding of human nature. Although much can be done to improve human behavior, only humans without selfish instincts for food, sex, money, power and pride could form a perfectly non-antagonistic society.

It is a physical body without these characteristics that cannot be explained.

This requirement for a qualitative change in human biology is matched by the requirement for a qualitative change in the structural propensities of human society. The New Testament is not so explicit about this but it can be worked out from the requirement that the social order is to be reversed as proclaimed in the passage from Matthew already quoted. 'You know that the rulers of the Gentiles lord it over them, and their great ones are tyrants over them. It will not be so among you; but whoever wishes to be great among you must be your servant, and whoever wishes to be first among you must be your slave' (Matthew 20:25-27). 'All who exalt themselves will be humbled, and all who humble themselves will be exalted' (Matthew 23:12).

If we are to take this reversal literally we will need to admit that the Kingdom is a call for humiliation not a change of structural propensities. As there is no hint in Jesus of a primary wish to humiliate, nor any hint in the continuing Christian hopes, then the literal does not seem the right interpretation. For instance, if the starving farmer and his family are elevated to kingship and the king and royal court are put in the position of the starving farmer this is only to replicate the same society that is complained about and the scene is set, not for the closure that is the goal of the gospels, but a repetitious cycle of complaint. The misery of starvation is a function of situation, not personality, as is the abuse of power. If The Kingdom is only to be, as it were, a game of musical chairs it has lost all claim as an object of the religious imagination.

The reversal of the social order can only be, just as the qualitative change in human biology, an imagined but unexplainable change in the structures of human society. Just as we cannot explain a body that does not need food and warmth so we cannot explain a society which does not generate the function of leadership and the advantage of one person over another. It is touching that the mother of the sons of Zebedee could not imagine this and wanted to use her influence with Jesus for the customary purposes of nepotism. Jesus has to let her down gently (Matthew 21:20). The theme of reversal of the social order is dear to apocalyptic. The Sibylline Oracle provides us with a fine illustration that this is a poetic vision based on qualitative change in the conditions of existence:

> But as for the others, as many as were concerned with justice and noble deeds, and piety and most righteous thoughts angels will lift them through the blazing river and bring them to light and life without care in which is the immortal path of the great God and three springs of wine and honey and milk. The earth will belong equally to all, undivided by walls or fences. It will then bear more abundant fruits spontaneously. Lives will be in common and wealth will have no division. For there will be no poor man there, no rich, and no tyrant, no slave. Further no one will be either great or small anymore. No Kings, no leaders. All will be on a par together. No longer will anyone say at all 'night has come' or 'tomorrow' or 'it happened yesterday' or worry about many days. No spring, no summer, no winter, no autumn, no marriage, no death, no sales, no purchases, no sunset, no sunrise. For he will make a long day (Sibylline Oracles 2:315-330).

To sum up, quantitative progression as the solution to the semi-final puzzle is excluded because a qualitative change is required for completion. The Kingdom is irreducibly a two component event. This is the inescapable characteristic that must be accommodated in any explanation of the social reality that the Kingdom represents.

12.6. The Social Reality Represented by the Kingdom of God
To summarize the evidence so far six prime characteristics of the
Kingdom of God have been elicited.

1. The character of the Kingdom is a society of perfectly amiable
   relations between humans.
2. The fulfillment of the Kingdom requires a qualitative change
   in human biology that can be imagined but not explained.
3. The fulfillment of the Kingdom requires a qualitative change
   in the structural propensities of human society that can be
   imagined but not explained.
4. The Kingdom is a society which can only be completed by a
   future event.
5. The Kingdom is a society which we must make strenuous
   efforts to achieve now.
6. Citizenship in the fulfilled Kingdom can only be obtained
   after judgment.

For the task ahead all six characteristics combined must be
convincingly incorporated in any social reality proposed as the
substrate of the supernatural and apocalyptic presentation of the
Kingdom.

In the course of discussion social realities corresponding to
the first four characteristics have already been given or implied.
The first factor is readily translatable. The Kingdom of God
represents a vision of the potential for perfection in human
relations. It represents the tragic contrast between what is and
what might be. This visionary status is confirmed by the next two
requirements. If the qualitative changes are necessary but
indescribable, then they have the status of unrealizable,
creatively imagined visions. They represent the knowledge that it
is the present qualities of human nature and human society that
produce the tragedy of human existence.

This visionary status is backed up by the typical form in

which apocalyptic literature is couched. Dreams, visions, secrets, signs, arcane knowledge, divinations, astrological calculations and revelations of the magical and fantastic tell us by their format that it is an ideal and not an actual Kingdom that is being presented. Schweitzer pinpointed the hyper-nature, the absolute idealism of the ethics of Jesus in contrast to the compromised status by which we commonly understand those ethics:

> We make him conceive of the Kingdom of God as if its historical realisation represented a narrow opening through which it had to squeeze before attaining the full stature which belongs to it. That is a modern conception. For Jesus and the prophets however, it was a thing impossible. In the immediateness of their ethical view there is no place for morality in the Kingdom of God or for the development of the Kingdom – it lies beyond the borders of good and evil; it will be brought about by a cosmic catastrophe through which evil is to be completely overcome. Hence all moral criteria are to be abolished. *The Kingdom of God is super-moral.* To this height of hyper-ethical idealism modern consciousness is no longer capable of soaring.[20]

The changed qualitative elements as a precondition of the Kingdom explain the condition that it is necessarily future. The qualitative changes cannot be engineered by the endeavor of humans. Hence the need for magical agency which brings in the qualitative change. The apocalyptic agency of God, or the Son of Man, represents the power that is beyond the possibility of the human.

With the first four characteristics of the Kingdom thus related to a social reality the outstanding matter is the semi-final puzzle. How does the present action of humans relate to the future action of God? If the future condition of the Kingdom may be taken as satisfactorily explained the remaining two essential problems can now be isolated. They are the need to qualify the present activity of humans in constructing the Kingdom together with the final condition of judgment. To put the question another way, if Christians cannot bring in this perfect ideal society why are they commanded to be busy and are in fact so busy in their efforts to achieve it in this world?

Perrin, in his summary, effectively identified this question as the second major outcome of the scholarly debate. 'What is the relationship between eschatology and ethics in Jesus' teaching?' [21] The apathetic misinterpretation of apocalyptic is driven to the answer, none, but our revised understanding of apocalyptic shows that the connection as fundamental. The injunction 'repent for the Kingdom of God has come near,' establishes that willingness personally to do all that one can to create the ideal society, in so far as it can be achieved by humans, is the precondition of entry to the future Kingdom. From this it can be concluded that of the two components to the ideal society one is within human grasp. The feature that one component is within human grasp must be so otherwise we would not be enjoined to attempt it.

Repent is an unfortunate translation of the original Greek because of its negative emphasis on past guilt and its association with evangelical overuse. The rendition in Spanish is infinitely preferable, *cambiad de actitud!* change your attitude! Change your attitude for the kingdom of heaven has come near! cries John. This is an active command to produce ideal relations. This is what the followers of John the Baptist are doing, sharing their coats and food. This is what the followers of Jesus are doing forgiving the brother they have fallen out with. This is what the congregations of Paul are doing making their collection to relieve famine at the Jerusalem Church. Christians everywhere and always have been engaged in such activity.

Luke's parable of the nobleman who entrusted a pound to each of his servants before going away explains that *the most important thing* is to use the individual talents that each of us possess for productive purposes (Luke 19:11). The Sermon on the Mount ends with the injunction to build a firm foundation for the coming Kingdom. 'Everyone then who hears these words of mine and acts on them will be like a wise man who built his house on rock. The rain fell, the floods came, and the winds blew and beat on that house but it did not fall, because it had been founded on rock' (Matthew 17:24).

But if Christians cannot complete the ideal society why are they attempting it? What fragment of that society are they building and with what hope of success? A clue to the answer can be picked up from the Humanist construction of the Kingdom of God. Humanists don't use the term but as they are cousins to the Christians in their vision of an ideal society it is no surprise that the character of the Kingdom should emerge in their literature albeit clothed in different language. The great analytic opportunity provided by the Humanist portrait of the ideal society is that, although it envisages just the same type of society as the Christian, it does not envisage supernatural agency to bring it in. Humanists, therefore, must propose, or at least provide as implicit, some method by which humans themselves are able to effect the qualitative changes that Christians consider could only be effected by magical agency. It is in this difference that the clue to the nature of the present Kingdom can be found.

The Humanist Kingdom of God can be drawn out of the three manifestos issued by the Humanist Association. Manifesto I appeared in 1933. Manifesto II was issued at the fortieth anniversary in 1973 and Manifesto III in 2003.[22] Manifesto I has a preamble which explains that doctrines of traditional religion have become powerless to 'solve the problem of human living in the Twentieth Century.' The Manifesto proposes re-founding a humanist religion that is capable of furnishing adequate social goals. It then goes on to affirm fifteen clauses. Most of these are intermingled with a concern to distance Humanism from the supernatural, but clauses eight, nine and fourteen reveal a mission identical to the Kingdom of God. Clause eight states, 'Religious Humanism considers the complete realization of human personality to be the end of man's life and seeks its development and fulfillment in the here and now. This is the explanation for the humanist's social passion.' Clause nine, 'The humanist finds his religious emotions expressed in a heightened sense of personal life and in a cooperative effort to promote social well-being.' Clause fourteen, 'The humanists are firmly convinced that existing acquisitive and profit-motivated society has shown itself to be inadequate and that a radical change in methods, controls, and motives must be instituted. A socialized and cooperative economic order must be established to the end that the equitable distribution of the means of life be possible. The goal of humanism is a free and universal society in which people voluntarily and intelligently cooperate for the common good.'

Manifesto II reflects the years of intervening history and has a preamble updating the horrors of Nazism and Stalinism. It confirms, 'The ultimate goal should be the fulfilment of the potential for growth in each human personality' and it offers a vision of hope, 'a set of common principles that can serve as a basis for united action... a design for secular society on a planetary scale.' Seventeen clauses are then given that set out the Kingdom of God. 'We are concerned for the welfare of the aged, the infirm, the disadvantaged, and also the outcasts, the mentally retarded, abandoned, or abused children, the handicapped, prisoners, and addicts, for all who are neglected or ignored by society... The preciousness and dignity of the individual person is a central humanist value.' We could be forgiven for suspecting that this clause had been lifted from Matthew's chapter five.

If the characterization of the humanist Kingdom is identical to the Christian so also are the elements of timing; urgency; the revolutionary end of an age; visionary faith and even an echo of the Hope of Israel. 'We have reached a turning point in human history.' 'World poverty must cease.' 'The world cannot wait for a reconciliation of competing political or economic systems to solve its problems.' 'War is obsolete.' 'We deplore the division of humankind on nationalistic grounds.' 'The true revolution is occurring in countless non-violent adjustments.' 'These affirmations are... an expression of a living and growing faith.' 'This new Humanist Manifesto is a vision of hope.'[23]

Humanism and Christianity can thus be seen to produce identical visions of an ideal human society. They are commonly referred to as utopian visions. But to call them utopian, if it means only some more or less unrealizable ideal, is a cliché that does not help in locating their special characteristic. There is a unique feature of the humanist Kingdom for which neither political theory nor sociology has a word and so it is necessary to invent one. It is what I call *transtopian*. This is the view that by a simple aggregation of individual actions structural change can be brought about in the society. The belief, faith even, is that somehow by a summation of individual direct action war or capitalism can be eliminated.

But the transtopian faith is naive. Nobody has yet found a way to end 'parochial loyalties and inflexible moral and religious ideologies'; nor to end 'destructive ideological differences among communism, capitalism, socialism, conservatism, liberalism and radicalism'; nor to end 'narrow allegiances of church, party, class, or race.' Transtopian faith is naive because these divisions are endemic. But for the Humanists such divisions can be eliminated. The seismic divisions listed in the manifesto are going to be 'transcended', 'overcome', 'superseded by broad-based cooperative efforts', 'by men and women of goodwill.' If any Christian is unconvinced of the difficulty in this, they have only to consider their home territory of divisions between the churches and the painful progress of ecumenism.

The transtopian impetus is a mistake but it is one that is easily made, and frustrating to people anxious for change. It seems obvious that because every action in the world is reducible to an individual action then if individual actions could be changed the summation would lead to a structural change. But this is not the case. Individual action is the necessary but not always the sufficient factor in any action. An analogy to grasp this situation is the relationship between chemistry and molecular biology. Every aspect of molecular biology is founded on the action of the individual elements of chemistry. This is a necessary but not sufficient explanation. The molecules built up out of the elements develop characteristics distinct from the individual components that make them and this leads to the myriad functions of enzymes and protein molecules that control organic life. Molecular biology has a set of characteristics independent of its chemical elements. It is an emergent property not present in its constituents. Human society likewise has a set of characteristics independent of its individual human elements. Simple aggregation of individual actions cannot effect structural change. Humans are faced with the obstinate fact that their societies have structural aspects that are beyond the control of the individual. The transtopian vision discounts this fact. The difference between the Humanist ideal society and the Christian Kingdom of God is that the Humanist vision is transtopian while the Christian is not. The Christian vision reserves a dimension to the action of God.

This matter of the impotencies of individual action brings the discussion back to Durkheim's social fact. Durkheim continued in the passage previously quoted to reinforce the concept with further illustration:

There is in every society a certain group of phenomena which may be differentiated from those studied by the other natural sciences. When I fulfil my obligations as brother, husband, or citizen, when I execute my contracts, I perform duties which are defined externally to myself and my acts in law and custom... Such reality is objective because I did not create them... The system of signs I use to express my thoughts, the system of currency I employ to pay my debts... the practices I follow in my profession function independently of my own use of them... Here, then, are ways of acting, thinking and feeling that present the noteworthy property of existing outside the individual consciousness. These types of conduct or thought are not only external to the individual but are, moreover, endowed with coercive power... since their source is not in the individual, their substratum can be no other than society.[24]

Durkheim's preface to the second edition expanded the analogy from chemistry:

The living cell contains nothing but mineral particles, as society contains nothing but individuals. Yet it is patently impossible for the phenomena characteristic of life to reside in the atoms of hydrogen, oxygen, carbon and nitrogen... The inanimate particles of the cell do not assimilate food, reproduce, and, in a word, live; only the cell itself as a unit can achieve these functions... Let us apply this principle to sociology. If, as we may say, this synthesis constituting every society yields new phenomena... these new phenomena cannot be reduced to their elements without contradiction in terms, since, by definition, they presuppose something different from the properties of these elements... social life cannot be explained by purely psychological factors, i.e., by states of individual consciousness.[25]

To take stock, what has emerged in the analysis at this point is that the Kingdom of God is an irreducibly two-component event. It consists of both qualitative and quantitative change. Human activity is similarly two-component. Some of our actions are socially constrained, some of our actions are discretionary. The transtopian belief evidenced by the Humanist vision of the ideal society attempts to efface both the two-component constitution of human activity and the two-component constitution of the Kingdom. It is in this two-component constitution that can be discovered the distinction between the religious and the political domain and the resolution of the semi-final puzzle of the Kingdom.

What is implied by Durkheim, although it is his concern to distance sociology from confusion with its opposite, is the reciprocal of the social fact. This is the sphere of human action in which the individual is not constrained and has the power to exercise free initiative. In moving toward a definition of the domain of religion this domain can be defined as *the reciprocal of the social fact*. The domain of religion is the discretionary individual creative power residual to the constraints of social facts.

Put in colloquial terms this is the creative power of the person. This corresponds with the magnetic appeal of the Bible which is a book of personal empowerment. Jesus always asks 'what are *you* going to do?' 'Will *you* take in this stranger?' 'Will *you* settle this dispute without going to court?' 'Will *you* forgive this injury?' 'Will *you* turn the other cheek?'

I want to appropriate the concept of the reciprocal of the social fact as a religious concept, distinct from the sociological. In opening this chapter the proposal was that the essential counterpart to the religious domain was the political domain, not the conventional counterpart the secular. The religious/political distinction replaces that of sacred/profane. A different understanding of the political was also proposed which brought it several stages down the hierarchy to the level of persons. To effect this different understanding of the political I propose to understand social facts as political facts. The purpose of this is to make it understood that the political is sited within the individual person just as the social fact is sited.

Some new terminology is needed to fix this understanding for two reasons. The word political cannot serve because it has too many unwanted associations. It is also unsatisfactory to define the religious domain by a negative. I name the reciprocal of the political fact, the discretionary creative power of the person as the *monosocial relationship*. The political fact, the constraint on the creative power of the person I name as the *polysocial relationship*. The monosocial relation is that power in the relation of two persons that is residual to the constraints of their polysocial relationship. The monosocial relation is the domain of religion. Every person is constituted by both the religious and the political domains. For an example, each of us in a monosocial capacity contributes our creative talents to our employment. At the same time we engage a polysocial structure. For no merit of our own, for reasons that we do not understand and for reasons that we have no power to dismantle, that employment in a developed country awards us twenty times the earth's resources than it does a worker in a developing country. To a worker in that circumstance we stand in a polysocial relationship. For another example, we serve in the army in response to a political fact. We play football with the enemy on Christmas Day, as some British troops are reported to have done, in response to a religious fact.

The absolute disjunction between the monosocial domain and the polysocial, between the relations of chemistry and the relations of molecular biology needs to be emphasized because of the temptation to think that the monosocial could somehow govern the polysocial. This is impossible. The case of Christian pacifism is an illustration. Cecil Cadoux undertook a study just prior to and at the start of the Second World War. He started the work with the hope that some synthesis could be found, that somehow there could be a pacifist solution to war. The blowing up of people's bodies with explosives is so absolutely against Christian principles that if there is to be any credibility to those

principles they must seem to offer a resolution. Cadoux's
conclusion was no conclusion. There is no synthesis to be found.
Cadoux was driven to adopt an apocalyptic resolution. The issue
is consigned to God's hands 'until the day of Jesus Christ.'[26]
Cadoux in this conclusion has confirmed the dual structure of
human existence. He discovered for himself the truth that
Machiavelli dared to speak openly and which shocked the
religious presumption of his day: A Christian society cannot be
established by Christian means, the religious and the political
domains of human existence are incommensurable.[27] It is this
dual social reality that is represented in the semi-final puzzle of
the Kingdom and it is this dual social reality that the Apocalypse
seeks to resolve.

Ironically for this apocalyptic result Cadoux is an anti-apocalyptic writer.[28] This irony makes the account of his journey
illuminating. He starts out from what is not in fact the Christian
position. He starts from a fantasy position of religiously inspired
political anarchism. Cadoux sets out thinking that an actual
resolution, a pacifist solution to war could be implemented. With
the dawning of the fact that this is not the case he then adopts the
realistic Christian religious apocalyptic position. Christians can
only do 'the best we know'[29] in the circumstances. Cadoux has
inadvertently recreated the semi-final two-component constitution of the Kingdom of God.

It is not necessary to take a voyage of intellectual discovery to
perceive what we know intuitively about war. The most heart
rending photos from the Second World War are those innocent
young men on all sides being thrown into the military machines.
Such photos are a portrait of the polysocial domination of the
monosocial.

Religion too bears within itself the stigma of this tectonic
fissure between the monosocial and polysocial domains. The
purpose of religion is inalienably monosocial but the operating
programs produce polysocial structures which contradict the

purpose. The mere thought structures set up divisions. The structures are peculiarly liable to hijack by other polysocial structures such as national, clerical or cultural. Christians and Muslims reach out to each other in their monosocial function. The polysocial program divides them. The Society of Friends, together with today's Super Ethic, fully understand in their intuitive manner the artificial divisions produced by the programs and the need for the purpose to fight back against the program.

The objection will be made that this separation of the religious from the political is a withdrawn, pietist, unnecessarily circumscribed definition of the religious domain. On the contrary the domain of religion resides in permanent tension with the political which is always a subtraction from the ideal envisaged by the monosocial relations. There is no doubt that some people will continue to engage in movements to political change inspired by their religious principles. The theory states only that this is not religious activity. It is a specialized activity. Politics cannot be religious because it is hierarchical, usually by class, education and gender. It is exclusive by temperament and aptitude. The religious domain by contrast is absolutely inclusive.

An example to illustrate the value of the new definitional apparatus would be useful. Melissa Raphael's work, *The Female Face of God in Auschwitz*,[30] provides this illustration. Raphael considers that although God appeared to have abandoned the Jews in Auschwitz she was still present. In the act of washing each other's filthy, vacated and beaten faces with urine or coffee, in the absence of sanitary facilities because the water supply was deliberately turned off, this irrepressible attempt to preserve dignity and caring human relationship showed the continued presence of God.

Some background is needed to place Raphael's line of thought. The holocaust provoked a challenge to Jewish theology with a call to abandon the supernatural God altogether. Richard Rubenstein argued that the holocaust was a radically new example of evil and that the traditional view that suffering is a punishment from God for breaking the covenant meant that God was, as he put it, 'Hitler's accomplice?!' For Rubenstein this conclusion is so awful that it is time for the Jews to abandon their three thousand-year-old tradition that there is a supernatural God looking after their nation. He announced the 'Death of God.'[31] On the other hand orthodox theology was untroubled by the event because it was nothing new. It repeated atrocious sufferings that have occurred many times in Jewish history. Eliezer Berkovits championed the traditional view. Zachary Breiterman encapsulated the tradition neatly: although the holocaust was historically unique, it was not theologically unique.[32] Faced with the stark alternatives of abandoning their cultural worldview, or accepting that God either actively murders innocent people or turns away from such matters, other theologians have tried to create some middle way. Emil Fakenheim tried to establish some positive lessons from Auschwitz. He salvaged from the experience a 'commandment to hope' and scraped together from the disaster some good points such as the creation of the state of Israel.[33]

Faced with alternatives that are either horrible, feeble, or reject God altogether, Melissa Raphael is concerned to establish a different vision of God. Her complaint against the prevailing theology comprises the additional dimension that it is male centered:

> Post-holocaust theology is disquieting not just because it relates catastrophe, but... by ultimately vindicating the sovereignty of God's name, it once more secures masculine religious territorial honour and standing. Although Holocaust theology has at least partially indicted God on account of his holocaustal absence, silence or... his abusiveness, it has not

questioned its own basic *model* of God, only certain failures of its attributes. It is my contention that it was a patriarchal model of God, not God-in God's-self, that failed Israel during the Holocaust. ...my critique... is... directed at a model of God which was reliant upon an idea of masculine power that simply could not withstand the actual masculine patriarchal power that confronted it. Theological analyses of the Holocaust that persist in using patriarchal categories of understanding are not identical, but are continuous with, the ideological conditions that produced the Holocaust and therefore cannot persuasively move beyond them.[34]

Raphael is concerned to rescue the religious witness of women from its erasure. She revives the Jewish principle of, 'the immanent God as Shekhinah, (the traditionally female image of the indwelling presence of God) which helps us trace God's redemptive presence in Auschwitz in ways which do not entail divine or theological complicity with evil.'[35] She proposes 'a theology of the face to face relation.'[36]

The hiddenness of God's masculine face in Auschwitz no longer looks like the reluctant withholding of interventionary power, but a dereliction of love, an abusive complicity, a permission for violence or a tacit admission of his non-existence. However, in so far as God's female face has always been occulted by the refusal or subjugation of the female dimension of God, the trope of hiddenness is not entirely dispensable. It helps us to ask how God might have been present but concealed in Auschwitz because her female face was yet unknowable to women... Yet hiddenness implies (undetectable) presence. And to be present is transitive; it is always and only a positioning of one to the other. So that Israel's god is nonetheless an accompanying God whose face or presence, as Shekhinah, 'She-Who-Dwells-Among-Us', goes with Israel, in mourning, into her deepest exile, even if Israel cannot see her in the terrible crush.[37]

To illustrate this Raphael draws on the memoirs of a number of survivors. She does not glamorize the experience. Under conditions of starvation, exhaustion, abuse, depersonalization and despair, meanness is manifested along with selfless generosity.

I hope Melissa Raphael will excuse me for taking her insight out of its local Jewish and feminist context in order to enlist it for my own purposes because it has universal potential. The significance of Auschwitz is that it presents the extreme polarization of the monosocial and polysocial relations. The monosocial was defined as the discretionary power of the individual as a residual of the polysocial. This means that the religious domain is a fluctuating arena. In Auschwitz, the possibilities of the monosocial were reduced toward zero as a matter of policy by the camp administration. The women were tattooed with numbers to deprive them of name. They were shaved and put in camp clothing to deprive them of identity. They were made fearful to exhibit kind actions through the terrorism of official reprisal. They were deprived of all the usual strength that we derive from family, friends and work relations. They were disorientated through uprooting from their homes. They were distraught at the loss of children and husbands. They had none of the material resources that we rely on to give help to others, fuel, clothing, bedding, food, soap, medicine; not even the water to clean the ubiquitous dysentery from their legs. The power of the polysocial, the system which subjected them, was as absolute as could be, without hope of change. As a microcosm of normal society with its balance between monosocial power and polysocial circumscription it was at the extremity of polarization. Yet nevertheless some irrepressible presence of God shone through. That was what Raphael saw in her 'theology of face to face.' It is a beautiful vision of God.

Raphael has effectively identified God in the ideal potential of the monosocial relationship. Her theology of face to face is the same as the theology of God discovered directly in the conditions of human relationships that was reviewed in chapter eight. The Shekhinah might be said to represent the extensive creative potency of monosocial relations that has been named in this work as psychosymbiosis.

Although monosocial is a novel word to define the sphere of relationships that comprise the religious domain the concept itself is perfectly current. It is the principle that defines a church. A church is a society of monosocial relations. Its members come together in voluntary association and leave their polysocial functions outside. Their relations are constituted on the egalitarian basis of persons unmixed with the relations of hierarchy in which they partake in the wider society. The church is thus an artificial partial society. It escapes the complication introduced by economic relations to the extent that it is not a real self-sufficient society. It remains dependent on its host society.

The understanding that the ideal potential of monosocial relations constitutes the present aspect of the Kingdom of God is already promoted in theology. This is the meaning of those who, since Augustine, consider the church to be the incipient Kingdom of God. In any society there *will always be* a polysocial order for better or worse. The point of the church as the present Kingdom of God is that the ideal potential of monosocial relations can be realized as a separate issue without reference to this prevailing order. Indeed if Christians had to wait for the fulfillment of some prior condition of society before they could begin work in the Kingdom they would be waiting for ever. This explains why Jesus is unconcerned with Roman rule. The present Kingdom of God has its own domain in which it is not short of work.

The question that started this discussion was, given the limitations on human possibility, what fragment of the two-component Kingdom are Christians commanded to build? Raphael's insight has answered this. Every person has a share of the creative power in relation to other people that is needed to produce the ideal in our monosocial relations. This is a capability under the free command of every person independent of the future qualitative change that would need to be brought in by God to complete the perfection. That perfection can only be finally realized by the elimination of the emergent property of polysocial relations.

To summarize, the semi-final puzzle of the Kingdom of God is resolved by that Kingdom's division into two components, one of which is within the capability of humans and the other of which is not. When Jesus makes that great statement recorded by Luke in chapter 17:20, 'The kingdom is not coming with things that can be observed; nor will they say "Look here it is!" or "there it is!" For in fact the kingdom of God is amongst you', (between you is a preferable translation), it is the sphere of monosocial relations that he is referring to. The social reality represented by characteristic five on the above summary list is the ideal potential of our monosocial relations. The apocalyptic vision of the Kingdom of God represents a protest against the tragedy of human existence which is permanently immersed in a struggle between its religious and its political domain.

12.7. The Social Reality Represented by Judgment

There remains to be identified characteristic six on the above list. What social reality is represented by the fact that citizenship in the fulfilled Kingdom can only be obtained after judgment?

It is no exaggeration to say that twentieth-century theology choked on the entry condition of judgment while nineteenth-century theology gloated over it. F.D. Maurice was dismissed from his professorship at King's College in 1853 for teaching dangerous doctrine that tended to lessen the horrible consequences attendant upon judgment. He made a distinction between eternal as a literary expression and endless as a literal one. Maurice denied that the bible literally prescribed endless punishment for the wicked. For him the matter was a poetic description.

The exclusive entry condition contradicts the inclusive sensibilities of twentieth-century democratic society and examples of refusal were given in the discussion of the Apocalypse. A further example is appropriate here specifically in relation to the Kingdom. Dodd, the father of the 'realized' Kingdom, which has been referred to here as the Socialist Kingdom successor to the Liberal Kingdom, did at least recognize that the issue of judgment was there in the record and had to be addressed. It is actually difficult in the context of a Kingdom that is to be produced on earth comprising the existing population to countenance any exclusionary basis. Any such qualification would reproduce something like Pol Pot's attempt at a pure peasantry, Mao's elimination of bourgeois professors, or the American era of eugenics. All such attempts at a purified population have been given up as horrific. Dodd's method of squaring the indelible fact of judgment stated in the record with the impossibility of twentieth-century acceptance of exclusion was to mollify it out of existence:

> Thus the coming Kingdom of God displayed its character of judgement, that is to say, as the testing and sifting of men. Though a drag-net may bring all kinds of fish to shore, they must be picked over before they can be marketed (as the fishermen disciples knew well). Harvest is both the ingathering of the crop *and* the separation of wheat from tares. So the multitudes who were brought by the preaching of Jesus within the scope of the Kingdom of God were sifted by the way things went. They passed judgement upon themselves, not by introspective self-examination, but by their reaction to the developing situation.[38] This self-selected exclusion is the

same principle as the annihilationism espoused today by Tom Wright.

Dodd may be on the right track. The possibility that judgment cannot be taken at its literal face value is opened up by its real role in the formation of community and the energization of the present as discussed in section 1.4. It is a typical aspect of sects that 'the elect' or 'the saints' are always envisaged to be inside the community. It is 'the others' who will be judged. The feature that turns this possibility that the face value is not what it seems into a certainty is the fact that as a literal concept judgment is absurd. It is impossible to assess the goodness of a human life in black and white terms of good or bad. The division into two classes of the righteous and the wicked is ridiculous. Although humanity may produce a proportion of obvious saints and sinners the majority are borderline cases. Were the attempt made to enforce the literal sense of judgment, on the basis say of 50 marks for a pass and 49 for a fail, then God is made into a ghastly bureaucrat with a relish for record keeping and inordinately detailed regulations. The borderline cases will clog up the offices of heaven with their appeals in search of that extra mark. Their friends will spend their time in heaven in an agony of concern for them. The result will be disgust with God. It would not be possible for God to escape this disgust by refining the procedure. No weighting system to calculate the value of individual transgressions could escape charges of arbitrary composition and so could not command consensus. The system would have to be imposed on the basis of unilateral authority with the only possible flexibility found in an appeal to forgiveness. This in turn would lead to endless resentful charges of personal favoritism. If this were avoided by universal application of forgiveness it would negate the principle first started with. Justice as the object of judgment is a fiction. The discrepancy between the sensational visionary status of judgment and its pedestrian literal status is too much to hold together any apparent value in the concept.

It is also necessary to take into account a peculiar unjust fact connected with judgment. A whole life of crime may be excused by a deathbed change of attitude. Clearance for entry can be obtained even at the very last hour at the cost of seeming unfairness to those who have been approved for longer, as the parable of the vineyard workers' wages portrays in Matthew chapter 20:1-16. With equal arbitrariness a whole life of good deeds may be vitiated by a last minute conversion to unbelief. The essential principle that is being expressed in these aspects is not justice it is voluntarism. Wright and Dodd's self-selection may be close to the mark as the real purpose of the feature. It is a condition of the ideal society that were anyone forced to join then it would no longer be an ideal society. Judgment is the condition that protects the status of the ideal society by preserving freedom of choice. It is necessary to respect the fact that some people may not care to enter the Kingdom. They are perhaps happy enjoying a mistress and exploiting their workforce and are prepared to take a chance on their inclusion.

This feature of freedom of choice is presented in the gospels through the circumstance that citizenship in the Kingdom is extended by invite:

> The kingdom of heaven may be compared to a king who gave a wedding banquet for his son. He sent his slaves to call those who had been invited to the wedding banquet, but they would not come. Again he sent other slaves, saying, 'Tell those who have been invited: Look, I have prepared my dinner, my oxen and my fat calves have been slaughtered, and everything is ready; come to the wedding banquet.' But they made light of it and went away, one to his farm, another to his business (Matthew 22:2).

Citizenship of the Christian Kingdom, to which the parables of the lost sheep and the prodigal son also give voice, has always been one of invitation, of any number of invites, of any number of refusals forgiven, of endlessly open acceptance and of joyful celebration at any change of heart. 'Son, you are always with me, and all that is mine is yours. But we had to celebrate and rejoice, because this brother of yours was dead and has come to life' (Luke 17:31). Dodd was right to exchange the sickle for sifting. The social reality expressed by judgment is that it is not possible to found any genuine religious community by coercion.

There remains the final question, what has this present task to do with the future? The incentive of judgment enjoins us to create the ideal monosocial society now. But why should we bother with that when in the new qualitative conditions of the future society all this will be swept away to irrelevance?

A clue to this lies in an omission from the qualitative changes to be engineered in the future Kingdom. The physical constitution of the human body will be different as also the structural propensities of the organization of society, but one thing that is not imagined to change is personal responsibility. It would in principle be possible to engineer the perfect future society by means of a qualitative change of mentality that produced lobotomized automatons without initiative. Were this to happen, however, the one essential part of human nature would have been obliterated. Whatever our complaints about the imperfection of human nature this is where a line is drawn. It is one thing we do not want to imagine about ourselves and from such a vision we recoil. This preservation of individual initiative means that the new gifts for the construction of the ideal society granted in the future Kingdom could still be subverted, *after judgment* by those who chose to negate them. The present Kingdom is therefore a *token in earnest* as a precondition of the completed Kingdom. Only those persons who have proved good use of their discretionary power are fit to be trusted. To use a modern analogy from the rules of driving, no teenager is going to get the keys to a superbike until they have passed the test on a moped. No parent would wish the procedure otherwise.

12.8. Conclusion

The two-stage implementation of the Kingdom of God is a faithful statement of the tragic condition of human existence. Humans are immersed in a bipartite social structure consisting of a religious and a political dimension. The tragedy is that although each of us individually is necessarily the creator of that political dimension, we are not individually the sufficient creator of it, and therefore do not control it. Humans are condemned by the twin structural levels of human existence perpetually to work for an ideal society that will never be accomplished. The social reality that the Kingdom represents is the contrast between the human nature that is and the vision of the human nature that can be imagined. To put the matter in more intuitive terms we each have the power to create our own slice of the Kingdom of God in our friendship groups, our families, our work relations and in our churches. This monosocial domain is what religion is. The Church, as the nascent Kingdom of God, has always recognized this partial mission. The rest, as the pacifism of Cadoux came up against, has to be left in the hands of God. The eventual revelation of God's justice, the Apocalypse, represents the dismantling of the emergent structure of human relations that humans are powerless to dismantle themselves. In the meantime there remains one immense and perpetual task to be undertaken that is by no measure secondary. It potentially exhausts every last ounce of every person's creative contribution. This is what religion serves to motivate. This is what unites the endeavor of Christians, Platonists, Mystics, Jesusologists, Humanists, plain Atheists and people of goodwill from any and every religion. This purpose is what religion is. It is the unifying basis of its various operating programs.

I propose Jesus for election to the Humanist council in order for him to introduce an element of realism into the program. The Humanist Manifesto believes that the Kingdom can be achieved by reason and thereby flies off into fantasy. Jesus knows that the perfect society can be only partially realized by human volition and, using the cultural expression of his times, he formulates the part that is beyond human engineering as something that can only be done by a creative force external to human society: an act of God.

Conclusion

The Manifesto of Social Theology

There have traditionally been two varieties of theology: Revealed Theology and Natural Theology. The premise of Revealed Theology is God revealed to humans through the mediating channel of other humans and embodied in texts. The premise of Natural Theology is God revealed to humans through the workings of the universe. These two traditions are united in the premise that transposes God as a source of moral command external to human relationships. The premise of Social Theology is that God arises directly from the dynamics of the human person in its creation by other persons. It names as God what is experienced within every person as the ideal potential of that creative relationship.

The Social Theology Manifesto

1 Religion is what is done not what is believed.
2 Life itself is the religious adventure. Each of us is a miracle of creative energy sprung from dust and to that dust we will return. During that brief span we have the free choice to use our creative power for a greater or a lesser good.
3 God is the invitation to join the enterprise of the greater good.
4 God is the equal value of every person in the creative enterprise of life.
5 God is the Friendship of No Authority between persons.
6 God is a celebration of the gift and potential of life.
7 God is perennial not eternal. We are trustees responsible for the renewal of God in every person in every generation.

It can be considered a failure of the radical theology of the past fifty years that it has contributed nothing to erase the gratuitously divisive distinction between believers and atheists. The division still plagues the liberal desire for non-exclusivity. Many people brought up in the environment of a Christian tradition, wanting to be part of the Christian community, people with religious feelings but doubtful about the supernatural agency of God, people who, on the measure of their wish for peace and goodwill to all people on earth, merit the title Natural Christians, are obliged to denominate themselves by a vocabulary of oxymorons, misnomers and negatives: Christian Atheists, Christian Agnostics, Christian Humanists, Non-theists, Non-realists and plain old fashioned Atheists. A whole generation of thoroughly religious young people are being brought up inarticulate in the expression of their innate religious feelings because they reject the traditional program that defines what it is to be religious. They lack the cultural apparatus with which to renew that program. Anthony Freeman felt obliged to adopt the misnomer Christian Humanism.[1] The collected testimony of twenty-seven Quaker Non-theists reluctantly compromised on that name as the least worst description on offer.[2]

The interviews with Christian Atheists undertaken by Brian Mountford testify to the awkward conceptual vortex in the wake of the departing supernatural God.[3] He refers to the 'odd paradox of Christian Atheism.' His interviewees grope among the broken conceptual apparatus for restatement in some form of 'secular mysticism'; depth, significance; the religious sense of sacred awe; wonder in the sublime beauty of art, music and literature. The resort to Tennyson's 'more faith in honest doubt' introduces a dubious clutching at straws; the intrinsic fuzziness of quantum physics possibly leaves a gap for God; revelation comes through ambiguity; both parties share common ground on God as, ultimately, a mystery

The disconcerting definitional awkwardness is accompanied

by awkwardness of membership; a sense of being an outsider; marginalization; half acceptance; placement as 'hangers on' and outright suspicion. Mountford attempts to close the gap by demonstrating that orthodox belief in God is more vaguely defined than is recognized and that atheists are more God inclined than they credit themselves, but in the end even his generous hand of friendship is equivocal in the description 'tangential... contributors.'[4]

Mountford undertook mission impossible. Given the terms of reference his result is inevitable. The metaphysical remnant defines all three positions of believer, atheist and agnostic. It is all encompassing. Even the atheists cannot escape it.

The task of Social Theology is to refuse the terms of reference. My preface stated the conviction that it is nonsense to say that life today is secular and not religious. The enterprise of life today is no less religious than it has ever been. The church is diffusive through the whole matrix of our social relations. The church is a voluntary monosocial community of people creating each other's lives on the basis of mutual assistance. That church does not necessitate a church building. It does not necessitate an institutionally structured church. It does not necessitate metaphysics. It does not necessitate authority or dogma. I like to think of Paul's churches as the model for impromptu friendship groups constituting a church, or the group of disciples that surrounded Jesus sharing meals together, or the Quaker refusal of liturgical formulas, gathered simply in quietness to draw strength from the spirit that flows between them.

There is no boundary to the diffusive extent of a church. Today's supportive church gatherings take place in the institution of the coffee bar; toddler's groups; the football ground; the pub; the treatment rooms of holistic practitioners and, still, fulfilling the necessary function of a formally open forum, the symbolic heart of the community, the parish church. These are the sites of the Church of the Super Ethic that sails over the quarrels of religion and its impeded morals.

As to the sacraments that articulate the stages of life the institutional church celebrates a limited set of seven key transitions to encompass the whole of life: birth day; confirmation day; marriage day; communion day; repentance day; ordination day and death day. Today's culture has comprehensively infused those sacraments of life into life. It has appropriated from the altar the sacrament of renewal and celebration of 'us together'. Communion has been invested in the arena of everyday life. The bread and wine of Galilee has been changed into the invitation to coffee or a beer. Communion now encompasses mother's day; father's day; wedding anniversary day; first day at school day; exam result day; leaving school day; first job day; starting university day; graduation day; moving out of home day; first flat day; moving house day; breaking a relationship day; promotion day; retirement day; welcome back from hospital day. This is an extended church celebration of the person. It is a supportive stock take of every stage post in the course of life. It is a sacramentalization of life to the extent that, those Quakers again are ahead of the game, the whole of life is the sacrament. As Gerald Priestland replied, dipping his biscuit into his cup of tea, in response to the Archbishop of Canterbury's concern about the Quaker refusal of communion, 'what do you think we are doing?'[5]

This is the new life of religion that Don Cupitt was trying to get at when he identified 'Life' as the word that has replaced 'God' in common language usage. This is the new religion that Charles Taylor groped toward when he cited the validation of everyday life and the subjective turn of the twentieth century. This is the everyday religion that Nancy Ammerman is struggling to uncover. This is the new religion of everyday life which is no different from the old religion which was always and only about everyday life. This is the newly revealed religion of Jeanne Warren's disqualified religious experience that people should 'not be left unprotected against the cold.'[6] It is the religion of the autonomy of the person that supports same sex marriages. It is the religion of fulfillment of the potential of the person that initiated the paralympics. It is the religion of empowerment that moved Val and Tony Bonnett and thousands like them on different projects, to raise money for fifteen years to build a sheltered block where their handicapped son and seven others could retain a degree of independence in adult life. It is the religion of the equal value of all persons that moved disenchanted social workers Margery and Bill Smith to start a gardening nursery for people with extra support needs. Their motto is 'we are all equal.'

These are actions pursued with faith, commitment and love. They are identical actions to religious actions. They should not be disqualified by the ethical parallel universe set up by the present terms of reference. They should not be disqualified as religious on account of the omission of the 'transcendent' or the supernatural fascia. This is the religion of what is done not what is believed. The sociologists of religion are on the threshold of rousing themselves to this consciousness. Grace Davie uses the analogy of an iceberg to describe her decentering that discovers the greater extent of religion beyond the tip of its institutions.[7] What is necessary to complete that decentering is the understanding that the sea itself is the religious medium.

Once upon a time it was acceptable language in this country to refer to people with dark skin as *niggers*. We have thankfully realized that it is not a descriptive word but a term of division. The word is an attempt to create exclusion by drawing an arbitrary cultural boundary between people. The word says nothing about the person to whom it is applied but does tell us the intention of the person who applies it. The word *secular*, with like purpose, was forged by Empire Christianity to police its borders. It has served in the armory of that regime of truth for the past fifteen hundred years. Sociology, the child of the church, picked up the usage because it knew no better example. It is time to banish our theological nigger word secular. I hope the day will come when secular will have its once upon a time, when it will be realized that secular was a culturally induced mirage.

It is time that the slumbering brains of theology and social science roused themselves from their dream world of ancient landscapes and woke up to the religion that is right in front of their noses.

Notes

Notes for Introduction and Preview

1   Acts 17.22-23 'Athenians, I see how extremely religious you
    are in every way. For as I went through the city and looked
    carefully at the objects of your worship, I found among
    them an inscription "To an unknown god." What you
    worship as unknown this I proclaim to you.' *The Holy Bible*,
    New Revised Standard Version, Oxford: Oxford University
    Press, 1995. All biblical quotations in this book are from this
    edition.

2   An early use of this name is in Charles Hartshorne and
    William Reese, Eds., *Philosophers Speak of God*. Chicago:
    Chicago University Press, 1953, p.2.

3   Michael Brierley, *Panentheism*, article in *The Encyclopaedia of
    Christianity*, Vol.4. Grand Rapids: Eerdmans Publishing,
    2005.

4   Quoted from a headmaster who wrote to John Robinson
    congratulating him on mediating the incomprehensible
    Tillich. Robinson and Edwards Eds., *The Honest to God
    Debate*, London: SCM Press, 1963, p.71.

5   Paul Tillich, *Systematic Theology*, Volume 1, Welwyn: Nisbet
    & Co., 1953, p.263.

6   'Schleiermacher's "feeling of absolute dependence" was
    rather near to what is called in the present system "ultimate
    concern".' *Systematic Theology* Vol. 1, p.47. 'When I first read
    Rudolf Otto's *Idea of the Holy*, I understood it immediately in
    the light of these early experiences, and took it into my
    thinking as a constitutive element. It determined my

method in the philosophy of religion, wherein I started with the experiences of the holy and advanced to the idea of God, and not the reverse way.' *Autobiographical reflections* in Kegley & Bretall Eds., *The Theology of Paul Tillich*, London: Macmillan, 1952.

7   Paul Tillich, *Ultimate Concern: Tillich in Dialogue*, D. Mackenzie Brown, Ed., London: SCM Press, 1965, p.191. This passage explains Tillich's problem of tact and use of parallel language.

8   'Over the next 79 years 'Paulus' was to continue his struggles, bearing a life-long dread of death, "the anxiety of being eternally forgotten".' Marion & Wilhelm Pauck, *Paul Tillich: His Life and Thought*, London: Collins, 1977. Tillich's autobiographical sketch *On the Boundary*, London: Collins, 1967, [1936]), recounts the many uncertainties of his life. *The Courage to Be*, Fontana, 1962, addresses 'the all-pervasive presence of the anxiety of doubt and meaninglessness in our own period.' p.166.

9   Stephen Sykes, *Friedrich Schleiermacher*, London: Lutterworth Press, 1971, Introduction.

10   B.A. Gerrish, *A Prince of the Church: Schleiermacher and the Beginnings of Modern Theology*, London: SCM Press, 1984, p.xiv.

11   Keith Clements, *Friedrich Schleiermacher: Pioneer of Modern Theology*, London: Collins, 1987, p.7.

12   Terence Tice, *Schleiermacher*, Nashville: Abingdon Press, 2006, p.xiii.

13   He is absent for instance from John Macquarrie, *Two Worlds are One: An Introduction to Christian Mysticism*, London: SCM Press, 2004. Bernard McGinn, *The Essential Writings of Christian Mysticism*, New York: The Modern Library, 2006. William Inge, *Christian Mysticism*, London: Methuen & Co., 1912

14   Rudolf Otto, *The Idea of the Holy*, Harmondsworth: Penguin,

1959.

15 Otto, *The Idea of the Holy*, p.125.

16 Otto, *The Idea of the Holy*, p.34.

17 John Robinson, *Honest to God*, London: SCM Press, 1963.

18 Don Cupitt, *The Way to Happiness*, Santa Rosa: Polebridge Press, 2005.

19 Otto, *The Idea of the Holy*, p.111.

20 Mircea Eliade, *The Sacred and the Profane*, San Diego: Harcourt Books, 1957.

21 Julian Huxley, *Religion without Revelation*, London: Watts & Co, 1941, p.83.

22 Thomas Altizer and William Hamilton, *The Death of God*, Harmondsworth: Pelican Books, 1968.

23 Don Cupitt, *Taking Leave of God*, London: SCM Press 1980. The Christian Buddhism proposed in this book together with the humanist inclination in *The New Christian Ethics*, London: SCM Press, 1988, tended to obscure the Nature God at the root of Cupitt's theology which was eventually revealed in his general theory of religion, *The Way to Happiness*, Santa Rosa: Polebridge Press, 2005.

24 Lloyd Geering, *Christianity without God*, Santa Rosa: Polebridge Press, 2002.

25 Letter to Eberhard Bethage April 30th 1944, Dietrich Bonhoeffer, *Letters and Papers from Prison*, London: Fontana, 1965, p.90.

26 Altizer and Hamilton, *The Death of God*, p.9.

27 Robinson, *Honest to God*, p. 22.

28 Robinson, *Honest to God*, p.13.

29 Karen Armstrong, *The Case for God*, London: Vintage Books, 2010. For further examples Catherine Keller, *On the Mystery: Discerning Divinity in Process*, Minneapolis: Fortress Press, 2008. Thomas Merton, *The Seven Storey Mountain*, San Diego: Harcourt Brace, 2002 [1948]. Matthew Fox, *The Coming of the Cosmic Christ*, San Francisco: Harper & Row,

1988. Matthew Fox, *Original Blessing*, Santa Fe: Bear & Company, 1983. Marcus Borg, *The God We Never Knew*, New York: Harper SanFrancisco, 1998. John Shelby Spong, *Why Christianity Must Change or Die*, New York: HarperCollins, 1999. Scotty McLennan, *Finding Your Religion*, New York: Harper SanFrancisco, 1999. Elizabeth Johnson, *She Who Is*, New York: Crossroad Publishing, 1992. Rosemary Radford Ruether, *Gaia & God*, London: SCM Press, 1992. Gordon Kaufman, *In Face of Mystery*, Harvard: Harvard University Press, 1995. John Macquarrie, *Principles of Christian Theology*, London: SCM Press, 1966. Neale Donald Walsch, *The New Revelations: A Conversation with God*, London: Hodder and Stoughton, 2003.

30   John Polkinghorne, Russell Stannard, Arthur Peacocke and Philip Clayton are examples of scientist theologians. The Schools of Theology at Chicago and later at Claremont have exercised a strong influence. See John Cobb and David Ray Griffin, *Process Theology an Introductory Exposition*, Philadelphia: Westminster Press, 1976. Also Philip Clayton and Arthur Peacocke Eds., *In Whom We Live and Move and Have our Being: Panentheistic Reflections on God's Presence in a Scientific World*, Grand Rapids: Eerdmans Publishing Co. 2004. Fritjof Capra's *The Tao of Physics*, London: Fontana, 1976, drew parallels between physics and mysticism but carefully drew a negative on any connection, p.338.

31   Alfred North Whitehead, *Process and Reality*, New York: Harper Torchbook, 1960.The extensive influence of process theology and its often overlooked influence underlying many thinkers, up to 1976, is illustrated in the guide to the literature Appendix B in John Cobb and David Ray Griffin, *Process Theology: An Introductory Exposition*, Philadelphia: Westminster Press, 1976.

32   'The picture of reality coming to us from contemporary science is so attractive to theology that we would be fools

not to use it as a resource for reimaging and reinterpreting Christian doctrine.' Sallie McFague, *The Body of God: An Ecological Theology*, London: SCM Press, 1993, p.74. See also Keller, *On the Mystery*.

33 Alasdair MacIntyre, *God and the Theologians*, Encounter, September 1963.

34 Keith Ward, *Holding Fast to God*, London: SPCK, 1982.

35 Anthony Freeman, *God in Us*, London: SCM, 1994.

36 Richard Harries, *The Real God*, London: Mowbray, 1994.

37 Alan Stephenson, *The Rise and Decline of English Modernism*, London: SPCK, 1984, p.198.

38 Sarah Coakley, Introduction, p.5. In Sarah Coakley and Charles Strang Eds., *Re-Thinking Dionysius the Aeropagite*, Chichester: Wiley-Blackwell, 2009.

39 'Paul Tillich is a theologian of our time who devoted much attention to the question of language about God, but I believe there is very little in Tillich's treatment of the matter that was not anticipated by Dionysius.' John Macquarrie, *Two Worlds Are Ours: An Introduction to Christian Mysticism*, London: SCM Press, 2004, p.90. The genetic line of descent has many strands. Oliver Davies for instance traces a different line through Proclus, Eckhart, Hegel and Heidegger. *Meister Eckhart Selected Writings*, London: Penguin Books, 1994.

40 John Hick, *Interpretation and Reinterpretation in Religion*, Chapter 4 in Sarah Coakley and David Pailin Eds., *The Making and Remaking of Christian Doctrine*, Oxford: The Clarendon Press, 1993.

41 Rosemary Radford Ruether, *Gaia & God: An Ecofeminist Theology of Earth Healing*, London: SCM Press, 1992, Introduction.

42 Enthusiasm: God and the Self are one.

43 Steve Bruce, *The Problems of a Liberal Religion*, in Mark Chapman Ed., *The Future of Liberal Theology*, Basingstoke:

Ashgate, 2002.

44   Coakley, *Re-Thinking Dionysius*, p.5.

45   Practices variously described, but these taken from Evelyn
     Underhill, *The Essentials of Mysticism* in Richard Woods Ed.,
     Understanding Mysticism, New York: Image Books, 1980.

46   Proposed by Wilfred Cantwell Smith, *Towards a World
     Theology*, Philadelphia: Westminster Press, 1981, Chapter
     nine *Interim Conclusion*. Taken up by John Hick, *An
     Interpretation of Religion*, Basingstoke: Macmillan, 1989, p.
     xiv, and adopted by Karen Armstrong, *The Case for God*,
     London: Vintage, 2010.

47   Coakley, *Rethinking Dionysius*, p.5.

48   Ernst Troeltsch, *The Social Teaching of the Christian Churches*,
     London: George Allen & Unwin, 1931.

49   Maurice Wiles, *The Remaking of Christian Doctrine*, London:
     SCM Press, 1974, p.106.

50   Adolf Harnack, *What is Christianity?* London: Williams and
     Norgate, 1912, p.8.

51   Karen King, *Back to the Future* in, *The Once and Future Jesus*,
     Santa Rosa: Polebridge Press, 2000.

52   John Hick, *The Second Christianity*, London: SCM Press, 1968,
     p.72.

53   John Hick, *The Fifth Dimension*, Oxford: Oneworld, 1999,
     p.84.

54   Keith Ward, *The Concept of God*, London: Collins, 1977, p.169.

55   John Hick, *Interpretation and Reinterpretation in Religion*,
     Chapter 4 in, Sarah Coakley and David Pailin Eds., *The
     Making and Remaking of Christian Doctrine*.

56   Don Cupitt, *Turns of Phrase: Radical Theology from A to Z*,
     London: SCM Press, 2011, p.14.

57   Don Cupitt, *The Way to Happiness*, Santa Rosa: Polebridge
     Press, 2005.

58   Armstrong, *The Case for God*, pp. 34, 43.

59   William Inge, *The Platonic Tradition in English Religious*

       Thought, London: Longmans, Green & Co., 1926, p.27.

60   William Inge, *The Philosophy of Plotinus*, London: Longmans
       Green & Co., 1923, p.54.

61   Inge, *Philosophy of Plotinus*, p.13.

62   David Strauss, *The Old Faith and the New*, London: Asher &
       Co., 1874.

63   Grace Davie, *The Sociology of Religion*, London: Sage
       Publications, 2007, pp. 19, 20.

64   Don Cupitt, foreword to Trevor Greenfield, *An Introduction
       to Radical Theology*, Ropley: O-Books, 2006.

65   Linda Woodhead, *Theology: The Trouble It's In*, in Gavin
       Hyman Ed., *New Directions in Philosophical Theology*,
       Basingstoke: Ashgate, 2004.

66   Franz Overbeck, *On the Christianity of Theology*, Trans.
       Wilson, Oregon: Pickwick Publications, 2002 [1873], p.92.

67   Martin Luther, *Treatise on Christian Liberty*, in John
       Dillenberger Ed., *Martin Luther a Selection of his Writings*,
       Doubleday Anchor, 1961, p.53.

8   Vladimir Lenin, *Left-Wing Communism, an Infantile Disorder*,
       Peking: Foreign Languages Press, 1975, [1920].

69   Alexander Berkman, *ABC of Anarchism*, London: Freedom
       Press, 1971, [1929].

70   Sayyid Qutb, *Milestones*, New Delhi: Islamic Book Service,
       2001, p.26.

71   Mahmoud Mohamed Taha, *The Second Message of Islam*,
       Translated by Abdullahi An-Na'im, New York: Syracuse
       University Press, 1996.

72   Don Cupitt, *The New Religion of Life in Everyday Speech*,
       London: SCM Press, 1999.

Notes for Chapter 1
The House of the Christians

1   Johannes Weiss, *Jesus' Proclamation of the Kingdom of God*,

Minneapolis: Fortress Press, 1971, [1895].

2   Albert Schweitzer, *The Quest of the Historical Jesus*, New York: Macmillan, 1960, [1910].

3   R.H. Charles, Ed., *The Apocrypha and Pseudepigrapha of the Old Testament*, Oxford: Clarendon Press, 1976, [1912].

4   R.H. Charles, *Eschatology: Hebrew, Jewish and Christian, A Critical History of the Doctrine of a Future Life*, London: Adam & Charles Black, 1898.

5   R.H. Charles, *Religious Development Between the Old and the New Testaments*, Oxford: Oxford University Press, 1914.

6   John Collins, Ed., *Apocalypse: The Morphology of a Genre*, Semeia 14, Atlanta: The Society of Biblical Literature, 1979.

7   Christopher Rowland, *The Open Heaven*, London: SPCK, 1982.

8   Charles, *Religious Development*, p.12.

9   Charles, *Religious Development*, p.110.

10   Charles, *Religious Development*, p.111.

11   Charles, *Religious Development*, p.69.

12   Charles, *Religious Development*, p.132.

13   Charles, *Religious Development*, p.18.

14   Charles, *Religious Development*, p.19.

15   Charles, *Religious Development*, p.23.

16   Charles, *Religious Development*, p.24.

17   Charles, *Religious Development*, p.24.

18   Charles, *Religious Development*, p.102.

19   Max Weber, *The Sociology of Religion*, London: Methuen & Co., 1963, p.139.

20   Weber, *Sociology of Religion*, p.143.

21   Weber, *Sociology of Religion*, p.142.

22   Weber, *Sociology of Religion*, p.145.

23   C. F. D. Moule, *The Birth of the New Testament*, London: Adam & Charles Black, 1962, p.103.

24   D.S. Russell, *Divine Disclosure*, London: SCM Press, 1982, p.14.

25   Moule, *Birth of the New Testament*, p.103.

26   Wolfhart Pannenberg et al., *Offenbarung als Geschichte, Kerygma und Dogma* Gottingen, Vandenhoeck & Ruprecht, 1965, p.96. Translated and quoted by H.D. Betz, *New Directions in the Study of Apocalyptic* in, *The Concept of Apocalyptic in the Theology of the Pannenberg Group*, Journal for Theology and the Church no.6, New York: Herder and Herder, p.193.

27   Ethelbert Stauffer, *New Testament Theology*, London: SCM Press, 1963, p.19.

28   George Caird, *The Language and Imagery of the Bible*, Gloucester: Duckworth, chapter fourteen.

29   George Caird, *The Revelation of St John the Divine*, London: Adam & Charles Black, 1966, p.292

30   Caird, *Revelation*, p.290.

31   Caird, *Revelation*, pp.292, 291.

32   Rowland, *The Open Heaven*, p.49.

33   Rowland, *The Open Heaven*, p.76.

34   Rowland, *The Open Heaven*, p.90.

35   Rowland, *The Open Heaven*, p.126.

36   Rowland, *The Open Heaven*, p.134.

37   Rowland, *The Open Heaven*, p.143.

38   Rowland, *The Open Heaven*, p.189.

39   Charles, *Religious Development*, p.12.

40   Caird, *Language and Imagery*, p.243.

41   Walter Kümmel, *Promise and Fulfilment*, London: SCM Press, 1957.

42   Kümmel, *Promise and Fulfillment*, p.152.

43   Kümmel, *Promise and Fulfilment*, p.153.

44   Kümmel, *Promise and Fulfilment*, p.151.

45   Kümmel, *Promise and Fulfilment*, p.154.

46   Kümmel, *Promise and Fulfilment*, p.146.

47   Kümmel, *Promise and Fulfilment*, p.155.

48   Saint Paul, 1 Corinthians, 15.35.

49   Saint Paul, Ephesians, 1.19, 1 Thessalonians, 4.15 and 1

Corinthians, 15.22-24.

50   J.H. Leckie, *The World to Come and Final Destiny*, Edinburgh: T & T Clark,1917, p.6. The Kerr Lectures to the Glasgow College of the United Free Church of Scotland.

51   William Inge, *The Philosophy of Plotinus*, London: Longmans Green and Co., Volume Two, p.7.

52   Russell, *Divine Disclosure*, p.9.

53   J.J. Collins, *Daniel, with an Introduction to Apocalyptic Literature*, Grand Rapids: Eerdmans, 1984, pp.2-3.

54   Robert Funk, *Honest to Jesus*, New York: Harper SanFrancisco, 1996, p.314.

55   Ernst Käsemann, *New Testament Questions of Today*, London: SCM Press, 1969, p.102.

56   John Hick, *Evil and the God of Love*, Basingstoke: Macmillan, 1985, preface.

57   Vernon White, *Life Beyond Death*, London: Darton Longman and Todd, 2006, p.38.

58   Jürgen Moltmann, *The Coming of God*, London: SCM Press, 1995, p.118.

59   Moltmann, *The Coming of God*, p.255.

60   Nicholas Thomas Wright, *Surprised by Hope*, London: SPCK, 2007.

61   Wright, *Surprised by Hope*, p.191.

62   Wright, *Surprised by Hope*, p.195, 6.

63   Wright, *Surprised by Hope*, p.172.

64   Wright, *Surprised by Hope*, p.183.

65   Wright, *Surprised by Hope*, p.181.

65   John Hick, *An Interpretation of Religion*, Basingstoke: Macmillan Academic, 1989, p.206,7.

67   Robert Funk, *Honest to Jesus*, New York: Harper SanFrancisco, 1996, p.314.

68   Cecil Cadoux, *The Historic Mission of Jesus*, p 345.

69   Wright, *Surprised by Hope*, p.193.

70   Hans Conzelmann, *An Outline of the Theology of the New*

Testament, London: SCM Press, 1969.

71   R. Meyer, *Prophets, in Theological Dictionary of the New Testament*, Ed., G. Friedrich, trans. G.W. Bromiley, Grand Rapids: Eerdmans, 1968.

72   T.F. Glasson, *Greek Influence in Jewish Eschatology*, London: SPCK, 1961.

73   S.B. Frost, *Old Testament Apocalyptic*, London: Epworth Press, 1952 and Paul Hanson, *Old Testament Apocalyptic Re-examined* in, Interpretation October 1971 Vol.XXV No. 4, Virginia Union Theological Seminary.

74   Gerhard Von Rad, *Old Testament Theology*, New York: Harper and Row, 1965.

75   W.D. Davies, *Christian Origins and Judaism*, London: Darton Longman & Todd, 1962

76   Frank Cross, *New Directions in the Study of Apocalyptic*, in Robert Funk Ed., *Journal of Theology and the Church*, Volume 6, New York: Herder and Herder 1969, note, p.165.

77   Leon Morris, *Apocalyptic*, London: Inter-Varsity Press, 1972, p.31.

78   Rudolf Bultmann, *Jesus and the Word*, London: Fontana, 1958, p.36.

79   Günter Bornkamm, *Jesus of Nazareth*, London: Hodder and Stoughton, 1960, p.67.

80   Paul Hanson, *Old Testament Apocalyptic Re-examined*, p.49, in Paul Hanson Ed., *Visionaries and their Apocalypses*, Philadelphia: Fortress Press, 1983.

81   Stephen Patterson, *The End of the Apocalypse: Rethinking the Eschatological Jesus*, Theology Today Vol.52, No1 April 1995, pp.11-12.

82   Marcus Borg, *A Temperate Case for a Non-Eschatological Jesus* in, *Jesus in Contemporary Scholarship*, Pennsylvania: Trinity Press 1994. (The essay appears as chapter three)

83   Saint Paul, 1 Corinthians, 7.25-31.

84   Stephen Liberty, *The Political Relations of Christ's Ministry*,

Oxford: Oxford University Press, 1916, preface.

85   Karl Kautsky, *Foundations of Christianity*, New York: Monthly Review Press, 1972, [1908].

86   Ernst Bloch, *Atheism in Christianity*, New York: Herder and Herder, 1972.

87   Jürgen Moltmann, *The Theology of Hope*, London: SCM Press, 1967. Bloch's Marxist Christian *Principle of Hope* was the foundational influence on Moltmann. Ernst Bloch *The Principle of Hope*, Massachusetts: M.I.T., 1986, [1938-47].

88   Moltmann never uses the word for his project as he dislikes apocalyptic and uses the term eschatology instead.

89   Morris, *Apocalyptic*, p.67.

90   Morris, *Apocalyptic*, p.74.

91   Morris, *Apocalyptic*, p.101.

92   Luke, 3.8-11. NRSV.

93   Paul Davies, *The Social World of Apocalyptic Writings*, p.268 in R.E. Clements, Ed. *The World of Ancient Israel*, Cambridge: Cambridge University Press, 1989.

94   Leckie, *The World to Come*, p.3.

95   Dale Allison, *Jesus of Nazareth Millenarian Prophet*, Minneapolis: Fortress Press, 1998, p.153.

96   Schweitzer, *The Quest*, p.285.

97   Weiss, *Proclamation*, Introduction by Richard Hiers and David Holland.

98   William Sanday, *The Life of Christ in Recent Research*, Oxford: The Clarendon Press, 1907, p.102.

99   Ernst Von Dobschütz, *The Eschatology of the Gospels*, London: Hodder and Stoughton, 1910, p.37.

100 Dobschütz, *Eschatology*, p.59.

101 Cadoux, *Historic Mission*, p.6.

102 Vladimir Simkhovitch, *Toward Understanding Jesus*, New York: Macmillan, 1927, p.65.

103 Frederick Grant, *The Gospel of the Kingdom*, New York: Macmillan, 1940, p.xi.

104 T.F. Glasson, *Jesus and the End of the World*, Edinburgh: The Saint Andrew Press, p.1.

105 Richard Horsley, *Jesus and Empire*, Minneapolis: Fortress Press, 2003, pp.80,81.

106 Caird, *Language and Imagery*, pp.252-4.

107 William Herzog, *Jesus Justice and the Reign of God*, Westminster: John Knox Press, 2000.

108 Nicholas Thomas Wright, *Who Was Jesus?*, London: SPCK, p.100.

109 Rowland, *The Open Heaven*, p.443.

110 Wright, *Who Was Jesus?*, p.100.

111 Morris, *Apocalyptic*, p.91.

112 Dobschütz, *Eschatology*, p.5.

113 Dobschütz, *Eschatology*, p.59.

114 Dobschütz, *Eschatology*, p.159.

115 Dobschütz, *Eschatology*, p.153.

116 Dobschütz, *Eschatology*, p.173.

117 Dobschütz, *Eschatology*, p.124.

118 Dobschütz, *Eschatology*, p.22.

119 Dobschütz, *Eschatology*, p.179.

120 Dobschütz, *Eschatology*, p.88.

121 Dobschütz, *Eschatology*, p.205.

122 Dobschütz, *Eschatology*, p.81.

123 Dobschütz, *Eschatology*, p.204.

124 Dobschütz, *Eschatology*, p.54.

125 Dobschütz, *Eschatology*, p.54.

126 Dobschütz, *Eschatology*, p.185.

127 Dobschütz, *Eschatology*, p.17.

128 Dobschütz, *Eschatology*, p.191.

129 T.W. Manson, *The Teaching of Jesus*, Cambridge: Cambridge University Press, 1951. p. 283.

130 Käsemann, *New Questions*, Norman Perrin, *Rediscovering the Teaching of Jesus*, London: SCM Press, 1967, Funk, *Honest to Jesus*.

131 John Dominic Crossan, *Jesus: A Revolutionary Biography*, New York: Harper Collins, 1994.

132 Amos Wilder, *Eschatology and Ethics in the Teaching of Jesus*, New York: Harper & Brothers, 1950,

133 Kümmel, *Theology of the New Testament.*

134 Nicholas Thomas Wright, *Jesus and the Victory of God*, London: SPCK, 1996,

135 Rudolf Otto, *The Kingdom of God and the Son of Man*, Lutterworth: Lutterworth Press, 1943, C.H. Dodd, *The Parables of the Kingdom*, London: The Religious Book Club.

136 Some of these elements can be found prefigured in English works for instance, in L.A. Muirhead, *The Eschatology of Jesus*, London: Andrew Melrose 1904. Scholars able to read the German literature of the period might confirm the full history of the repertoire.

137 Charles, *Religious Development*, p.30.

138 Käsemann, *New Testament Questions*, chapter V.

139 Klaus Koch, *The Rediscovery of Apocalyptic*, London: SCM Press, 1972.

140 William Beardslee, *New Testament Apocalyptic in Recent Interpretation*, in, Interpretation, October 1971 Vol. XXV No.4 Virginia: Union Theological Seminary.

141 Koch, *Rediscovery*, p.129.

142 Koch, *Rediscovery*, p.110.

143 Grant, *The Gospel of the Kingdom*, p.181. Grant did spoil the idyll with his opinion that the only obstacle to its fulfillment was the 'crime of contaminating the nation's blood-stream' with low-grade children who could not be supported, p. 187. For Leroy Waterman prophetic religion is modelled on American democracy and the Kingdom of God, which is to be achieved on earth will follow suit. Leroy Waterman, *The Religion of Jesus*, New York: Harper Brothers, 1952. Where the Kingdom of God is expected to be achieved on earth then the American national pride noted by De Tocqueville is

bound to assert itself.

144 Wright, *Jesus and the Victory of God.*

145 Christopher Rowland, *Christian Origins*, London: SPCK, 1985 p.285, section III.2,1 and III.4,2b

146 Martin Werner, *The Formation of Christian Dogma*, London: Adam & Charles Black, 1957, p.6.

147 Werner, *Formation*, p.31. Werner's italics.

148 Werner, *Formation*, p.25.

149 Werner, *Formation*, p.105.

150 Werner, *Formation*, p.142.

151 Werner, *Formation*, p.327.

152 Werner, *Formation*, p.304.

153 Werner, *Formation*, p.329.

154 Werner, *Formation*, p.330.

155 Werner, *Formation*, p.327.

156 Werner, *Formation*, p.329.

157 Rowland, *Origins*, p.293.

158 Rowland, *Origins*, p.291.

159 Wright, *Surprised by Hope*, p.54.

160 Wright, *Surprised by Hope*, p.169

161 Oscar Cullmann, *The Christology of the New Testament*, London: SCM Press, 1963, p.316.

162 Cullmann, *Christology*, p.321.

163 Kümmel, *Theology of the New Testament*, p.330.

164 Moule, *The Birth of the New Testament*, p.5.

Notes for Chapter 2
The House of the Platonists

1 Charles Bigg, *The Origins of Christianity*, Oxford: Oxford University Press, 1909, p.412.

2 Bigg, *Origins*, p. 405.

3 Coined by Karl Christian Krause (1781-1832). Michael Brierley, *Panentheism*, p.22.

4   Charles Hartshorne and William L. Reese, Eds., *Philosophers Speak of God*, Chicago: University of Chicago Press, 1953. A selection of writings from fifty philosophers. These authors present a graded scheme of philosophical Gods using five qualifying attributes. Their claim is that only Gods with all five, that is panentheist definitions, 'stand out as the truth.'p.514.

5   Miriam Simos, (Starhawk), *Dreaming the Dark*, Boston: Beacon Press, 1982 and *The Spiral Dance: A Rebirth of the Ancient Religion of the Great Goddess*, New York: HarperSanFrancisco, 1989.

6   Rosemary Radford Ruether, *Gaia & God: An Ecofeminist Theology of Earth Healing*, London: SCM Press, 1993.

7   Simos, *The Spiral Dance*, p.3.

8   Simos, *The Spiral Dance*, p.7.

9   Simos, *The Spiral Dance*, p.9.

10   Plato, *Timaeus and Critias*, translated by Desmond Lee, Harmondsworth: Penguin Books, 1971, p.124.

11   Plato, *Timaeus*, p. 42.

12   Jane Harrison, *Prolegomena to the Study of Greek Religion*, London: Merlin Press, 1980.

13   Harrison, *Prolegomena*, p.xi.

14   Harrison, *Prolegomena*, p.425.

15   Harrison, *Prolegomena*, p.455.

16   Harrison, *Prolegomena*, p.473.

17   Harrison, *Prolegomena*, p.471.

18   Harrison, *Prolegomena*, p.630.

19   Harrison, *Prolegomena*, p.633.

20   Harrison, *Prolegomena*, p.635.

21   Harrison, *Prolegomena*, p.654.

22   Harrison, *Prolegomena*, p.657.

23   Harrison, *Prolegomena*, p.657.

24   Harrison, *Prolegomena*, p.589.

25   Harrison, *Prolegomena*, p.591.

26 Harrison, *Prolegomena*, p.531.

27 Harrison, *Prolegomena*, p.581.

28 John Macquarrie, *Principles of Christian Theology*, London: SCM Press, 1966.

29 Kitty Ferguson, *Pythagoras*, London: Icon Books, 2011.

30 Bertrand Russell, *History of Western Philosophy*, London: Unwin, 1979, p.56.

31 Ferguson, *Pythagoras*, p.159.

32 Alfred North Whitehead, *Process and Reality*, New York: Harper Torchbooks, 1957, p.63.

33 Russell, *History of Western Philosophy*, Pythagoras, Chapter III.

34 Russell notes that the conception of a reality behind the passing illusions of sense originates with Parmenides on the basis of a logical argument as to the impossibility of not-being. The contention that the world of sense is illusory is for Russell the product of fallacious reasoning but difficult to disentangle. Bertrand Russell, *Our Knowledge of the External World*, London: George Allen & Unwin, 1961, p.171.

35 Richard Livingstone, *Selections from Plato*, Oxford: Oxford University Press, 1937, pp.xvi-xviii.

36 Elizabeth Johnson, *She Who Is*, New York: Crossroad Publishing, 1994, p.113

37 Ralph Inge, *The Philosophy of Plotinus*, Vol II, London: Longmans Green and Co, 1948, p.43.

38 Inge, *Plotinus*, p.27. Quote from Spinoza.

39 Inge, *Plotinus*, p.43. From Fifth Ennead of Plotinus.

40 Inge, *Plotinus*, p.101. Inge expressing his own view.

41 Gordon Kaufman, *In Face of Mystery*, Massachusetts: Harvard University Press, 1993, p.265.

42 For an example 'For God is ultimately one, and that means that each of us is part of this oneness."My me is indeed God." The mystics are right. They are people of a deeper consciousness. There is only one consciousness, but self-

conscious people alone can know it.' John Spong, *Eternal Life: A New Vision* New York: HarperOne, 2009, p.209.

43   Whitehead, *Process and Reality*, preface.

44   Whitehead, *Process and Reality*, pp. xi and 63.

45   Catherine Keller, *On the Mystery*, Minneapolis: Fortress Press, 2008, p.xii.

46   Keller, *Mystery*, p.x.

47   Keller, *Mystery*, p.18.

48   'a mystical divine... unquestionably the greatest prophet of contemplative mysticism.' Inge, *Christian Mysticism*, p.305. Praised also by Don Cupitt, as resonating his own cosmic consciousness. Don Cupitt, *The Way to Happiness*, Santa Rosa: Polebridge Press, 2005, p.72. 'My favorite way of describing divinity was in the terms William Wordsworth had used in his poem "Tintern Abbey".' McLennan, *Finding Your Religion*, p.174.

49   William James, *Varieties of Religious Experience*, New York: New American Library, 1958, p.321.

50   William Inge, *Christian Mysticism*, London: Methuen, 1948, p.105.

51   Reported in the Acts of the Apostles, 17:16-32.

52   *Address of Tatian to the Greeks*, in, *The Ante Nicene Fathers*, Edinburgh: T&T Clark, Grand Rapids: Eerdmans, Vol. II, 1994, p.65.

53   Henry Chadwick, *The Early Church*, Harmondsworth: Penguin, 1967, p.10.

54   Taking up Paul's boast that he will make known the unknown God of Greek worship. (see note 1 Introduction). Clement of Alexandria, *The Stromata*, in, *The Ante Nicene Fathers*, Roberts and Donaldson Eds., Edinburgh: T&T Clark, Grand Rapids: Eerdmans, 1994, p.321.

55   Clement, *Stromata*, Book 1 chapter xxi. The Jewish institutions and laws of far higher antiquity than the philosophy of the Greeks.

56 Clement, *Stromata*, Book 1 chapter xxvi. 'Moses rightly called a divine Legislator, and, though inferior to Christ far superior to the great legislators of the Greeks.'

57 Clement, *Stromata*, Book 1 chapter xxiv.

58 Clement, *Stromata*, Book 2 chapter ii.

59 Clement, *Stromata*, Book 1 chapter xxii.

60 Clement, *Stromata*, Book 5 chapter i, p.446 'The philosophers of the Greeks are called thieves, inasmuch as they have taken without acknowledgment their principal dogmas from Moses and the prophets.'

61 Cleveland Coxe, in Roberts and Donaldson, Eds., *The Ante Nicene Fathers*, p.342.

62 Cleveland Coxe, *The Ante Nicene Fathers*, p.125.

63 Clement, *Stromata*, Book 5 chapter xi p.462.

64 Clement, *Stromata*, Book 5 chapter xiv p.468.

65 Clement, *Stromata*, Book 5 chapter xiv p.468.

66 Clement, *Stromata*, Book 5 chapter iii p.448.

67 Clement, *Stromata*, Book 5 chapter xiv p.471.

68 Clement, *Stromata*, Book 5 p.475.

69 Justin Martyr, *Hortatory Address to the Greeks*, chapter xxix, p.285 in Roberts and Donaldson Eds. *Ante Nicene Fathers*, Volume 1 Grand Rapids: Eerdmans Publishing Company, 1979.

70 Justin Martyr, *Hortatory Address*, chapter xxii.

71 Justin Martyr, *Hortatory Address*, chapter vii.

71 Chadwick, *The Early Church*, pp.95, 96.

73 Robert Berchman, *Porphyry Against the Christians*, Leiden: Brill, 2005, p.45.

74 A confession of God in Platonist terms is made in book 5 chapter xii.

75 A.H. Armstrong, *Plotinus*, New York: Collier Books 1962, p.18.

76 Elmer O'Brien, *The Essential Plotinus*, New York: Mentor Books, 1964, p.15.

77   O'Brien, *Plotinus*, p.18.

78   O'Brien, *Plotinus*, p.18.

79   Armstrong, *Plotinus*, p.19.

80   Armstrong, *Plotinus*, p.19.

81   John Bussanich, *The Ethicization of Rebirth Eschatology in Plato and Plotinus*, www.academia.edu.

82   Inge, *Plotinus* Vol II p.x.

83   Brierley, *Panentheism*, p.23.

84   Irenaeus, *Against Heresies*, in Roberts and Donaldson Eds., *The Ante Nicene Fathers*, Volume 1 Grand Rapids: Eerdmans Publishing Company, 1979.

85   Emile Durkheim, *The Elementary Forms of the Religious Life* in W.S.F. Pickering Ed., *Durkheim on Religion* London Routledge & Kegan Paul, 1975, p.111.

86   Durkheim, *Elementary Forms*, p.123.

87   Durkheim, *Elementary Forms*, p.130.

88   Durkheim, *Elementary Forms*, p.130.

89   Durkheim, *Elementary Forms*, p.132.

90   Durkheim was well aware of the Nature God but was concerned to dismiss it in his challenge to the two leading conceptions of elementary religion of his day, the *animism* of Tylor and the *naturism* of Max Müller, respectively chapters two and three of *The Elementary Forms of the Religious Life*. Durkheim has a double blindness to the Nature God. In his desire to prove all religion to be a social fact derived from a social fact he had to dismiss any suggestion that it might derive from a non-social reality or an individual condition of human existence. He is also temperamentally unsympathetic to the power, mystery, energy, and fate involved in nature. 'What characterises the life of nature is monotonous regularity' (p.73). 'Whatever we do, if expressing the forces of nature is the chief purpose of religion, it is impossible to see religion as anything but a system of misleading fictions whose survival is incomprehensible' (p.71). The

Philosophized Nature God is also dismissed. 'If we remove from the religions of the past everything involving the notion of Gods as cosmic agents, what is left? The idea of divinity itself, of a transcendent power that has created man and to which he is subject? But this is a philosophic and abstract conception that was never embodied as such in any historical religion; it has no importance for the science of religions' (p.72). Emile Durkheim *The Elementary Forms of the Religious Life*, translated by Carol Cosman, Oxford: Oxford University Press, 2001.

91 Brierley, *Panentheism*.

92 Michael Brierley, *Naming a Quiet Revolution: The Panentheistic Turn in Modern Theology*, in Philip Clayton and Arthur Peacocke Eds., *In Whom we Live and Move and Have Our Being*, Grand Rapids: Eerdmans Publishing, 2004, pp.5-12.

93 Keller, *On the Mystery*, p.23.

94 Whitehead, *Process and Reality*, p.525.

95 Clayton and Arthur Peackoke Eds., *In Whom we Live and Move and Have our Being*.

96 Gordon Kaufman, *Reconstructing the Concept of God: De-reifying the Anthropomorphisms*, p.107, in Sarah Coakley and David Pailin Eds., *The Making and Remaking of Christian Doctrine.*, Oxford: The Clarendon Press, 1993.

97 Arthur Koestler, *The Sleepwalkers: A History of Man's Changing Vision of the Universe*, Harmonsworth:Pelican Books, 1964, p.27.

98 Gerd Ludemann, in, *The Once and Future Jesus*, Santa Rosa: Polebridge Press, 2000, p.158.

99 Charles Bigg, *The Christian Platonists of Alexandria*, (The Bampton Lectures of 1886) Oxford: Clarendon Press 1913, p.354.

100 Bigg, *The Christian Platonists of Alexandria*, p.87. quoting from Clement *Stromateis* vii, 9.53.

101 Plato, *Republic*, Book Three 414e-415c.

102 Bigg, *Christian Platonists*, p.183.

103 Macquarrie, *Two Worlds*, p.70

104 Armstrong, *Case for God*, p.311.

105 William Inge, *The Platonic Tradition in English Religious Thought*, London: Longman and Todd, 1926, 115.

106 Michael Goulder and John Hick, *Why Believe in God*, London: SCM Press, 1983, p.32. My italics.

107 C.E. Rolt, *The Divine Names and the Mystical Theology*, London: SPCK 1957 [1920] p.26.

108 Scotty McLennan, *Finding Your Religion*, New York: HarperCollins, 1999, p. 102.

109 McLennan, *Finding Your Religion*, p.20

110 Julian Huxley, *The Perennial Philosophy*, London: Triad Grafton, 1985 [1946] p.198.

111 Huxley, *Perennial*, p.76, 77.

112 Thomas Merton, *The Seven Storey Mountain*, New York: Harcourt Brace, 1998, p.191.

113 Merton, *The Seven Storey Mountain*, p. 189.

114 Rowan Williams' response to John Spong, Church Times 17th July 1998

115 Rolt, *Divine Names*, p.207.

116 Inge, *Philosophy of Plotinus*, p.63.

117 Maurice Wiles, *Reason to Believe*, London: SCM Press, 1999, p.64.

118 Marcus Borg, *The God We Never Knew*, New York: Harper SanFrancisco, 1998, p.2, note 1.

119 Matthew Fox, *The Coming of the Cosmic Christ*, New York: Harper & Row, 1988, p. 42.

120 Inge, *Platonic Tradition*.

121 Franz Overbeck, *On the Christianity of Theology*, Trans. John Wilson Oregon: Pickwick Publications, 2002 [1873], p.69.

122 Macquarrie is an admirer of Rudolf Otto whose schematization of the rational by the irrational is paralleled in

different terms by Macquarrie's structure.

123 Macquarrie, *Principles*, p 314.

124 Macquarrie, *Principles*, p.318.

125 Macquarrie, *Principles*, p.330.

126 Armstrong, *Plotinus*, p.24.

127 Keith Ward, *The Concept of God*, Glasgow: Collins, 1977, p.38.

128 Fox, *Original Blessing*, p.26.

129 Fox, *Original Blessing*, p.316.

130 Scotty McLennan, *Jesus was a Liberal*, Basingstoke Palgrave Macmillan 2009, p.60.

131 Keller, *On the Mystery*, p.88.

132 Inge, *Christian Mysticism*, p.261.

133 John Hick, *The Fifth Dimension*, Oxford: Oneworld Publishing, 1999, p.86.

134 Altizer, *The Gospel of Christian Atheism*, London: Collins 1967, p.40.

135 Altizer, *The Death of God*, p.134.

136 John Spong, *A New Christianity for a New World*, New York: Harper SanFrancisco, 2001, p.8.

137 Armstrong, *The Case for God*, p.311, 8.

138 Inge, *The Platonic Tradition*, p.27.

139 The Gospel of Mark 1:14. NRSV Oxford: Oxford University Press, 1995.

140 Marcus Borg, *Jesus and Buddha*, Berkeley: Ulysses Press, 1997 p.xiv, xv.

141 Spong, *Why Christianity Must Change or Die*, pp.100-107.

142 McLennan, *Jesus was a Liberal*, p.8. (my italics).

143 Friedrich Schleiermacher, *The Life of Jesus*, Philadelphia: Fortress Press, 1975, p.131.

144 Paul Tillich, *Systematic Theology*, Vol.1, Welwyn: Nisbet & Co., 1953, 263.

145 Altizer and Hamilton, *Death of God*.

146 Altizer, *Gospel*, 10.

147 Borg, *The God we Never* Knew, 24.

148 Scotty McLennan, *Jesus Was a Liberal*, p.59.

149 Lloyd Geering, *Christianity without God*, Santa Rosa: Polebridge Press, 2002, 58.

150 Armstrong, *The Case for God*, p. 5.

151 Michael Hampson, *God without God*, Winchester: O-Books, 2008, pp. 9, 27.

152 Kaufman, *In Face of Mystery*, p.39.

153 Plato, *Republic*, 509a, Translated by Robin Waterfield, Oxford: Oxford University Press, 1998.

154 The ineffable nature of ultimate concern he likened to the color red: you can point to it but never define it. D. MacKenzie Brown, ed., *Ultimate Concern; Tillich in Dialogue*, London: SCM Press, 1965, p. 44.

155 Although one lineage has been picked out, the genetic path of Tillich's Platonist DNA is multi-routed. Oliver Davies in his work on Eckhart takes a line from Proclus (an elaboration of Plotinus). through Eckhart to Hegel's rediscovery of Eckhart then from Hegel into Heidegger. Oliver Davies, *Meister Eckhart*, London: Penguin Books, 1994. Davies stops here as he is not concerned with Tillich but, in the discussion of 'Being', Tillich's home territory has already been reached. Tillich was a colleague of Heidegger at Marburg. Macquarrie traces another ancestor. He spots in Heidegger a passage from Bonaventure's mystical reflection of God as Being, which he attributes to Heidegger's saturation with scholastic philosophy of which he was professor at Freiburg. John Macquarrie, *Two Worlds are Ours*, London: SCM Press, 2004, p.132.

156 Thomas Altizer, *The Gospel of Christian Atheism*, London: Collins, 1967.

157 John Caputo and Gianni Vattiimo, *After the Death of God*, Columbia: Columbia University Press, 2007.

158 Caputo, *After the Death*, p 53.

159 Caputo, *After the Death,* p51.

160 Caputo, *After the Death,* p.56.

161 Caputo, *After the Death,* p.51.

162 Caputo, *After the Death,* p.53.

163 Caputo, *After the Death,* p.70.

164 Caputo, *After the Death,* p.21.

165 David Strauss, *The Old Faith and the New,* p.169.

166 Don Cupitt, *The Way to Happiness,* Santa Rosa: Polebridge Press 2005.

167 Macquarrie cites his philosophical theology as an apologetic to counter objections to faith from atheists. *Principles,* p.39. Armstrong accuses the atheist triumvirate Dawkins, Hitchens and Harris of basing their attack on poor theology, *The Case for God* p.8.

168 Joseph Hoffmann, *Porphyry's Against the Christians,* Amherst: Prometheus Books, 1994, p.14.

169 Hoffmann, *Porphyry,* p.9.

170 Porphyry constructed a parallel text of the gospels to display the inconsistencies and worked out the late origin of the Book of Daniel and of 'Moses.' In so doing he originated the first Christian attempts at defense on the same terms. Berchman, *Porphyry,* p.65.

171 Christian Buddhism makes an early appearance in Don Cupitt, *Taking Leave of God,* London: SCM Press 1980, xii, and pervades Don Cupitt, *Turns of Phrase Radical Theology from A-Z,* London: SCM Press, 2011.

172 Ross Thompson, *Buddhist Christianity,* Winchester: O-Books, 2010, contains a bibliography of much current Christian/ Buddhist dialogue.

Notes to Chapter 3
The Christian Mystics

1 Louis Bouyer, *Mysticism: An Essay on the History of the Word,*

p.53, in Richard Woods Ed., *Understanding Mysticism*, New York: Image Books, 1980.

2   William Inge, *Christian Mysticism*, London: Methuen & Co., 1948, p.78

3   Charles Bigg, *The Origins of Christianity*, Oxford: The Clarendon Press, 1909, p.415

4   Discussed by George Pattison, *The End of Theology and the Task of Thinking about God.* London: SCM Press, 1998, p.13. Made use of also by Kaufman, *In Face of Mystery*, p. 29.

5   H. A. Armstrong, *Plotinus*, New York: Collier Books, 1962, p. 28.

6   Keith Ward, *Holding Fast to God: A Reply to Don Cupitt*, London: SPCK 1982

7   Thomas Merton, *The Seven Storey Mountain*, New York: Harcourt Brace, 1948.

8   Bernard McGinn, *Christian Mysticism*, New York: Random House 2006, p. xiv.

9   Alan Segal, *Paul the Convert*, Yale: Yale University Press, 1990.

10   William Inge, *Christian Mysticism*, London: Methuen, 1948, p. 77.

11   Bertrand Russell, *Mysticism and Logic*, London: George Allen & Unwin, 1918, p. 8.

12   Matthew Fox, *Confessions*, New York: HarperCollins, 1996, p. 95.

13   Fox, *Confessions*, p. 58.

14   Fox, *Confessions*, p. 55.

15   Fox, *Confessions*, p. 24.

16   Fox, *Confessions*, p.129.

17   Matthew Fox, *The Coming of the Cosmic Christ*, San Francisco: Harper & Row 1988.

18   Fox *Cosmic Christ*, p.73.

19   Michael Hampson, *God Without God*, Winchester: O-Books, 2008, pp.13, 26.

20   John Hick, *An Interpretation of Religion*, Basingstoke: Macmillan, 1989.

21   John Hick, *The Fifth Dimension*, Oxford: Oneworld, 1999, 67.

22   Hick, *The Fifth Dimension*, p.245.

23   Diasetz Suzuki, 1979 *Mysticism Christian and Buddhist*, London: Unwin Paperbacks, p.5.

24   Suzuki, *Mysticism*, pp.1 to 4.

25   Tarjei Park, *The English Mystics*, London: SPCK, 1998, p. 3.

26   McGinn, *Christian Mysticism*, p. xiv.

27   Oliver Davies, *Meister Eckhart: Selected Writings*, London: Penguin Books, 1995, title page.

28   Hans Lewy, Ed., *Selected Writings of Philo of Alexandria*, New York: Dover Publications, 2004.

29   Lewy, *Philo*, p.8.

30   Lewy, *Philo*, p.15.

31   Lewy, *Philo*, pp. 22, 23.

32   Lewy, *Philo*, p.24.

33   Lewy, *Philo*, pp.12, 13.

34   Lewy, *Philo*, p.13.

35   Lewy, *Philo*, p.11.

36   Lewy, *Philo*, p.16.

37   McGinn, *Christian Mysticism*, 482.

38   John Macquarrie, *Two Worlds are Ours: An Introduction to Christian Mysticism*, London: SCM Press, 2004, p. 6.

39   Macquarrie, *Two Worlds*, pp.19,21.

40   Macquarrie, *Two Worlds*, p.28.

41   Macquarrie, *Two Worlds*, p.266.

42   Bouyer, *Mysticism: An Essay on the History of the Word*.

Notes to Chapter 4
The Jesusologists

1   Thomas Sheehan, *From Divinity to Infinity*, In, The Jesus Seminar, *The Once and Future Jesus*, Santa Rosa: Polebridge

Press, 2000.

2   Walter Wink, *The Son of Man*, In, *The Once and Future Jesus*,
     p.167. (Wink's italics).

3   Lloyd Geering, *Christianity without God*, Santa Rosa:
     Polebridge Press, 2002, p 96.

4   Don Cupitt, *The Debate about Christ*, London: SCM Press,
     1979, p.69.

5   John Knox, *The Humanity and Divinity of Christ*, Cambridge:
     Cambridge University Press, 1967, p.67. The controversy
     that was brewing up crystallized in the collection of essays,
     John Hick Ed., *The Myth of God Incarnate*, London: SCM
     Press, 1977.

6   Thomas Altizer, *The Gospel of Christian Atheism*, London:
     Collins, 1967, pp.11, 20.

7   Dominic Crossan, *The Historical Jesus*, New York: Harper
     Collins, 1992.

8   Marcus Borg, *Jesus A New Vision*, New York: Harper Collins,
     1991, preface.

9   For examples, Geering defers to the work *Christianity
     Without God*, p.119, 117. For Borg Crossan is 'the premier
     Jesus Scholar in the world today.' Marcus Borg, *Jesus and
     Buddha*, Berkeley: Ulysses Press, 1997, p. xii. Don Cupitt is
     an admirer too. Don Cupitt, *The Meaning of the West*,
     London: SCM Press 2008, p 92 and Don Cupitt, *Free
     Christianity*, in Colin Crowder Ed., *God and Reality*, London:
     Mowbray, 1997, note 55.

10   Borg, *Jesus: A New Vision*, pp 13, 16.

11   This begins with Friedrich Engels stated in his introduction
     of 1895 to Karl Marx, *Class Struggles in France 1848-1850*,
     London: Lawrence and Wishart, 1895. It continues with Karl
     Kautsky's mission to reclaim a revolutionary Jesus sold out
     by clerics in the interest of their sinecures. Karl Kautsky,
     Foundations of Christianity, New York: Monthly Review
     Press, 1972. This follows through to Ernst Bloch, *Atheism in*

Christianity, New York: Herder and Herder, 1972. Through Bloch's influence on Jürgen Moltmann the influence feeds back into Christianity and seventies liberation theology.

12 William Herzog, *Jesus, Justice and the Reign of God*, Westminster: John Knox Press, 2000, p.32.

13 Herzog, *Jesus, Justice and the Reign of God*, p.32.

14 Robert Funk, *Honest to Jesus*, New York: HarperCollins, 1997, p.168.

15 Funk, *Honest to Jesus*, p.79, 146.

16 Funk, *Honest to Jesus*, p.74.

17 Funk, *Honest to Jesus*, p.70.

18 Dominic Crossan, *Jesus: A Revolutionary Biography*, New York: HarperSanFrancisco, 1994, pp. 54, 55.

19 The connection of Jesus with John the Baptist is one of the great pieces of historical information preserved in the Gospel of John. 'After this Jesus and his disciples went into the Judean countryside, and he spent some time with them and baptized. Now a discussion about purification arose between John's disciples and a Jew. They came to John and said to him, "Rabbi, the one who was with you across the Jordan, here he is baptizing, and all are going to him."' John 3:22-25. NRSV.

20 Maurice Wiles, *Reason to Believe*, London: SCM Press, 1999, p.54.

21 John Hick, *The Second Christianity*, London: SCM Press, 1983, p.50.

22 John Hick, *The Fifth Dimension*, Oxford: OneWorld, 1999, p.165.

23 Matthew Fox, *The Coming of the Cosmic Christ*, San Francisco: Harper and Row, 1988, p.72.

24 Fox, *Cosmic Christ*, p.67.

25 Borg, *Jesus: A New Vision*, p.29.

26 Borg, *Jesus: A New Vision*, p.16.

27 Borg, *Jesus: A New Vision*, p.97.

28   Geering, *Christianity without God*, p.132.

29   Geering, *Christianity without God*, p.60.

30   John Spong, *A New Christianity for a New World*, New York: HarperSanFrancisco, 2001, p.126.

31   Thomas Altizer, *The Gospel of Christian Atheism*, London: Collins, 1967, p.44.

32   Marcus Borg, *The God We Never Knew*, New York: HarperSanFrancisco, 1998. A panentheist manifesto.

33   John Hick, *The Metaphor of God Incarnate*, London: SCM Press, 1993, p.6.

34   Hick, *The Metaphor*, p.60.

35   Hick, *The Metaphor*, p.70.

36   Hick, *The Metaphor*, p.126.

37   Hick, *The Metaphor*, p.158.

38   Leroy Waterman, *The Religion of Jesus*, New York: Harper Brothers, 1952.

39   Waterman, *The Religion of Jesus*, p.112

40   Catherine Keller, *On the Mystery*, Minneapolis: Fortress Press, 2008, p.52.

41   In Brierley's standard theological terminology panentheism is defined by degree Christology. Michael Brierley, *Panentheism*, article in *The Encyclopedia of Christianity*, Vol.4. Grand Rapids: Eerdmans Publishing, 2005.

42   Hick, *The Second Christianity*, p.79.

43   Reimarus, *Fragments*, Philadelphia: Fortress Press, 1970.

44   David Strauss, *The Old Faith and the New*, London: Asher and Co.1874, p.4.

45   Franz Overbeck, *On the Christianity of Theology*, Oregon: Pickwick Publications, 2002, p.90.

46   Hick, *The Second Christianity*, p.12.

47   Hick, *The Second Christianity*, p.13. Hick was quoted as a mystic in the last chapter and a Jesusologist in this. The connection should become clear later in the chapter. The 'vast creative process' is a clue to the presence of the nature

God.

48   John de Gruchy, *Being Human: Confessions of a Christian Humanist*, London: SCM Press, 2006, p.53.

49   Julian Huxley, Introduction in, Teilhard de Chardin, *The Phenomenon of Man*, New York: HarperCollins, 1975.

50   Teilhard de Chardin, *The Phenomenon of Man*. A diagrammatic representation appears on page 192.

51   Sheehan, *From Divinity to Infinity*, p.35.

Notes to Chapter 5
Can Liberal Theology Save Religion for the Twenty-First Century?

1   Wilfred Cantwell Smith, *Towards a World Theology*, Philadelphia: The Westminster Press, 1981, p.185.

2   Wilfred Cantwell Smith, *Faith and Belief: The Difference Between Them*, Princeton, 1979.

3   Smith, *Towards a World Theology*, pp, 186/7

4   Smith, *Towards a World Theology*, p.182.

5   John Hick, *An Interpretation of Religion*, Basingstoke: Macmillan, 1989, p.xiii.

6   Hick, *An Interpretation*, p.2.

7   Scotty McLennan, *Jesus was a Liberal*, New York: Palgrave Macmillan, 2009, pp108, 9.

8   McLennan, *Jesus was a Liberal*, p.123.

9   Miriam Simos, *Dreaming the Dark*, Boston: Beacon Press, 1988.

10 Scotty McLennan, *Finding Your Own Religion*, New York: HarperSanFrancisco, 1999, p.38.

11 John Spong, *A New Christianity for a New World*, New York: HarperSanFrancisco, 2001, p.179

12 Spong, *A New Christianity*, p.182.

13 Spong, *A New Christianity*, p.137.

14 Michael Hampson, *God without God*, Winchester: O-Books,

2008, p.10.

15   Thomas Altizer, *The Gospel of Christian Atheism*, London: Collins, 1967, p.34.

16   Altizer, *The Gospel of Christian Atheism*, p.55.

17   John Macquarrie, *Principles of Christian Theology*, London: SCM Press, 1966, p.134.

18   Maurice Wiles, *Reason to Believe*, London: SCM Press, 1999, pp.65, 80.

19   Marcus Borg, *The God we never Knew*, New York: HarperSanFrancisco, 1998, pviii.

20   Borg, *The God we never Knew*, p.viii.

21   Matthew Fox, *The Coming of the Cosmic Christ*, San Francisco: Harper and Row, 1988, p.229.

22   Karen Armstrong, *The Case for God*, London: Vintage Books, 2010, p.20.

23   Armstrong, *The Case for God*, p.119.

24   Armstrong, *The Case for God*, p.8.

25   Paul Tillich, *Christianity and the Encounter of the World Religions*, Columbia: Columbia University Press, 1963, p.96.

26   Alan Watts, *The Way of Zen*, New York: Pantheon Books, 1961, p.45.

27   Watts, *The Way of Zen*, p.19.

28   Watts, *The Way of Zen*, p.vi.

29   Stephen Katz, Ed., *Mysticism and Philosophical Analysis*, London: Sheldon Press, 1978, p.35.

30   Katz, *Mysticism*, p.41.

31   Katz, *Mysticism*, p.45.

32   Raphael Demos, *Journal of Philosophy* Vol XLIV, No. 22 October 1952, reprinted in, In Memoriam Paul Tillich *Journal of Religion* Vol XLVI Jan 1966, University of Chicago Press.

33   Gabriel Vahanian, *The Death of God*, New York: George Brazillier, 1957, p.xx.

34   David Jenkins, *Guide to the Debate About God*, Lutterworth: Lutterworth Press, 1966, p.47.

35   Plato, *Timaeus and Critias*, Translated by Desmond Lee, Harmondsworth: Penguin, 1965, 4.34.

36   Bertrand Russell, *Our Knowledge of the External World*, London: George Allen & Unwin, 1949, p.38.

37   Bertrand Russell, *History of Western Philosophy*, London: Unwin Paperbacks, 1979, p.788.

38   Jenkins, *Guide to the Debate about God*, p.47.

39   Tilllich *Christianity and the Encounter*, 58.

40   John De Gruchy, *Being Human: Confessions of a Christian Humanist*, London: SCM Press, 2006, p 130.

41   Macquarrie, *Principles*, p.193.

42   Marcus Borg, *Meeting Jesus Again for the First Time*, New York: HarperSanFrancisco, 1994, p.61.

43   Fox, *Confessions*, p.70.

44   Fox, *Confessions*, p.96.

45   Keith Ward, *The Concept of God*, London: Collins, 1977, p.29.

46   Ward, *The Concept of God*, p.116.

47   McLennan, *Finding Your Religion*, p.108.

48   Catherine Keller, *On the Mystery*, Minneapolis: Fortress Press, 2008, p.52.

49   John Hick, *The Fifth Dimension*, Oxford: OneWorld, 1999, p.224.

50   William Inge, *The Philosophy of Plotinus*, London: Longmans Green & Co., 1923, Vol II p.222.

51   David Pailin, *Probing the Foundations*, Kampen: Kok Pharos Publishing, 1994, p.21.

52   Keller, *On the Mystery* p.62.

53   Fox, *Confessions*, p.106.

54   Fox, *Confessions*, p.117.

55   Spong, *A New Christianity*, p.57

56   Spong, *A New Christianity*, p.83.

57   John Spong, *Why Christianity Must Change or Die*, New York: HarperSanFrancisco, 1998, p.4.

58   Karen Armstrong, *The Spiral Staircase*, London:

HarperCollins, 2004, p 329.

59   Armstrong, *The Case for God*, p.185.

60   Armstrong, *The Case for God*, p.5.

61   Armstrong, *The Case for God*, p.130 quoting St Anselm.

62   Borg, *The God We Never Knew*, p.49.

63   Aldous Huxley, *The Perennial Philosophy*, London: Triad Grafton, 1985, quoting John of the Cross. p. 44.

64   Thomas Merton, *The Seven Storey Mountain*, New York: Harcourt Brace, 1998, p.191.

65   Wiles, *Reason to Believe*, p.ii.

66   Macquarrie, *Principles*, p.95.

67   Macquarrie, *Principles*, p.163

68   Ward, *The Concept of God*, p.184.

69   Macquarrie, *Principles*, p.264.

70   Keller, *On the Mystery*, p.61.

71   George Pattison, *The End of Theology*, London: SCM Press, 1998, p.94.

72   Ward, *Concept of God*, p.99.

73   Fox, *Confessions*, p.158.

74   Fox, *The Coming of the Cosmic Christ*, pp 60-67.

75   William Inge, *Christian Mysticism*, London: Methuen &.Co., 1948, p. xv xiv.

76   Inge, *Christian Mysticism*, p. 252.

77   Inge, *Christian Mysticism*, p. xvi.

78   Inge, *Christian Mysticism*, p.114.

79   Inge, *Christian Mysticism*, p.115.

80   Inge, *Christian Mysticism*, pp.17, 14.

81   Armstrong, *The Spiral Staircase*.

82   Jeanne Warren, *Search for Meaning*, p.118, in, David Boulton Ed., *Godless for God's Sake*, Dent: Dales Historical Monographs, 2006.

83   Hick, *Fifth Dimension*, p.163.

84   Rufus Jones, *Spiritual Reformers of the 16th and 17th Centuries*, London: Macmillan & Co., 1928, p.xxi.

85 Fox, *Cosmic Christ*, p.44.

86 John Macquarrie, *Two Worlds are Ours*, London: SCM Press, 2004, p 112.

87 Harnack quoted in Inge, *Christian Mysticism*, p.21.

88 Michael Goulder & John Hick, *Why Believe in God?* London: SCM Press, 1983, p 11.

89 Goulder, & Hick, *Why Believe in God?* p.4.

90 Goulder, & Hick, *Why Believe in God?* pp 60, 61.

91 Hick, *The Fifth Dimension*, p.112.

92 Goulder & Hick, *Why Believe in God?* p.40.

93 Don Cupitt, *Turns of Phrase: Radical Theology from A-Z*, London: SCM Press, 2011, p.79.

94 Borg, *The God We Never Knew*, p.112

95 McLennan, *Finding*, p.19.

96 McLennan, *Finding*, p.27.

97 McLennan, *Finding*, p.63.

98 McLennan, *Finding*, p.65.

99 McLennan, *Finding*, p.208.

100 Goulder & Hick, *Why Believe in God?* p.100.

101 Goulder & Hick, *Why Believe in God?* p.44.

102 Armstrong, *The Spiral Staircase*, p.339

103 Armstrong, *The Spiral Staircase*, p.336

104 Aldous Huxley, *The Perennial Philosophy*, London: Triad Grafton, 1985, p.14.

105 Huxley, *The Perennial Philosophy*, p.98.

106 Huxley, *The Perennial Philosophy*, p.11.

107 Huxley, *The Perennial Philosophy*, p.53

108 Albert Einstein *My Credo*, in Michael White and John Gribbin, *Einstein: A Life in Science*, London: Simon and Schuster, 1997, p.263.

109 William Inge, *The Platonic Tradition in English Thought*, London: Longmans Green & Co., 1926, p.115.

110 Cupitt states that 'The whole architecture of "traditional" religious belief is *philosophically* ruined.' *Turns of Phrase*, p.ix.

111 Don Cupitt, *The New Christian Ethics*, London: SCM Press, 1988, p.59.

112 Cupitt, *The New Christian Ethics*, pp. 22, 23.

113 Alan Watts, *Beyond Theology*, New York: Pantheon, 1964, pp.89, 155.

114 David Boulton, *The Trouble with God: Religious Humanism and the Republic of Heaven*, Alresford: O-Books, 2002.

115 Edmund Gosse, *Father and Son*, London: Heinemann, 1941.

116 Michael Hampson, *God Without God*, Ropley: O-Books, 2008, Title page.

117 Borg, *The God We Never Knew* p.67. There is no intention to set up a rivalry between Catholic and Protestant portraits of God with the implication that this God is either exclusive to or uniform within Protestantism. Liberal writers with a Catholic background may suffer the same syndrome. The Catholic Karen Armstrong is a refugee from the damaging self-abnegation of the convent. Armstrong, *The Spiral Staircase*. Matthew Fox is in reaction against original sin. Fox *Original Blessing*. Some protestant liberals such as Tillich and Robinson seem to have happy childhood memories of God.

118 Altizer, *The Gospel of Christian Atheism*, p.22.

119 Altizer, *The Gospel of Christian Atheism*, p.93.

120 Altizer, *The Gospel of Christian Atheism*, p.80.

121 Altizer, *The Gospel of Christian Atheism*, p.97.

122 Borg, *The God We Never Knew*, p.61.

123 Borg, *The God We Never Knew*, pp.64 to 71.

124 Borg, *The God We Never Knew*, pp.71 to 79.

125 A vote of thanks to my mother Marie Rock and to the Order of Saint Francis.

126 Cupitt, *The New Christian Ethics*, p.9.

127 Cupitt, *Turns of Phrase*, pp. 64-6.

128 Cupitt, *Turns of Phrase*, p.39.

129 Cupitt, *Turns of Phrase*, p.112.

130 Cupitt, *Turns of Phrase*, p.64.

131 Cupitt, *Turns of Phrase*, p.90.
132 Cupitt, *Turns of Phrase*, pp.98, 103,103.
133 Cupitt, *Turns of Phrase*, p.106.
134 Cupitt, *Turns of Phrase*, p.106.
135 Cupitt, *Turns of Phrase*, p.102.
136 Cupitt, *Turns of Phrase*, p.xi.
137 Cupitt, *Turns of Phrase*, p.1.
138 Cupitt, *Turns of Phrase*, p.3.
139 Keller, *On the Mystery*, p.19.
140 Daphne Hampson, *After Christianity*, London: SCM Press, 1996.
141 Keller, *On the Mystery*, ch.4.

Notes for Chapter 6
The Sociology of Religion is the Puppet of Plato

1 Linda Woodhead, *Five Concepts of Religion*, Revue Internationale de Sociologie, 2011, volume 21, issue 1, p.138.
2 Woodhead, *Five Concepts of Religion*, p.129.
3 Steve Bruce, *Why Are Women More Religious than Men*, Oxford: Oxford University Press, 2012, p.106.
4 Paul Heelas and Linda Woodhead, *The Spiritual Revolution*, Oxford: Blackwell, 2005.
5 Bertrand Russell's definition of metaphysics. *Mysticism and Logic*, Longmans Green, 1918.
6 Edward Evans-Pritchard, *Theories of Primitive Religion*, Oxford: Oxford University Press, 1965, p.100.
7 Edward Evans-Pritchard, *Theories of Primitive Religion*, Oxford: Oxford University Press, 1965, p.314.
8 Clifford Geertz, *The Interpretation of Cultures*, New York: Basic Books, 1973, p.87.
9 Thomas Luckmann, *The Invisible Religion*, New York: Macmillan, 1967, p.18.
10 Malcolm Hamilton, *The Sociology of Religion*, London:

Routledge, 1995, p.viii.

11   Grace Davie, *Religion in Britain since 1945: Believing not Belonging*, Oxford: Blackwell, 1994, pp.84, 90.

12   Grace Davie, *The Sociology of Religion*, London: Sage Publications, 2007, p.4.

13   Garnett, Grimlet, Harris, Whyte and Williams, Eds., *Redefining Christian Britain*, London: SCM Press 2006, pp.14, 289.

14   Don Cupitt, *Turns of Phrase: Radical Theology from A-Z*, London: SCM Press, 2011, p.5.

15   Don Cupitt, *The Meaning of It All in Everyday Speech*, London: SCM Press, 1999, Introduction.

16   Steve Bruce, *God is Dead: Secularization in the West*, Oxford: Blackwell, 2002, p.42.

17   Bruce, *God is Dead*, p.202.

18   Davie, *Sociology of Religion*, p.25.

19   Emile Durkheim, Translated by Carol Cosman, *The Elementary Forms of the Religious Life*, Oxford: Oxford University Press, 2001, pp.88, 94.

20   Edward Evans-Pritchard, *Nuer Religion*, New York: Oxford University Press, 1956, p.313.

21   Will Herberg, *Protestant, Catholic, Jew*, New York: Doubleday & Company, 1955. Winthrop Hudson, *American Protestantism*, Chicago: University of Chicago Press, 1961.

22   Durkheim, *The Elementary Forms of the Religious Life*, p.311.

23   Durkheim, *The Elementary Forms of the Religious Life*, p.105.

24   Steven Lukes, *Émile Durkheim: His Life and Work*, London: Peregrine, 1975, p.7.

25   'There is then a great variety of evidence to show that the type of religion which is founded on kinship, and in which the deity and his worshippers make up a society united by the bond of blood, was widely prevalent and that at an early date, among all the Semitic peoples... this was the original type of religion out of which all other types grew... This, I

apprehend is good evidence that the fundamental lines of all Semitic religion were laid down long before the beginnings of authentic history, in that earliest stage when kinship was the only recognised type of permanent friendly relation between man and man, and therefore the only type on which it was possible to frame the conception of a permanent friendly relation between a group of men and a supernatural being. That all human societies have developed from this stage is now generally recognised.' W. Robertson Smith, *The Religion of the Semites*, The Burnett Lectures 1888-89, London: Adam and Charles Black, 1914, p.50.

26 Robertson Smith, *The Religion of the Semites*, p.55.

27 There is a question here that cannot be taken up but ought to be highlighted in passing. A distinction needs to be made between the propitiation of nature/fate and the governance of human social relations. These two fundamental dependencies of human existence have been identified as founding the two religions in Christianity. Both these substrates and their respective structures are at present lumped together in the word religion. For clarity I propose that only the governance of human relations should be allocated the word religion. The rites of nature propitiation should be known by a different term. Of course the two interact. That interaction would be a useful study in its own right. Sociology already records a magnificent example of the clear separation of nature propitiation from social relations by Malinowski, although he did not theorize the matter as such. The Kula Ring of absolutely important but economically irrelevant exchange of tokens formed the social religion. The rites of nature propitiation, such as blessing the canoes and appeasing the witches of the sea formed an ancillary support to that social religious enterprise. Bronislaw Malinowski, *The Argonauts of the Western*

Pacific, London: Routledge, 1978, [1922]

28 Durkheim, *The Elementary Forms*, p.36.

29 Durkheim, *The Elementary Forms*, p 38.

30 Durkheim, *The Elementary Forms*, p.39.

31 Durkheim, *The Elementary Forms*, Chapter one, subheading one. This was Tylor's definition adopted in *Primitive Culture*.

32 Durkheim, *The Elementary Forms*, p.32.

33 See discussion in Lukes, *Emile Durkheim*, p.26.

34 W.E.H. Stanner, *Reflections of Durkheim and Aboriginal Religion*, p.229, in Maurice Freedman Ed., *Social Organization: Essays Presented to Raymond Firth*, London: Frank Cass & Co., 1967.

35 Stanner, *Reflections on Durkheim*, p.230.

36 Stanner, *Reflections on Durkheim*, p.229.

37 Stanner, *Reflections on Durkheim*, p.234.

38 Stanner, *Reflections on Durkheim*, p.226. Quoted from *La Determination du Fait Moral*, 1907.

39 Mircea Eliade, *The Sacred and the Profane: The Nature of Religion*, New York: Harcourt, 1959. Eliade was chairman of the department of the history of religions at the University of Chicago and at one time it was calculated that ex-pupils of Eliade held the majority of US professorships in the sociology of religion.

40 Eliade, *The Sacred and the Profane*, p.11.

41 Woodhead, *Five Concepts of Religion*, p.132.

42 Peter Berger, *The Social Reality of Religion*, Harmondsworth: Penguin Books 1973, p.180. Published originally under the name *The Sacred Canopy*, New York: Doubleday, 1967.

43 Peter Berger, *A Rumour of Angels*, New York: Doubleday, 1969.

44 Berger, *The Social Reality of Religion*, pre title page.

45 Robert Bellah, *Religion in Human Evolution: from the Paleolithic to the Axial Age*, Cambridge Massachusetts: Harvard University Press, 2011.

46 Bellah, *Religion in Human Evolution*, p.xix.
47 Jeffrey Cox, *The English Churches in a Secular Society 1870-1930*, New York: Oxford University Press, 1982.
48 Bellah, *Religion in Human Evolution*, p.11.
49 Bellah, *Religion in Human Evolution*, p.2.
50 Robert Bellah, *The New Religious Consciousness and the Crisis of Modernity*, p.348, in Robert Bellah Ed., *The New Religious Consciousness*, Berkeley: University of California Press, 1976.
51 Marta Trzebiatowska and Steve Bruce, *Why are Women More Religious than Men*, Oxford: Oxford University Press, 2012.
52 Trzebiatowska and Bruce, *Why are Women*, p.106.
53 Trzebiatowska and Bruce, *Why are Women*, p.176.
54 Steve Bruce, *Defining Religion: A Practical Response*, Revue Internationale de Sociologie, Volume 21, issue 1, 2011.
55 Bruce, *Defining Religion*, p.118.
56 Sarah Williams, *Religious Belief and Popular Culture in Southwark c1880-1939*, Oxford: Oxford University Press, 1999.
57 Jeffrey Cox, *The English Churches*, p.97.
58 Charles Booth, *Life and Labour of the People in London*, London: Macmillan, 1902.
59 Williams, *Religious Belief*, p.117.
60 Williams, *Religious Belief*, p.119.
61 Williams, *Religious Belief*, p.107
62 Williams, *Religious Belief*, p.113.
63 Williams, *Religious Belief*, p.113.
64 Williams, *Religious Belief*, p.115.
65 Williams, *Religious Belief*, p.108
66 Williams, *Religious Belief*, p.117.
67 Williams, *Religious Belief*, p.119.
68 Williams, *Religious Belief*, p.118.
69 Williams, *Religious Belief*, p.119.
70 Williams, *Religious Belief*, p.120
71 Williams, *Religious Belief*, p.139.

72   Williams, *Religious Belief,* p.141.

73   Williams, *Religious Belief,* p.116.

74   Williams, *Religious Belief,* p.142.

75   John Macmurrary, *The Search for Reality in Religion,* Swarthmore Lecture 1965, London: George Allen and Unwin, 1965.

76   Macmurray, *The Search for Reality in Religion,* p.5

77   Macmurray, *The Search for Reality in Religion,* pp. 7, 8.

78   Macmurray, *The Search for Reality in Religion,* p.14. A footnote makes due allowance for youthful exaggeration here.

79   Macmurray, *The Search for Reality in Religion,* pp.15-17.

80   Macmurray, *The Search for Reality in Religion,* p.20

81   Macmurray, *The Search for Reality in Religion,* p.20.

82   Macmurray, *The Search for Reality in Religion,* p.21.

83   John Macmurray, *The Form of the Personal,* in two volumes, *The Self as Agent,* and *Persons in Relation,* London: Faber and Faber, 1957.

Notes for Chapter 7
By What Authority? Is this the End of Theology?

1   Linda Woodhead, *Theology: The Trouble It's In,* p.183 in Gavin Hyman Ed., *New Directions in Philosophical Theology,* Ashgate, 2004.

2   Linda Woodhead, *Theology: The Trouble It's In,* in Gavin Hyman Ed., *New Directions in Philosophical Theology,* Ashgate, 2004, p.179.

3   Woodhead, *Theology: The Trouble It's In,* p.184.

4   Paul Heelas and Linda Woodhead, *The Spiritual Revolution: Why Religion is Giving Way to Spirituality,* Oxford: Blackwell, 2005, p.5.

5   Heelas and Woodhead, *The Spiritual Revolution,* p.4.

6   Heelas and Woodhead, *The Spiritual Revolution,* p.4.

7   Thomas Hobbes, *Considerations upon the Reputation, Loyalty,*

Manners & Religion of Thomas Hobbes by Himself, William Molesworth Ed., *The Collected Works of Thomas Hobbes,* Volume 4. London: Routledge, 1997 [1839-45].

8   Linda Woodhead, *What People Really Believe about God, Religion and Authority,* p.51, in, Linda Woodhead, Guest Editor, *Modern Believing,* Volume 55, issue 1, 2014. This volume of the Journal is a handy overview of an extensive survey published in two volumes, Linda Woodhead, *Religion and Personal Life,* and *Religion and Public Life,* London: Darton, Longman and Todd, 2014.

9   David Jenkins, *The Calling of a Cuckoo,* London: Continuum, 2002, p.136.

Notes for Chapter 8
God Derived from the Dynamic of the Person

1   The concept of mother and maternal is not restricted to biological definition but is taken here to include in the broadest sense anyone of either gender or generation who has responsibility for the upbringing of children. The digest in what follows is taken from Deborah Blum, *Love at Goon Park: Harry Harlow and the Science of Affection,* New York: Basic Books, 2002, Chapter Two, *Untouched by Human Hands.*

2   Blum, *Love at Good Park,* p.32.

3   Jeremy Holmes, *John Bowlby & Attachment Theory,* London: Routledge, 1993.

4   Blum, *Love at Goon Park,* p.217.

5   Quoted in Holmes, *John Bowlby,* from Joan Rivière, *The Unconscious Phantasy of an Inner World Reflected in Examples from Literature,* in M Klein, P. Heiman and R Money-Kyrle, Eds., *New Directions in Psychoanalysis,* London: Hogarth Press, 1955.

6   Alasdair MacIntyre, *Dependent Rational Animals,* Chicago: Open Court Publishing, 1999, p.xi.

7   MacIntyre, *Dependent Rational Animals*, p.105.
8   MacIntyre, *Dependent Rational Animals*, pp.96,7.
9   MacIntyre, *Dependent Rational Animals*, p.95.
10   MacIntyre, *Dependent Rational Animals*, p.120.
11   John Rawls, *A Theory of Justice*, Cambridge Massachusetts: Harvard University Press, 1972.
12   Corinthians 12.27, Romans, 12.5, Ephesians, 4.25.
13   Michael Battle, *Reconciliation: The Ubuntu Theology of Desmond Tutu*, Cleveland Ohio: The Pilgrim Press, 1997.
14   Robinson, *Honest to God*, p.26.
15   John MacMurray, *The Search for Reality in Religion*, The Swarthmore Lecture 1965, London: George Allen & Unwin, 1965, p.9.
16   Robinson, *Honest to God*, p.18.
17   Gerald Priestland, *Reasonable Uncertainty*, London: Quaker Home Service, 1982.
18   Gerald Priestland, *Priestland's Progress*, London: BBC Publications, 1981, p.9.
19   Grace Davie, *Religion in Britain since 1945. Believing not Belonging*, Oxford: Blackwell, 1994.
20   A fuller explanation of this can be found in Hugh Rock, *The Marriage of Two Temperaments in the Theology of Honest to God*, Modern Believing, Volume 54.3, 2013.
21   Robinson, *Honest to God*, p.27.
22   Alan Stephenson, writing the history of English Modernism, spotted the influence of Wren Lewis on Robinson and cited him as the real beginning of the new radicalism despite the prominence given to the Teutonic thinkers. Stephenson remarked Wren Lewis' booklet gathering dust on the library shelf at his theological college and never referred to. Alan Stephenson, *The Rise and Decline of English Modernism*, London SPCK, 1984, pp.185-187.
23   Dewi Morgan, Ed., *They Became Anglicans*, London: Mowbrays, 1959, p.161.

24   Morgan, *They Became Anglicans*, p.170.

25   Morgan, *They Became Anglicans*, p.172.

26   Morgan, *They Became Anglicans*, p.171.

27   Morgan, *They Became Anglicans*, p.175.

28   Morgan, *They Became Anglicans*, p.168.

29   John Wren Lewis, *Return to the Roots: A Study in the Meaning of the Word God*, London: Modern Churchmen's Union, 1956, p.10.

30   Wren Lewis, *Return to the Roots*, p.16.

31   Wren Lewis, *Return to the Roots*, pp.9-11.

32   Robinson, *Honest to God*, p.49.

33   John Robinson & David Edwards Eds., *The Honest to God Debate*, London: SCM Press, 1963, p.60.

34   Don Cupitt, *The Sea of Faith*, London: BBC Publications, 1985, p.35

35   John Macmurray, *The Form of the Personal*, published in two volumes, *The Self as Agent* and *Persons in Relation*, London: Faber and Faber, 1995, [1961].

36   Macmurray, *The Self as Agent*, introduction by Stanley Harrison.

37   Macmurray, *The Self as Agent*, p.37.

38   Macmurray, *Persons in Relation*, p.17.

39   Macmurray, *The Self as Agent*, p.71.

40   Macmurray, *Persons in Relation*, p.51.

41   Macmurray, *Persons in Relation*, pp.211, 2.

42   Macmurray, *The Self as Agent*, p.70.

43   John Macmurray, *The Structure of Religious Experience*, London: Faber and Faber 1936, p.10.

44   Macmurray, *Persons in Relation*, p.206.

45   Macmurray, *The Self as Agent*, p.72.

46   Macmurray, *Persons in Relation*, p.164.

47   Macmurray, *The Structure of Religious Experience*, p.32.

48   Macmurray, *The Structure of Religious Experience*, pp. 43-46.

49   Daphne Hampson, *After Christianity*, London: SCM Press,

1996, p.238.

50   Hampson, *After Christianity*, p.242.

51   Hampson, *After Christianity*, p.253 quoting Linell Cady, *Relational Love: A Feminist Christian Vision*, in P.M. Cooey, S.A. Farmer, and M.E. Ross, Eds., *Embodied Love: Sensuality and Relationship as Feminist Values*, San Francisco: Harper and Row, 1983, pp.144-5.

52   Hampson, *After Christianity*, chapter VI.

53   Hampson, *After Christianity*, p.212.

54   Hampson, *After Christianity*, p.2.

55   Hampson, *After Christianity*, p.6.

56   Hampson, *After Christianity*, p.10.

57   Hampson, *After Christianity*, p.10.

58   Hampson, *After Christianity*, p.10.

59   Hampson, *After Christianity*, p.111.

60   Hampson, *After Christianity*, p.110. Quoting E. Haney, *What is Feminist Ethics? A Proposal for Continuing Discussion.* Journal of Religious Ethics, 8, 1980, pp 115-124.

61   Hampson, *After Christianity*, p.251.

62   Hampson, *After Christianity*, p.214.

63   Hampson, *After Christianity*, p.214.

64   Hampson, *After Christianity*, p.244.

65   Hampson, *After Christianity*, p.235.

66   Hampson, *After Christianity*, p.255.

67   Hampson, *After Christianity*, p.256.

68   Hampson, *After Christianity*, p.247.

69   Reported in Gerald Priestland, *Priestland's Progress*, London: British Broadcasting Corporation, 1981, p.48.

70   Priestland, *Priestland's Progress*, p.53.

71   John Spong, *Why Christianity Must Change or Die*, New York: HarperSanFrancisco, 1994, p.64.

72   John Spong, *A New Christianity for a New World*, New York: HarperCollins, 2001, p.71.

73   Spong, *A New Christianity for a New World*, p.240.

74 Matthew Fox, *Original Blessing*, Santa Fe: Bear & Company, 1983, pp.35,53.

75 *The Oxford Dictionary of the Christian Church*, F. Cross and E.A. Livingstone Eds., Third Edition Oxford: OUP, 2005.

76 *Catechism of the Catholic Church*, London: Burns and Oates, 1999, p.276.

77 Adc Marc 2.9, quoted in *The Oxford Dictionary of the Christian Church.*

78 *The Oxford Dictionary of the Christian Church.*

Notes for Chapter 9
God Hidden in the Invisible Religion of Today's Culture

1 Thomas Luckmann, *The Invisible Religion: The Transformation of Symbols in Industrial Society*, New York: Macmillan, 1967.

2 Sarah Williams, *Religious Belief and Popular Culture in Southwark, c.1880-1939*, Oxford: Oxford University Press, 1999.

3 Charles Taylor, *A Secular Age*, Harvard: Harvard University Press, 2007.

4 Don Cupitt's quest to identify the new religion was published in a trilogy. *The New Religion of Life in Everyday Speech*, 1999, *The Meaning of It All in Everyday Speech*, 1999, *Kingdom Come in Everyday Speech*, 2000. All three published London: SCM Press.

5 Geoffrey Ahern and Grace Davie, *Inner City God*, London: Hodder and Stoughton, 1987.

6 Paul Heelas and Linda Woodhead, *The Spiritual Revolution*, Oxford: Blackwell, 2005. Several more writers could be included in this review but the selection is sufficiently representative of the whole.

7 Jeffrey Cox, *The English Churches in a Secular Society: Lambeth 1870-1930*, Oxford, Oxford University Press, 1982.

8 Margaret Penn, *Manchester Fourteen Miles*, London: Futura,

1982.

9   Luckmann, *The Invisible Religion*, p.92.

10   Luckmann, *The Invisible Religion*, p.109.

11   Luckmann, *The Invisible Religion*, p.107.

12   Luckmann, *The Invisible Religion*, p.105.

13   Luckmann, *The Invisible Religion*, p.103.

14   Williams, *Religious Belief*, p.2.

15   Williams, *Religious Belief*, p.3.

16   Williams, *Religious Belief*, p.vi.

17   Williams, *Religious Belief*, p.1.

18   Williams, *Religious Belief*, p.167

19   Williams, *Religious Belief*, p.176.

20   Williams, *Religious Belief*, See definition on page 11.

21   Steve Bruce, *God is Dead: Secularization in the West*, Oxford: Blackwell, 2002.

22   Grace Davie, *The Sociology of Religion*, London: Sage, 2007, pp.19,20.

23   Nancy Ammerman, Ed., *Everyday Religion*, Oxford: Oxford University Press, 2007, p.10.

24   Ahern and Davie, *Inner City God*, p.39.

25   Ahern and Davie, *Inner City God*, p. 114.

26   Ahern and Davie, *Inner City God*, p.80.

27   Ahern and Davie, *Inner City God*, p.104.

28   Cupitt, *The New Religion of Life*, pp.1, 2.

29   Cupitt, *The New Religion of Life*, p.13.

30   Cupitt, *The New Religion of Life*, p.15.

31   Don Cupitt, *Kingdom Come in Everyday Speech*, p.89.

32   Cupitt, *Kingdom Come in Everyday Speech*, p.62.

33   Charles Taylor, *A Secular Age*, p.395 ff.

34   Charles Taylor, *Sources of the Self*, Harvard: Harvard University Press, 1989, p.224.

35   Taylor, *Sources of the Self*, chapter 21.

36   Taylor, *Sources of the Self*, p.390.

37   Taylor, *Sources of the Self*, p.507.

38   Taylor, *Sources of the Self*, p.402.

39   Taylor, *Sources of the Self*, p.518.

40   Heelas and Woodhead, *The Spiritual Revolution*, p.5.

41   Heelas and Woodhead, *The Spiritual Revolution*, p.29.

42   Heelas and Woodhead, *The Spiritual Revolution*, p.27, 28.

43   Heelas and Woodhead, *The Spiritual Revolution*, p.110.

44   Heelas and Woodhead, *The Spiritual Revolution*, p.106.

45   Quentin Skinner, *The Foundations of Modern Political Thought*, Volume two, Cambridge: Cambridge University Press, 1978.

46   Vernon White, *Identity*, London: SCM Press, 2002, p.72.

47   Brian Turner, *Religion and Social Theory*, London: Sage Publications, 1983, p.197.

48   Rowan Williams, *On Christian Theology*, Oxford: Blackwell, 2000, p.34.

49   Section nineteen of this Act.

50   Callum Brown, *What Was the Religious Crisis of the 1960s?* Journal of Religious History, Volume 34, Number 4, December 2010.

51   Robert Bellah, *The New Religious Consciousness*, California University Press, 1976. Taylor, *A Secular Age*, p.473. Charles Taylor, *The Ethics of Authenticity*, Harvard: Harvard University Press, 1991.

52   Linda Woodhead, *Conclusion; A Values Profile of Great Britain*, pp.69, 70, in *Modern Believing*, Volume 55 issue 1, 2014.

53   Peter Berger, *A Rumour of Angels*, London: Allen Lane, 1970, p.119.

Notes for Chapter 10
God in the Christian Practice of the Authority of No Authority

1   Genesis, 38:3-10.

2   Samuel, 6:1-7.

3   1 Samuel, 15.

4   Genesis, 34.

5   *Quaker Faith & Practice,* The book of Christian discipline of
     the Yearly Meeting of the Religious Society of Friends in
     Britain, 1999, section 24.15.

6   Yearbook 24.02 Quoted from Barclay, Robert. 1678 *Apology
     for the true Christian Divinity.*

7   Leo Tolstoy, *A Confession and What I believe,* Oxford: Oxford
     University Press, 1921 [1884], pp.107-116

8   Tolstoy, *A Confession,* p.ix and note on page 123.

9   Leo Tolstoy, *The Kingdom of God is Within You,* New York:
     Dover Publications, 2006 [1894], p. ix.

10   Yearbook, section 1.02.17. In deference to the spirit of the
     Society it must be noted that quotations from the book do
     not represent established doctrine. Although entries have
     passed through a process of consensus they remain contri-
     butions to an ongoing discussion.

11   Yearbook, 23.36.

12   Yearbook, 15.20.

13   Yearbook, chapter 24.

14   George Fox, Ed., Rufus Jones, *The Journal of George Fox,*
     Richmond: Friends United Press, 1976, p.451.

15   Yearbook, 24.04.

16   Fox, *Journal,* p.327.

17   Yearbook, 19.37. Quoted from Joseph Besse, *A Collection of
     the Sufferings of the People called Quakers,* 1753.

18   Fox, *Journal,* p.248.

19   Yearbook, 19.40. From Thomas Ellwood, *History of the Life,*
     1714

20   Yearbook, 19.42

21   Fox, *Journal,* p110. Fox was normally more circumspect and
     took advantage of the customary privilege to start a
     discussion after the sermon was finished.

22   Yearbook, 1.02.14

23   Tolstoy, *The Kingdom of God,* p.60.

24 Fox, *Journal*, p.318.

25 Yearbook, 2.83.

26 Yearbook, 23.73

27 There is a certain self-deception in this. The doctrine of the Society is the Equality of All Persons.

28 See discussion in John Macmurray, *The Search for Reality in Religion*, London: George Allen & Unwin, 1965, pp. 67-75.

Notes for Chapter 11
God in the Religious Vision of Political Anarchism

1 Emma Goldman, *Living My Life*, Pluto Press, 1988, p.84.

2 Quoted in Woodcock and Avakumovic, *The Anarchist Prince*, Boardman and Co, 1950, p.112.

3 Leonard Shapiro, *The Rise of the Communist Autocracy*, Harvard: Harvard University Press, 1965.

4 Vladimir Lenin, *Left-Wing Communism, an Infantile Disorder*, Peking: Foreign Languages Press, 1975, [1920]

5 Lenin, *Left-Wing Communism*, p.39.

6 Vlesovod Voline, *The Unknown Revolution*, Solidarity Black and Red, 1974, p.99.

7 David Footman, *Nestor Makhno*, in Footman Ed., *Soviet Affairs*, St Antony's Papers Number 6, Chatto and Windus 1959, p.86.

8 Footman, *Nestor Makhno*, p.106.

9 Footman, *Nestor Makhno*, p.84.

10 Footman, *Nestor Makhno*, p.101.

11 Voline, *The Unknown Revolution*, pp.460-463.

12 Voline, *The Unknown Revolution*, pp. 289-295.

13 Voline, *The Unknown Revolution*, p523.

14 Tolstoy, *The Kingdom of God is within You*. Dover 2006 [1894], pp 249-256.

15 p 256.

16 Tolstoy, *The Kingdom of God*, p.147.

17 Tolstoy, *The Kingdom of God*, p.271.
18 Tolstoy, *The Kingdom of God*, p.274.
19 Tolstoy, *The Kingdom of God*, p.181.
20 Tolstoy, *The Kingdom of God*, p.271.
21 Tolstoy, *The Kingdom of God*, p.314.
22 Tolstoy, *The Kingdom of God*, pp. 244, 245.
23 Birkbeck MSc. 2008.
24 Franz Borkenau, *The Spanish Cockpit*, Faber and Faber, 1937, p.22.
25 Borkenau, *The Spanish Cockpit*, p 298.
26 James Joll, *The Anarchists*, Methuen, 1964, p.12.
27 George Woodcock, *Anarchism*, Harmondsworth: Pelican, 1962, p 23.
28 Gerald Brenan, *The Spanish Labyrinth*, Cambridge: Cambridge University Press, 1943, p.188.
29 Brenan, *The Spanish Labyrinth*, pp.191, 192.
30 Peter Kropotkin, *Memoirs of a Revolutionist*, Swan Sonnenschein & Co 1906, p.144.
31 Kropotkin, *Memoirs*, p.157.
32 Kropotkin, *Memoirs*, pp.201, 2.
33 Kropotkin, *Memoirs*, pp.375, 372
34 Alexander Berkman, *ABC of Anarchism*, Freedom Press, 1971 [1929].
35 Berkman, *ABC*, p.9.
36 Berkman, *ABC*, p.2.
37 Berkman, *ABC*, p.14.
38 Berkman, *ABC*, p.22.
39 Berkman, *ABC*, p.25.
40 Berkman, *ABC*, p.22.
41 Berkman, *ABC*, p.23.
42 Berkman, *ABC*, p.15.
43 Berkman, *ABC*, p.18.
44 Berkman, *ABC*, p.24.
45 Berkman, *ABC*, p.68.

46 Berkman, *ABC*, p.76.
47 Berkman, *ABC*, p.15.
48 Berkman, *ABC*, p.28.
49 Berkman, *ABC*, p.9.
50 Berkman, *ABC*, p.xv.
51 Berkman, *ABC*, p.34.
52 Berkman, *ABC*, p.xv.
53 Berkman, *ABC*, p.41.
54 Berkman, *ABC*, p.59.
55 Berkman, *ABC*, p.42.
56 Berkman, *ABC*, p.83.

Notes for Chapter 12
The Distinction between the Religious and the Political Domains – What is the Kingdom of God?

1 Emile Durkheim, *The Rules of Sociological Method*, Illinois: University of Chicago Press, 1938, p.1.
2 Durkheim, *The Rules of Sociological Method*, p.3.
3 Joan Taylor, *The Immerser: John the Baptist within Second Temple Judaism*, Grand Rapids: Eerdmans, 1997.
4 Charles Dodd, *The Parables of the Kingdom*, London: Collins, 1965, p.34.
5 Lundstrom, G. (English translation Joan Bulman) *The Kingdom of God in the Teaching of Jesus*, Oliver and Boyd, 1963. Norman Perrin, *The Kingdom of God in the Teaching of Jesus*, London: SCM Press, 1963. Bruce Chilton, *The Kingdom of God in the Teaching of Jesus*, London and Philadelphia: SPCK/Fortress, 1984.
6 Perrin, *The Kingdom of God*, p.159.
7 Chilton, *The Kingdom of God*, p.21.
8 Chilton, *The Kingdom of God*, p.21.
9 Bruce Chilton, *God in Strength*, in Chilton Ed., *The Kingdom of God*, London: SPCK, 1984, p125

10   There is an unquantifiable snag in ascribing to Jesus what he
     and his audience could or could not have understood on the
     basis of scripture. This discounts the prime feature of charis-
     matic personalities that they use traditional materials
     creatively to forge compelling new understandings that
     could not have been predicted. Paul is the great example of
     playing fast and loose with scripture. Without having the
     written evidence before us the interpretation of Jesus as the
     seed of Abraham could never be credited. The fact that Jesus
     has to do so much explaining about the Kingdom indicates
     that he was not a simple purveyor of preconception and that
     something novel was afoot.

11   John Meier, *A Marginal Jew: Rethinking the Historical Jesus,*
     Anchor Yale Bible Reference Library, 1991-2009, Vol. 2 1994,
     Mentor, Message, Miracles, p.452.

12   Johannes Weiss, *Jesus' Proclamation of the Kingdom of God,*
     Philadelphia: Fortress Press, 1971, p.73.

13   Weiss, *Proclamation,* p.74.

14   Albert Schweitzer, *The Quest of the Historical Jesus,* New York:
     Macmillan, 1960, p.239.

15   Chilton, *The Kingdom of God,* p.21.

16   Dodd, *Parables,* p.207.

17   'Jesus consciously chose to indicate that the display of
     miraculous power in his own ministry constituted a partial
     and preliminary realization of God's kingly rule, which
     would soon be displayed in full force. It was to underline the
     organic link between his own ministry in the present and the
     full coming of God's eschatological rule in the near future
     that Jesus chose to employ "the kingdom of God" for both.
     That much, I think, can be inferred from the strange double
     usage of Jesus. Perhaps like the parables this paradoxical
     usage was meant to be something of a riddle, aimed at
     teasing the mind into active thought (to borrow the famous
     words of C.H. Dodd). In my view this is all that we can say.

To go beyond this minimal explanation of the kingdom present yet future is to leave exegesis and engage in systematic theology.' *A Marginal Jew*, Vol. 2 p.453.

18   Meier, *A Marginal Jew*, Vol. 2 p.11.

19   Joachim Jeremias, *Rediscovering the Parables*, London: SCM Press, 1966.

20   Albert Schweitzer, *The Mystery of the Kingdom of God*, London: A & C Black, 1925, p.101.

21   Perrin, *The Kingdom of God*, p.158.

22   www.americanhumanist.org/about/manifesto.

23   Manifesto II.

24   Durkheim, *The Rules of Sociological Method*, pp.1-3.

25   Durkheim, *The Rules of Sociological Method*, Author's preface to second edition, pp.viii, xlix.

26   Cecil Cadoux, *Christian Pacifism Re-examined*, Oxford: Basil Blackwell, 1940, p.229.

27   Isaiah Berlin, *The Originality of Machiavelli*, in *Against the Current; Essays in the History of Ideas*, Isaiah Berlin Selected Writings, Volume 3, Oxford: Oxford University Press, 1981.

28   Cecil Cadoux, *The Historic Mission of Jesus*, Lutterworth: Lutterworth Press, 1941.

29   Cadoux, *Christian Pacifism*, p.229.

30   Melissa Raphael, *The Female Face of God in Auschwitz*, London: Routledge, 2003.

31   Richard Rubenstein, *After Auschwitz*, Indianapolis: Bobbs-Merrill, 1966.

32   Zachary Braiterman, *(God) After Auschwitz*, Princeton: Princeton University Press. 1998, p.13.

33   Emil Fackenheim, *God's Presence in History*, Canada: HarperCollins, 1970.

34   Raphael, *Female Face of God*, p.5.

35   Raphael, *Female Face of God*, p 5.

36   Raphael, *Female Face of God*, p15.

37   Raphael, *Female Face of God*, p 6.

38   Dodd, *Parables of the Kingdom*, p.202.

Notes to the Conclusion
The Social Theology Manifesto

1   Anthony Freeman, *God in Us*, London: SCM Press, 1993.

2   David Boulton, *Godless for God's Sake: Nontheism in Contemporary Quakerism*, Cumbria: Dales Historical Monographs, 2006, p.6.

3   Brian Mountford, *Christian Atheist: Belonging without Believing*, Winchester: O Books, 2011.

4   Mountford, *Christian Atheist*, p.129.

5   Gerald Priestland, *Something Understood*, London: Arrow Books, 1988, p.265

6   Jeanne Warren, *Search for Meaning*, p.118, in David Boulton Ed., *Godless for God's Sake*, Dent: Dales Historical Monographs, 2006.

7   Grace Davie, *Vicarious Religion*, p.28. in, Nancy Ammerman, Ed., *Everyday Religion; Observing Modern Religious Lives*, Oxford: Oxford University Press, 2007.

CHRISTIAN
ALTERNATIVE

Throughout the two thousand years of Christian tradition there have been, and still are, groups and individuals that exist in the margins and upon the edge of faith. But in Christianity's contrapuntal history it has often been these outcasts and pioneers that have forged contemporary orthodoxy out of former radicalism as belief evolves to engage with and encompass the ever-changing social and scientific realities. Real faith lies not in the comfortable certainties of the Orthodox, but somewhere in a half-glimpsed hinterland on the dirt track to Emmaus, where the Death of God meets the Resurrection, where the supernatural Christ meets the historical Jesus, and where the revolution liberates both the oppressed and the oppressors.

Welcome to Christian Alternative... a space at the edge where the light shines through.